Urban Unrest in the Middle East

SUNY Series in the Social and Economic History of the Middle East
Donald Quataert, editor

Issa Khalaf, *Politics in Palestine: Arab Factionalism and Social Disintegration, 1939–1948*

Rifaʿat ʿAli Abou-El-Haj, *Formation of the Modern State: The Ottoman Empire, Sixteenth to Eighteenth Centuries*

M. Fuad Köprülü, *The Origins of the Ottoman Empire*, translated and edited by Gary Leiser

Guilain Denoeux, *Urban Unrest in the Middle East: A Comparative Study of Informal Networks in Egypt, Iran, and Lebanon*

*Prepared under the auspices of the
Center of International Studies,
Princeton University*

Urban Unrest in the Middle East

A Comparative Study of Informal Networks
in
Egypt, Iran, and Lebanon

Guilain Denoeux

State University of New York Press

Published by
State University of New York Press, Albany

© 1993   State University of New York

For information, address State University of New York
Press, State University Plaza, Albany, NY 12246

Production by Dana Foote
Marketing by Fran Keneston

Library of Congress Cataloging-in-Publication Data

Denoeux, Guilain.
    Urban unrest in the Middle East : a comparative study of informal
networks in Egypt, Iran, and Lebanon / Guilain Denoeux.
       p. cm. — (SUNY series in the social and economic history of
the Middle East)
    Includes bibliographical references and index.
    ISBN 0–7914–1523–6 (hc : acid-free) : ISBN
0–7914–1524–4 (pb : acid-free)
    1. Middle East—Social conditions. 2. Protest movements—Middle
East. 3. Social networks—Middle East. 4. Urbanization—Middle
East. I. Title. II. Series.
HN656.A8D44   1993
306'.0956—dc20   92–25353
                                                                                          CIP

10 9 8 7 6 5 4 3 2 1

Contents

Figures

Acknowledgments

This book owes much to the generous advice of John Waterbury and Samir Khalaf, and their willingness to share their expertise with me. John's profound understanding of the Middle East, combined with his grasp of the comparative politics literature, served as an inspiration. Samir, who provided the initial idea for this study's focus on informal networks, repeatedly drew my attention to some of the more subtle sociological and anthropological aspects of Middle Eastern politics. More importantly, both John and Samir gave generously of their time, and never tired of reading successive versions of the manuscript (one of which was eleven hundred pages). Many of the suggestions they made have been incorporated into the book. I am deeply indebted to both of them.

For the material dealing with Iran, I benefited greatly from many discussions with Ahmad Ashraf, who was always ready to share with me his encyclopedic knowledge of that country. Henry Bienen, whose own work on urbanization and political instability helped orient my research, also made very useful contributions to the manuscript. His constant encouragement is deeply appreciated. Kay Warren read sections of chapters 11 and 12, and her incisive comments on them enabled me to sharpen the anthropological and cultural dimensions of the study. I also wish to express my gratitude to the institutions that funded my work: Princeton University, Princeton's Center of International Studies and Council on Regional Studies, the Sternberg Fund, and the John D. and Catherine T. MacArthur Foundation.

In preparing the book for publication, I benefited from the help of several other individuals, including four anonymous reviewers, whose perceptive remarks did much to improve the manuscript. My two research assistants at Colby College, Margaret Russell and Kyle Lissack, were diligent and conscientious, and deserve much of the credit for the computer-generated diagrams, charts, and "graphs from hell"—as Margaret called one file. I am also deeply appreciative for the useful comments and suggestions offered by Rosalie Robertson, Donald Quataert, Dana Foote, and Wendy Nelson, at the State University of New York Press. I feel very privileged indeed to have benefited from their professionalism for my first book.

From the beginning, my wife, Eliza, was there to provide love and encouragement. I am very grateful to her for enduring with patience and understanding the time I spent hidden in my study researching and writing (and rewriting) this book.

Finally, I thank Pergamon Press for the permission to reprint from Henry Bienen's article, "Urbanization and Third World Stability," *World Development*, Vol. 12, No. 7 (July 1984).

Note on Transliteration

This book uses a simplified version of the transliteration system adopted by the *International Journal of Middle East Studies,* but with no diacritical marks, except for *hamza* (') and *'ayn* ('). Words in Arabic or Persian are in italics, except for proper names, and those that are now commonly used in newspapers and magazines, and which are treated here as English terms (e.g., ulama, Shiite, Sunni, shaykh, or bazaar). Place names, too, are usually spelled in the English fashion (e.g., Beirut and not Bayrut), as well as a few well-known personal names (e.g., Nasser and not Nasir). Words in European languages other than English are also in italics.

A mes parents,
Gérard et Claudine Denoeux

Introduction

Woe to the cities in whose midst lies tinder!
The people, breaking their chains,
Take to self-help in terrible ways.

—Schiller (quoted in Tilly et al. 1975, 1)

Our Middle Eastern city is far from being an harmonious environment
and the Middle Eastern Man is too tormented by the ravages of war and
conflict all around him to make his transition to modernity smoothly
and with a minimum of anguish.

—Crown-Prince Hassan Bin Talal of Jordan
("Keynote Address," in Saqqaf 1987)

And these three things abideth—class, role, and network—
and the greatest of these is network.

—(Quoted in Mitchell 1969, 1)

I first realized the true vitality of informal networks in the mid-1980s, after I had been assigned to Baghdad for sixteen months at the height of the Iran-Iraq war. Even in that suffocating police state, where the pressure of formal cadres was truly terrifying, informal ties and loyalties survived in a dormant state, sustained by roots that reached deep into the region's past. In fact, as the fear of a possible Iraqi defeat gripped the population, and as the traumatic shock of Iran's repeated missile attacks spread through the Iraqi capital, informal networks rose to provide the social and psychological support that Saddam Hussein's totalitarian machine could not deliver.

Back in the United States, my interest in the political significance of informal networks was further stimulated by the discovery of a growing literature on this subject by sociologists, anthropologists, students of Third World urbanization, and Middle East specialists. At the same time, I found myself drawn to the study of urban protest movements in the Middle East. Out of these various interests developed this book, which analyzes the contribution of informal groups to urban unrest in Egypt, Iran, and Lebanon, with particular emphasis on the period from the 1940s through the 1980s. This is, therefore, a comparative and interpretive work, focused on the intersection of three areas of investigation: informal networks, urban unrest, and the relationship between rapid urbanization and political instability.

Political unrest has become so prevalent in the Middle East that mere reference to the region often brings to our minds images of widespread turmoil and political disorder. To capture the ongoing political upheaval in the Middle East, one need only think of some of its most dramatic manifestations: the protracted and violent conflict in Lebanon (1975–90), the Palestinian uprising (*intifada*) in the Israeli-occupied territories (which has been going on since December 1987), the Iranian revolution of 1977–79, some of the more belligerent manifestations of the so-called Islamic revival, and a variety of riots, usually motivated by cost-of-living issues (Iran, 1992; Jordan, 1989; Algeria, 1991, 1988, and 1986; Morocco, 1984 and 1981; Sudan, 1985 and 1982; Tunisia, 1984 and 1978; Egypt, 1977).

Clearly, these instances of political turmoil differ greatly in their underlying causes, scope, and significance. In most cases, however, it has been in cities, and especially in the largest ones, that the unrest has taken place.

This observation certainly applies to Egypt and Iran, two of the three countries we will investigate. In Iran, the 1977–79 revolution was almost exclusively an urban phenomenon, and so were the 1963 uprising and the turmoil of the 1951–53 period. Similarly, much of the unrest that occurred in Egypt in the 1970s and 1980s took place in cities—especially in Cairo, but also sometimes in the rapidly expanding provincial capitals of Upper Egypt, such as Minia and Assiut.

Lebanon presents us with a somewhat different picture, in that, between 1975 and 1990, no area, whether urban or rural, was spared the carnage. Fighting raged in Beirut, Tripoli, and Sidon, but also in the mountains of the Shuf, the valleys of the Bekaa, and the villages of the south. Yet even in the Lebanese case, it is in the cities, and especially in Beirut, that the key battles occurred, and that the destruction caused by the civil war was most visible. Repeatedly, events in the capital had a determining influence on the course of the civil war, and it is often their outcome that provided the background for further clashes in other parts of the country.

Beyond the experiences of Egypt, Iran, and Lebanon, however, this book focuses on cities because the predominantly urban nature of unrest in the Middle East is bound to become even more pronounced, given the rapid urbanization of Middle Eastern countries. Of all the major regions in the world, the Middle East and North Africa displayed the highest annual urbanization rates during the period 1950–80, a trend that should continue for the rest of this century.[1]

Unfortunately, despite the spectacular growth of Middle Eastern cities over the last thirty years, and despite the fact that these cities, especially the largest ones, are becoming ever more clearly the centers of intense political struggles, the study of urban politics in the Middle East has received surprisingly little attention, whether from Middle East specialists or from comparativists.[2] Thus, the books, anthologies, and journals dealing with the politics of rapid urbanization in developing countries include relatively few works on the Middle East. Furthermore, the lack of comparative concerns that characterizes the few existing studies on Middle Eastern urban politics stands in sharp contrast to similar research on Latin America. In an attempt to partially fill these gaps in the existing literature, this book makes an explicit effort to apply to the Middle East ongoing debates among scholars of Third World urbanization, and to compare the politics of several Middle Eastern cities (instead of focusing on any one of them).

My examination of urban unrest in the Middle East will be conducted from the perspective of informal networks. I use the word *network* here to refer to groups of individuals linked to one another by highly personal, noncontractual bonds and loyalties. Four specific types of networks—clientelist,[3] occupational, religious, and residential—will be singled out for systematic attention.

One of the factors that prompted this focus on informal networks was the existence of a large number of studies showing that, throughout the Third World, rapid urbanization in the 1950s, 1960s, and 1970s had promoted the multiplication of informal associations, and that the stabilizing role played by these networks was one of the main reasons why, by and large, Third World cities had not experienced the kind of sociopolitical upheaval that had been anticipated by earlier writers.[4]

As an observer of the Middle East in the 1980s, I felt intrigued by such conclusions, if only because the political turmoil gripping cities across the region was at significant variance with the optimistic picture portrayed by this literature. Many colleagues, furthermore, were often quick to mention rapid urbanization as a primary cause of instability in that part of the world, and saw the dramatic growth of Middle Eastern cities as one of the major forces behind the development of Islamic fundamentalism.[5] Thus, was one to conclude that there is something specific about urbanization in the Middle East that makes it a more destabilizing process than in other areas of the world? Or is there actually no causal link between rapid urbanization and instability in the Middle East?

I decided that one way to address these questions was to examine the politics of a few significant Middle Eastern cities through the prism of informal groups. Such an approach seemed particularly appropriate, given the widely acknowledged importance of informal groups and loyalties in Middle Eastern politics, and given that networks play a central role in the arguments of those who have attempted to explain why rapid and massive urbanization has not generated widespread political unrest in the Third World. Would a focus on the Middle East (a region neglected by students of the politics of Third World urbanization) yield different conclusions?

An emphasis on informal networks also offered the attractive prospect of connecting the long-standing debates on the premodern Middle Eastern city, with more recent ones on the contemporary megalopolis. Such a linkage has rarely been attempted.[6] On the one hand, indeed, urban historians of the Middle East continue to be fascinated by the subject of the "Islamic City," but they rarely address broader political and sociological questions and usually fail to explore the extent to which the features they see as characteristic of the traditional Middle Eastern city can shed light on the late-twentieth-century urban phenomena in the Middle East. On the other hand, political scientists tend to focus exclusively on contemporary urban forms. They are concerned primarily with the issue of whether city and government can cope with the massive loads created over the last few decades by staggering urban growth and mounting social, economic, and political problems. Accordingly, the kinds of processes on which they concentrate include rapid rural-to-urban migrations, the transformation of urban economies, the development of the "informal sector," acute housing shortages, inadequate transportation facilities, problems of income distribution and city management, class formation, and political unrest.[7]

Thus, while historians are often tempted to stress the uniqueness of the Islamic, Arab, or Oriental city, political scientists emphasize that the problems faced by contemporary Middle Eastern cities can be found, in more or less similar forms, in Asian, Latin American, and African cities. Also, while historians concentrate on the continuities that Middle Eastern cities displayed throughout much of the premodern period, political scientists highlight the rapid transformations of urban politics in the region.

Clearly, the political scientist's approach is more likely to enable us to understand contemporary urban society. It is also deliberately comparative, which permits us to see contemporary Middle Eastern cities against the background of today's Third World cities in general. Political scientists, however, usually fail to look at Middle Eastern cities in the light of these cities' own pasts. Most often, they do not even care to get into the major issues that historians have identified about the historic Middle Eastern city.[8] They seem to assume that contemporary Middle Eastern cities have changed so much over the last fifty years that there is little to be gained from the analysis of their premodern antecedents, if one's primary objective is to understand modern urban society and politics. Significantly, even when the study of a contemporary Middle Eastern city by a political scientist begins with observations on the traditional Middle Eastern city, one often gets the impression that these observations are perfunctory and unrelated to the rest of the work.

This absence of an explicit dialogue between historians and political scientists was also one of the factors that prompted this book's focus on networks. Since both historians and political scientists appeared to agree that informal groups have always been a building block of the Middle East's urban political economy, these networks seemed to offer a natural perspective from which one might analyze both continuities and changes in the Middle East's urban scene and therefore establish much needed bridges between the works of historians and those of political scientists.

Finally, an analysis of the role of informal networks in Middle Eastern politics also held the prospect of averting another weakness in the field of Middle Eastern studies: the tacit division of labor between political scientists, who focus primarily on macroprocesses, and anthropologists, who tend to favor studies of local communities. Few studies so far have endeavored to connect explicitly the concerns of anthropologists and sociologists with those of political scientists.[9] In this respect as well, an emphasis on networks seemed to have the potential of yielding new insights.

While a focus on networks looked therefore like a potentially very productive endeavor, it was not without problems. Some of these need to be mentioned briefly here, if only because they hampered my own research. Most significantly, precisely because of their informal nature and organization, networks are inherently more difficult to describe than groups such as political parties and trade unions, which have a clearly established membership, ideology, program, and organizational structure. An observer, for instance, often will find it difficult to identify the exact boundaries of the membership of a network or to understand how that network operates. Such obstacles, in turn, explain why the study of politics continues to center on institutional processes and structures, why so many scholars seem to remain unaware of the essential role that informal groups play in the lives of ordinary people, and why, as a result, so little energy has been invested in the systematic gathering of information on Middle Eastern networks. In this context, finding sources of information was in many ways the most difficult problem I faced. Informal networks— let alone their impact on political stability—are rarely made an explicit object of research. Information did exist, but it was usually scattered throughout a myriad of works. My main task was to try to piece this information together to present a coherent picture of what urban networks look like, and to develop hypotheses on the relationship between these networks and political stability.

Finally, although Middle East specialists have emphasized repeatedly the centrality of informal networks to political processes in the region,[10] they rarely have described networks in any detail. Too often, one gets the feeling that networks are invoked in the abstract, as a sort of invisible and mysterious force that explains, to some extent at least, the volatility, unpredictability, and fluidity of Middle Eastern politics. In contrast, this book not only describes particular networks, but also investigates systematically their impact on the urban political order. Similarly, although scholars have emphasized the key role that informal networks play in Middle Eastern elite settings,[11] they have paid much less attention to informal networks in the population at large, or to informal networks in the hands of counterelites. It is on these networks, and more generally on the politics of the street and the politics of counterelites, that this study focuses.

Having decided to examine urban unrest through the lenses of informal networks, I selected a few countries for comparisons. Since the Middle East is such a rapidly urbanizing area, it seemed particularly important to study the role of informal networks in some of the region's largest cities. In this respect, Cairo and Tehran were logical choices, because they were the largest two urban concentrations in the region between 1950 and 1990 (since then, Istanbul has overtaken Tehran). By 1990, according to the *very conservative* estimates of the United Nations, Cairo's population was well above nine million, while Tehran's was only slightly below seven million (see the Appendix, figure A.1).

Cairo and Tehran were also attractive choices because of their sharply different political evolution in the late 1970s. From 1977 to 1979, Tehran became the main theater of a mass-based, popular revolution that put an end to what had often been portrayed as the strongest regime in the region and replaced it with the world's first Islamic republic. No comparable sociopolitical upheaval took place in Cairo, despite the tumultuous student riots of 1972–73, the industrial strikes and demonstrations in the early to mid-1970s,[12] the January 1977 explosion, and various manifestations of Islamic militancy, leading up to Sadat's assassination on 6 October 1981.

In fact, even a cursory look at Egypt in the 1970s and 1980s reveals no serious and sustained challenge to the regime's stability, and points to the fragmented character and limited intensity, scope, and success of urban protest movements under Sadat and during the first decade of Mubarak's rule (1981–91). This is not to deny the problems that the Egyptian regime has had to face because of the existence of small but determined and violent Islamic fundamentalist groups. If anything, the assassination of Anwar al-Sadat was a dramatic demonstration of what the fundamentalist opposition can achieve. Moreover, while radical Islam was on the wane in Egypt between 1981 and 1985, it has picked up again since then.[13]

Nevertheless, throughout the 1970s and 1980s, the Egyptian government consistently defeated the attempts by Islamic militants to confront the ruling elite directly, as in April 1974, January 1977, June and October 1981, and March 1986. Despite Sadat's assassination, the regime that issued from the 1952 coup has remained intact under Mubarak. Even if the Egyptian regime were to collapse tomorrow, one would still be faced with the task of explaining its extraordinary resilience during the 1970s and 1980s, despite the accumulation of economic difficulties and mounting demographic pressures.

Against this background, a comparison between Egypt and Iran (and Cairo and Tehran in particular) seemed to be ideally suited to test hypotheses regarding the impact of informal networks on urban political stability. Since Cairo and Tehran were comparable in size throughout the 1970s (with a clear but diminishing advantage in favor of Cairo), and since they also happened to differ considerably in terms of unrest at the end of that decade, they seemed to provide a reasonable basis from which one might assess the impact of informal networks on political outcomes. Of course, by focusing on informal networks, I would have to downplay or ignore many other variables that also affect internal politics. Nevertheless, as became rapidly clear, urban informal networks and their relationships to the central authorities seemed by themselves to go a long way toward explaining the resilience of the political order in Egypt and its demise in Iran.

For different reasons, I also found myself drawn to the Lebanese experience. After all, Beirut was the site of a ferocious civil war that lasted for fifteen years, and anyone interested in contemporary manifestations of urban unrest in the Middle East could hardly fail to note the significance of what happened in that country. Yet Lebanon was also obviously a unique case, and one that could not be compared directly to the other two. Three variables at least pointed to the peculiarity of the Lebanese situation. One was the very small size of the country and its population (about four million in the 1970s). Another factor was the special nature of Lebanon's "confessional" political system, in which each religious sect was assigned a fixed proportion of all governmental offices in the country. The third variable was the consistent and dramatic impact that international events and foreign actors had on Lebanese politics in the 1970s and 1980s. Here, one need only think of the role that regional rivalries and the Palestinian presence in the country played in the initial outbreak of hostilities, of the 1982 Israeli invasion and Iran's subsequent support of radical Shiite groups, or of Syria's growing involvement in the country's internal affairs, culminating in its virtual takeover of Lebanon in 1990–91.

These peculiarities notwithstanding, it seemed that, as in the other two countries, network analysis offered a perspective that was potentially very helpful in understanding both the initial breakdown of political order in 1975 and the intensity and protracted character and violence that ravaged Lebanon for the following fifteen years. Beirut was also interesting because of its staggering development after World War II. Between 1960 and 1970, in particular, the growth of Beirut and its suburbs alone accounted for about two-thirds of the increase in Lebanon's urban population, and the population growth rate of the Lebanese capital reached 6.5 percent per year (Tabbarah 1978, 5). As Tabbarah has noted, "Comparable rates for urban agglomerations varied mostly between 1.5 and 4.0 percent in the developed countries and between 2.5 and 6 percent in most of Asia and Latin America. Significantly higher rates for this period (1960–70) could only be found in the unusual circumstances of such boom towns as Baghdad (9.4 percent) and Kuwait city (12.2 percent)." By 1975, Beirut's population had reached 1.5 million, almost half of Lebanon's total population. In a way, Lebanon had become a city-state (Hourani 1988, 6). Thus, it was primarily as a result of Beirut's growth that, in less than one generation, Lebanon was transformed from one of the least urbanized countries in the Arab world to the most urbanized one outside the Gulf region (see the Appendix, figure A.3).

Finally, the choice of Egypt, Iran, and Lebanon also reflects this study's interest in the relationship between urbanization—more specifically, that part of it due to rural-to-urban migration—and urban unrest. In each of the three countries, rural-to-urban migration has greatly contributed to the growth of its capital, which makes it possible to investigate the extent to which migrants are a destabilizing force.

Granted, in the case of Cairo, the greater part of city growth (about two thirds) is now due to natural increase, and it is also true that a large and growing proportion of migrants to Cairo probably come from urban areas (figures are unavailable). Nevertheless, Cairo has remained an attractive destination for rural migrants. By one account, every year in the 1980s, at least another one hundred thousand rural Egyptians moved to the Egyptian capital—that is, twice as many as two decades earlier.[14] Thus, rural-to-urban migration may now constitute "only" about a third or even a quarter of the demographic growth of Greater Cairo, as opposed to 50 percent twenty-five years ago, but this must be balanced against the fact that Cairo's population is now more than twice what it was then. In the districts located on the northern and northwestern belts of Greater Cairo, the annual rate of increase in the 1980s ranged between 10 and 20 percent (Ayubi 1991, 168).

The case of Iran is equally interesting. In 1950, Iran's urban population was below five million, and the proportion of urban to total population about 28 percent. By 1990, however, some thirty-one million people, or about 57 percent of the country's population, lived in urban areas (see the Appendix, figure A.2). Therefore, the great majority of Iran's urban population is a product of the last thirty years. And cities would not have grown so fast had it not been for unprecedented rural-to-urban migrations. By one estimate, from the mid-1960s to the mid-1970s, migrants accounted for as much as 50 percent of the increase in Iran's urban population (Walton 1980, 282). Furthermore, in the two decades that preceded the Iranian revolution, "step migration—from village to town, then town to city—was no longer common; villagers were moving directly from communities of a few hundred to cities of over a million" (Mottahedeh 1985, 348). The figures are, once again, all the more staggering when one looks at the capital. In 1976, there were more than two million migrants in Greater Tehran, and an estimated 371,450 of them had moved to the Iranian capital in the preceding five years. The percentage of migrants in total population rose from 11 percent in 1956 to 12.9 percent in 1966 and to 15 percent in 1976.[15]

Finally, regarding Lebanon, rural-to-urban migrations were undisputably the driving force behind Beirut's staggering growth in the 1960s and 1970s. For Lebanon as a whole, estimates of the share of rural-to-urban migration in urban growth vary from 65 percent for the period 1965–80, to 44.4 percent between 1970 and 1975, and 82.1 percent between 1970 and 1982.[16]

Organization of the Following Chapters

Part 1 (chapters 1 and 2) develops the major theoretical and comparative issues that form the background for this study.

Part 2 (chapters 3 through 7) puts the argument in historical perspective, by providing an overview of the role of informal networks in the politics of Middle Eastern cities from the medieval period up to the nineteenth century. More specifically, it demonstrates that while informal networks usually provided the "glue" that held together mosaic-like cities in which institutions were relatively weak, they also could operate, at times, as channels for political dissent.

Part 3 (chapters 8 through 10) constitutes the heart of this study. By using examples drawn from the political histories of Lebanon, Egypt, and Iran from the 1940s through the 1980s, it suggests that while informal networks often integrate individuals and groups into urban society, they also can provide paths through which alienated counterelites and marginalized segments of the lower classes can disrupt social peace.

The Conclusion summarizes the book's main implications, which are in the following five areas: (a) the changing features of urban networks in the Middle East, and their continuing relevance to the region's politics; (b) the ability of informal groups to function as effective vehicles for collective resistance to the authorities; (c) the conditions under which networks can change their role from system-supportive to system-challenging; (d) the independent impact of Islam on contemporary forms of urban violence in the Middle East; and (e) the relationship between urbanization and political stability.

For those who do not require parts 1 and 2, a secondary pattern of reading would be to start directly with part 3 and the Conclusion, and then consult parts 1 and 2 for any further historical or theoretical background that might be needed.

Part I

Theoretical and Comparative Issues

1

Informal Networks and Political Stability: Old and New Perspectives

In any society, individuals participate in public life through webs of personal relationships and connections to other individuals. Since these social networks constitute the background against which urban unrest in the Middle East will be examined, some of their essential characteristics should be defined from the outset. To do so, one may contrast informal networks with the formal institutions and organizations that have come to play such a prominent role in the modern world.

Informal Networks versus Formal Organizations

Formal groups operate according to written rules and regulations. No such rules and regulations exist in the case of informal groups, which display a much greater degree of spontaneity, a greater reliance on personal ties in the transmission of authority, and a much looser and more amorphous structure. Similarly, whereas the goals of formal groups tend to be clearly established and explicitly stated in a written program, ideology, charter, or constitution, the objectives of informal groups are much less rigidly set. Thus, informal groups depend much more than formal groups on the individual initiative of their members. This reliance on personal initiative as opposed to sustained, corporate effort also tends to make informal groups more transient and vulnerable to external pressures than formal organizations.

The reasons for joining formal groups also frequently differ from those that typically lead to membership in informal networks. Members of a formal group are normally held together by common interests, shared goals, or the ideology they want to promote. Thus, two individuals may strongly dislike one another and still belong to the same formal group, such as a political party, because the personal relations among the group's members are not as important as the objectives of the group, its ideology, or the common interests of its members. By contrast, personal ties and commitments play a determining role in informal networks, even when members also hope to gain goods and services from associating with the network. When they exist, these hopes and material motivations will usually be less explicitly stated in networks than in formal groups, and typically they will be cloaked in the language of friendship, kinship, or ethnicity. It is this emphasis on personal contacts and primary relationships that actually explains why informal groups have little use for written programs, ideologies, and internal administrative structures and regulations. It also means that two individuals who share considerable animosity toward one another will find it much more difficult (although not impossible) to belong to the same informal group than to the same formal group.

Such distinctions notwithstanding, "informal networks" and "formal organizations" are only ideal types, and most groups in reality fall on a continuum from more formally organized entities to groups in which informal features are predominant. On the one hand, truly formal organizations rarely exist. Thus, political scientists and sociologists have repeatedly pointed to the survival of personal ties in large-scale and presumably formal organizations. Students of administrative behavior, for instance, have shown that the seemingly most impersonal bureaucracies actually revolve around personalistic networks. The vast literature on political patronage even suggests that formal organizations offer fertile ground for the multiplication of patron-client relationships, as individuals who have access to the resources of these organizations can distribute them in exchange for political loyalty.

On the other hand, informal groups often present, in an attenuated form, some of the attributes that are characteristic of more formally organized groupings. For instance, they are rarely totally devoid of internal structure. Furthermore, like the Hizballah in Lebanon, they sometimes might be seen as the representatives of a particular ideology or program, part of which may even be available in written form. Finally, shared interests may play as important a role in determining membership in a network as in a formal group.

In this context, the following chapters will look upon informal networks and formal groups less as dichotomies than as poles on a continuum, and their main objective will be to investigate the functioning of groups that approximate, in varying degrees, the ideal type of informal network described above, focusing more specifically on four types of networks: patron-client clusters, networks based on occupational ties, religious associations, and networks built on residential affiliation (street, quarter, neighborhood).

Urbanization, Informal Networks, and Political Stability: Old Theories and Misconceptions

Ever since the nineteenth century, there has been a strong tendency to view urbanization as destructive of informal groups that mediate between the individual and the larger environment. Popular conceptions still hold that cities tend to replace intimate relationships by impersonal ties and substitute formal organizations for voluntary associations and circles of kin, neighbors, and friends.

Within the largely conjectural literature that developed around this theme over the years, one basic perspective recurs again and again under different guises. This viewpoint argues that the destruction of intermediate groups creates isolation, loneliness, normlessness, alienation, and anomie. It then contends that such social atomization and personal disorientation greatly increases the possibility of extremist, "deviant," or "marginal" political behavior, and that it tends to make masses very receptive to radical ideologies expressed by demagogic leaders who try to exploit the socially dislocated population's longing for a new sense of community.[1]

When applied to the Third World, arguments of this variety focus on the recent migrants to the city, particularly slum and shantytown dwellers, who are seen as "uprooted, disoriented, and isolated...torn out of the tightly knit and tradition-sanctioned social structure of their rural or small-town society and cast adrift in the impersonal, bewildering environment of the big city...[and therefore] tinder for radical movements of the right and left, or for the appeals of any irresponsible demagogue" (Nelson 1979, 110).[2] Such assumptions were essential to Oscar Lewis's concept of a "culture of poverty," as well as to the notion of "marginality" as it was developed in some Latin American circles in the 1960s.[3] In a similar vein, early explanations of the ghetto riots of the mid-1960s in the United States frequently emphasized the presumed inability of recently urbanized black populations to adjust to their new environment, and the disruption of traditional ties and mechanisms of social control resulting from these populations' move to the cities.[4]

Urbanization, Informal Networks, and Political Stability: New Perspectives

For several decades now, sociologists and political scientists have known that the empirical evidence tends not to support the theory that has just been summarized. Far from destroying social groups, urbanization in fact appears to strengthen them (Fischer 1984). This seems to be particularly true in the Third World.

The last three decades of research on the politics of rapid urbanization in developing countries have pointed to the vitality of informal associations in Third World cities, especially among the poor.[5] Throughout the Third World, the lack of political organizations enjoying wide popular support has led informal groups and associations to assume functions—including mediating disputes, allocating resources, conveying information, and providing for order and social integration—that, in more institutionalized political settings, have become the responsibility of formal organizations. Since formally organized political groups such as parties, unions, and youth and women's associations are often tightly controlled by the regime, networks provide avenues for genuine participation in public life, and they can act as effective instruments for the representation of the population's actual interests and needs. Not surprisingly, in most developing countries, the urban population has sought to present its requests and grievances to the state essentially through community associations, brokers, and patron-client networks (Nelson 1987).

The structure of Third World economies also promotes the development of informal networks, since these economies remain dominated by small-scale activities and self-employment, in which personal relations and contacts are essential, whether they are between peers, between employers and employees, or between sellers and buyers. Furthermore, the pronounced fragmentation and high mobility of the work force hampers the development of class consciousness and class-based organizations and increases the likelihood that the population will engage in social and political action by using informal networks based on personal ties and loyalties.[6] In this context, the Middle Eastern state's attempt to tax, control, and regulate economic activities in the last thirty years has often forced people into the parallel or "informal" economy, which in turn has been one of the most powerful forces generating informal networks in the region.[7] Similarly, in Mexico, the debt crisis and the economic downturn of the 1980s led to a contracting of economic opportunities in the formal sector, both private and public. This phenomenon forced individuals to move into the informal economy, which in turn contributed to a booming informal organizational life (Eckstein 1990, 170–71). Thus, contemporary economic forces such as the Third World's debt crisis and the modernizing state's attempt to control the economy can magnify the role of informal networks in developing countries.

Throughout the Third World, therefore, the existence of a multiplicity of informal associations based on shared interests or on ethnic, religious, residential, or occupational affiliations, challenges earlier assumptions about the rural migrants' presumed psychological and social isolation in impersonal urban environments. Furthermore, leading students of Third World urbanization have tended to see these networks as one of the main reasons why earlier expectations of widespread political explosions in Third World cities have not materialized.[8] Their view is that informally organized groups facilitate the adjustment of the urban poor and rural migrants to their environment and constitute a barrier against socially and politically destabilizing phenomena, for several reasons.

First, networks (especially patron-client clusters) tend to cut across social classes, and they therefore preempt or dilute class loyalties and consciousness among the poor. Second, networks shelter the poor against the anomie, normlessness, and alienation that earlier writers had predicted. They provide individuals with arenas for socialization and enable them to develop a sense of community and collective identity. In so doing, they help integrate the poor and recent migrants into the urban political order.[9] Third, and perhaps most importantly, circles of kin, neighbors, and friends, or access to a powerful patron, are valuable sources of aid and assistance. In fact, individuals often are drawn into these groups because of their ability to deliver material support in ways that are perceived as more personal and effective than many official institutions that are explicitly designed to help the population economically.[10] In situations characterized by widespread unemployment, low wages, physical vulnerability, and material scarcity, networks provide essential channels for securing food, shelter, jobs, licenses, permits, medical aid, credit, and other vital necessities. Frequently, for instance, individuals will pool their resources together to create informal credit associations that they can use at times of emergency or in order to save for a much-needed item.

The literature on urban politics in the Third World has paid particular attention to the stabilizing role played by patron-client relationships, noting that patronage networks usually operate as channels through which Third World governments can respond to the limited demands of the urban poor and therefore diffuse their destabilizing potential.

> Demands are often highly localized and parochial, and governments respond to them through patron-client networks, keeping the organizations of the urban poor very localized and dependent on middlemen who are part of the government apparatus. Where independent leaders spring up, they may be coopted or coerced by government. Thus, political participation may be going on and demands being made, but the demands are not radical, and to the extent that the government can provide some goods and services or hold out the hope that goods and services will be forthcoming, they are not destabilizing. (Bienen 1984, 669)[11]

Joan Nelson goes even farther to assert that "participation through patrons or brokers is inherently conservative and 'within the system'" (Nelson 1979, 394). This "conservative bias," according to Nelson, emerges from the fact that "neither traditional leaders nor patrons are likely to use the political power inherent in their followings to bring about substantial change, since such change would almost surely undermine their own positions" (Nelson 1979, 166). In any case, she notes, "parties, including radical parties, seldom make sustained and vigorous efforts to win support among the urban poor" (Nelson 1979, 166). Likewise, Huntington believes that the urban poor are primarily concerned with obtaining immediate benefits, and that these benefits "can only be secured by working through, rather than against, the existing system" (Huntington 1968, 280). He adds:

> Like the European immigrant to nineteenth-century urban America, the rural migrant to the modernizing city today is fodder for political machines and bosses who deliver the goods rather than for ideological revolutionaries who promise the millennium. (280)

Finally, Wayne Cornelius's work on low-income neighborhoods in the periphery of Mexico City deserves special mention. It describes in a very detailed fashion how the government, through patron-client ties, coopts and controls the leaders of popular communities, who are known as *caciques* (Cornelius 1975, 1977). By acting as brokers between their respective communities and higher officials in the government-party apparatus, *caciques* promote the integration of local communities into the state and thereby dampen the destabilizing potential of rapid urbanization in Mexico.[12] What emerges from Cornelius's work is the "functionality" of the *cacique* for the Mexican political system.[13] The *cacique* mobilizes his followers, many of whom are recent rural migrants who have no detailed knowledge or understanding of national politics, for regular displays of public support for the government (Cornelius 1977, 347). His role, however, does not stop there.

> [He] is also expected to maintain 'control' of his settlement—to keep order, avoid scandals and public demonstrations embarrassing to the government, and head off any other type of occurrences which might disrupt social tranquility or undermine confidence in the regime. He also has obligations to 'orient' his followers politically (i.e., propagandize on behalf of the regime and strengthen local identification with it) and to organize the participation of his followers in elections, voter registration campaigns, and other forms of officially prescribed political activity. Finally, the *cacique*

is expected to assist the regime in minimizing demands for expensive, broad-scope benefits which might 'load' the political system beyond its responsive capabilities. (Cornelius 1977, 347–48)

To sum up, scholars recently have been inclined to downplay the political dangers traditionally associated with rapid urbanization. Not denying the association between urbanization and political mobilization, they do question the nature and organizational bases of such mobilization. They maintain, for example, that contrary to theories widespread in the 1960s, the increase in participation that accompanies social mobilization does not rest on class and sectoral interests. Instead, they assert, such participation is more likely to express itself through informal networks based on residential, tribal, ethnic, sectarian, or patron-client relationships (Nelson 1987). Participation within such networks, they continue, takes place within, not against, the established political system. It is also more likely to take the form of bargaining and negotiation for access to goods and services—water, sewers, electricity, garbage removal, schools and teachers, health facilities, and so on—rather than a recalcitrant and boisterous call for a radical restructuring of society.

Thus, study after study describes the urban poor as optimistic, pragmatic, responsible individuals who not only accept the system but actively participate in it to achieve their own ends. In settings that are predominantly authoritarian, the poor are understandably very reluctant to engage in large-scale disruptive activities. Instead, they see the city as an opportunity for upward social mobility and attempt to improve their situation through individual and group action. Informal groupings and associations, in this context, become channels through which the poor organize and try to lobby the state for concrete advantages and benefits.[14] In the process, networks contribute to the neutralization of the lower classes' revolutionary potential.

2

Urban Networks as Destabilizing Forces

As the preceding chapter documented, leading scholars of urbanization in the Third World have concluded that one of the major reasons why the urbanization process in the Third World has not been as politically destabilizing as earlier writers had anticipated is because it is accompanied by a strengthening of informal networks. Numerous case studies suggest that these networks are supportive of the existing political order because they shelter the migrants and the urban poor against personal disorientation, provide them with access to vital goods and services, and facilitate their integration into the urban political order. Scholars of Third World urbanization, and certainly Joan Nelson and Henry Bienen, do not deny that networks can be used for destablilizing purposes, but they pay no attention to that possibility.

In contrast, this book's primary goal is to show that, while informal networks can indeed provide for social cohesion and integration, they can also operate as ideal bases for the articulation of grievances in the political arena. Before we turn to a historical and comparative documentation of this phenomenon in a Middle Eastern context, the approach that will underlie the presentation of the evidence in the subsequent chapters must first be presented. To do so, it is convenient to distinguish between patron-client clusters, on the one hand, and networks based on religious, ethnic, and neighborhood ties, on the other hand.

Clientelist Networks as Vehicles for Political Protest

It is hard to deny that, for the reasons that were examined in the preceding chapter, patron-client networks usually reduce the potential for political conflict. Yet, in their rush to describe the stabilizing features of clientelism, scholars of Third World urbanization have paid insuffcient attention to several kinds of situations in which clientelist networks are far from playing the integrative role usually attributed to them.

To begin with, very rapid socioeconomic and political changes can have destabilizing effects that clientelist structures cannot contain. As will be shown later, many of the strains that the Lebanese polity experienced as early as the 1950s can be analyzed in this light. The collapse of the political system in Lebanon in 1975 can in part be traced back to the inability of the clientelist structure of control in Beirut to cope with the political consequences of rapid urbanization and with the emergence of an aspirant elite that could not be absorbed into the existing patronage networks. Lebanon also illustrates the dangers of clientelism in multiconfessional or weakly institutionalized societies, which seem to encourage the emergence of a disruptive form of clientelism. Finally, the Lebanese experience demonstrates that at times patrons can lose control over their clients and brokers, and that in such circumstances, violence may become extremely difficult to control.

More importantly, evidence from both Lebanon and Iran suggests that, under certain circumstances, patrons may use their followings in a highly destabilizing way. Thus, while one might agree that, more often than not, patronage systems uphold established power structures, one might still question statements such as "Participation through patrons or brokers is inherently conservative and 'within the system,'" and "Neither traditional leaders nor patrons are likely to use the political power inherent in their followings to bring about substantial change, since such change would almost surely undermine their own positions" (Nelson 1979, 394, 212). In fact, we will examine many situations in which urban patrons have used their followings to attempt to bring about a radical change in the existing sociopolitical system.

It seems that authors who suggest that clientelism is always stabilizing have a very specific kind of patron in mind—actually only one of many possible types. By "patrons" they essentially mean individuals who belong to the established authorities and whose interest it is to back the power structure. Not all patrons are of that kind, however. In both Iran and Lebanon, for instance, large segments of the urban poor have consistently escaped the control of the establishment, and they sometimes have followed a counterelite that has worked not within, but against, the system.

Nonclientelist Networks

In turning to informal networks based on religious, ethnic, occupational, or residential ties, can we assume that they too are inherently stabilizing because they dilute class perceptions, shelter the poor against anomie and isolation, and provide them with access to vital goods and services? Part 3 will show that, at times, such networks, instead of acting as buffers against militancy, may in fact provide the poor with the determination and the resources to become destabilizing political actors. Although they provide some of the economic, social, and psychological support needed to absorb the tensions associated with rapid socioeconomic change, informal networks also offer channels for the articulation of grievances and for the mobilization of the poor into destabilizing political activities. Here, it might be useful to put this study's argument concerning such networks in historical perspective.

We saw earlier that some writers had predicted that rapid urbanization would lead to political unrest, because they anticipated that urbanization would be accompanied by the destruction of intimate social circles based on kinship, friendship, or ethnic, religious, residential, and occupational ties. These writers' line of reasoning as summarized in chapter 1 is shown in figure 1.

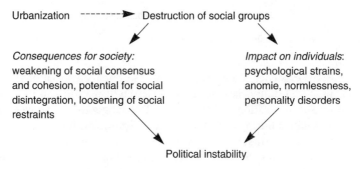

Figure 1. From Social Atomization to Instability

We also saw, however, that research on Third World cities in the 1960s and 1970s has shown that urbanization in fact strengthens informal networks. As they move into the cities, populations create or recreate social circles. Such networks, according to recent studies, facilitate the adjustment of these pre-dominantly poor populations to their environment, and therefore constitute one of the primary reasons why Third World cities have not experienced any massive and sustained turmoil. The line of reasoning, here, is something like that shown in figure 2.

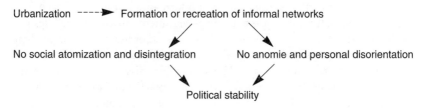

Figure 2. Networks as Stabilizing Forces

Against this background, I suggest the scenario described in figure 3 may in fact take place in many instances:

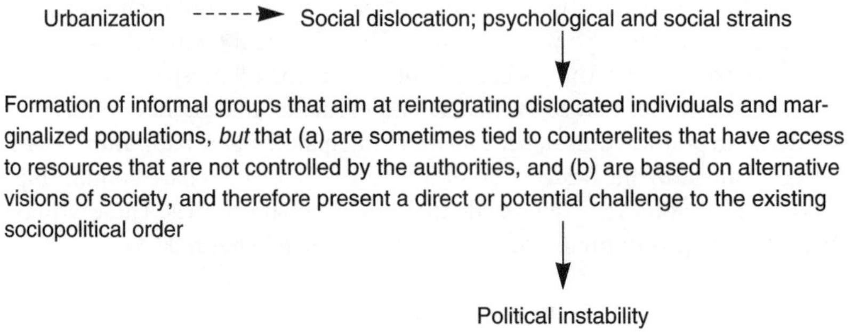

Urbanization   -----▶ Social dislocation; psychological and social strains

                                                      ↓

Formation of informal groups that aim at reintegrating dislocated individuals and marginalized populations, *but* that (a) are sometimes tied to counterelites that have access to resources that are not controlled by the authorities, and (b) are based on alternative visions of society, and therefore present a direct or potential challenge to the existing sociopolitical order

                                                      ↓

                          Political instability

Figure 3.   Networks as Destabilizing Forces

Thus, the existence of a dense network of secondary associations among the poor may well dilute class perceptions, lessen alienation and uprootedness, reduce social isolation, provide access to vital goods and services, and therefore facilitate adjustment to the urban environment. It does not necessarily follow, however, that these networks are always stabilizing.

To the above, one should add that, because of their small size, networks are sometimes in a better position to ensure personal effort and commitment than are large, formal organizations. In a small group, an individual can more easily believe that his or her participation will make a significant difference, and she or he can more easily be punished (through both symbolic and physical sanctions) for failing to contribute to the group's objectives. As a result, small groups minimize Olson's "free-rider" problem and therefore can facilitate political mobilization.[1]

Networks offer several other elements needed for successful collective action. They strengthen trust and solidarity among their members and can provide a population with the minimum degree of internal structure required for political mobilization. They also offer meeting places, contacts, and channels for the circulation and communication of information. Moreover, because of their informal nature, they are hard for governments to control and locate. Therefore, where repressive regimes make it difficult or impossible for political opposition to express itself through the channels of formal organizations such as political parties, labor unions, and interest groups, dissent is likely to take the form of small, personalistic groups based on informal ties and loyalties. In other words, preexisting social networks that are nominally nonpolitical constitute in fact very precious resources for insurgents against authoritarian governments.

Under repressive regimes, furthermore, informally organized groups of peers, friends, coreligionists, or neighbors are sometimes the only social bodies to enjoy a substantial degree of autonomy from the central authorities. By participating in these networks, therefore, the poor may develop ways of resisting the cultural hegemony that those in power usually exert. They may begin to reflect on their situation, and, given the new sense of empowerment they may also derive from active involvement in these groups, they might conclude that oppression and injustice are not inevitable and can be eliminated through political action.

The relevance of informal networks to political protest also stems from their potential contribution to community building. When individuals participate in dense and overlapping social circles, they often come to form a community, endowed with a sense of collective identity and purpose. Historically, such cohesive communities have been much better able than dislocated groups and unanchored masses to pose a threat to a regime. It is in this light that the networks of the Iranian bazaar and religious community will be examined.

Finally, the possibility that rapid urbanization may strengthen distinctive subcultures and social worlds that subsequently may clash with one another deserves perhaps special emphasis. One might anticipate that, as city size increases, especially in ethnically or religiously divided societies, the networks that will be formed among recent migrants will be based on already existing cultural cleavages. If so, networks will enhance the internal solidarity of each of the communities that constitute the country, but they might also increase the social distance between these communities and therefore weaken the population's attachment to urban society and the country as a whole. Micro-loyalties to sect or ethnic group may come to supersede the macro-loyalty to the nation. The more rapid and the more pronounced the urbanization process, the larger the size of the cohesive urban subcommunities that make up the city, and perhaps the greater the potential of conflict between them. The city and its growth can therefore have an independent impact on political conflict, and this impact can be exercised through the multiplication of networks that urbanization often brings about. As Claude Fischer has noted:

> Cities...*intensify* the distinctiveness of their subcultures. The very numbers of people in any social location means that they are more likely to reach the 'critical mass' it takes to become worlds unto themselves: to support institutions such as clubs, stores, and newspapers; to provide the entirety of an individual's social needs so that relations with outsiders are unnecessary; to enforce cultural norms; and to provide a clear identity. Moreover, so many

distinct subcultures compressed into a small geographical area inevitably means contact, confrontation, and conflict between people with differing styles of behavior and belief....In these encounters, fealty to one's own way of life is usually reaffirmed and subcultural boundaries are buttressed. Thus cities, as cities, make themselves into those pluralistic mosaics of "little worlds." (Fischer 1982, 12)

As will be seen, such connections among rapid urbanization, the multiplication of networks, and the development of increasingly coherent and separate subcultures that turn the city into a mosaic of distinct social worlds have obvious implications for the Lebanese case. More generally, the previous considerations clearly suggest that while networks usually play a stabilizing role, they also have the potential to become vehicles for political protest. In this context, the key question is: Under which conditions do informal groups become destabilizing? The following chapters, which look at the politics of several Middle Eastern cities both in historical times and during the more recent period, will provide answers to this essential question.

Part II

Informal Networks
in the
Traditional Middle Eastern
Urban Political Economy

The 'institutional' history of Middle Eastern and Islamic urban societies is not to be understood in terms of formal political, legal, and social structures, but rather in terms of informal relations among individuals, classes, and groups. (Lapidus 1984, xiv)

3

Informal Networks as Integrative Force and Medium of Government in the Historic Middle Eastern City

For two reasons it is difficult to generalize about Middle Eastern cities in historical times. First, these cities differed considerably across a region that stretches over several thousand square miles. Second, they changed significantly over time, depending on factors such as shifting trade routes, the fortunes of ruling dynasties, wars, epidemics, and the evolution of crafts. Yet despite the different physical environments and periods in which they developed, Middle Eastern cities shared certain distinctive political characteristics, which one encounters from one end of the region to another and from the ninth century (when a distinctive urban civilization first arose in the Arab-Muslim Empire) to the early nineteenth century (when the first seeds of modernization and Westernization were introduced into the region).

Accordingly, the following chapters refer to "the historic Middle Eastern city" in an attempt to capture the essence of what constituted urban politics in the premodern Middle East. Inevitably, the concept of a historic Middle Eastern city oversimplifies very complex situations, events, and processes and downplays regional and historical variations. Indeed, it may even offend historians, well attuned to these differences. Yet the outside observer who takes a broad look at the Middle East prior to the region's dramatic encounter with an expanding Europe in the nineteenth century is struck less by the differences she or he expects when dealing with such a vast area over a millenium than by the relative unity and distinct political style and institutions that transcended these divisions.

A major feature of Middle Eastern urban society in historical times was the lack of formally organized political groups and of elected municipal bodies representing the collective interests of the city.[1] As one looks at the historic Middle Eastern city, it becomes apparent that, although Middle Eastern cities saw the development of groups that often became somewhat more structured and formally organized over time,[2] these groups never developed into full-blown corporate entities similar, for instance, to the municipal councils or the guilds in medieval Western Europe.[3] Accordingly, historians have emphasized the fluidity, the "looseness" (Stern 1970, 26), the "relative openness" (Hodgson 1974, 64), and the lack of "corporativeness" (Moore 1974) of premodern Middle Eastern urban societies.[4]

The salience of informal networks in the historic Middle Eastern city is directly correlated to the weakness of formal groups. Indeed, although the urge to belong to intimate and tightly knit social groups is a universal phenomenon, it is inevitably more pronounced in societies where there are few formally organized groups capable of satisfying collective needs, of protecting individuals against violence and deprivations, and of acting as intermediaries between them and society at large (Cahen 1959b). Before proceeding any farther, it is necessary to discuss briefly why Middle Eastern societies belonged to this category of societies.

Islam and the Political Salience of Informal Networks

The "uninstitutionalized" or "unincorporated" nature of groups and group loyalties in the historic Middle Eastern city was not primarily due to cultural factors. Instead, it was a natural product of two essential political characteristics of the region in premodern times. Most important was the unwillingness of Middle Eastern states and city authorities to tolerate the rise of independent and tightly structured bodies. Thus, the substantial power of the state's bureaucracy and army thwarted the possibility that groups attempting to represent their own interests could develop formally organized institutions autonomous from those of the authorities.[5] A second significant factor was the absence or weakness of a full-fledged indigenous bourgeoisie.[6] This factor proved important; in the West after all, it was the commercial bourgeoisie that acted as the dynamic force behind the emergence of the cities as distinct and largely autonomous political entities, with separate powers and privileges, their own councils, assemblies, parliaments and courts.

Overall, therefore, culture cannot be said to be the major cause of the salience of informal networks in the historic Middle Eastern city. This conclusion, however, needs to be qualified by considering a series of conjectural but plausible hypotheses concerning the influence of Islam on the sociopolitical structure of premodern Middle Eastern cities. Thus, leading scholars of the Middle East, such as Claude Cahen, Albert Hourani, and Marshall Hodgson, have suggested that Islam—somewhat ironically for a religion that aimed at universality—may have promoted a degree of fragmentation in the city and heightened the prominence of informally organized groups that were parochial in orientation. The next few pages will now turn to an examination of these hypotheses.

At the heart of Islamic doctrine is the notion that each man stands in a direct, unmediated relationship to God. Thus, unlike their Christian counterparts, for example, Muslim men of religion were never said to have the power to intercede with God on behalf of believers or to grant God's forgiveness for past sins. More generally, the Quran made it clear that Islam and its scriptures were under the guardianship of the community as a whole, not of one particular group among the faithful, such as the clergy. Muslim clerics, therefore, were never really seen as essential to the survival of Islam. Partially as a result, they were never organized into a highly structured, centralized, and hierarchical church. Thus, unlike Christianity, Islam offered no religiously sanctioned model for the building of formally organized groups. In fact, as will be argued subsequently, given Prophet Muhammad's heavy reliance on informal ties and loyalties to spread the faith, early Islamic history would seem to provide some cultural legitimation for organizing public life around informal networks.

More decisive was probably the role of Islamic law (the *shari'a*). The difference between Muslims and non-Muslims was always at the very heart of Islamic doctrine. Accordingly, Islamic law and Islamic societies provided individuals with different rights and privileges, depending on whether or not they belonged to the *umma*, the community of Muslim believers. Therefore, while residential segregation according to religious background antedates the rise of Islam, the sharp legal distinctions that Islamic law made between Muslims and non-Muslims must have accentuated the tendency to divide urban space according to religious affiliation. This segmentation of the urban population into Muslim and non-Muslim quarters, in turn, might well have contributed to the strengthening of small local groups that were based on overlapping neighborhood and religious affiliations.

Furthermore, as Albert Hourani correctly points out, "Islamic law did not recognize corporate personality except in a limited sense, and the whole spirit of Islamic social thought went against the formation of limited groups within which there might grow up an exclusive natural solidarity hostile to the all-inclusive solidarity of an *umma* based on common obedience to God's command" (Hourani 1970, 14).[7] This unwillingness to recognize any formal intermediaries between man and God stands in sharp contrast to the recognition, in Roman law, of the idea of legal associations and of juridical persons (Stern 1970, 47). In medieval Western Europe, this recognition presumably facilitated the development of formally organized, corporate structures. One suspects that the absence of such recognition in the Middle East contributed to the lack of comparable developments.

Similarly, while the population of late medieval Western towns could draw on the notions of legal associations and juridical persons in Roman law to get the rulers to grant privileges (the charters) to municipal bodies, Middle Eastern populations could not find in the *shari'a* equivalent concepts that might have enabled them to engage in a drive toward urban autonomy (Shoshan 1986, 211). Considerations such as these may help explain why Middle Eastern cities never developed the equivalent of those communal assemblies and councils that, in the West during the later medieval period, were instrumental in enabling the cities to acquire a substantial degree of autonomy vis-à-vis the feudal lords in the neighboring countryside.

More generally, Islamic law in traditional Middle Eastern societies did not provide for, or encourage, the individual's incorporation into formally organized bodies or a system of stratification that once and for all determined his or her place in society and his or her accompanying rights and privileges. The contrast with India and its caste system, and with the feudal order of medieval Europe, could hardly be starker (Hodgson 1974, 63–64). Such a situation implied very substantial benefits for the individual: a high degree of personal liberty and potential mobility in the social structure. Its major drawback, however, is that it also left the individual relatively isolated and therefore quite vulnerable and insecure (Hodgson 1974, 64). It is partly to compensate for such isolation, vulnerability, and lack of integration into a community, that the individual was drawn to the informal networks that constitute the focus of this study.

A look at the relationship between the individual and what we would now call "the state" yields similar conclusions. Medieval Middle Eastern societies, in fact, never developed a true concept of state or public law—perhaps, once again, partly because of Islam (Cahen 1959a). In these societies, there was, in theory at least, only one legitimate and unalterable source of law, the *shari'a*, which had been bestowed once and for all by God, in the form of the Quran. The government was not the source of this sacred Law. It was not even seen as its primary custodian, since the duty of defending and upholding the Law fell on the community of believers as a whole. The ruler's duty, theoretically at least, was limited to creating conditions under which the *shari'a* could be preserved, and Islamic values, ethics, and ways of life flourish.

Given such religious beliefs, and the extent to which they were embraced by the population, the state could only be seen as a superstructure with which the population felt in fact very little solidarity—the more so since the rulers were often foreigners who did not even speak the local language, and since they often acted in ways blatantly contrary to Islamic precepts (Cahen 1959a, 26). For its part, the state felt it had only minimal obligations toward the populations over which it ruled. Against such a background, it was all the more essential for individuals to belong to some tightly knit and private grouping on whose unconditional support they could rely for purposes of defense, protection, and mediation with an otherwise impersonal urban environment (Cahen 1958b; Hodgson 1974, 106). In this respect as well, therefore, Islam may have contributed to the salience of informal networks in the Middle East's traditional urban political economy.

Finally, unlike religions that are closely associated with a specific tribe, territory, or ethnic group (one thinks here in particular of Judaism), Islam is a faith that deliberately aims at universalism and that specifically condemns allegiance to a specific territory.[8] Thus, within the Islamic community, Islam encouraged cosmopolitanism as opposed to the kind of local civic solidarity that, in medieval Western Europe, proved conducive to the emergence of formally organized structures (municipalities, communes, etc.) whose explicit aim was to embody and defend the rights and interests of the town as a corporate entity. In fact, Islam tended to promote a situation in which cities were interconnected (through men who moved from one end of the Islamic world to another in search of religious knowledge, and through the general feeling that cities belonged to the same moral community formed by those who shared a belief in the faith), while there existed a substantial degree of fragmentation within the cities themselves. Local corporate entities did not thrive in Muslim lands, in part because, as Hodgson has correctly observed, "they presumed differential rights according to class and territorial status. That is, a man had rights and duties as member of a commune or of a municipality which an outsider could not have....Under Islam, with its cosmopolitan outlook, such parochial rights and duties were not judicially recognized. A person was not a citizen of a particular town, with local rights and responsibilities determined by his local citizenship; as a free Muslim he was a 'citizen' of the whole Dar al-Islam, with responsibilities determined by his presence before God alone. Legally, there was no true boundary line between the territory of one town and that of another, nor between a town and the surrounding countryside; and movement was free" (Hodgson 1974, 108).

In its cosmopolitanism as well, therefore, Islam tended to discourage the emergence of formally organized groups and institutions. By the same token, it also reinforced the need for individuals to belong to informally organized networks that provided for a degree of security and integration into the urban sociopolitical order.

Thus, although the vitality of small networks built around personal ties and loyalties, and the existence of loosely knit groups that are often parochial in orientation, are phenomena that are hardly peculiar to the Islamic world or to the Middle East, and although it is also true that the Middle East saw such groups proliferate and flourish much before the rise of Islam,[9] Islam may have provided a particularly favorable terrain for the development of such associations, while also making it difficult for them to evolve into truly corporate, formal entities (Cahen 1958b, 26).

While political authoritarianism, the absence of a significant indigenous bourgeoisie, and the independent impact of Islam thwarted the development of formal institutions, councils, or self-governing bodies, Middle Eastern populations devised other ways of participating in public life and of preserving social cohesion, order, and a sense of community. Thus, in the absence of formal political organizations, informally organized groups that had not been formed for explicitly political purposes were called on to perform vital political tasks (Hodgson 1974, 68).

Observers of the traditional Middle Eastern city again and again have been struck by the effectiveness with which these networks held society together and guaranteed a high level of public activity. Hodgson (1974) emphasizes their part in providing "means of maintaining social norms and of achieving social goals: of mediating between the individual and a vast impersonal social environment" (106). Similarly, Le Tourneau notes their instrumental role in binding together, and creating a balance between, the various cells and groups that constituted Fez before the French protectorate. In Fez, as in other cities, this integrative power, while not backed up by institutions, was nevertheless strong enough to have lasted for centuries (Le Tourneau 1957, 45–46; Le Tourneau 1949, 211–73). Overall, the vitality of informal networks in the historic Middle Eastern city suggests an image that differs significantly from the lingering and simplistic view of a "Middle Eastern despotism," in which a Leviathan-type state rules over apathetic, atomized, and powerless societies, deprived of collective will and of any ability to resist the exactions of predatory governments.

The informal networks through which the dynamism of civil society expressed itself belonged to two overlapping categories. The first consisted of those informal ties that ran from members of the governing elite down to commoners, through key intermediaries (such as ulama, wealthy merchants, and leaders of quarters and sufi orders). These ties worked as important channels of communication between the regime and the population. The second type of informal network was, on the whole, independent of direct participation by members of the governing elite. It consisted of various voluntary associations based on quarter, kinship, religious, or occupational affiliations.

The Stabilizing Role of Patron-Client Networks

In the historic Middle Eastern city, the barriers that always separate the rulers from the ruled were unusually high. For instance, from about the tenth century onward, the local elite was usually of Turkish origins and Turkish-speaking, while the population over which it ruled was Arabic- or Persian-speaking (Hourani 1970, 17). Thus, the local rulers were essentially outsiders who had no long-standing ties to, and little knowledge of, native society. Often, as mentioned earlier, they did not even speak the local language. In the Mamluks' case, Staffa notes, "it was [even] considered a degradation for a man in high office to have great familiarity with the language of the country" (1977, 120).

As a result, individuals, by and large, did not identify with their rulers. Nor did they expect the authorities to embody the community's aspirations and ideals. They were content with seeing the local elites defend the community against outside threats, supply food, ensure public order, and engage in some minimal infrastructure works. In other words, they simply expected the authorities to create the general sociopolitical and economic conditions in which the community might best pursue its moral and religious values, free from interference by the state (Mottahedeh 1980, 187–88). The local government, by and large, conformed to these expectations, and adopted a laissez-faire attitude toward society.

In such a context, it is not surprising that contacts between elite and masses should have been primarily of a clientelist nature. Given the linguistic and ethnic barriers that often separated the elite from the population, the government had to rely on local leaders in its dealings with the community. Even when the distance between rulers and ruled diminished, as in the Ottoman period, the authorities found it easier and more effective to use prominent individuals and middlemen than to attempt to set up a bureaucratic administration.

The vitality of patronage networks between rulers and ruled also reflected technological constraints. Given the still-limited capacity of the instruments of control and government available to it, the urban elite had to rely on personal ties to achieve its goals (Staffa 1977, 5). Between rulers and ruled, it is only natural that such ties should have taken primarily the form of an exchange of favors, goods, and services in return for political obedience and loyalty.

Historians have spoken of a "politics of notables" to describe the public life of societies in which clientelist ties between the regime and the population loomed so large.[10] As the leading members of local society, the "notables" represented the community and operated as mediators between it and the local, military elite. They and their respective families often entered into alliances and coalitions among themselves, creating in the process an informal urban leadership structure.

In the absence of formal mechanisms and institutions capable of ensuring the government's control over the population, the notables were key intermediaries between state and society. They made the people accessible to the government, and the government somewhat more accessible to the people. They helped overcome the lack of direct communication between ethnically alien elites and the local population and were one of the most important integrative forces in society.

As a rule, the notables exerted a stabilizing and moderating influence on urban politics. After all, the basic attribute of these dignitaries and leading personalities was that, under normal circumstances, they could deliver the cooperation of their followers to the authorities. Moreover, they were usually quite content to play the role of middlemen and had no ambition of substituting themselves for the authorities. Staffa (1977, 393) has put forward several very plausible hypotheses to explain this cautious political behavior.

First, the notables (al-a'yan) knew that the elite (al-khassa) would not hesitate to crack down on them if it felt threatened by them. Al-a'yan were supposed to be a link between the elite and the commoners (al-'amma)—not a rival to the elite. The notables understood this. They were not willing to risk losing the considerable power they already had as brokers and mediators by overstepping the boundaries within which the elite was willing to tolerate their power. It was, after all, from their position as key intermediaries between state and society that they derived a great deal of their influence and sometimes even wealth. Al-a'yan were also very much aware of their dependence on the military authorities to keep the trade routes open, bring in the food supply from the rural hinterland, and, if need be, restore order and social peace by the force of arms.

The notables also knew that they were hardly a match for the elite, which had a quasi monopoly over military force and a propensity for using it ruthlessly if necessary. By and large, in any case, the notables were ill prepared to assume the leadership of an armed movement. Neither were they, by disposition, inclined to violence. Most importantly, perhaps, "elite regimes came and went and elite houses came and went faster. The notables, on the other hand, went on" (Staffa 1977, 393). In other words, in the long run it was safer and more profitable to belong to al-a'yan (the group of notables) than to al-khassa (the elite). The rewards were fewer, but one was likely to enjoy them longer.

Some Historical Examples of Patron-Client Networks

In his study of Damascus, Cairo, and Aleppo under the Mamluk dynasty (1258–1517), Lapidus showed how the Mamluks established ties of patronage that linked them directly to all groups in urban society, including the lower social classes. The ties between the Mamluk governing elite and the Muslim clerics, the ulama, were probably the most important ones. The Mamluks, who were alien to local society, had to rely on the ulama for several reasons: (1) because the ulama were the official interpreters of the law in a society where the *shari'a* (Islamic law) regulated almost every aspect of daily life; (2) unlike the Mamluks, the ulama were familiar with local traditions; (3) their religious learning and sometimes ancestry often commanded the population's respect; and (4) they controlled the *awqaf* (religious endowments), which provided them with a strong economic base.

Thus, the ulama were in the best position to become brokers between the regime and the population, and they happily fulfilled that role. The relationship between the Mamluks and the ulama remained essentially a clientelist one, and it worked to the benefit of both partners. On the one hand, the state provided the ulama with official recognition, state support for religious institutions, as well as employment as administrators, judges, notaries, and the like. On the other hand, the ulama contributed to the legitimation of Mamluk rule and dealt with the authorities on behalf of the population in matters of public order, security, taxation, the provision of essential foodstuffs, and the maintenance of public facilities (Lapidus 1973b, 56).

The ulama's role as intermediaries between the regime and the population was perhaps most manifest at times of tension between the government and the population. At that point, the local population would ask the ulama to present its grievances to the authorities and to press for the rescission of unpopular measures. The Mamluks, in turn, would use the ulama to restrain the population.

The Mamluks also established links of a patron-client nature with members of the merchant class, especially the most prominent ones. The wealthiest merchants stood to benefit most from public projects and from the considerable expenses of the ruling household. In addition, they frequently performed important functions for the state, including money lending, and sometimes even managed specialized departments in the central administration (Lapidus 1984). In return for this privileged access to the state, the Mamluks expected the leading merchants to use their influence to implement government directives in the marketplace.

The Mamluks also strove to establish direct channels of communication with the commoners (*al-'amma*). Several concerns must have justified such a strategy. First, of course, was a desire to prevent any potential union of the notables and the lower classes against the regime. Equally important, perhaps, direct access to the lower classes gave the Mamluks the option of playing the masses against the notables in order to check the latter's political ambitions.

The Mamluks' ties to the lowest social classes—what Marxists would call the "lumpenproletariat"—played a particularly important role in their general strategy of balancing social forces against one another. For one, the Mamluks could always, implicitly or explicitly, threaten the notables and the commoners with unleashing against them the violence inherent in the paramilitary groups and gangs known as *zu'ar*.[11] Competing factions within the Mamluk elite would even use the *zu'ar* as a weapon to settle their disputes. The *zu'ar* were only too happy to cooperate, and in Cairo, for instance, they would frequently "hire themselves out as auxiliaries of the Mamluk factions in times of civil war for the sake of gifts and above all for a free hand to plunder the quarters and markets" (Lapidus 1984, 173–74).

Such clientelist strategies continued after the Mamluks. Under the Ottomans (1517–1914), especially, the role of the notables in urban politics reached its zenith, particularly in the cities of geographical Syria (including present-day Lebanon) and Palestine. This was perhaps a natural development, insofar as a rather weak central authority in Istanbul could hardly hope to maintain any control over faraway cities without acknowledging the power of the dominant local forces and relying on them to govern. Even as late as the second half of the nineteenth century, when the Ottomans began to implement reforms (the *tanzimat*) aimed at strengthening central control over the provinces of the empire, local politics continued to revolve around patron-client networks. In Damascus, for instance, these reforms fostered the development of a group of "landowner-bureaucrats": members of locally prominent, large, landowning families, who were often thriving as a result of agrarian commercialization, and who were also moving into important positions in the rapidly expanding Ottoman bureaucracy. As these individuals suddenly found themselves in an enhanced position to dispense "favors or benefits in the form of jobs, contracts, and access to and protection from government,...patronage networks were extended and diversified, and a certain stability, unknown in Damascus for generations, reigned in the city and its provinces" (Khoury 1983b, 47).

Attempts by the ruling elite to govern through the distribution of patronage and the manipulation of informal relations between individuals and groups were not phenomena limited to the Arab world or to Sunni societies. They likewise apply to Shiite Iran under the Safavid (1501–1786) and Qajar (1779–1924) dynasties.

To control the population of Iran's major cities, the Safavids relied primarily on key individuals who acted as transmission belts between state and society: the *qadis* (judges), the *Imam jom'ehs* (the leaders of the Friday prayer), the *shaykh al-Islams* (presidents of the religious courts, and chief religious officials of the cities), the *kalantars* (sorts of mayors), and the *kadkhudas* (guild and district leaders). Under the Qajars, in the late eighteenth and nineteenth centuries, this system of rule was not significantly altered. In fact, a now weaker central authority increased the freedom of maneuver of the notables. As Abrahamian (1968, 184) emphasizes, "The Qajar dynasty based its power not on a standing army, nor on an extensive bureaucracy, for it had neither, but on the readiness of the magnates, the ulama...the judges, and the guild masters to enforce the shah's will, and the disposition of the subjects to submit to his authority."

The networks of patronage controlled by the Qajars and by the notables in the provinces rested largely on the gifts, pensions, jobs, offices, and salaries that this tiny upper class dispensed to it faithful clients. The direct or indirect dependence of so many people on the largess and conspicuous consumption of the central and provincial elites was a powerful weapon in the rulers' hands. During periods of turmoil, for instance, the elite would often mobilize its clients, retainers, and servants against political insurgents. Significantly, following the first Iranian revolution of 1905–6, which forced the Qajar dynasty to accept the election of a parliament and a constitution that established limits on the monarch's power, the royalist crowds protesting against the newly installed parliamentary regime included large numbers of individuals whose livelihood had been seriously threatened by that regime's decision to impose cuts in the expenses of the royal court and of the aristocracy (Abrahamian 1968, 195–96). Such incidents highlight how important the uninterrupted flow of patronage was in the maintenance of sociopolitical order.

Religious Ties and Networks as an Integrative Force

Over the millenium covered in this part of the book, religion was one of the very few constants in people's lives. In the absence of strong institutions reaching deep into society, Islam held Middle Eastern urban society together by providing spiritual guidance, accepted norms of behavior, and ways of conducting private and commercial transactions. By offering a common reference point in an environment in which parochial loyalties were otherwise very strong, Islamic ideals helped preserve a certain cultural and moral unity in urban society (Lapidus 1984). The search and respect for religious knowledge (*'ilm*) also created important bonds among individuals. Finally, the shared Islamic values of the rulers and the ruled, and the elite's professed commitment to the defense of the faith, helped compensate somewhat for ethnic and lifestyle differences between the elite and the masses.

Religious solidarities expressed themselves most directly through membership in informally organized religious circles, sectarian groups, and religious brotherhoods. These groups—more than the vague sense of belonging to the universal *umma*—provided the believers with concrete opportunities to experience Muslim solidarity.

In particular, from the eleventh century onward, the appearance and development of the Sufi orders (*turuq*, sing. *tariqa*) had a profound influence on Islamic society.[12] Although many of these religious brotherhoods did become more structured over time, most remained loosely organized bodies. Significantly, the term *tariqa* itself "literally means a 'way' or 'path,' and refers to a mode of conduct, not to a formal association" (Bill and Springborg 1990, 92). The *turuq* relied primarily on personal ties among their members. In fact, one essential reason for the success of the Sufi orders was the intense personal devotion of the disciple (*murid*) to his master (*shaykh* or *pir*), as well as the sense of solidarity that united a *tariqa*'s members from one end of the Islamic Empire to another.

Sufi brotherhoods fulfilled vital charitable, educational, administrative, legal, and economic functions that we would now associate with the government. In addition, they provided much-needed psychosociological support, by offering social arenas in which worldly constraints did not apply. Like other religious groups and circles, they operated as a beneficent source of coherence, order, and meaning in lives otherwise dominated by uncertainty and insecurity. Especially for their lower-class members, they were a refuge from chaos and alienation.

More importantly, because Sufism is a form of mysticism that emphasizes group experience, it drew people together and therefore acted as a very important unifying force. In the *zawiyyat* (lodges where the disciples of a particular saint or Sufi shaykh would gather), the *turuq* often brought together rich and poor, and rulers and ruled. Thereby, they helped bridge the existing cleavages in society. Finally, leaders of brotherhoods were often part of the religious establishment, which was itself tightly integrated into the power structure. In such instances, the *turuq* provided channels for the sociopolitical control of the lower classes by the elite.

Professional Networks and Government Supervision of the Marketplace

In the historic Middle Eastern city, men who practiced similar crafts and trades often shared a comparable outlook on life and identified with one another. Even where and when guilds did not exist, fellow merchants and craftsmen were linked to one another through kinship, by social and economic networks of reciprocal ties and obligations, and by membership in informal religious circles. By and large, these networks promoted sociopolitical cohesion and order, in that they fostered a sense of collective identity and community among artisans and shopkeepers.

The authorities also could easily exploit professional ties and solidarities to facilitate government control over the trades and crafts. For instance, from among the more influential craftsmen and merchants, they would frequently select individuals to whom they delegated the responsibility of implementing government directives concerning the trading and manufacturing professions.[13] These individuals inevitably were chosen because of their status in the profession, and because of their prominent positions in the various networks that bound tradesmen and craftsmen to one another. This somewhat unique position made them very valuable to the government, which could expect them to deliver the cooperation of their fellow tradesmen and craftsmen at a minimal cost to the authorities.[14]

The Integrative Aspects of Neighborhood Solidarities and Networks

Living quarters were the building blocks of social life in the traditional Middle Eastern city. Called *hara* (e.g., in Cairo, Damascus, and Sanaʿa), *mahalla* (e.g., in Aleppo, Mosul, and Baghdad), or *hawma* (e.g., in Algiers and Tunis), they were more sociopolitical entities than physical or geographical units. Accordingly, while it was not always easy for outsiders to recognize the physical boundaries of a given neighborhood, insiders had a very precise knowledge of where their quarter stopped.

The population of a given district often shared the same ethnic and religious background. Sometimes, a large segment of the neighborhood's male population also exercised the same profession. Furthermore, relations of patronage often bound individuals and families inside the quarter to one another. Such overlap between residential, ethnic, religious, professional, and patron-client ties inevitably accentuated the distinct identity of each section of the city. They also enhanced social solidarity inside the neighborhood and made it easier for quarter-based networks to develop. More specifically, neighborhood-based feelings and networks had several important stabilizing effects on politics.

Individuals felt a sense of loyalty and attachment to their respective quarters. The quarters' relatively small sizes fostered a feeling of intimacy among their inhabitants, and neighborhood streets, houses, baths, and coffee-houses offered primary avenues for socializing.[15] Overall, this sense of belonging helped contain the potential for social disorder.

The quarters' limited populations also provided for effective policing and sociopolitical control. In societies where the state delivered few public services, neighborhoods and neighborhood-based groups often took upon themselves functions that, in other contexts, are performed by the central government. In addition to the social control already mentioned, tasks commonly carried out by neighborhoods included distributing water, cleaning the streets, providing lighting, and maintaining order and security.

The authorities were often too eager to relegate such responsibilities to the quarters and frequently attempted to strengthen neighborhood solidarities from above. By doing so, they probably hoped to exert a less centralized and costly, yet more effective, control over the quarters' populations. Thus, the government often appointed informal leaders of quarters, variously called *shaykh, ra'is, sharif, muqaddam, muharrik* (in Tunis), or, in Iran, *kadkhuda* (a term also used for village headmen and guild leaders). When central authority was strong, these individuals and their assistants would act almost as agents of the central government. They collected taxes, provided the authorities with information about the quarter, implemented government directives, maintained order, and settled disputes. The authorities, in turn, held the leader of the quarter responsible for potential problems caused by its inhabitants.[16]

Perhaps the most crucial and distinctive feature of neighborhoods is that they ensured the protection and physical security of their populations. They often did so through informal associations of young men from the quarter. These groups were found throughout the region between the ninth and the fifteenth centuries, and they frequently took on paramilitary features.[17] These youth gangs, known as *ahdath, 'ayyarun, zu'ar, 'usab,* or *shuttar,* could easily lapse into extortion and *caciquismo.* Nevertheless, they also frequently policed "their" respective quarters against thieves and protected them against outside threats (including those represented by the many exactions of the state). At times, the authorities even used these gangs as a kind of local militia.

In addition, *ahdath, 'ayyarun,* and their like sometimes engaged in welfare and charitable activities and generally endeavored to promote the conditions of the poor and less privileged elements in urban society. Because they could be coopted and manipulated by the authorities, they also ensured some form of sociopolitical control over many young, restless elements in the lower classes. Finally, by providing a focus for political loyalty and a refuge from marginality, they helped integrate the lower-class youth into urban society.

After the sixteenth century, one hears not so much of groups, but of a few powerful individuals acting as informal leaders and protectors of their respective quarters. In Cairo, such individuals became known as *futuwwat*. Similarly, in Qajar Iran, the *lutis*—who in several ways were the heirs of the *'ayyarun*[18]—often played an active role in urban politics.[19] Although there were "good" and "bad" *lutis* (Robin Hood–like heroes and hooligans), one may adopt Floor's usage of the word *luti* to refer exclusively to a folk hero, and the word *awbash* to refer to the "bad *lutis*" or criminals (Floor 1971, 112–13). In this context, the *lutis* can be described as young individuals, primarily but not exclusively from a lower-class background,[20] who made a very conscious attempt to live up to the code of honor embodied in the *javanmardan*—an important image.

> In its classical or ideal sense, *javanmardan* meant a man who pos-
> sessed noble qualities; one who had a sense of identity...carried
> out his promises, spoke the truth and developed such virtues as
> perseverance, valor and purity in thought, desire, and action. He
> avoided bringing harm to anyone, championed the weak, and
> opposed cruelty....[He was expected] to demonstrate such quali-
> ties as generosity, hospitality, gratitude, chastity, directness in
> behavior and thought, honor, and self-integrity. (Arasteh 1961a,
> 47–48)[21]

The *lutis*, like their predecessors, did not constitute an "organization" in the formal sense of the word. Rather, they formed a series of informal circles loosely connected to one another. The *lutis* of a given quarter usually stuck together, but associations of *lutis* from different quarters of the city were also in touch with one another. Within each circle of *lutis*, meetings were conducted informally, and status and influence were based on informal criteria.[22] For instance, the leaders of *luti* groups (known as *baba-shamal*) were acknowledged as such on an informal basis by their fellow *lutis*. Around 1866, there were an estimated fifteen such leaders in Tehran alone, and these leaders "were treated as if they belonged to the notables of the city" (Floor 1971, 111).

Informally organized as they were, the *lutis* could be very helpful to the populations of their respective quarters. As in the case of the groups that preceded them, the *lutis'* ideals and values led them to undertake various charitable and welfare activities that benefited the population of the quarter, particularly the most deprived elements in it.[23] More importantly, in times of crisis, especially when religious factionalism led to clashes between quarters associated with different sects or religious schools, *lutis* defended their quarter against outside threats. At times, *lutis* from different quarters could even pool their resources together to protect the city as a whole. For example, during the Constitutional Revolution at the beginning of the twentieth century, groups of *lutis* played a key role in defending Tabriz against the Royalist troops sent by the central government (although some *lutis* were also involved on the side of the Royalists).[24]

4

Networks as Vehicles for Political Protest in the Historic Middle Eastern City

Middle Eastern history offers many examples of informal associations, and the ties and loyalties that sustained them, leading to political unrest. We now turn to an examination of some of these examples, since they show very clearly that, while networks usually fulfilled the integrative and stabilizing functions highlighted in the preceding chapter, they also could operate, at times, as destabilizing forces.

Neighborhood Solidarities and Networks as Bases for Political Unrest

The neighborhood-based youth associations that we encountered earlier, and that, from the dawn of Islamic history through the Ottoman period, strengthened social identification with the quarter and protected it against outside threats, were not always stabilizing forces. For one, these groups were quarrelsome and often fought with one another. After all, one of the major reasons behind their appeal was their ability to provide young men in the lower classes with channels for asserting their personal independence. A certain rebelliousness was inevitably associated with this feature. These associations' quasi-military discipline and their frequent association with violent sports—as in Iran, where the *'ayyarun* and the *lutis* used gymnasiums (*zurkhanehs*, literally, "houses of strength") as headquarters—tended to reinforce both the violent character of many of these youth gangs and their effectiveness in the political arena.[1]

Furthermore, *zuʿar*, *ʿayyarun*, and their like often recruited heavily from among criminal elements and independent-minded youths who often were alienated from, and at odds with, the dominant sociopolitical order (Hodgson 1974, 128). Not surprisingly, these groups were frequently involved in all sorts of illegal activities, such as smuggling, gambling, racketeering, and plundering. The rich, however, were their primary targets. In a way, therefore, the members of these associations were "social bandits," Robin Hood–like heroes who, through their often violent actions, expressed their bitterness at what they felt was the injustice of the authorities and of the sociopolitical order in general.[2]

Most importantly, however, the major reason why youth gangs were stabilizing at the level of the quarter was also precisely the one that always made them potentially destabilizing at the level of the urban political system as a whole: By strengthening the internal solidarity of the neighborhood, and by fostering the development of a distinctive subculture within it, residential networks expressed and enhanced a communal, locally based solidarity that was distrustful of outside forces and could easily be turned against the political authorities or against members of rival associations in other quarters.

In particular, the group feelings that united the members of a given quarter often translated themselves into feelings of animosity toward the inhabitants of other quarters, especially neighboring ones, who were easily identified as collective enemies. Thus, intense rivalries and bloody clashes between neighborhoods and neighborhood-based associations abound in Middle Eastern history. At several points in the ninth and tenth centuries, such confrontations led to the total destruction of the cities involved (Cahen 1959a, 27). Centuries later, during the Ottoman period, pitched battles between rival quarters and their youth associations remained a traditional feature of life in cities such as Cairo, Baghdad, and Mosul (Raymond 1985, 304–5).

Neighborhood-based youth gangs also frequently clashed with the authorities in order to protect the quarter's population against the abuses of the government, have some unpopular measure rescinded, or simply keep the government at bay and preserve the quarter's autonomy. In fact, youth associations at times played the role of an extralegal political opposition. They acted as popular militias that helped the quarter protect itself against oppression and state attempts to interfere with the behavior, the lifestyles, and the values of the quarter's inhabitants.[3]

Religious Networks and Political Mobilization

In the historic Middle Eastern city, Islam was not only the unifying force described earlier. The same religious ideals that promoted social order also fostered certain disintegrative tendencies within urban society. Thus, conflicts between quarters associated with different schools of Islamic law, different branches of Islam, or rival Sufi brotherhoods often had disastrous effects on the social fabric.[4] Islamic ideals also could serve as a basis for insurrection against the authorities, since a counterpart to the population's willingness to obey the city government was that the rulers were expected to live up to certain moral standards, grounded in Islamic doctrine. When the elite could be blamed for what appeared as a major violation of this tacit, Islam-based moral and social contract between rulers and ruled,[5] the population frequently rebelled.[6]

More importantly from this study's perspective, networks built around Islamic places, institutions, and personnel offered the organizational resources, the political entrepreneurs, and the followings without which collective action is impossible. In particular, since they were sacred and therefore inviolable places (*hurum*, sing. *harim*), mosques, shrines, *zawiyyat*, and the houses of leading religious figures provided safe havens for the expression of popular discontent.[7] Thus, for example, the Great Mosque (the mosque where the Friday prayer took place) was a focal point in the incidents of urban unrest that affected Cairo and Damascus at the end of the eighteenth century.[8]

For several reasons, religious brotherhoods could serve as particularly effective channels for mobilization against the authorities. They usually enjoyed financial and organizational independence from the state. They were somewhat secretive and therefore could easily operate underground. They often had tremendous popular appeal, as in eighteenth-century Cairo, where, at times of crisis, the Sufi orders could mobilize as many as eighty thousand men (Marsot 1972, 151). Since the brotherhoods also recruited among members of all classes, their influence was felt at all levels of society. Finally, *zawiyyat* operated as a series of interconnected cells, which could pass on political information from one end of the Islamic world to another. These attributes explain why Sufi orders were always potentially destabilizing forces and repeatedly rose against the authorities, as in eighteenth-century Egypt, late-nineteenth-century Algeria (against the French), or during the early years of the Turkish Republic. It is not surprising, therefore, that, in the nineteenth and twentieth centuries, modernizing governments bent on centralizing and concentrating power in their own hands have sought to bring the Sufi orders under the control of the state.

Finally, religious networks also could provide political entrepreneurs for demonstrations, that is, individuals willing to spend time and effort on the organization of a protest movement. Although ulama participation in urban uprisings was, on the whole, a relatively rare occurrence,[9] and although the higher ulama tended to be very moderate and cautious in their political behavior,[10] lesser ulama—a group that included seminary students, the prayer leaders of the smaller mosques in the city, shrine attendants, marriage notaries (*ma'dhuns*) and clerks of *shari'a* courts—sometimes played a quite active role in urban protest movements (Baer 1984, 23).[11]

Unlike the higher ulama, the lesser ulama lived close to the people, whose aspirations and needs they were in a better position to understand. It is the lesser ulama, for instance, who decided matters of personal law, and directed the religious ceremonies held at times of birth, marriage, death, and religious holidays and festivals. They also taught children basic educational skills in the *kuttab* (religious schools), presided over informal religious gatherings, and distributed charities and welfare. It is this multiplicity of contacts, exchanges, and reciprocal influences between the lesser ulama and the lower classes that largely explains the lower-ranking clerics' ability to instigate popular revolts, "albeit without giving [these revolts] leadership and direction" (Baer 1977, 242). For instance, lesser ulama were prominent in the 1798 rebellion against the French in Egypt. Similarly, mullas were highly involved in the popular movements that shook Iranian cities (especially Isfahan) throughout the nineteenth century. Preachers also played an important role in informing, agitating, and mobilizing public opinion during the Constitutional Revolution in Iran (Fathi 1980).

Occupational Networks and Solidarities as Vehicles for Political Protest

When the authorities made decisions that were particularly arbitrary and harmful to the interests of the trading and manufacturing classes—from creating new taxes or imposing low price ceilings in times of food shortages to simply stealing the supplies they wanted—occupational networks could facilitate the emergence of protest movements.[12] Thus, even when guilds did not exist, the absence of formal organization among shopkeepers and artisans did not constitute an insurmountable obstacle to their ability to engage in collective action, which typically involved the shutdown of the bazaar. The various networks that bound craftsmen and merchants to one another in medieval times constantly heightened solidarity and the awareness of shared interests and values in the bazaar. Accordingly, they provided the population of the crafts and trades with the sense of collective identity required for successful political mobilization. Furthermore, commercial networks and contacts could be used to pass on political as well as economic information, and therefore offered lines of communication and ways of ensuring coordination that could be used by political insurgents.

Later on, when guilds did exist, they sometimes provided urban protest movements with some structure. To be sure, guilds usually were too tightly controlled by the government to serve as avenues of political dissent. Nonetheless, in some instances they did contribute to sociopolitical upheavals. The example of the Constitutional Revolution in Iran immediately comes to mind. The revolution was first and foremost a movement of the bazaar, in which the guilds provided financial support, organizational resources, and the rank and file of the demonstrations (Abrahamian 1968, 192–93). Similarly, guilds played an important part in the popular movements that shook Cairo in the late eighteenth and early nineteenth centuries, especially the butchers' guild in the al-Husayniyya quarter, and the vegetable sellers' guild in the Rumayla neighborhood (Raymond 1968, 108–9). This was particularly true during the 1805 uprising that brought to power the founder of modern Egypt, Muhammad Ali.

The contribution of the guilds to protest movements such as these, however, ought to be clarified. First, historians do not show that what enabled the guilds to act as powerful political forces was their *organizational structure*. On the contrary, chroniclers insist on the spontaneous nature of the uprisings. Thus, one feels that it probably was not the guilds themselves, but rather the informal ties and networks that sustained them, that proved decisive. Furthermore, the guilds rarely operated alone. Although our knowledge of the exact connections among guilds, Sufi brotherhoods, and quarters is still very sketchy, it seems clear that all three sources of solidarity were concomitantly involved in many of the protest movements that shook Ottoman cities. In eighteenth-century Cairo, for example, the Husayniyya quarter, the butchers' guild, and the Bayumiyya Sufi order appear to have been bound to one another by a dense web of informal networks and ties.[13] According to Raymond, it is this feature that largely explains the political dynamism that the Husayniyya quarter displayed throughout the eighteenth century (Raymond 1968, 107). Under the leadership of the Shaykh of the Bayumiya, Ahmad Salim al-Jazzar ("The Butcher"), al-Husayniyya rebelled twice when the Ottoman authorities imposed Murad Bey as Governor in 1786 and 1790. Al-Husayniyya was also instrumental in Muhammad Ali's rise to power in 1805 (Staffa 1977, 269).[14]

The Limits of Clientelism
as a Medium for Ensuring Urban Order

Patron-client networks always fell short of guaranteeing stability in the premodern Middle Eastern city. One reason was that the lower classes included a population that was not normally part of the clientelist system of control, or whose integration into the clientelist structure was tenuous at best. This population was made up of either unemployed or underemployed individuals with few or no skills. While most of them probably resided in the city on a permanent basis, some were peasants whom changes in the rural economy drew back and forth between the city and its hinterland (Hourani 1970, 19). This "underworld," and the informal associations that were formed in its ranks, lived on the fringes of society and represented an unstable element. They are referred to in historical sources by terms that demonstrate very clearly the fear that they inspired in commoners and notables alike: *aradhil al-ʿamma* (the lowest of the common people), *al-awbash* or *awbash al-ʿamma* (riffraff of the common people), *al-ghawghaʾ* (the troublemakers), *al-harafish* (the beggars), *al-suqa* (the rabble of the towns), or *aradhil al-suqa* (the lowest of the people professionally involved in the market, e.g., street vendors, hawkers, water carriers, porters, servants, beggars, prostitutes, etc.).[15] The authorities could not count on controlling such groups more than temporarily, and control was always far from total. It is significant perhaps that, although successive Middle Eastern regimes repeatedly cracked down on them, these associations of the underprivileged kept on reappearing, sometimes under different names, whenever circumstances would allow them to do so—as during periods marked by widespread turmoil or a weakening of central authority.[16]

Given this study's interest in the relationship between urbanization and political protest, one might wonder whether these groups were composed of old urban populations, or whether their members were primarily recent migrants from the countryside. The answer to this question is not easy to find, in part because our knowledge of incidents of urban unrest in which the "rabble" played an important part remains sketchy, and in part because it is once again difficult to generalize about the history of a whole region over several centuries. The available evidence, however, indicates that the politically most restless and subversive segments of the lower classes were generally not recent migrants to urban areas, but individuals well integrated into the city. After all, the *ahdath, zuʿar, ʿayyarun, lutis,* and their likes were often seen as the representatives of the old solidarities and traditions associated with their respective quarters. We can also take a clue from Baer, who tells us that, in Ottoman Cairo, the *fellahin* (peasants) recently arrived from the countryside generally did not take part in Cairo's popular revolts. In particular, during Cairo's most tumultuous years in the eighteenth century, "rural elements were not connected in any way with the numerous revolts [in the Egyptian capital]" (Baer 1977, 216).

Nevertheless, one also finds in the literature sparse evidence to indicate that, at times, recent migrants to the cities did play a part in popular protest, even though their role appears to have been limited to providing the rank and file of movements whose inspiration and leadership lay elsewhere. Sabari (1981, 89), for example, claims that the frequency and scope of popular upheavals led by the *'ayyarun* in Abbassid Baghdad was due to the fact that the city's economy "had been unable to absorb the huge mass that had gathered in the capital." Similarly, Salibi (1968, 193–95) has argued that much of the bloodshed in Damascus in 1860 was produced by a union between the traditional Damascene rabble and recently urbanized and semiurbanized Druze. There is also evidence that, in Aleppo and Damascus in the eighteenth and early nineteenth centuries, rural migrants joined the ranks of the militias of the locally recruited janissaries and contributed to these groups' ability to challenge the authorities and the dominant families.[17] More generally, in his effort to document what he calls "the long-drawn conflict between city and country" in Syria, Batatu (1981, 337) speaks, for that period, of "a phenomenon that repeats itself: rural people, driven by economic distress or lack of security, move into the main cities, settle in the outlying districts, enter before long into relations or forge common links with elements of the urban poor, who are themselves often earlier migrants from the countryside, and together they challenge the old established classes."

In addition to the existence of marginal elements and groups only very incompletely incorporated into the clientelist structure of political control, there was another major limit to the ruling elite's ability to control popular forces through the manipulation of patron-client ties. This limit was the always present possibility that notables would suddenly lose their grip over their clienteles. In such cases, the best local leaders could do was to adopt a strategy of damage control.

It is easy to understand why local leaders were frequently bypassed. Theoretically at least, the only accepted way for commoners to protest against the abuses of the elite was to submit *mazalim* (requests) to the elite through the notables. There were numerous cases, however, when the population was so outraged at some official decision that it could not bear with the rather lengthy and cumbersome process of going to the notables, explaining popular complaints to them, asking them to plead the population's cause with the authorities, and waiting for the elite to do something about what had brought about the discontent in the first place. In such cases, or when central authority was seen as weak or internally divided and therefore unable to respond adequately to popular requests, sudden outbursts of popular violence were likely. It is important to emphasize, however, that violence was not randomly exercised, but typically focused on government buildings, jails,[18] and the houses of high officials and profiteering merchants. The population usually regarded these acts not as crimes, but as a way to seek redress against the wrongdoings of the elite.

We know of several instances in which the notables lost control over their clients. For example, the 1800 and 1805 revolts in Cairo were marked by the emergence of popular leaders who acted in opposition to the traditional patrons and largely supplanted them (Baer 1977, 242). In Aleppo, in 1770 and again in 1819, popular uprisings forced many of the notables, who had become too closely identified with the authorities, to flee the city (Meriwether 1981, 245–46).

From a different perspective, notables proved unable to prevent the anti-Christian violence that shook the cities of Syria and Palestine in the mid-nineteenth century.[19] In Aleppo, Antioch, Beirut, and Jaffa, local leaders tried to restrain the crowd and stop the bloodshed, but they did not succeed (Ma'oz 1968, 230). Similarly, the massacre of Christians in Damascus in 1860 took place despite many notables' courageous attempts to protect the Christians and even fight the rioters. That the traditional leaders revealed themselves unable to stop the carnage is highly significant of the dangers of relying on clientelism as the main strategy of political control. As Khoury puts it, "The interesting point is that the Damascus nobility—believed to be the strongest social and political force in the city—proved to be incapable of controlling the situation" (Khoury 1983b, 9). For a variety of reasons well examined by Khoury, the traditional urban leadership had become estranged from the local population. Thus, when the riot occurred, many of the notable families that traditionally had maintained control over their respective quarters proved unable to restrain their clients, and new and more radical leaders from within the populace itself were able to emerge and stir up the population into the atrocities that took place (Khoury 1983b).

When Clientelist Networks Became Destabilizing

In the historic Middle Eastern city, clientelist networks not only fell short of ensuring urban order, but at times they even could become vehicles for activities against the existing political system, as local leaders would mobilize their respective constituencies against each other or against the government. For instance, between the tenth and the twelfth centuries, leaders of prominent notable families in the cities of Syria and Upper Mesopotamia would often recruit an armed following among popular elements and then use it to force the political authorities—governors or princes who were not natives of the city—to acknowledge their power, and sometimes to appoint them as "head of the city" (*ra'is al-balad*).[20] In eighteenth- and early-nineteenth-century Syria, too, it was common for local notables, particularly the leaders of the *ashraf* and of the locally recruited janissaries (*yerliyyan*), to instigate popular rebellions against other notables, the imperial janissaries (*kapikuli*), or the various Turkish governors.[21]

There were three main situations that were especially conducive to the notables acting as leaders of popular upheavals.[22] The first situation was a weakening of central authority, because it provided the local leaders with an opportunity to step into the power vacuum, and because a weak central authority that could no longer deliver order, security, and favors no longer constituted an attractive partner for the notables. Such hypotheses might help explain the ulama's repeated involvement in popular disturbances in Egypt in the eighteenth century, as Mamluk factions competing with one another proved unable to maintain order, at the same time when Mamluk exactions and abuses of power increased dramatically (Marsot 1972, 160–61).

When local dignitaries had access to their own resources, independent of those controlled by the authorities, their ability to act as destabilizing agents was greatly enhanced, since they did not have to fear that a challenge to the government would jeopardize their access to goods and services and therefore undermine their ability to maintain their position as patrons.[23] In such instances, the authorities could do little to prevent local leaders from using their autonomous control over goods to incite their followings in a destabilizing fashion. Instances that seem to fit this perspective include the leading role played by many *mujtahids* (most prominent religious leaders) and other clerics during the nineteenth-century urban disturbances in Iran, as well as the involvement of some prominent ulama not tied to al-Azhar in the protest movements of the late eighteenth and early nineteenth century in Egypt. These ulama, prominent among whom were the leaders of important *turuq* and the *naqib al-ashraf*,[24] had built large patronage networks and drew their power from their independent control over resources, both symbolic (religious learning and ancestry) and material (e.g., *awqaf, iltizams*,[25] and other personal and corporate properties). For instance, it is such resources, in addition to a contribution levied from "the wealthier citizens," that enabled Umar Makram, the *naqib al-ashraf*, to buy arms, turn them over to the populace, pay individuals "a daily wage, as indemnity for leaving their trade and turning soldiers," and, therefore, be able to "call upon nearly forty thousand men" (Marsot 1968, 274).[26]

A second situation in which notables could act as leaders of popular upheavals arose when government decisions threatened the interests of substantial segments of the urban population, which would then exert pressure on the local leaders to become involved on their side and seek redress from the authorities. As a result, the notables would find themselves in a delicate situation: Despite their reluctance to confront the authorities, they could not give the impression of being insensitive to popular complaints without risking the loss of their followings. Such considerations may explain the involvement, during the 1798 uprising in Cairo, of some prominent ulama who until then had cooperated closely with the authorities (Baer 1977, 229). As the exactions of the Mamluks became more frequent, and as the population's ability to tolerate such abuses wore very thin, the ulama became more assertive in their opposition to the Mamluk *beys* (governors).[27]

Finally, notables frequently stirred up the populations they controlled whenever they felt their interests and positions of power to be imperiled by government decisions, the interference of outside forces, or the emergence of alternative sources of patronage that threatened to attract their clienteles. In Mamluk Cairo, for example, the al-Azhar mosque/religious university complex was the hub of patronage networks that linked al-Azhar's most prominent ulama (the patrons) to large numbers of impoverished religious students and to masses of assisted people, such as the beggars and the blind, who received rations of grain and vegetables. Whenever their interests were threatened, al-Azhar's leading clerics could easily rouse this volatile population into destabilizing political action.[28] In fact, it was largely the fear that the French might establish in Egypt a new sociopolitical order in which clerical influence would be considerably reduced that drove some prominent ulama to play an active part in the 1798 nationalist uprising against the French.

Similarly, in Syria and Palestine in the mid-nineteenth century, local leaders often gave their blessings to sectarian violence, and sometimes even incited it. In Aleppo in 1850, for instance, the leaders of the janissaries and the *ashraf* joined ranks to stir up the Muslim population against the Christians. Six years later, in Nablus, the local ulama led the anti-Christian rioting, while in Damascus several prominent Muslim personalities instigated and presided over the 1860 massacre of Christians. Here as well, Muslim notables tolerated and even sometimes encouraged anti-Christian violence because their sociopolitical position was being undermined, in this particular instance by Ottoman reforms and European penetration.[29] Europe's increasing involvement in the affairs of the Empire, in particular, saw the emergence of the Western consuls as powerful individuals on the local scene, and therefore as rivals to the *a'yan*. By manipulating anti-European and anti-Christian feelings, Muslim leaders probably hoped to demonstrate to the authorities their continued power over the masses, as a way to reestablish their diminished status and be recognized once again as the regime's natural brokers with the street.

Urban Networks, ca. 1800–ca. 1940: Contrasting Egypt and Iran

B ecause of their attempt to cover a time frame stretching from the ninth through the eighteenth century, the preceding two chapters downplayed differences between countries and changes over time. As we move closer to the 1940s–1980s period, which will be the focus of part 3, it is necessary to show how trends that began in the nineteenth century had a very different impact on the political resilience of urban informal networks in each of the three countries that constitute the focus of this study. It is from this particular angle that the present chapter compares Iran and Egypt. In chapter 7, an attempt will be made to summarize the very different historical process that, in Lebanon, led to the establishment of a political system entirely built around informal ties and loyalties.

From Regional Trends to the Egyptian and Iranian Cases

The modern Middle East was born in the nineteenth century, when the face of the region was radically altered by governmental efforts to centralize authority and by the progressive integration of the area into the world economy. In most countries, one of the consequences of these trends was a sharp erosion of the role of informal networks in urban politics. For example, as guilds were weakened or disappeared altogether, the old networks built around the crafts and trades lost much of their earlier vigor and relevance to politics. Similarly, as modernizing states deprived religious institutions of most of their former prerogatives and autonomy, religious networks became less visible and significant. By contrast, bureaucracies and formally organized political groups based on new, "modern," and essentially forward-looking ideologies began to play an increasingly active role.

These trends notwithstanding, it is difficult to generalize. A closer look at the region reveals that the resilience of informally organized groups based on religious, occupational, or neighborhood-based ties varied greatly from one country to another. In this respect, the cases of Egypt and Iran stand in sharp contrast to one another, since the vitality and political significance of informal networks remained much more pronounced in the latter country than in the former.

Perhaps the major reason for this difference was that the forces of political centralization and economic modernization were felt much later in Iran than in Egypt. Iranian society and politics really did not change substantially until Reza Shah's modernization drive in the 1920s. Dramatic as they were, however, many of the reforms introduced by the first Pahlavi monarch occurred so late and over such a short period of time (1925–41) that they were not irreversible.[1] Thus, it really was not until the 1960s and Muhammad Reza Shah's program of economic modernization from above that Iran experienced large-scale and sustained efforts to break radically with the past.

Egypt presents us with a very different picture, since it was heavily exposed to the effects of modernization as early as the beginning of the nineteenth century. Instrumental in this process was the critical impact on Egypt of Muhammad Ali and his modernizing programs. Although many of Muhammad Ali's projects ended in failure, they created a basis on which subsequent rulers built. By the turn of the twentieth century, considerable exposure to the West and the modernizing efforts of Egypt's rulers (including the British after 1882) had already transformed the country dramatically. As will now be shown, one of the main consequences of these changes was a very substantial reduction of the role of informal networks in Egyptian society at large.

Contrasting the Evolution of Muslim Religious Networks and Institutions in Egypt and Iran

The story of the dispossession of the Egyptian ulama by Muhammad Ali is well known, and need not be retold here.[2] Suffice it to say that, in the early nineteenth century, Muhammad Ali dealt a fatal blow to the political influence that the ulama had painfully accumulated over the preceding two centuries. By the end of the nineteenth century, the ulama had been deprived of most of their educational and judicial functions and had lost much of their former wealth, autonomy, and sociopolitical influence in Egyptian society. By clinging ever more tightly to their traditions, and by refusing to adjust to the new conditions in society, they became more and more of an anachronism and rapidly made themselves vulnerable to the charge of "medievalism" soon leveled against them by the reformers.[3]

The Sufi orders went through a very similar evolution. As shown earlier, the leaders of the main *turuq* exerted considerable autonomous power in eighteenth-century Egypt. Thanks to their control over *awqaf*, shrines, and *iltizams*, as well as to the influence they derived from religious ancestry and learning, they could mobilize a large crowd at a moment's notice. Such a situation was not to the taste of Muhammad Ali, who rapidly brought the Sufi orders under the control of the state.[4]

The Egyptian ulama's irreversible decline throughout the nineteenth century stands in sharp contrast to the substantial increase of the political autonomy and influence of their Iranian counterparts during the same period. In fact, prior to the establishment of the Islamic Republic in 1979, the ulama in Iran never wielded as much independent political power as during the period from the mid-nineteenth century to the Constitutional Revolution of 1905–6, when mosque-centered networks repeatedly displayed their ability to act as vehicles for political protest. The next section will examine the general background against which popular movements led by the higher ulama, the Shiite *mujtahids*, took place. The objective, here, is simply to convey an idea of the types of networks controlled by the *mujtahids* and to show the destabilizing part that these networks played during the nineteenth century. In this context, it is appropriate to keep in mind that "the influence of the ulama was primarily on urban populations and exercised in an urban environment" (Algar 1969, 53). The phenomena described below, therefore, are specifically urban.

In nineteenth-century Iran, there existed two groups of ulama (Keddie 1977, 128). The first was formed by government-appointed, and therefore largely government-controlled, ulama. It included in particular the *shaykhs al-Islam*, *qadis*, and *Imams jom'eh* of the major cities. The state used this group to exert influence over religious jurisdiction, to legitimize Qajar rule, and to try to maintain control over the mosque and the population (Algar 1969, 123).

A second group, however, was largely independent of the government. It was made up of those ulama who, in Algar's words, "[persisted] in their traditional reluctance to be polluted by the touch of royal power" (Algar 1969, 123). Among them were a few prominent *mujtahids*—those ulama whose learning and prestige entitle them to undertake *ijtihad*, or independent reasoning to interpret the Shiite law. Unlike the government-appointed ulama, these *mujtahids* drew their power not from their occupation of a formal office, but from the loyalty and legitimacy granted to them by the population at large. Despite their informal organization,[5] independent *mujtahids* wielded much more power than the government-appointed ulama, in part because close connection to the authorities was considered to be a sign of corruption.

Here it is pertinent to disclose some of the key factors that laid the foundation for the constitution of *mujtahids*-led networks and made it possible for these networks to play a destabilizing role. One essential development was the rise, in the eighteenth and nineteenth centuries, of a Shiite school of thought known as *usuli*. The *usuli* doctrine argued that only *mujtahids* could interpret the foundations (*usul*) of the faith, and, therefore, that each believer had to follow the edicts of a living *mujtahid*.[6] The *usuli* school thus established a clear division within the Shiite community between the many seeking guidance, known as *muqallids*,[7] and the few allowed to provide such guidance in the absence of the Hidden Imam, the *mujtahids* (Algar 1969, 35). By the nineteenth century, the *usuli* philosophy had imposed itself as the hegemonic school of thought within Shiism. This, in turn, encouraged each believer to look to a living *mujtahid* for sociopolitical leadership and guidance. By heightening the status and the authority of the leading clerics in Iranian society, the triumph of *usuli* doctrine provided the more politically inclined *mujtahids* with the ideological basis to justify their repeated involvement in sociopolitical matters (Keddie 1981a, 21–22).

Important as well was the Qajars' willingness to consent to each *mujtahid*'s right to collect directly charitable contributions (*zakat*) and religious dues (*khums*) from his followers. As a result, unlike in the neighboring Sunni countries, each leading Iranian cleric became financially independent both from the government and from the rest of the religious establishment (Keddie 1981a, 17; Arjomand 1988, 14). Because of the strengthening of the bonds between the mosque and the bazaar, voluntary contributions and religious taxes from the merchants to the ulama became more substantial as the nineteenth century wore on (Algar 1972, 236). The resulting financial strength and autonomy of the *mujtahids* were further buttressed by their independent control over numerous *awqaf*, many of which were located in the Iraqi shrine cities of Kerbala, Najaf, and Samarra and therefore lay outside the direct reach of the shah (Keddie 1977, 127).

Three additional developments contributed to an increase in the sociopolitical power of the *mujtahids* under the late Qajars: the progressive disengagement of the ulama from the state, the increasing alienation of the population from the Qajar elite, and closer links between civil society and the ulama. These trends were clearly interrelated. For instance, the ulama's dwindling access to state patronage, which was both a manifestation and a cause of their disassociation from the state, could only increase the incentive for them to pose as spokesmen for the interests of the population at large (De Groot 1983, 21). Similarly, by the late nineteenth century, the ulama derived much of their heightened power and influence from being regarded as a potential refuge from the government's tyranny and as embodiments of the nation against the state (Algar 1969). Fueling this perception were the clerics' closer ties to the population, which themselves were a product of the clerics' growing involvement in the everyday life of the common people, either through participation in informal religious gatherings, as in the case of the *mullas*, or by providing goods, services, and political and social leadership, as in the case of the *mujtahids*. Proceeding as they were from a wider financial base, the ulama became better able to dispense protection and offer material support to their clients among the lower classes.

Within this context, one better understands the constitution, especially in the largest urban centers, of vast networks controlled by the *mujtahids*. Figure 4 illustrates a "typical" network. What kept this informal structure together were the webs of informal contacts among *mujtahids*, as well as the personal bonds running from each *mujtahid* to his *muqallids* (followers) through key intermediaries—*mullas, lutis, sayyids* (descendants of the Prophet through the male line), *bazaaris* and *talabehs* (seminary students).

To exert influence over the population, a *mujtahid* could draw on two types of resources: material (access to goods, services, and means of physical coercion) and symbolic (control and manipulation of religious symbols). In theory, symbolic resources were the decisive ones, since a follower chose to attach himself to a given *mujtahid* on the basis of his assessment of the *mujtahid*'s learning and piety.[8] Because it is not easy for the average believer to assess the piety and learning of religious scholars, particularly from a distance, *mullas* and *sayyids* were instrumental in spreading the reputation of a *mujtahid* and in acting as a physical indication of the scope of each *mujtahid*'s influence. (*Mullas* and *sayyids* also often enforced the *mujtahid*'s judicial pronouncements.)

An important resource of the *mujtahid* was the *ijaza* he could bestow upon an aspirant *mujtahid*. The *ijaza* was (and remains) a certificate attesting to the piety and religious knowledge of an aspirant *mujtahid*. The *ijaza* was significant not only for the one receiving it, but also for the *mujtahid* giving it. One should remember, here, that there was no formal process of establishing who was a *marja'-i taqlid* (literally, "source of imitation"), that is, a very prominent *mujtahid* who, because of his superior knowledge and learning, was recognized as worthy of imitation. Thus, any *mujtahid* who aspired to become a leading *mujtahid* and perhaps even a *marja'-i taqlid*, had to have as many followers as possible. Only a large group of followers, many of whom were dedicated former students, could testify to the *mujtahid*'s piety and learning. In this context, conferring an *ijaza* was one of the resources available to a *mujtahid* to build a reputation for himself, since aspirant *mujtahids* would

eventually move on to become themselves scholars and teachers, and therefore opinion makers in the religious community. In other words, *mujtahids*
were patrons, and, like all patrons, they needed as many clients as possible to
establish and spread their reputation.

Yet substantial as these symbolic resources were, they played only a secondary role in a religious scholar's ability to attract a large popular following
for himself. Most likely, only those *muqallids* interested in and conversant
with the details of scholastic knowledge must have ascribed a significant role
to learning in their choice of a given *mujtahid*. Such *muqallids*, who formed
the *mujtahid*'s "educated public," must have consisted primarily of educated
bazaar merchants, *talabehs*, and *mullas*. For other *muqallids*, much more
important were the material resources controlled by the *mujtahid*: the proceeds from the *awqaf* and from the collection of *khums* and *zakat*, the judicial
functions of the *mujtahid*, and his power to offer *bast* (sanctuary).

The *mujtahid* acted very much as a patron in redistributing the proceeds
of the *awqaf* and the religious dues and charitable contributions he received
personally as a representative of the Imam (*na'ib al-imam*). Typically, some of
these proceeds would go to the upkeep of religious institutions and to charitable causes. Another part would be spent on financial support for seminary students and poor *mullas*. A great deal, in any case, was distributed at the *mujtahid*'s discretion, and this distribution of largess was an essential element of
the *mujtahid*'s power, especially important in recruiting crowds and *lutis*—
although the crowds were often mobilized by the *lutis* themselves, and
although strong anti-government feelings in the lower classes often made it
easy for *mujtahids* or *lutis* to recruit a popular following (Floor 1971, 116).

Lutis also welcomed the *mujtahids*' ability to provide them with *bast*
(sanctuary) in religious places. In exchange for "services" (usually involving
coercion) that the *lutis* rendered them, the *mujtahids* would sometimes not
only overlook acts of plunder and robbery by the *lutis*, but even provide them
with asylum and other forms of protection against government retribution
(Algar 1969, 19).[9]

Material rewards played a key role in securing the loyalty of even the
mujtahid's educated public. One suspects that the financial support a *mulla*
received from a *mujtahid* was an important force sustaining the relationship
between the two men. The same applied to the religious students, the *talabehs*.
Securing the loyalty of a large number of *talabehs* was relatively easy, since *talabehs* were badly in need of material support. It was also essential, since, as
noted earlier, *talabehs* would subsequently be in a position to influence a *mujtahid*'s reputation when they themselves became *mullas*, teachers, or even
mujtahids. Furthermore, the *talabehs* traditionally formed an unruly group,
which a *mujtahid* could easily spur to violent action. Thus, "the control of a

madrasa [religious seminary] was doubly desirable—it offered the financial power of the *awqaf* and the physical strength of the *talabehs* (Algar 1969, 19).[10]

The *lutis*, too, constituted a restless lot. Thus, a *mujtahid* could rely on both *lutis* and *talabehs* to enforce his *fatvas* (religious pronouncements) and, if need be, to confront the authorities, other *mujtahids*, or "religious deviants" and "heretics," such as the Sufis and the Babis (subsequently Bahais). Together with a large number of *mullas*, many of whom were not averse to physical fighting, the *lutis* and the *talabehs* made up the core of the *mujtahids'* private armies or "shock troops." They formed, in Algar's words, "the executive arm of clerical authority" (Algar 1969, 109). Finally, the *sayyids*, too, would at times engage in violent activities on behalf of the *mujtahids*. Whether these *sayyids* were real descendants of the Prophet or imposters, the *mujtahids* often tolerated their levying religious taxes on the population in exchange for the *sayyids'* willingness to enforce clerical authority when needed (Algar 1969, 19).

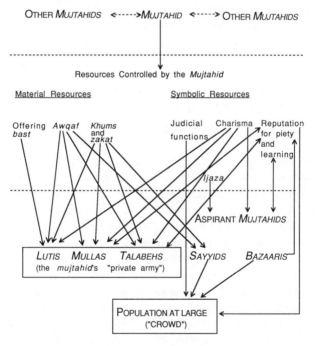

Figure 4. A *Mujtahid*'s Network (only the most important corrections [indicating means of influence] are shown)

In retrospect, nineteenth-century Iranian history appears to have been marked by an increasingly intense struggle between the ulama and the state. At first, this struggle took the form of repeated clashes in the provinces

between governors and individual *mujtahids.* As the century wore on, however, the conflict assumed nationwide dimensions. The ulama emerged as
national leaders and representatives of civil society against a state increasingly
seen as corrupt, oppressive, and associated with foreign powers encroaching
on Iran. It was, in fact, their fear of foreign influence and their common alienation from the state that brought ulama and nation closer together. This
process culminated in the Constitutional Revolution of 1905–6, in which the
ulama played a leading role. In many ways, however, the revolution was also
the ulama's swan song. Not until the 1970s were they able to play again such
an activist and prominent role. In any case, after 1907 the majority of them
withdrew their support from the Constitutionalists. They became disappointed with the turn of events and frightened by the ascendancy of the Westernized intellectuals. Unable to comprehend the nature of the challenges facing Iran and to devise a political strategy to deal with these challenges,
incapable of acting as one single political force, and in any event unwilling to
seize control of the state and play a permanent role in political affairs, the
ulama essentially returned to their books and seminaries.[11]

Bazaar-Mosque Networks and Protest Movements: The Case of Nineteenth-Century Iran, and a Comparison with Eighteenth-Century Egypt

The preceding chapters emphasized the close relationship that often
existed between the bazaar and the mosque in the historic Middle Eastern city.
In Egypt, as late as the eighteenth century, a dense web of informal ties and
contacts linked the ulama, the guilds, and the Sufi orders to one another.
Ulama and guild shaykhs met frequently on an informal basis, while craftsmen, merchants, and even ulama themselves often belonged to the same
turuq.[12] In addition, although the vitality of religious rites and traditions in the
guilds seems to have declined after the seventeenth century, religious symbolism continued to play an important role in the life of many guilds, particularly
during ceremonies of initiation.[13] More generally, the life of artisans and
craftsmen remained imbued with religiosity. Finally, Al-Azhar's proximity to
the Qasaba, Cairo's commercial artery at the time, further solidified the networks between ulama and members of the guilds and the *turuq.* Thus, in the
relatively limited area formed by the al-Azhar/Qasaba complex, there existed a
fairly large and concentrated population that constituted a very receptive
audience for the opinions of the leading Sufi shaykhs, the ulama, and the guild
leaders.

Al-Azhar and the craftsmen and merchants of Cairo were also linked to one another through family ties. Several shaykhs of al-Azhar were sons of modest shopkeepers and craftsmen, and intermarriages between ulama families and leading dynasties of *tujjar* (prominent merchants) were very common.[14] Furthermore, the heads of families that possessed an hereditary leadership of important Sufi *turuq* had close connections with the Muslim merchants engaged in the Nile and Red Sea trade.[15] Most importantly, perhaps, ulama and merchants shared economic interests. For instance, many shops and workshops were *awqaf,* and prominent ulama were often successful and wealthy businessmen, highly involved in the management of their *awqaf* and *iltizams.* Other ulama may not have been quite as successful economically, but they nevertheless were active participants in the world of trades and crafts.[16]

As noted earlier, the political relevance of the networks built around trades, crafts, guilds, ulama, and *turuq* was clearly demonstrated by the uprising against the French in Cairo at the turn of the nineteenth century. Looking at these events, one sees a tacit "*zawiyya*-mosque-bazaar coalition," in some respects similar to the bazaar-mosque alliance that would emerge in Iran a few decades later. However, this incipient alliance, which one might have expected to play a lasting role in Egyptian politics, was nipped in the bud for at least two reasons.

The first and undoubtedly determining factor was the undisputed control that Muhammad Ali soon achieved over Egypt. Within years of Muhammad Ali's rise to power, the ulama and the Sufi orders fell under the control of the state. Meanwhile, a much stronger central government tightened its grip over the bazaar, thus depriving merchants of much of their earlier autonomy. As the nineteenth century wore on, Egypt's administration became better organized and more efficient. The government, increasingly determined to centralize power in its own hands, came to feel it could dispense with the guilds, since government agencies could now carry out the functions that guilds had performed until then, including tax collection, the issuing of professional permits, and the policing of the activities of craftsmen and shopkeepers (Baer 1970, 27).[17]

A second critical factor that accounts for the failure of a bazaar-mosque alliance to take hold in Egypt was the considerable weakening of the indigenous Muslim Egyptian merchant and manufacturing classes throughout the nineteenth century. While Egyptian Muslims probably remained dominant in handicraft production, trade, especially the profitable import-export trade, fell into the hands of foreigners (Europeans, Greeks, Lebanese, Cypriots, and Maltese) and members of the religious minorities (Copts and Jews).

In Cairo, the integration of Egypt into the world economy also greatly accelerated what Abu-Lughod has called "the decentering of the economic core of the city." As retail activities spread throughout the city during the second half of the nineteenth century, the former commercial center, the Qasaba, lost its predominance in the world of trade. Furthermore, following Ismail's return from the Exposition Universelle in Paris, in 1867, the recent business district at Azbakiyah was enlarged, and a new quarter, Ismailiyah, was created.[18] Small-scale crafts did survive in the traditional city. The Qasaba, however, was increasingly marginalized by the commercial ascendancy of the Western quarters, where Europeans, Greeks, Lebanese, Maltese, Cypriots, Copts, and Jews controlled most of the trade activities. Thus, by the turn of the century, Cairo's bazaar had lost much of its former physical integrity and socioeconomic importance, and therefore its role as a focus of vibrant commercial networks.

While in Egypt the potential for a lasting union between the bazaar and the mosque failed to materialize after 1805, the circumstances prevailing in nineteenth-century Iran did bring about such an alliance. This was a momentous process, and its consequences for Iranian politics would be felt as late as the 1970s. To begin to account for it, one needs to consider that, while in nineteenth-century Egypt most branches of trade were progressively being taken over and reorganized by foreigners, merchants in Iran remained predominantly natives of the land. Significantly, "by 1914, Egypt had some 250,000 European residents, while Iran had only some hundreds" (Keddie 1972a, 59). Furthermore, even though Jews and Bahais were actively involved in Iranian commerce, members of the religious minorities played a much less pronounced and visible role in Iran than in Egypt. Thus, even though the Iranian merchant community remained quite fragmented along ethnic and regional lines, it still formed a relatively homogeneous group, especially by comparison with its Egyptian counterpart. Religious and national homogeneity, in turn, was one of the factors that spurred Iran's merchant community to defend its collective interests in face of European economic encroachment, which was seen as a threat to both Islam and Iranian sovereignty.

The experience of collective action further heightened the sense of collective identity and the assertiveness of the Iranian merchant community, and made it easier for it to close ranks and overcome the splits that had divided it until then. In the late nineteenth century, merchants repeatedly coordinated their political activities on a nationwide scale. Ervand Abrahamian captures the essence of this transformation when he points out that "in 1800, the middle class was sharply fragmented into small locally bound communities; by 1900, it was transformed into a broad statewide force conscious, for the first time, of its common personality" (1982, 58).

Moreover, Iran's craft production was not as hard hit by the import of manufactured goods as Egypt's (Keddie 1981b, 779). Although foreign commercial penetration did hurt some traditional Iranian handicrafts, many Iranian merchants were also quick to take advantage of the new economic opportunities presented by the increase in trade with Europe. Significantly, the nineteenth century saw the development of a group of extremely wealthy and increasingly assertive bazaar merchants (Ashraf and Hekmat 1981, 734-35).

By the mid-nineteenth century, therefore, the situation of the *bazaaris* and the ulama had improved substantially. Both groups were now in a better position to challenge the state. In this context, the West's encroachment on Iran and the policies of the late Qajars became catalysts for the constitution of an informal alliance between the two groups. As in later instances when ulama- and bazaar-based networks would be mobilized against the authorities, both material interests and cultural concerns played a key role in turning these networks into vehicles for political protest.

Culturally, the religiously oriented *bazaaris* feared the damage to Islamic values and lifestyles that the growing European involvement in the affairs of Iran could only provoke. At another level, the *bazaaris* resented the extraterritorial rights and privileges (including exemption from most taxes, and immunity from local courts and laws) that the Iranian government had granted to foreign merchants and industrialists operating in the country. They also opposed foreign control of essential national resources, both for nationalistic reasons and because this control could only hurt the interests of Persian traders.

Compounding these concerns was the increasingly inefficient, despotic, and arbitrary nature of Qajar rule, which had particularly adverse effects on the merchant community. The deterioration of order in the provinces endangered the security of the trade routes and made the bazaar an easy prey for bands of thieves (Ashraf and Hekmat 1981, 730). Meanwhile, the government subjected the *bazaaris* to numerous exactions, confiscations of property, intimidation measures, insults, and bastinadoes (one of which was the catalyst for the Constitutional Revolution of 1905–6). At times, government forces themselves would plunder provincial bazaars (Ashraf and Hekmat 1981, 728). Understandably, the *bazaaris* became increasingly resentful of a regime that not only oppressed them, but also failed to protect domestic manufacturing against the competition of European products, and appeared to be selling out the country to the infidels. In the ulama, whose alienation from the state was growing as well, the merchants were soon to find an ideal partner to engage in collective action against the Qajar dynasty.

Indeed, the ulama themselves also felt threatened by the Qajars' policies. Ulama grievances revolved around state attempts to control the revenues from *awqaf*, to limit the right of sanctuary (*bast*), and to restrict the role of the *shariʿa* and the ulama in the judicial system. The reduction of state allowances to the clergy, and the incipient development of a modern, secular education system molded after the West's, also caused great concern in the religious establishment.[19] Most important perhaps, the ulama feared that the presence of foreigners in the country would have perverting, impure, and corroding influences on the social fabric of "the Abode of Islam," as Iran was still often referred to by Persian writers and publicists in the late nineteenth century.[20] Such apprehensions, for instance, were instrumental in clerical mobilization against the tobacco concession granted to a British subject, Major General Talbot.

Against this general background, the ulama and the *bazaaris* took advantage of the administrative and military weakness of the Qajars to lead several protest movements against the state. They were ideally suited partners. Nobody was better qualified than the ulama to speak against the intrusion of nonbelievers in the abode of Islam and in favor of the restoration of just and righteous rule—which, to the great majority of Iranians at the time, still meant Islamic rule (Lambton 1970, 268–69). As for the *bazaaris*, they could provide both the economic clout and the large numbers of demonstrators that protest movements needed to be effective.

Elements of the bazaar-mosque alliance can already be discerned in the early 1870s, in the opposition to the Reuter concession.[21] The alliance, however, became most visible and effective during the Tobacco Movement of 1891–92.[22] For the first time, *bazaaris* and ulama acted in concert on a nationwide scale. Having discovered the power they could muster, they became much more assertive in the following years. This process culminated in the Constitutional Revolution, during which the ulama provided spiritual and political leadership, and the *bazaaris* the rank and file, the financing, and the economic leverage (the shutdown of the bazaar) of the movement.

Parallel to the progressive consolidation of the bazaar-mosque network, informal ties and contacts were multiplied between some clerics eager for change and segments of the Westernized intelligentsia aware of the mobilizing potential of religion. Groups of intellectuals, merchants, and ulama began to coordinate their attacks on the Qajar dynasty. By the turn of the twentieth century, some of them met in informal circles known as *anjumans*, or associations. A few years later, during the Constitutional Revolution, the network of interlocking *anjumans* proved very effective, not only in providing lines of communication between religious leaders, intellectuals, and *bazaaris*, but also in organizing large segments of the politically active population against the regime (Miller 1969b, 344). In fact, an observer of Iran's 1905–6 Constitutional Revolution claimed that "the *anjumans* were the cause of the victory....They had drawn the people together and united them in one common cause, and had organized their strength to such an extent that in the day of trial tyranny found, to its surprise, a united front against it" (Browne 1910, 167–68).[23]

Despite its remarkable success, the bazaar-mosque alliance began to experience serious tensions after 1907–8. By then, for reasons already examined, the majority of the ulama had become disillusioned with Constitutionalism and even hostile to it. Most *bazaaris*, by contrast, remained faithful to the Constitutionalist cause, which in fact became identified almost exclusively with the interests and aspirations of the bazaar and the Westernized intellectuals. Thus, the political paths of the *bazaaris* and the ulama began to diverge significantly. After 1925, the bazaar-mosque alliance, already under stress, was unable to oppose significantly Reza Shah's authoritarian policies. Yet even during the trying years of Reza Shah's rule, the long-standing networks linking the bazaaris and the ulama did, at times, manifest themselves on the political scene. In 1926–27 and again in 1935–36, there were some demonstrations organized around the bazaar, the guilds, and the mosque in some of Iran's largest cities, including Tehran, Qum, Shiraz, and Isfahan (Abrahamian 1982, 152). Despite Reza Shah's frontal attack against the ulama and the slow and incipient development of a modern economic sector, many of the conditions that had allowed the bazaar-mosque alliance to develop remained in place. In the 1950s, and on a much larger scale in the 1970s, one would again see the *bazaaris* and the ulama coordinating the activities of a national movement directed against the state and foreign influences in the country.

The Erosion of Neighborhood Solidarities and Networks

Between Muhammad Ali's accession to power (1805) and the Second World War, neighborhood-based networks lost much of their former political significance in Cairo. One major cause of this phenomenon was what political scientists would now call an increase in "state capacity." From the late nineteenth century onward, Egypt's centralizing governments became better able to oversee the daily activities of a population that, in turn, came to rely more heavily on the state to provide vital goods and services, especially order and security. Consequently, the need to secure mutual aid and assistance from informally organized groups, including neighborhood-based ones, became less pressing.

Thus, functions that neighborhood networks and informal leaders had performed became the direct responsibility of the state. For instance, in the course of the nineteenth century, the fiscal and police duties of the *shaykh al-hara* were transferred to government departments (Baer 1968, 145). Similarly, as the state expanded its role to include not only tighter control of the streets but also the distribution of welfare services, government agencies came to assume many of the functions formerly carried out by the informal leaders of

Cairo's quarters, the *futuwwat* (El-Messiri 1977, 242). The *futuwwat*'s role was further diminished as a result of two factors. First, the range of services that the *futuwwat* were capable of delivering did not keep pace with Cairo's dramatic growth and its population's increasing needs (El-Messiri 1977, 251). Second, from the time of Muhammad Ali onward, the state made a conscious effort to control the *futuwwat* and deprive them of their former insurrectionary power.

Yet another development that contributed to the weakening of neighborhood-based ties and networks in Cairo was the high rates of migration into the capital. Once again, this process would not reach dramatic proportions until the 1940s and 1950s. Nevertheless, from the late nineteenth century onward, rural-to-urban migrations brought together people with different religious backgrounds (Muslims and Copts) and regional origins (Upper Egypt versus Lower Egypt), and mixed them together and with the indigenous population of the quarters, the *awlad al-balad*. Meanwhile, there was an overall widening of socioeconomic cleavages in society, as a result of rapid modernization, heightened commercial and cultural contacts with the West, the inflow of foreigners into Cairo and Alexandria, and, after 1882, direct British rule. Consequently, people with different lifestyles, social status, and occupations came to coexist in the same quarters (Baer 1968, 145–46).

The time when quarters were inhabited predominantly by individuals sharing similar religious, regional, and occupational backgrounds was gone. In the end, these changes could only erode neighborhood solidarities and networks. Thus, it is doubtful that one can speak of "quarters" in any corporate sense for Cairo after the nineteenth century. Significantly, interquarter rivalries—which were so important in fostering a sense of common identity among the members of a given quarter—diminished considerably throughout the 1800s (Baer 1968, 145). One also looks in vain in the literature to find instances of quarters or quarter-based groups participating in movements directed against the political authorities. The last spectacular popular movement in which quarters as such played an important role occurred in 1800. In a similar vein, after 1805, "historical sources are silent as to the participation of the *futuwwat* in revolts or movements such as the 1919 uprising" (El-Messiri 1977, 250).

Little evidence exists to document the evolution of neighborhood solidarities and networks in Iran. One surmises, however, that, in the absence of the two trends—high rates of migration and early centralization of authority—that led to their dramatic weakening in Egypt from the nineteenth century onward, neighborhood solidarities and networks remained stronger in Iran, up to the Second World War at least. Especially significant perhaps was Iran's slow pace of urbanization in the 1800s and early 1900s. It really was not before the 1950s that Iran began to experience very high rates of urbanization. In these conditions, neighborhood solidarities, and the informal networks based on them, probably remained more vibrant in Iran than in Egypt. The weakness of Qajar rule also made it relatively easy for these networks to assume destabilizing manifestations. As was seen earlier, *lutis* continued to play an active and often destabilizing political role throughout the nineteenth and early twentieth centuries—that is, at a time when, in Egypt, neighborhood gangs and informal leaders had already been forced to recognize the supremacy of the state. Even during the 1920s and 1930s, when, under the authoritarian rule of Reza Shah, *lutis* were forced to take a low profile, they did not disappear altogether. In the 1940s and 1950s, their heirs, the *chaqu-kashan*, were still active in public life.

To anticipate the 1940s–1980s period, which will be the focus of part 3, the increasing socioeconomic, ethnic, and religious heterogeneity of neighborhoods over the last fifty years has produced, throughout the region, a considerable decrease in urban-based *'asabiyya* (group feeling). While some of the older quarters still retain a distinctive identity, and while their residents sometimes still draw a sense of collective identification from living there,[24] the significance of quarters as units of sociopolitical organization is now much diminished. Government agencies now perform such tasks as the resolution of disputes, the maintenance of law and order, the levying of taxes, and the management of public services, which once were fulfilled by informal leaders of quarters (*shaykh al-hara, ra'is, muqaddam, kadkhuda, futuwwat, lutis*), by quarter-based youth groups (*ahdath, zu'ar, 'ayyarun*), or by other informally organized associations based on residential affiliations. More generally, modern offices, factories, schools, universities, and the bureaucracy have replaced the neighborhood as the main avenues for the constitution of social networks, except among lower-class women.

As a result, the following kinds of phenomena have by and large disappeared from the urban scene in most Middle Eastern countries: the existence of powerful elite families that dominate the social and political life of their quarters through vast patronage networks, the political rivalries between neighboring quarters, clashes opposing youth groups from rival neighborhoods, quarter-based challenges to the central authorities, or quarters' bearing the main burdens of ensuring the security and defense of their populations. Although one may still identify neighborhood-based networks,[25] there has been a sharp decline in the strength, scope, and density of these networks, as well as in the functions they fulfill. Overall, while quarters, especially poor ones, may still display a certain solidarity, sustained by shared living conditions or common kinship or regional origins, they no longer operate, as in the past, as quasi corporate social and political entities, interacting with the state or even opposing it. The accompanying weakening of neighborhood-based networks as potential sources of unrest or opposition to the central authorities explains why I make no attempt in part 3 to examine the political functions of these networks in the post–World War II period.

6

The Politics of Informal Networks in the Historic Middle Eastern City: Concluding Observations

Before we turn to an examination of the sui-generis Lebanese case, it is already possible to summarize some of the findings of part 2. In historical times, as we have seen, informally organized groups based on patron-client, residential, kinship, occupational, and religious ties had dual effects on Middle Eastern urban society. On the one hand, they provided for a substantial degree of order, cohesion, and solidarity in a context where institutions were too weak to do so. On the other hand, since they formed the basic units of public life, they naturally imposed themselves, in troubled times, as vehicles for political protest.

Networks as Vehicles for the Political Expression of Urban ʿasabiyat: Solidarity versus Factionalism in the Historic Middle Eastern City

There was at least one fundamental element built into many of these networks that always made them potentially destabilizing: the particularly intense group feelings (ʿasabiyat) on which they were built, and the local concerns that they embodied. These groups were endowed with a keen sense of separateness from the rest of urban society, and they usually were anxious to preserve and assert their local autonomy and independence. Thus, while the primordial loyalties and the common outlook, interests, and life experiences that sustained networks provided for solidarity among their members, they also often reflected and fostered animosity toward members of other networks. In other words, locally circumscribed bases of solidarity provided for cohesion at the group level, but also for factionalism and a spirit of separatism that would recurrently threaten the unity of the city. As Helen Staffa has noted:

> It is significant that in…[historical] texts, Muslim writers do not speak of *'asabiya* or 'solidarity' in the singular but rather use the plural, *'asabiyat.* Based upon personal relationships and nearly always associated with residence, *solidarity* was inseparable from *factionalism.* For the majority of the population, it is safe to say that kinship, ethnic ties, and patronage were not only primary elements in the establishment of group feeling but fostered competition with other groups organized on like principles.…The word 'solidarity' has a positive connotation, but 'factionalism' was the unavoidable opposite side of the coin. (Staffa 1977, 223–24)

In an environment where the state had few responsibilities and where politics was inevitably local and revolved around parochial issues and concerns, the informal groups through which most individuals participated in public life could not but foster "us-versus-them" feelings and attitudes. This phenomenon was perhaps particularly true of the informal associations based on residential solidarities that were examined earlier. These informal networks promoted a strong sense of collective identity among local groups primarily by exaggerating the specificity and uniqueness of the group and by downplaying its ability to live peacefully with other similar groups. In the end, membership in the network often thwarted the integration of its members into the larger urban community. Politics could then easily degenerate into clashes between antagonistic, narrowly based, urban *'asabiyat.*

The Defensive Nature of Protest Movements

One is also struck by the essentially defensive nature of most of the cases of urban unrest examined in part 1. To use Tilly's distinction between "reactive" and "proactive" forms of collective action (Tilly 1975, 507), urban collective action in the traditional Middle East was usually clearly reactive. Its purpose was not to advance new claims, but to resist the perceived or real new claims of others: the state, foreign powers, or members of the religious minorities.

By the same token, urban protest movements in the traditional Middle East were essentially past-oriented. They were against real or perceived challenges to situations sanctioned by tradition and, especially, by religion: against the infidels' encroachment on the "Abode of Islam," against the political emancipation of the religious minorities, and against state attempts to do away with the rights and privileges traditionally conferred on a group in society. The leaders of these movements, particularly when they were the ulama, had no long-term program or specific blueprint for the future. Their objective, more often than not, was to restore an order they felt had been unjustly upset.

The population's tolerance of oppression and exactions, it is appropriate to note, was very high. Spontaneous popular uprisings, in this context, were rare events. More frequent were popular movements encouraged by one or several strategically located groups or individuals.[1] Typically, such individuals and groups, too, would act defensively.[2] They were spurred into collective action by the assumption that ongoing developments endangered their very integrity and power as a group, and that the state unjustly tolerated or even encouraged these developments. These groups would then proceed to use their networks of informal contacts with other strata in the population to launch a rebellion.[3]

In historical times, therefore, the two main features of urban protest movements in the traditional Middle East appear to have been their informal organization and their defensive nature. Given the authorities' superior coercive power, the population was reluctant to confront the local elite. Therefore, as long as the elite's violations of the implicit covenant that bound rulers and ruled remained within tolerable limits, popular protest was unlikely to take place. It is only at times of great crisis—and especially when the community or an influential group in it perceived its very existence, values, and way of life to be "under siege" by inimical forces—that informal networks would finally come to play a destabilizing role. Crises and threats would crystallize the social solidarities sustaining those networks and provide the sense of urgency needed to turn them into instruments for political unrest. In a way, therefore, informal networks functioned as a latent and intermittent political opposition, whose power manifested itself only in exceptional circumstances.

There is also a clear relationship between the defensive nature of many urban protest movements in historical times and their distinctive Islamic character. The mobilization of informal networks against the authorities or against foreign encroachment often took place when Islam itself appeared to be in danger, as during the 1798 and 1800 uprisings against the French in Cairo, the popular movements in the late nineteenth and early twentieth centuries in Iran, and the communal riots in the Syrian provinces in the mid-nineteenth century. Furthermore, Islam was the only force that transcended the more parochial allegiances to quarter, profession, family, and friends, and it therefore represented a symbol of the sociocultural unity of the urban community. Combined with the fact that it was also the focus of a variety of overlapping informal networks (those controlled by the ulama, the *ashraf*, the Sufi brotherhoods, etc.), this factor explains why popular perceptions of real or imagined threats to Islam were particularly conducive to generating strong, large-scale movements, which would frequently assume violent, xenophobic, and sectarian overtones.

The Costs of Informal Politics

This part of our exploration cannot conclude without noting that the predominantly informal nature of politics in the historic Middle Eastern city goes a long way toward explaining the ineffectiveness of the region's urban elites in confronting an expanding Europe in the late nineteenth and early twentieth centuries. Middle Eastern notables, the natural leaders of the population, never really understood the importance of organization in conducting the anticolonial struggle. By disposition, training, outlook, and experience, they were unprepared to create strong and formally organized political machines. As a result, they were unable to mobilize effectively the indigenous population against militarily, technologically, and organizationally superior European powers.

It is not surprising, therefore, that the focus of resistance to colonialism was the countryside, not the city (e.g., Algeria between 1830 and 1847, or Syria and Iraq in the 1920s), or that the urban-based political elites, which in the 1940s found themselves in control of the newly independent states of countries such as Syria and Iraq, proved unable to hang on to power (the situation was somewhat similar in Egypt). These elites, indeed, revealed themselves to be incapable of breaking decisively with the pattern of urban politics that traditionally had prevailed in the Middle East. To try to maintain their dominant sociopolitical position, they continued to rely mostly on the manipulation of informal networks and on the personal prestige that they and their families had accumulated over the centuries and during the struggle for independence. By the 1940s and 1950s, such a strategy had become inadequate to keep control over cities, especially capitals, that were experiencing tremendous growth and in which the population was becoming rapidly politicized under the impact of socialist and pan-Arab ideals. Predictably, in Egypt, Iraq, and Syria, the experiment with parliamentarian systems lasted only a few years. The urban political elites that had occupied the forefront of the political scene during these countries' liberal experiments fell victim to better organized groups, often military cliques composed of individuals of rural background, whose relative unity was often sustained by primordial solidarities based on regional and sectarian affiliations (Salamé, 1988).

The Politics of Informal Networks and Loyalties in the Making of Modern-Day Lebanon

This is not the place to present a summary of Lebanon's complex history before independence (1943).[1] Rather, this chapter provides some of the necessary historical background to illuminate the particular post-1943 developments that will be explored in part 3. Given this study's focus, special attention is paid to three phenomena: the politics of rapid urbanization in nineteenth-century Beirut, the increasing reliance on the manipulation of clientelist and communal networks to provide for political stability in the emerging Lebanese polity, and the dual effects of these networks on the urban political order.

The Politics of Rapid Urbanization in Nineteenth-Century Beirut

The sudden and spectacular rise of Beirut in the nineteenth century was accompanied by a dramatic increase of sectarian tensions in a city that, until then, had been known for its tolerance and for the intercommunal harmony that prevailed in it. The growing European commercial and diplomatic presence and influence in the city, combined with rapid and massive migrations of Christians from the mountain districts to Beirut, upset the city's delicate political balance between sects (Fawaz 1983; Chevallier 1968). By the late nineteenth century, clashes between Christians and Muslims had become so common that "hardly did a week go by without an assassination, or a year without a [sectarian] riot" (Fawaz 1983, 115).

The strong-arm men and folk heroes known as *qabadayat* (sing. *qaba-day*) played an active role in communal feuds. A *qabaday*'s power base was usually the quarter in which he resided and whose solidarity he embodied. Thus, identification with one's quarter and with the quarter's *qabaday* or *qabadayat* were inextricably mixed, and neighborhoods frequently were known by the *qabaday* or *qabadayat* active in them. Although *qabadayat* usually acted as individuals, they also could operate, at times, as the informal leaders of loosely organized groups of youth that recognized them as the legitimate and natural leaders of their respective quarters. In several respects, therefore, the *qabadayat* resembled the *lutis* examined earlier. They, too, wore a distinctive apparel[2] and were known for their physical strength and propensity to use it in feuds. They, too, often lived just on the right side of the law, were engaged in semilegal or illegal activities, and were not reluctant to confront the authorities. Finally, they, too, benefited from the protection of more powerful figures, for whom they frequently served as bodyguards and intermediaries with the population.

More importantly, the *qabadayat*, as the *lutis* and their historical predecessors, had both positive and negative influences on the social fabric. They protected their quarters against outside threats, settled disputes, and acted a transmission belts between the notables and their clients, but they also were quarrelsome and violent and often preyed on the populations they claimed to defend.

In one fundamental respect, however, the *qabadayat* were much more destabilizing than the *lutis*. In a society where sectarian tensions were on the rise, *qabadayat* in late-nineteenth- and early-twentieth-century Beirut were definitely perceived as communal champions, and, in order to maintain their image, they frequently instigated religious riots. Thus, while notables made attempts to stop or prevent communal fighting, *qabadayat* could often be seen exacerbating sectarian tensions in the city. This phenomenon is only part of a more general process that we shall see at work in Lebanon throughout this study: In a country as sharply divided along religious lines as Lebanon, informal groups and their leaders usually cannot but take on a sectarian character. The distinct sectarian orientation of networks, in turn, exacerbates these networks' destabilizing potential and gives the resulting unrest a definite religious nature.

Although sectarian conflict in late-nineteenth- and early-twentieth-century Lebanon was most pronounced in the lower classes, it existed among the notables as well, albeit in a less visible and violent form. In Leila Fawaz's words, "While the common people openly fought, the merchants and notables channeled their energies into political maneuvering, struggles for influence, and outdoing one another in charitable largess" (Fawaz 1983, 116–17).

It is therefore no coincidence that, under the leadership of the notables of the city, the second half of the nineteenth century witnessed the establishment of an unprecedented number of schools, hospitals, colleges, clubs, associations, and benevolent societies, each of which catered exclusively to the members of a specific sect. In creating these institutions and networks, the local leaders were inspired in part by philanthropic motives, in part by a sense of communal loyalty, and in part by the desire to institutionalize their patronage, so as to widen and better control their clienteles.

Institutions and networks created in this context had both stabilizing and destabilizing effects. They were stabilizing to the extent that, in a society undergoing rapid socioeconomic change, they fostered a sense of collective identity and cohesion among their members and distributed much-needed material support (Fawaz 1983, 117). On the other hand, they were destabilizing in several respects. By making membership, and therefore access to the goods and services they delivered, conditional upon religious affiliation, they could not but sharpen the already pronounced sectarian divisions in society. Benevolent societies and clubs became instruments in the competition among sects and among notables. Significantly, they often were established in reaction to each other's creation. For instance, the leading Beiruti Sunnis who, in 1878, founded the charitable association known as the Maqasid,[3] were reacting to the establishment of schools and other facilities by the Protestant missionaries in Lebanon and hoped to overcome the educational gap between Sunnis and Christians.[4]

Yet despite the new rivalries between them, the Muslim and Christian elites in Beirut endeavored to cooperate with one another, so as not to threaten their common interest in Beirut's continued prosperity. In particular, they strove to prevent sectarian feelings from degenerating into armed confrontations among members of the lower classes. Whenever communal clashes occurred in the streets, notables would promptly intervene to try to mediate and put an end to the fighting. Muslim and Christian leaders also sat together on public committees and courts and often belonged to the same private societies and clubs (Fawaz 1983, 118–20). Thus, cooperation at the elite level was preserved, and it usually proved effective in maintaining order and stability in the city.

Therefore, even before the First World War, politics in Beirut already presented several characteristics that were to remain distinctive of Lebanon as a whole until much after World War II. Two such features, particularly pronounced among the lower classes, were the substantial overlap between political and communal affiliations, and the latent hostility toward members of other sects. Since this sectarian hostility was largely sustained by religious institutions and networks, it would remain difficult for the observer to determine whether conflict should be attributed to the networks themselves (the engines of violence) or merely to sectarian antagonisms (the fuel of violence). Late-nineteenth-century Beirut also already shows the somewhat ambiguous status of patronage networks, as both instruments for the competition among notables (notables often exerting conscious pressures on the population to think of itself in sectarian terms) and as instruments for the preservation of order. Clearly, while sectarian hostility and competition among notables promoted fragmentation and strife, the intra-elite consensus and the patrons' control over their respective clienteles strengthened the existing sociopolitical system. It was evident early on, however, that it would be difficult to maintain such a precarious balance between the stabilizing and destabilizing attributes of sectarian and patronage networks.

Informal Networks in the Emerging Lebanese Polity: From the Creation of "Greater Lebanon" (1920) to the "National Pact" (1943)

From the very moment the French created Greater Lebanon, in 1920, the new country was faced with at least three fundamental problems. These problems have to be examined, albeit briefly, not only because they would continue to haunt Lebanon, but also because they constitute the backdrop for this study's focus on urban networks.

First, the Maronites had been the only community to welcome unambiguously the establishment of Greater Lebanon (and the French Mandate). Although large segments of the Sunni community, especially its upper strata, did eventually reconcile themselves to the idea of being "Lebanese," the tension between allegiance to Lebanon and membership in the wider "Arab nation" remained latent among many Sunnis, especially in the lower and middle classes. At times, as in 1958, this tension would prove very destabilizing and would provide a catalyst for the mobilization of Muslim networks against the state.

A second major problem involved in the creation of Greater Lebanon was the sectarian diversity of the new country. In Mount Lebanon, the problem of sectarian coexistence had been relatively easy to manage, since the area was primarily Maronite (more than 60 percent) and secondarily Druze (about 15 percent), with a lesser number of Greek Catholics (almost 10 percent) and Greek Orthodox. In Greater Lebanon, however, Sunnis and Shiites now represented almost 40 percent of the population—a percentage that not only was greater than that of the Maronites (30 percent), but that also was bound to increase rapidly over time, because of substantially higher birth rates among

Muslims. The situation was further complicated by the fact that by 1920 these various sects already had a history of bitter rivalries and confrontations with one another.

The third major problem facing the new country from its inception was the existence of pronounced regional cleavages. Greater Lebanon brought together at least five different regions: Mount Lebanon; the coastal cities, especially Beirut, Tripoli, Sidon, and Tyre, and these cities' immediate hinterlands; ʿAkkar in the north; the Bekaa Valley in the east; and Jabal ʿAmil in the south. These regions were inhabited by populations that differed greatly in their outlook, ways of life, and socioeconomic and political organization.[5] These regional differences overlapped partly with sectarian ones, but geography was a centrifugal force of its own. From the very beginning, it pulled Greater Lebanon in opposite directions.

Perhaps the most important rivalry was that between the *ahl al-jabal* (the people of the mountain) and the *ahl al-sahil* (the people of the coast [coastal cities]).[6] Given this study's interest in the politics of rapid urbanization, the importance of this basic dichotomy between "the mountain" and "the city" needs to be highlighted, especially since, after World War II, the rapid and staggering growth of Beirut led, in a way, to the conquest of the city by the mountain.

In the late nineteenth and early twentieth centuries, the city, and Beirut in particular, became the locus of a variety of ideologies and worldviews that stressed liberalism, tolerance, and the possibility that communities that differed greatly in their beliefs and ways of life could nevertheless coexist peacefully and benefit from mutual interaction. The city became characterized by a certain curiosity and openness to the outside world, and first presented to the world the image, later to become that of Lebanon as a whole, of a pluralistic, open, and tolerant society, dominated by trade, culture, and service activities and operating as a cultural and commercial bridge between the West and the East (Hourani 1976, 39).

In Mount Lebanon, however, a different view of the world prevailed. Over the centuries, Mount Lebanon's primarily Maronite population had been concerned first and foremost with preserving its autonomy by keeping outsiders out. The mountain, therefore, showed little of the openness and curiosity found in the city. It instead promoted an essentially defensive, inward-oriented, and conservative mentality. Neither did it put much emphasis on sectarian diversity and peaceful coexistence between sects, since, as Hourani emphasizes, the "ideologies of the mountain" were also specifically ideologies of the Maronite community (1976, 36).[7]

The mountain and the city also differed greatly according to the types of politics that traditionally had prevailed in them. In the city, it was "the politics of the notables." Mountain politics, by contrast, had always been dominated by family, clan, and quasi tribal solidarities and feudings. Furthermore, whereas the city abhorred violence (the politics of the notables was precisely aimed at diminishing its likelihood), violence—particularly to defend the family or the clan's "honor"—had always been an integral part of political life in the mountain. Finally, the mountain and the city were largely hostile to one another. The city, predictably, looked down on the mountain as a place filled with hicks and religious fanatics. The mountain, for its part, distrusted the city, the traditional seat of the Ottoman governors who had always been ready to interfere in the internal affairs of the mountain. It also disdained the constant compromises and bargaining among groups that urban life and the politics of the notables involved.

To think of the emerging Lebanese polity from the late 1800s through the French mandate as divided between the people of the mountain (*ahl al-jabal*) and the people of the coastal cities (*ahl al-sahil*) is to greatly simplify a complex reality, but it does emphasize a fundamental cleavage that was at least as salient as the sectarian one, with which it overlapped (the people of the mountain were primarily Maronites, while the population of the coastal cities was predominantly Sunni). Significantly, during the mandate period, Lebanese commentators repeatedly used the expressions *ahl al-jabal* and *ahl al-sahil* to refer to these two distinct populations (Buheiry 1987, 17). Moreover, during the 1930s, the cleavage between the mountain and the city reflected itself in the rivalries between political institutions that represented the respective concerns of these two constituencies. The official institutions of the Republic of Greater Lebanon, as well as those of the French mandatory power, stood primarily for the mountain and the Maronite population of Beirut. The interests of the population of the coastal cities, by contrast, expressed themselves in rather informal forums such as the "Conference of the Sahil and the four Qadas," the Maqasid, the Beirut Chamber of Commerce, the Association of Muslim Youth, the National Muslim Congress, and so on (Buheiry 1987, 16–18). Even though the French Mandate provided "a controlled forum for a rapprochement between the *ahl al-Jabal* and the *ahl al-Sahil*, provoking in some degree the Beirutisation of the 'Old Lebanese' and the Libanisation of the Beirutis" (Buheiry 1987, 20), the outlook, modes of political action, and aspirations of the people of the mountain and the people of the city remained far apart, particularly among the lower classes. Rivalries between the mountain and the city would continue to plague Lebanon's existence.

Thus, from the very moment Greater Lebanon was created, no observer could ignore the tremendous problems that the country was bound to face in the future. To some extent, the Mandatory authority and the Maronite leadership recognized these problems and attempted to devise an institutional framework that would increase the country's chance of success. Accordingly, the Constitution of 1926 established a parliamentary system whose purpose was to accommodate the interests of the various communities, factions, notables, and regions and to water down the impact of sectarian divisions on national politics.[8]

Yet Muslims began to participate fully in the Lebanese polity only after the adoption, in 1943, of the National Pact (*al-mithaq al-watani*), which created the "confessional system," in which positions in government, the bureaucracy, and the administration are distributed according to the proportion of each sect in the population, as determined by the 1932 census.[9] From the perspective of our concern with informal networks, however, the confessional system had two most unfortunate consequences.

First, it made sectarian affiliation the official basis for political participation. Thus, far from weakening sectarian identities and loyalties so as to erode their disintegrative potential, the confessional system not only reinforced them, but politicized them as well. By the same token, it made the political process more dependent upon religious affiliations. At times of crisis, in particular, there would be an inevitable tendency to think in terms of Muslims versus Christians, and some sects against others.

More specifically, by putting such a premium on religious loyalties as a basis for political participation, the confessional system also brought the informal networks through which these loyalties expressed themselves to the heart of the formal political scene. Combined with the inability or unwillingness of successive Lebanese leaders to build up the institutions of the state, this phenomenon helps explain why the formal political institutions never acquired a reality and logic of their own, but instead continued to work primarily through the mediation of informal networks, especially those based on patron-client and sectarian ties. Significantly, the presidents themselves (with the possible exception of Shihab) would behave less as chiefs of state than as the supreme patrons of a predominantly clientelist and sectarian system. This is but one of the many factors that, in turn, reinforced the belief among many Muslims that the state and its institutions were merely the instruments of Christian dominance in the country. This phenomenon goes a long way toward explaining the lack of legitimacy of the state in Muslim eyes and why the urban Sunni population, which had at its disposal a variety of sectarian, kinship, neighborhood-based, and patron-client networks, withdrew around these networks to participate in politics. In the end, by making the political life of the country dependent upon the workings of informal networks, the confessional system made Lebanese politics vulnerable to the phenomenon that constitutes the focus of this book: the double-edged effects of networks on political stability. This feature would prove all the more destabilizing in that a weak state with little independent structure, legitimacy, or logic of its own would often be incapable of intervening decisively in times of crisis.

A second major shortcoming of the confessional system was its overreliance on the formation of an intra-elite consensus to hold together the various sects, regions, and factions that constituted Lebanon. The continued stability of the system, therefore, rested on two assumptions: that the various components of the elite would be able to keep control over their clients, and that, through a process of bargaining and mutual adjustment in their ranks, they could preserve the intra-elite consensus. In the long run, as will be shown in part 3, these assumptions proved hasty. Rapid social mobilization and politicization made it increasingly difficult for the respective sectarian elites to control their clienteles, especially in the Muslim community. Similarly, on such basic issues as relations with the West or the "Arab character" of Lebanon, the illusion of consensus within the elite would prove increasingly difficult to maintain.

Part III

Informal Networks and Urban Unrest: Evidence from Egypt, Iran, and Lebanon since the 1940s

8

The Changing Organizational Bases of Urban Unrest in the Middle East since World War II: An Overview, with Special Reference to Egypt, Iran, and Lebanon

A s shown in part 2, in historical times it was primarily through informally organized groups that urban dwellers in the Middle East were involved in destabilizing political activities. However, one may legitimately wonder whether informal networks continued to provide effective vehicles for political dissent after World War II, given the dramatic socioeconomic and political changes that have taken place in the region over the last fifty years.

The Changing Features of Protest Movements in Middle Eastern Cities

The organizational basis of Middle Eastern urban protest movements has changed considerably in this century, especially since World War II. This change is inextricably linked to the broader transformations that have affected the ideology, grievances, participants, and modes of action characteristic of these movements. For instance, growing labor activism and the higher incidence of strikes reflect the advance of a politically conscious and sometimes radical industrial labor force that often uses formally organized trade unions and political parties to advance its interests.

More generally, the configuration of Middle Eastern urban protest movements has been greatly affected by the ever-increasing integration of the Middle East in the world economy, the centralization of authority, the processes of industrialization, secularization, Westernization, and modernization, and the cities' rapidly changing infrastructure, economy, and social structures. Such processes led to the marginalization or disappearance of some of the actors who had played a prominent role in urban uprisings until the nineteenth century (notables, guild leaders, Sufi shaykhs, lower-ranking ulama, *tullab, lutis,* and *futuwwat,* to name just a few). They promoted, however, the emergence of new social strata—professionals, civil servants, Westernized intellectuals, and industrial workers—that often became attracted to new, forward-looking ideologies (socialism, communism, baʿathism, nationalism, and pan-Arabism) and adopted new forms of collective action, including mass demonstrations, strikes, and boycotts.

More importantly, these groups, whose lives revolved around universities, high schools, factories, and modern offices, did not usually engage in politics through the old networks built around the mosques, the quarters, and the crafts and trades. Instead, they were attracted to better organized, more recently established, and modern-looking entities, such as political parties, trade unions, and syndicates. Unlike the networks examined in part 2, these new vehicles for political action provided bases for the formation of alliances extending far beyond narrow circles of coreligionists, clients, and neighbors. As a result, the first half of the twentieth century saw the unmistakable tendency toward the formation of broadly based movements of political protest (Burke 1986).

The Development of Formal Organizations as Vehicles for Political Protest in Iran, Egypt, and Lebanon since the Second World War

The rise of formally organized political groups, and these organizations' ability to provide effective channels for political dissent, was manifested most dramatically in Iran during the 1940s and early 1950s. Throughout the turbulent period stretching from the abdication of Reza Shah in 1941 to the coup d'état of 1953, Iran witnessed the growth of mass-based political parties and trade unions. The National Front and the Tudeh[1] played particularly active and visible roles during those years. While the National Front remained a loosely organized group of prominent nationalist politicians and never was able to develop into a well-organized party, the Tudeh rapidly became, in the 1940s, the single most important political force in the country. Endowed with a nationwide organization and an elaborate structure, the party was well implanted in the country's largest urban centers, especially Tehran, around the oil fields, and in industrial areas. It even had branches in smaller cities and towns (Abrahamian 1982, 290–305). The Tudeh drew its strength not only from its own active membership, which may have been as high as 100,000 in 1946, but also from the unions it controlled through the Central Council of Federated Trade Unions of Iranian Workers and Toilers (CCFTU), which claimed some 335,000 members in 1946 (Abrahamian 1982, 303).

Underlying the rise of the Tudeh, the unions, and the National Front was the development of new social strata in Iran's cities. Thus, throughout the 1940s and early 1950s, the modern middle class, the intelligentsia, and the industrial working class often proved more active than the shopkeepers, craftsmen, apprentices, journeymen, militant lesser ulama, and theology students who until then had formed the core of Iranian protest movements. This phenomenon contributed greatly to the growth of the mass-based political parties and the unions, which, more than the old Islamic networks that revolved around the mosque and the bazaar, became the primary vehicles for the political mobilization of these new, more modern, and often better-educated segments of the Iranian population.

Largely because of these transformations, the scope of protest movements in Iran's cities was broadened dramatically. Whereas the demonstrations of the beginning of the twentieth century in Iran usually involved only a few thousand persons,[2] some one hundred thousand individuals participated in the fifth-anniversary celebrations of the Tudeh, in October 1946 (Abrahamian 1968, 190). More generally, in the mid-1940s and early 1950s, the Tudeh and the CCFTU were able to organize what would be, until the late 1970s, the largest demonstrations and strikes in the country's history. Demonstrations and strikes of several tens of thousands were common events during the Tudeh's peak years, 1945–46 and 1951–53.[3]

However, following the CIA-sponsored 1953 coup, which put an end to the nationalist government of Prime Minister Mossadegh and which brought the shah back to power after a self-imposed exile that lasted only a few days, the Tudeh and the trade unions were crushed. With Muhammad Reza Shah's rapid consolidation of power in the late 1950s and early 1960s, these once impressive and powerful organizations were totally dismantled. Independent political parties, labor unions, and professional associations were outlawed, while a system of state-run trade unions was established.[4] Therefore, from the mid-1950s until the Iranian revolution that brought Ayatollah Khomeini to power, the shah dominated the political arena, unconstrained by formally organized opposition groups. The second National Front's life was brief (1960–62) and uneventful. Similarly, the small underground guerrilla organizations created in the early 1970s, especially the Marxist Fadaʿiyan-i Khalq and the Islamic Mujahedin-i Khalq, proved more of a nuisance to the regime than a serious threat to it. Although they were able to carry out a few spectacular actions—assassinations of prominent government officials and of a few Americans, kidnapings, bombings of government buildings, attacks of police stations, and clashes with the police and the security forces—they failed to generate mass support, and their appeal remained limited to segments of the young intelligentsia. More importantly, by 1977 they not only had suffered from important internal splits, but essentially had been decimated by SAVAK, with their leaders either dead or languishing in jail (Milani 1988, 129). Thus, on the eve of the revolution, while there was considerable hatred of the shah, there also existed no formally organized group in a position to challenge his regime.

Like Iran, Egypt in the 1940s experienced the rise of mass-based and relatively structured political organizations that rapidly moved to challenge the actors who, until then, had monopolized the political arena: the monarchy (supported by the British) and a narrow-based, weakened, and largely discredited *Wafd* party. Particularly important was the Muslim Brotherhood (*al-Ikhwan al-Muslimin*), which, at its peak in the late 1940s, had evolved into a nationwide organization with some two thousand branches and half a million members (Mitchell 1969). Similarly, Young Egypt, with its strong infrastructure, disciplined membership, and mobilizing ideology imbued with fascist overtones, revealed itself to be a very dynamic political force. Finally, various communist groups were able to attract Western-educated intellectuals and segments of the growing industrial working class, while an assertive labor movement, whose history is just beginning to be written, also began to develop.[5]

However, the seizure of the state apparatus by a group of military officers on 26 July 1952 radically altered the political prospects of the Muslim Brotherhood, the political parties, and the trade unions. Following the coup, the new leaders rapidly outlawed all political organizations except for the Muslim Brotherhood, which for two years was allowed to operate. By 1954, however, the Muslim Brotherhood, too, had been banned and driven underground. Then, between 1954 and 1956, the Free Officers endeavored to curb the labor and student movements through a mixture of repression and co-optation.[6] Syndicates, too, were brought under control. By 1956, a one-party, authoritarian-corporatist system was in place. Thus, as occurred in Iran around the same time, formal political organizations independent of the regime disappeared from the political spotlight.

Some two decades later, Egyptian President Anwar al-Sadat engaged in a cautious process of political liberalization (1975–79), which after his death was revitalized and expanded by his successor, Husni Mubarak. As a result, formal political organizations in Egypt have been able to provide some limited avenues for the expression of political dissent. For instance, the left-wing National Progressive Unionist Party, or *Tagammuʿ*, has repeatedly criticized the government for its concessions to the private sector, for its Western orientation and pro-American foreign policy, and for straying from Nasser's commitment to social justice and equity. Similarly, throughout the 1980s, the right-of-center New Wafd party was quite successful at mobilizing the educated public behind issues of government corruption, abuses of human rights, and lack of respect for personal freedoms (Makram-Ebeid 1989, 427). Finally, professional associations, especially the bar association and the journalists' syndicate, were at different points actively involved in opposing the course of Sadat's policies, especially after 1978, and they remained vocal in the 1980s.

In Lebanon, finally, formally organized groups have also been active in oppositional politics since the country gained its independence from the French in 1943. Before the outbreak of the civil war, this was, for instance, the case with the Syrian Social Nationalist Party (PPS),[7] a tightly and hierarchically organized, highly disciplined party, endowed with a nationwide infrastructure.[8] The Baʿath and the Lebanese Communist Party (LCP) were also able to provide vehicles for articulating the grievances of a rapidly growing young intelligentsia against a political system denounced as corrupt, anachronistic, unfair, and insensitive to the lot of the underprivileged. The LCP's appeal even expanded beyond the confines of the educated public, and the party developed important power bases in the textile industry, in the transportation sector, and in the shipping industry. It was well implanted among the longshoremen of the port of Beirut and, in Tripoli, among the port workers in the harbor area, al-Mina (Picard 1988, 97; Petran 1987, 341).

In addition, the post–World War II period in Lebanon saw the growth of a formally organized trade union movement.[9] While this movement remained relatively weak and fragmented,[10] unions nevertheless gave Lebanese workers some experience with rational organizations, and they can boast an impressive record in terms of their ability to secure substantial concessions from both employers and the government in the areas of wages, working conditions, and labor legislation. Such successes might explain the continuous growth of the trade union movement, whose membership in 1980 represented perhaps as high as one quarter of the country's work-force (Hanf 1988, 174–75). One should also emphasize the resiliency and adaptability of the trade union movement, even under the most inhospitable conditions. Throughout the civil war, the movement remained unified—even as the government bureaucracy, the army, political parties, and educational institutions were being torn apart by political and sectarian hatreds—and was able to secure important gains for its members (Hanf 1988, 174–76).[11]

In addition to the labor unions, student unions also contributed to the turmoil of the early 1970s, especially at the Lebanese University, where "the student union...became the backbone of the entire student movement...", took a real part in the conflicts erupting throughout the country, and developed into a force the government could not wholly ignore" (Petran 1987, 141). More recently, in the second half of the 1980s, syndicates and professional associations played a significant role in trying to mobilize their members and the population at large in movements of protest against the "war society" and the "reign of the militias."

The militias themselves provide the best example of formally organized entities used for destabilizing political purposes. By the late 1970s, these militias had become highly effective politicomilitary machines, endowed with large and sophisticated bureaucracies that had taken over over a whole array of "public" services, including tax collection, education, health, and the management of hospitals, schools, economic enterprises, ports, and radio and television stations.[12]

To summarize the argument presented so far, therefore, there have been many instances since World War II in which formally organized entities have provided segments of the Egyptian, Iranian, and Lebanese populations with effective vehicles for political protest. The same phenomenon has been observed in other Middle Eastern countries. For instance, Batatu (1978) has shown the key role played by the Iraqi Communist Party during the 1940s and 1950s in organizing and mobilizing the urban educated youth. Similarly, politicized trade unionism in the port of Aden (Yemen) operated as a catalyst for the uprising against British rule in the 1950s and 1960s (Halliday 1974, 180–88). Trade unions also have been an important part of the political history of Morocco ever since the First World War. In the 1960s, the Union Marocaine du Travail (UMT, or Moroccan Labor Union) was particularly active. More recently, the newly formed and more radical Confédération Démocratique des Travailleurs (CDT, or Democratic Workers Confederation) played a leading role in organizing the 1978–79 and June 1981 strikes that shook several cities.[13] Unions also were highly involved in the unrest and unprecedented waves of strikes that Turkey experienced in the late 1970s (Margulies and Yildizoglu 1984). Finally, in some countries, professional associations have been able to provide the educated public with instruments to voice its grievances. The example of Egypt has already been mentioned. Significant as well is the case of Sudan, where syndicates, especially those of the doctors and lawyers, were instrumental in the collapse of the Nimeiri government in March 1985 (Seddon 1989, 121–23). Most recently, during the unrest in Jordan in April 1989, professional associations, particularly those of physicians and engineers, participated in the protests that forced Premier Rifaʿi to step down.

Considering such evidence, can we assume that collective action through informal networks has become, or is in the process of becoming, a thing of the past? Have formally organized parties, unions, and syndicates displaced ad hoc groups based on personal ties as the main vehicles for opposition to the authorities? Or have formal organizations and informal networks tended to coexist as modes of organization of the resistance of civil society to the state? Has one particular mode (formal/informal) tended to prevail in specific periods? If so, in which circumstances have formal organizations prevailed over informal networks, and vice versa? It is now time to address these questions.

Informal Networks and Political Unrest in the Contemporary Middle East

The last forty years have shown that informal networks remain potent bases from which to organize political dissent in the Middle East. One of the main reasons for this phenomenon is the authoritarian nature of most Middle Eastern regimes, because the absence of formal channels to express opposition to the government often has turned informally organized associations into the most readily available vehicles for the airing of grievances. Throughout the region, the state's relentless drive to impose its hegemony over the political arena and its enhanced ability to handle open forms of protest (strikes, demonstrations, riots) have turned groups that operate in an informal manner and under the surface of the political system into "zones of autonomy" that political opponents can use to organize against the regime.

Moreover, even when opposition political parties and trade unions have been allowed, their ability to recruit and mobilize has been seriously impeded by the state's ability to coopt or coerce social forces through the distribution of patronage and the threat to use force. Even in the more open political systems of North Africa, the population understands that opposition parties and trade unions possess neither the independence nor the resources to provide clear alternatives to the existing regimes. In this context, informally organized groups have continued to frequently be channels for the expression of political dissent, as can be shown through a brief overview of their contribution to the political unrest that Iran, Egypt, and Lebanon experienced from the 1950s through the 1980s.

Although Iran in the 1940s and early 1950s saw a few formal organizations play an unprecedented part in mobilizing public opinion against the monarchy and British influence in the country, it did not witness the demise of the oppositional role of the old mosque- and bazaar-based networks. Thus, while the Tudeh displayed great success at mobilizing organized labor, National Front and Royalist politicians harnessed to their respective advantage the political energy of the more amorphous "street" by manipulating the informal networks under the control of clerics or of strong-arm men known as *chaqu-kashan*. In addition, networks led by radical clerics with a power base in the lower echelons of the bazaar and among the urban poor often revealed themselves to be very destabilizing, as in the case of the Fada'iyan-e Islam or during the 1963 urban uprising. More fundamentally, the shah's consolidation of power after 1953, and the increasingly authoritarian character of his regime, had the effect of turning the informal networks under the influence of the religious and *bazaari* communities into the most efficient vehicles for the expression of political dissent. In this context, as will be seen later, the informal networks organized around the cohesive worlds of the mosque and the bazaar made the 1977–79 revolution possible.

In turning to Egypt during the 1940s and 1950s, the previous description of the Muslim Brotherhood (MB) as a mass-based political "organization" must now be qualified. The qualification concerns not the mass-based character of the MB, but the extent to which it was an "organization" in the formal sense. Significantly, the MB never registered as a party. Officially, it always remained a benevolent association. Its success was, to a very large extent, a result of its ability to resort to centuries-old methods of recruitment, using mosques, sermons, and personal contacts to expand its membership and influence. The MB also relied heavily on personal ties for purposes of internal organization, since the entire movement was built around small, semi-independent cells geared to the particular needs and aspirations of their members. The vocabulary used to refer to these various cells is revealing of the MB's attempt to capitalize on intimate feelings as a way to enhance the movement's cohesion and effectiveness. Thus, after 1943, the most basic unit of the MB was called the "family" (*al-usra*). It included only five, subsequently ten, members, and was headed by an elected chief (*naqib*) who represented the "family" before the leadership of the local branch (Mitchell 1969, 197). Similarly, *al-'ashira*, which literally means "clan," referred to the unit formed by four families. It is also significant that the word used to describe the movement's message was *al-da'wa*, "the call," a word that is imbued with religious significance and has operated as a rallying cry for many messianic movements in Islamic history.

If one now looks at the period ushered by the 1952 coup, which overthrew the monarchy and brought to power the regime that still rules the country, it becomes clear that no political party, union, or professional association has ever been able to pose a real threat to the regime, including during the relatively tolerant Mubarak era. Thus, while the policy of political liberalization initiated by Sadat in the mid-1970s and broadened by Mubarak since 1981 has led to the development of opposition parties, these parties suffer from considerable structural weaknesses. Most importantly, their social base is restricted to a small segment of the bourgeoisie and the intelligentsia. Even the left-wing *tagammu*, which claims to speak for workers and peasants, is in fact composed primarily of students, journalists, writers, and academics and is "marred by too many 'prominent intellectuals' and armchair leftists" (Hendriks 1987, 29).[14]

In addition, opposition parties only have limited access to the state-controlled media, and they lack an effective grassroots infrastructure and the financial and organizational resources to act as a counterweight to the distribution of state patronage through the government bureaucracy and the public firms. Their freedom of maneuver is also strictly constrained by the government. Thus, even under the relatively liberal climate of the Mubarak regime, election fraud, intimidation, and harassment of opposition parties and their members remain common practice. When all is said and done, opposition parties operate only by the goodwill and sufferance of the Mubarak government, and they remain very vulnerable to an always-possible state crackdown.

Opposition parties also suffer from a high degree of internal fragmentation, and from debilitating ideological and personal feuds and rivalries. In addition, they are divided among themselves—a feature that the state has become expert at using to its own advantage.[15] Most fundamentally perhaps, the effectiveness of opposition parties is structurally constrained by the Egyptians' reluctance to participate in the formal, official political scene. This phenomenon, which reflects the population's cynicism toward the government and its general disillusionment with the political system, manifests itself most dramatically through voter apathy. It is noteworthy that nonregistration and abstention are especially pronounced in urban areas, where voter turnout rarely exceeds 25 percent (Springborg 1989, 163). In fact, it seems that the bigger the city, the lower the electoral participation. Significantly, in both the 1984 and the 1987 legislative elections, the lowest voter turnouts were registered in Egypt's three largest cities (Post 1987, 22). In 1987, in some areas of Cairo as little as 14 percent of the eligible population bothered to vote (Makram-Ebeid 1989, 432.)

This, however, does not indicate that Egyptians are politically inactive. It means, rather, that most of them participate in politics not through formal organizations but through religious, patron-client, and neighborhood- and kin-based informal networks. The party system in Egypt operates only on the surface of politics. More important and better established political forces are at work in the country—including the Islamic movement, especially its moderate wing, which penetrates deeply in society through a multiplicity of informally organized associations and clubs that provide the Egyptian population with essential social services. The fact that political parties court Islamic groups and try to capitalize on the existence of strong Islamic feelings in the population only underscores the weakness of these parties' own capacity to mobilize the public (Roussillon 1987–88, 332). By the same token, it also highlights the political power of informal networks in Egyptian politics.

Thus, although since 1968 Egypt has been shaken by several waves of popular discontent, real challenges to the regime have not emerged from formally organized entities, whether political parties, trade unions, or syndicates. Instead, they have come from spontaneous riots,[16] or from a variety of underground Islamic networks that, unlike opposition parties, are perceived as offering a clear alternative to the current government. By the early 1990s radical Islamic groups had been unable to seriously threaten the survival of the regime, but they had nevertheless proved to be the most destabilizing political force in Egyptian society, by encouraging sectarian strife, harassing local Christians, burning churches, provoking the authorities, attacking police stations, shops, clubs, discos, and bars, and engaging in kidnapings and assassination attempts against prominent individuals associated with the government or against secularist politicians and journalists.

In turning finally to Lebanon during the period from the country's independence to the outbreak of hostilities in 1975, one cannot but notice the structural weaknesses displayed by opposition organizations that tried to transcend networks. The appeal of formally organized parties such as the PPS, the Ba'ath, and the Lebanese Communist Party remained limited to a tiny segment of the Lebanese population, primarily students, intellectuals, and professionals (Yamak 1966a: 153–54). Lacking grassroots support and often forced to operate clandestinely, these parties remained on the fringes of the political system.

Furthermore, even self-styled progressive or revolutionary parties in Lebanon often remained little more than loosely organized political factions built around prominent individuals and families who used these parties to consolidate, widen, and mobilize their respective clienteles. The case of Kamal Jumblatt's Progressive Socialist Party (PSP) is particularly revealing. It is true that, in the 1960s and early 1970s, the PSP was able to capitalize on its leader's charisma and progressive rhetoric to expand its membership beyond the narrow confines of the Druze community and attract large numbers of Muslims alienated from their traditional *zu'ama'*. Yet for the majority of his followers, Kamal remained first and foremost a Jumblatti, the scion of one of the two leading Druze families, and only secondarily a "progressive socialist" (Khalaf

1985, 91–92). His political power, in other words, continued to be sustained more by primordial allegiances than by an ideology or a specific program. It is significant perhaps that Kamal Jumblatt's Druze followers would refer to him as "the Lord of Mukhtara," a title that Kamal never repudiated (Abu-Khalil 1985, 32). It is also significant that, following Kamal Jumblatt's death, his son Walid automatically inherited the party's leadership, as if the party was only one of the family's many holdings (Abu-Khalil 1985, 32).

Overall, between 1943 and 1975 the vehicles used by most Lebanese to engage in destabilizing activities or political protest against the political system were not formally organized parties, trade unions, and syndicates, but loosely organized groups based primarily on patron-client ties and sustained by a mixture of sectarian, regional, kinship, clannish, and/or neighborhood loyalties. The armed clashes that punctuated Lebanese political life during this period were thus usually a product of rivalries between contending *zuʿamaʾ*. In particular, the opposition to Chamoun's government during the 1958 uprising was mobilized almost exclusively through the networks controlled by influential but dissatisfied political bosses.[17] Although these *zuʿamaʾ* were helped during the crisis by the Baʿath and the Lebanese Communist Party,[18] the leading role in the opposition was played by *zuʿamaʾ*, not by parties. As Hottinger points out, these *zuʿamaʾ* may have been old-fashioned in their way of operating—relying as they did on personal ties and loyalties—but they nevertheless proved very effective in challenging the government.

The outbreak of the civil war in 1975 did not trigger the demise of networks, even though, as noted earlier, it brought to the fore a new kind of highly organized politicomilitary machine: the militia. Thus, while the militias played an important role in perpetuating violence, so did a multiplicity of smaller and loosely organized groups sustained by a variety of narrow-based allegiances, such as patron-client, clannish, or kinship ties, or loyalty to a particular religious figure.[19] Moreover, the civil war, and the heightened sectarian consciousness it promoted, weakened the already limited internal structure and cohesion of the self-professed left-wing political parties that earlier had tried to mobilize the Lebanese public against the inequities of their system. In the late 1980s, for example, the Lebanese Communist Party was riddled with sectarian divisions, especially between Greek Orthodox and Shiites. The PPS, too, was split into loosely organized and competing factions based on sectarian affiliations. In Druze areas, the PPS had even become the instrument used by the Yazbaki family to contain the influence of the better established Jumblattis (Abu-Khalil 1988, 178–84).

Patron-Client Networks and Urban Unrest in Iran, Lebanon, and Egypt

Although one of this book's objectives is to demonstrate that, under certain conditions, patron-client networks can operate as effective vehicles for political protest, it is hard to deny the stabilizing influence that clientelism usually exerts on urban politics (and, for that matter, on rural politics). In fact, the political histories of Lebanon, Egypt, and Iran since World War II provide much evidence to demonstrate the integrative nature of urban patronage systems.

The Effectiveness of Clientelism as a Structure of Political Control

Perhaps more than any other Middle Eastern country in the recent period, Lebanon from 1943 to the early 1970s demonstrates that clientelism can make an essential contribution to the maintenance of political order and social peace. Indeed, it is largely on the basis of the demonstrated ability of clientelism to work as a structure of political control that many students of Lebanon in the 1960s and early 1970s proclaimed their confidence in the stability of the country.[1] Lebanon was then a country in which the basic ingredients of politics were not formally organized, ideologically oriented political parties debating issues and programs, but loosely organized factions dominated by patrons called *zu'ama'* (sing. *za'im*), an Arabic term that can also be translated as "chiefs," "heads," "leaders," or "strongmen" (Hottinger 1961, 128).[2]

Prior to 1975, the *zu'ama'* usually were the most prominent members of the country's rich notable families, and they derived their power from their wealth, influence, and access to the government. These political bosses protected their clients, often found employment for them, and interfered on their behalf with the bureaucracy or with powerful individuals to whom the clients needed access. In return for such services, a client owed political allegiance to his patron. At elections, the client would vote for his *za'im* or for the candidate his *za'im* had chosen. Needless to say, a *za'im* also had the power to speak for his clients as a group. He could commit them to specific causes and tasks, and even call upon them to take arms and fight other *zu'ama'* and their followings (Hottinger 1961, 128).

In the cities, a *za'im*'s network was typically made up of four concentric circles as shown in figure 5. The circle closest to the *za'im* included his immediate household (his family, servants, and other dependents and their families). The second circle was represented by the patron's most trusted agents and administrators, and by a group of very influential neighborhood leaders, sometimes called *ru'asa'* (sing. *ra'is* or *rayyis*), or "chiefs," to indicate their prominent status among *qabadayat*. These neighborhood leaders were usually former minor *qabadayat* who, through years of service for their patron, had become successful businessmen and well-established political bosses in their own rights. In Beirut, a *za'im* generally had fifteen to twenty such *ru'asa'* (Johnson 1986, 88).

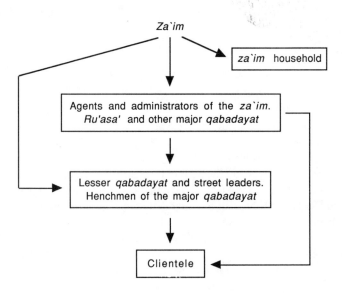

Figure 5. A *Za'im*'s Network

These major *qabadayat*, in turn, relied on a third circle, a group of henchmen and lesser *qabadayat* and street leaders, who played a key role in directly recruiting, policing, organizing, and mobilizing the *za'im*'s clientele. These lesser *qabadayat* were often thugs who were involved in racketeering and smuggling operations, and their influence was more locally circumscribed and limited than that of the major *qabadayat*. In exchange for their services, *zu'ama'* (or the *ru'asa'* working for the *zu'ama'*) would protect these lesser *qabadayat* against arrest and help them in their "business" operations. (Outside of the largest cities and in the case of relatively minor *zu'ama'*, a *za'im* would frequently be forced to deal directly with minor gang leaders and *qabadayat*.)

Finally, the clientele, quantitatively the largest component of the *za'im*'s following, formed the fourth circle. This outlying circle included all those who were indebted to the *za'im* because he once had rendered them or their family a service, because they worked in companies owned partially or totally by the *za'im*, or because allegiance to the *za'im* simply represented a sort of insurance against physical harassment or material deprivation (Hottinger 1961, 129).

The *zu'ama'* strove to keep their clients in a state of dependence. Although most individuals had to rely on a powerful patron for access to goods and services, the greater the individual's deprivation, the more limited his skills and access to resources and power, the more he had to depend on a patron for help and protection (Hottinger 1966, 98). Class solidarity, therefore, was the weakest among the lower classes. Thus, from the *za'im*'s viewpoint the system was particularly effective, in that it hampered collective action precisely for those who stood to benefit most from such action.

Two additional factors buttressed the position of the *zu'ama'*. First, patron-client clusters most often linked members of the same sect. In such a context, patrons could always manipulate to their profit the emotions and sentiments of solidarity associated with sectarian affiliations. Second, since patrons made ample use of *qabadayat* to act as brokers between them and their clients, and since *qabadayat* were often perceived as symbols of their respective quarters, neighborhood solidarities were also harnessed to strengthen feelings of loyalty to a given patron. This process, in turn, further thwarted the development of horizontal solidarities in the urban population. As Johnson (1986, 94–95) has observed, "By effectively forcing clients to approach him through their quarter or family *qabaday*, the *za'im* encouraged the individual client to see himself as a member of a particular locality or family, and discouraged the formation of other social groups which might have posed a threat to the status quo."

Political bosses also endeavored to promote individualism and fragmentation among the lower classes by refusing to grant favors and concessions to class and interest organizations, such as trade unions. Consequently, the urban poor were forced to compete among themselves for access to the *zuʿamaʾ* and to the goods and services only *zuʿamaʾ* could deliver. Even the *qabadayat* were condemned to work for individual advancement in the shadows of their respective bosses (Johnson 1986).

In addition to the domination of each sectarian community by an elite that exerted tight control over its flock by monopolizing access to jobs, goods, and services, another essential characteristic of the Lebanese clientelist structure was the existence of a broad consensus between the various sectarian elites. The system rested on the premise that elite accommodation at the level of the country as a whole would mitigate intersectarian conflict. Whenever lower-class Christians and Muslims would clash on the streets, the leaders of each community would use their authority to bring their respective followings back into the fold. As long as some form of compromise could be worked out between the various sectarian elites, the system would be stable. Lebanon, in this context, was often presented as an example of "consociational democracy," that is, "government by elite cartel designed to turn a democracy with a fragmented political culture into a stable democracy" (Lijphart 1969, 216).

Until the early 1970s, this clientelist structure of control proved remarkably effective. In a country where the state traditionally had done very little, the greater part of the nation's resources were channeled through the personalized networks of the clientelist system. The ubiquity of the system and its acceptance by a population socialized in it seemed to augur well for its future.

The different political evolutions of Iran and Egypt in the 1970s also bear witness to the stabilizing influence of urban patronage networks. In 1970s Iran, no networks existed to provide a bridge between the regime and the urban population, and to compensate for the absence of formally organized political groups binding the monarchy to the modern middle class, the *bazaari* and religious communities, the working class, and uprooted peasants.[3] Eventually, coercion and the selective distribution of economic rewards fell short of ensuring the population's loyalty. Not surprisingly, it was in the cities, where political control traditionally has been more difficult to achieve than in rural areas, that the shah's failure to rely on effective political organizations and/or well-established patronage networks, proved fatal to his regime.

Meanwhile, although the Egyptian regime has consistently failed to develop institutions capable of mobilizing the mass public, it nevertheless has displayed greater links between state and civil society. Of course, urban-based clientelist structures are only one element in such elite-mass linkages. More important, perhaps, has been the existence of corporatist organizations that had no counterparts in the shah's Iran and that were expanded under Sadat and especially Mubarak. By the late 1980s, these organizations had become key points of contacts between the regime and strategic urban constituencies, including businesspeople, labor, professionals, and civil servants (Bianchi 1989b). To be sure as well, the relatively limited scope of patron-client networks in Egyptian cities needs to be emphasized. For instance, in at least two essential respects, Egypt's urban patrons have been considerably weaker than their counterparts in pre-civil-war Lebanon. First, their freedom to maneuver has been greatly limited by the existence of a relatively strong state, with which they can cooperate but against which they cannot rise. Second, both the scope of clientelist networks (which encompass only a small share of Egypt's urban population) and the control that patrons exert over the life of their clients are much more limited in urban Egypt than in the cities of pre-civil-war Lebanon (Springborg 1975, 90). Overall, Egyptian urban bosses—who may be either Westernized professionals or, as in the *baladi* districts, traditional notables[4]— create only tenuous links between the urban population and the larger political system (Hinnebusch 1985, 248).

Nevertheless, urban clientelist structures also have contributed to the stability of the Egyptian government, which has been able to establish ties to segments of the urban population by co-opting local notables in the ruling NDP, or by relying on subelites active in local government councils, unions, neighborhoods, and benevolent and professional associations (Hinnebusch 1985). Furthermore, in many neighborhoods the direct presence of the state remains limited. This feature enables prominent personalities in the neighborhood to function, with the government's encouragement, as brokers between the local community and a rather distant bureaucratic authority. Thus, urban clientelist networks, however limited in scope they might be, have consolidated webs of personal loyalties, reciprocal commitments, and shared interests between the political elite and local urban communities, and they too help explain the resilience of the political order in Egypt (Hinnebusch 1985, 127).

The Limits of Clientelism in Cities

In turning from an examination of the political effectiveness of patronage to an analysis of its limits, we may note, first, that, while patron-client networks help maintain political order both in cities and in the countryside, clientelism tends to be much less stable in urban than in rural areas. There are several reasons for this. First, an urban patron usually has less control over the economic, social, and political life of his or her client than a rural patron (who typically is a large landowner). For their livelihood, physical security, and access to the government, peasant populations often remain highly dependent on the few landowner-notables who dominate the area where they live and who possess a monopoly over local resources. Accordingly, relations between peasants and their landlords are usually "multiplex": They are not limited to specific exchanges, but tend to be all-encompassing. By contrast, an urban dweller often has a choice between several sources of access to jobs, goods, and services. He or she is unlikely to remain dependent on one single patron for a long period of time. Instead, he or she will try to establish contacts with several patrons or brokers, as a way of increasing his or her options and security. This is one of many ways in which the city, in many Third World countries, renders the individual freer than he or she was back in the village.

Similarly, the connection between an urban patron and his client is likely to rest more exclusively on the distribution of favors than is usually the case in the relationship between landlord and peasant, as the peasant's loyalty to the landlord is often seen as stemming not only from the benefits he owes his patron, but also from a more general feeling of moral commitment, passed down over the years and through the family. This feature, too, explains why the hold of the city boss over his clientele is usually considerably less secure than that of his rural counterpart, since patron-client loyalties in the urban environment will tend to fluctuate with the flow of resources. As one scholar puts it, "It may be the death knell of clientelist ties when they cease to be cloaked in the vernacular of friendship, honor and moral or sacred obligation" (Waterbury 1979, 223).

In part because of the factors already mentioned, and in part because of the inherently more fluid and unpredictable nature of urban politics, the patronage arena also tends to be more competitive in the cities than in the countryside. City bosses constantly have to vie with one another to consolidate and widen the base of their patronage and to try to extend their respective spheres of influence beyond the circles of people who are directly dependent upon them. Because of the resulting rivalries in their ranks, and because of the more politicized nature of the constituencies to which they try to appeal, urban patrons often will resort to ideological slogans (on Lebanon, see Hottinger 1966, 96). Thus, while personal loyalties remain the essence of clientelism in urban areas (individuals support less a program or an ideology than a person perceived as capable of dispensing protection and favors), patronage is usually more politically oriented in the city than in the village. This difference, as will be shown below, also tends to make the urban patronage arena more susceptible to destabilization than its rural counterpart.

Lebanon throughout the period from independence to the outbreak of the civil war illustrates many of the points just mentioned. For instance, one may contrast the "feudal" Shiite *zu'ama'* of southern Lebanon (e.g., the As'ad, 'Usayran, Hamadeh) and the Sunni *zu'ama'* of the coastal cities of Beirut, Tripoli, and Sidon (e.g., Saeb Salam in Beirut, Rashid Karamé in Tripoli, or

Ma'ruf Sa'ad in Sidon). In the 1940s, 1950s, and 1960s, the feudal Shiite *zu'ama'* never had much problem reproducing their power, as each parliamentary election would see them reelected for yet another term. This phenomenon was merely the political translation of the poor peasants' continuing dependence on their *zu'ama'* to find jobs and secure vital goods and access to government officials. The position of the Sunni *zu'ama'* of the coastal cities was much more precarious, particularly in the capital. It was not uncommon for segments of the urban population to switch allegiance from one patron to another. As a result, even the most prominent *za'im* could always be challenged, as the political demise of Sami al-Sulh in the late 1950s demonstrates.

Some Dangers of Clientelism in a Multiconfessional Society: Lebanon as Example

In pre-1975 Lebanon, patron-client clusters tended to link members of the same sect. Although a few politicians were able to extend the base of their clientage much beyond the borders of their own religious community—Kamal Jumblatt[5] and Najah Wakim[6] immediately come to mind—such *zu'ama'* were the exceptions that confirmed the rule. Usually patron and client belonged to the same sect. In numerous instances, this overlap between clientelism and communalism proved very destabilizing, since conflicts between patrons could degenerate into bloody and nasty sectarian strife. More importantly, the stability of the system rested on the ability of each sectarian elite to contain the latent or manifest religious hostility, particularly pronounced among the lower classes, that might result in sectarian strife.[7] While, historically, cooperation between notables of various sects had been able to contain intersectarian conflict, the sectarian elites did at times lose control over their flocks, most spectacularly during Lebanon's first civil war, in 1958, and less than two decades later, in 1975–76, when the second civil war broke out.

The *zu'ama'* themselves were neither free from sectarian prejudices nor always wise enough to play by the rules of consociationalism. Indeed, consociational solutions assume that sectarian or ethnic leaders are enlightened enough to realize that the societies in which they live are prone to destabilization and that caution must be exerted at the elite level to preserve stability. The success of consociationalism also rests on the premise that the various elites are sufficiently aware of their common interests in the survival of the system that they eventually will be able to contain whatever differences might erupt in their ranks. From the late 1960s onward, the sectarian elites proved incapable of living up to these high standards. (The fact that one key actor, the Palestinians, was not part of the consociational framework made the situation more difficult to control.) Under the presidencies of Charles Helou (1964–70) and Suleiman Franjieh (1970–76), the Maronite leadership stubbornly resisted the moderate and legitimate requests of its Sunni coalition partners for increasing the Muslims' share of power in the political system, in line with the country's demographic evolution. In fact, Franjieh openly tried to undercut the power of his Sunni prime minister, who was excluded from key decisions (Petran 1987, 119–20).

As the political crisis reached disturbing proportions in 1973–74, the Kata'ib stepped into the fray. Spurred by the issue of the Palestinian presence in the country, as well as by the alliances between Palestinian organizations and predominantly self-professed leftist Lebanese groups, the leadership of the Kata'ib refused to abide by the rules of the intra-elite game. From the early 1970s onward, the Phalange became increasingly sectarian in its outlook and slogans; it abandoned its earlier moderation and commitment to fostering cross-confessional unity and became unwilling to compromise. Even John Entelis, whose 1974 book provides a sympathetic portrayal of the Kata'ib, recognizes that the party leadership's response to the situation in Lebanon in the mid-1970s was "drastic, indeed fanatical" (Entelis 1981, 240). In fact, the party used its following, organization, and military power to escalate the conflict and make a political solution to the fighting difficult to reach (Hudson 1976, 117).[8]

The Maronite establishment was not solely responsible for the slide toward chaos. From the late 1960s onward, a new group of younger and more militant Muslim leaders proved insensitive to the growing concerns of the Maronites. Not only was the de facto politicomilitary alliance between the Palestinians and the Lebanese left a direct violation of the 1943 National Pact,[9] but, more generally, the behavior and rhetoric of the leaders of the self-professed leftist groups became increasingly provocative. Significant was the case of Kamal Jumblatt, who in the late 1960s and early 1970s began to advocate an increasingly radical political agenda (al-Khazen 1988, 187–90). Even as the country was obviously drifting into civil war, many Muslim leaders saw the growing unrest as an opportunity to expand their power bases by outdoing their traditional rivals with the use of inflammatory rhetoric. (Jumblatt, in his open defiance of the established Sunni leadership, is once again a good example.)

There are several lessons to be learned from Lebanon's political evolution in the late 1960s and early to mid-1970s. First, the quality of the political class is an important mediating variable if one wants to assess the chance of success of confessional solutions. The Lebanese elite's lack of civility, emphasized early on by Shils (1966), proved to have disastrous consequences. Second, in a country characterized by very pronounced religious or ethnic divisions, elites may not be impermeable to sectarian or ethnic prejudices or to the weight of centuries of ethnic/religious violence. Hafiz al-Assad saw Jumblatt's behavior in the mid-1970s as merely "a matter of revenge, which dates back 140 years" (al-Khazen 1988, 182). While this interpretation may be exaggerated, it undoubtedly captures part of Jumblatt's motives. The same reasoning applies to the Maronites' old fears and prejudices, which go a long way toward explaining their leadership's intransigence and fanatic reaction in 1975.

When one looks at societies with highly fragmented political cultures, how safe is it to assume, as advocates of consociationalism do, that the respective elites will remain immune to the prevailing divisions? At times of crisis, sectarian or ethnic prejudices can always resurface at the elite level, and, combined with other sources of tension and conflict, they may make intra-elite bargaining and consensus an elusive process. This was shown in 1958, 1975–76, and repeatedly ever since. In Lebanon, an unfavorable domestic and regional situation in the early 1970s gave rise to increasingly violent intra-elite feuds, which eventually led to a breakdown in communication among the country's leading politicians. The personal estrangement between Lebanon's old *zu'ama'* often grew more intense over the years. This phenomenon demonstrates, as Walid Khalidi (1979, 97) has put it, that "if there is such a thing as learning the rules of the game...which enables leaders to acquire the knack of consensual politics in open but divided societies, there is also a process of unlearning these rules."

Overall, therefore, clientelism is more likely to be disruptive in plural than in homogeneous societies. Furthermore, in countries where primordialism cannot be wished away, consociationalism's reassuring facade may be very misleading. Finally, while the political engineering associated with consociationalism may not always be a solution to the inherent instability of plural societies, its chance of success will be heavily influenced by the quality of the political class.

Clientelism in a Weak State

The collapse of many patron-client networks in Lebanon in 1975–76 shows that, although patronage can provide the much-needed lubricant of a political system whose stability rests primarily on the existence of a strong central authority, clientelist networks by themselves cannot be relied upon to provide for political order in large, politicized, and modern cities. Lebanon in this respect was unusual, in that few modern polities operate almost exclusively along clientelist lines. In most countries, urban patrons either are agents of the central bureaucracy or, at a minimum, work under its auspices and watchful eyes. Typically, the informal leader of a community will be coopted in the ruling party, or a member of the ruling party or central bureaucracy will impose himself as a local leader through his ability to deliver vital goods and services. In either case, clientelism provides the degree of personalism and flexibility necessary for the smooth but effective articulation of local communities and the state machinery.

Yet the existence of a strong central authority in the background is as vital as the clientelist structure itself in ensuring the stability of the system. Patrons and brokers know that they have to operate within the boundaries fixed by the national elite. Attempts by local actors to abuse their freedom to maneuver usually will be met by an almost instantaneous reaction of the central authority. Local patrons inevitably will be defeated in such confrontations, since they are fragmented among themselves and can match only a few, if any, of the organizational resources that the state can muster against them.[10]

Furthermore, where central authority can make and unmake patrons, the latter are denied the temptation of establishing their credentials as leaders through a demagogical exploitation of popular prejudices and moods. In contrast, in postindependence Lebanon, an urban patron could best carve out a place for himself by being recognized as a leader by "the street." This feature heightened the unstable nature of the Lebanese clientelist system by creating strong incentives for various brands of political demagogues either to manipulate pseudomodern, radical ideologies or to whip up religious prejudices for the sake of immediate political advantage.

A strong state also provides a sense of purpose, permanence, and continuity and tends to smooth or prevent internecine strife between patrons. In 1970s Mexico, for instance, the existence of corporate organizations of peasants and workers provided those who reached the top levels of the political system with readily available power bases. As Purcell notes, "This frees the circulating elites from having to devote their energies to building, and possibly mobilizing, ever larger individual followings. Such activities, after all, could ultimately destabilize the political system by increasing competition among the elites (thereby fragmenting them) and encouraging dangerously high levels of mobilization. Instead, the provision of permanent corporate power bases to the pool of circulating elites encourages the elites to spend their time constructing and improving relationships with other elites, so as to increase their chances of profiting from each other's promotions" (Purcell 1981, 205). In Lebanon, however, the political system provided little incentive for political bosses to cooperate with one another. Patronage was more of a zero-sum game, in which independent patron-warlords were concerned primarily with undercutting each other's influence and with maintaining or expanding their own power bases. *Zu'ama'*, furthermore, were engaged in a shortsighted search for immediate political advantage, and they were often heedless of the long-term impact such a strategy would have on the political system.

Similarly, in relatively strong states, government officials, patrons, and brokers usually belong to the same structure (indeed patrons and government officials often are the same individuals). This situation tends to minimize the possibility that patrons will work at cross-purposes with one another. In post-1958 Lebanon, by contrast, state-sponsored patrons, the more autonomous patrons, and the *qabadayat* appeared as three largely distinct actors who more often than not, through shifting coalitions, worked to undercut each other's power.

Most importantly perhaps, the effectiveness of Lebanese clientelism as a system of political control rested on the ability of the major *zu'ama'* to reach some minimal consensus. This consensus was attained through informal procedures and tacit agreements and could survive only as long as the major participants in the system benefited from it. There was little that the state—itself essentially a coalition of the most influential *zu'ama'*—could do to arbitrate between patrons and prevent them from settling their differences by resorting to violence. In fact, in a culture prone to violence and imbued with the values of honor and machismo, armed confrontations between patrons mobilizing their respective followings were frequent occurrences. Significantly, on at least two occasions in the recent period, 1958 and 1975–76, the absence of a strong central authority capable of arbitrating between competing elites contributed both to the outbreak of civil hostilities and to the reliance of the major participants on outside help.

In 1958, Chamoun's narrow-based government was more one of many factions involved in a contest for power than a government in the real sense of the term. It could not depend on the army, which early on in the conflict announced its neutrality. Moreover, while the police did provide some support for the government, it was poorly equipped and ill-prepared to deal with a major uprising. In any event, the police itself was divided over the attitude it should take, and many policemen deserted to join the insurgents (Qubain 1961, 83; Petran 1987, 51). The state, in other words, did not have at its disposal the power either to restore order by force or to mediate between competing warlords and force them to accept a compromise. This situation explains why Chamoun had to rely on the intervention of an outside force (the fourteen thousand U.S. Marines who landed in Beirut) and on the Kata'ib and the PPS.

In 1975–76 again, dissension in the ranks of the elite—and, more precisely, the Sunni leadership's inability to persuade its Maronite counterpart to accept a compromise—once again led to a breakdown of order, which the government found itself unable to prevent or contain. This time around, however, there would be no return to the status quo ante.

The only serious effort to create a stronger state in Lebanon took place during the presidencies of Fouad Shihab (1958–64) and Charles Helou

(1964–70)—particularly under Shihab. In the aftermath of the 1958 conflagration, Shihab set out to increase the power and the effectiveness of the government in Lebanese politics. To do so, he surrounded himself with foreign
experts, young technocrats, and army officers. These individuals had few or
no ties to the traditional patron class, and they were highly critical of the
waste, corruption, and inefficiencies associated with confessionalism and the
politics of notables. Accordingly, Shihabism is often presented as an authoritarian attempt to reform the system from above, by enhancing the autonomy
and power of the executive branch and by circumventing the *zu'ama'* who
controlled parliament.

To some extent, this description is accurate. In addition to his achievements in the fields of social reforms and economic modernization (development of the south, extension of water and electricity to poor areas of the country, reduction of inequalities, etc.), President Shihab also made an earnest
effort to curtail the power of the traditional notables in the country.

Yet it is also important to underline the limits of Shihabism. As Johnson
(1986, 140) puts it, "Ultimately, Shihabism remained a prisoner of the clientelist system." To undermine the traditional *zu'ama'*, Shihab established direct
links between the army's internal security agency, the Deuxième Bureau, and
qabadayat who until then had worked under the shadows of their respective
zu'ama'. Thus, Shihab's policies were directed more against the traditional
zu'ama' than against clientelism as such. By promoting *qabadayat* and
younger rivals to the traditional *zu'ama'*, the Lebanese president himself
resorted to the manipulation of clientelist networks. At no point did Shihab
embark on any serious attempt to create a political party or movement aimed
at destroying clientelism or the sectarian system.[11] His policy remained based
on the largely contradictory and self-defeating strategy of using patron-client
networks to weaken clientelism in the country. It is perhaps revealing of the
informal nature of politics in Lebanon that an attempt to enhance the political
autonomy and strength of the state should take the form of a manipulation of
informal structures.

In the end, as he himself acknowledged, Shihab proved unable to reform
the system (Petran 1987, 59). The traditional *zu'ama'* emerged victorious
from their fight with him, and they even were able to defeat the pro-Shihabist
candidate (Elias Sarkis) in the presidential election of 1970.[12] Shihab's failure
was to have dramatic consequences. For one, by the early 1970s the patronage
system had become wholly inadequate to govern a city like Beirut. The
absence of a real central authority endowed with a monopoly over the exercise
of legitimate violence and capable of providing solutions to the basic infrastructural, economic, and social problems faced by a rapidly growing city
proved fatal. Albert Hourani has put it eloquently.

One important factor...which was missing in the analyses of Lebanese politics 20 years ago [Hourani refers more specifically to the 1966 volume edited by Binder] was a sense of the ways in which Lebanon had become a city-state, and in which the government of a city-state differs from that of a republic of villages. In the villages of the mountain valleys, government can be carried on—and perhaps it can only be carried on by political manipulation within limits which leave the local power of the lords of the valleys untouched. In a city, however, the government has other tasks: to maintain the public utilities without which life is impossible—transport, electricity, water, drainage—and to channel wealth by means of taxation into social services, education and popular housing. All this involves something more than political manipulation; it needs direct bureaucratic control, and this in turn demands a government with a solid basis of authority. (Hourani 1988, 6)

At a conference organized in September 1987 by the Center for Lebanese Studies in Oxford, Hourani linked the absence of centralized authority and the rise of the militias. The militias, he suggested, emerged to assume some of the functions that the central government had proved unable or unwilling to perform. There is much evidence to support Hourani's hypothesis. For instance, faced with the growing paralysis of the Lebanese government between 1973 and 1975, the Kata'ib clearly tried to substitute itself for a state that it had come to see as incapable of maintaining order and the country's unity. Similarly, a few years later the Lebanese Forces emerged primarily "in response to the vacuum created by the collapse of the central government, and particularly in response to the total absence of internal security and other essential government services" (Snider 1984, 1). Significantly perhaps, "many activities undertaken by the Lebanese Forces began as efforts to persuade or pressure various government bureaucracies to perform the services which by law they are charged to provide" (Snider 1984, 1). By 1977, the Kata'ib and the Lebanese Forces were busy competing with each other and with the state for the loyalty of the Christian population. Both posed as the enforcers (for the Christian population at least) of law, order, and national sovereignty—collective goods that the state could no longer be expected to deliver.

Imam Sadr's Movement of the Disinherited and its Amal militia were born in 1974 in a similar context. Initially, the movement contented itself with lobbying the government for an improvement of living conditions in the south (Ajami 1986; Norton 1987). After 1975, however, confronted with the breakdown of state authority and the increasingly aggressive behavior of the heavily armed, rightist Maronite militias, the Movement of the Disinherited was forced to rely on its own militia to ensure the physical security of its members. As in the Christian community, but with a time lag of three to four years, Amal began to assume functions that the state had proved unable to fulfill.

By 1980, the militias, especially the better organized and largest ones, had become the real locus of power in the country. In the Maronite community, where the "militia phenomenon" had benefited from an early start, militias raised taxes, operated checkpoints, drafted individuals, and managed firms and ports. Faced with the formidable politicomilitary organizations of the Maronites, other communities had little choice but to attempt to organize themselves along similar lines, and this phenomenon goes a long way toward explaining the cancerlike growth of the militias and the spread of warlordism in the country. In retrospect, however, what really paved the way for the militias was simply a delusion on the part of Lebanon's ruling oligarchy—the delusion that a modern, large, and heavily politicized Arab capital located in a particularly hostile environment could still be governed primarily through the manipulation of patron-client networks.[13]

Social Mobilization and the Erosion of Urban Patronage Networks in Lebanon

Lebanon's recent history demonstrates that clientelist networks can fail to shelter the political system against the destabilizing consequences of rapid social mobilization. For instance, as lower-class Sunnis in Beirut, Sidon, and Tripoli became attracted to Nasserism and pan-Arab ideologies in the 1950s, the position of the traditional Sunni politicians became increasingly delicate. Nasserite slogans of social justice, reform, and equity threatened the Sunni *zu'ama'*, whose neofeudal and hereditary power represented a constant denial of the sociopolitical ideals for which Nasser seemed to stand. By reviving the pan-Arab dream, the Egyptian president was also lessening the identification of the Sunni population with the Lebanese entity. In 1943, however, the Sunni establishment had committed itself to the preservation of Lebanon's independence, sovereignty, and territorial integrity. In addition, Sunni leaders were fully aware that the survival of their power depended on the continued existence of Lebanon as a separate state, in which Christians and Muslims lived peacefully.

Thus, the leading Sunni politicians were caught between two imperatives. On the one hand, they had to profess allegiance to some form of pan-Arab goals and doctrines if they were to keep the support of the Sunni street.

On the other hand, in order to maintain a working relation with their Maronite coalition partners, they had to refrain from offending the Maronites' susceptibilities and dedication to a sovereign, independent Lebanon, distinct from the Arab world and uninvolved in regional wars and ideological quarrels. Eventually, the imperatives of political survival forced the Sunni *zuʿama*' to make concessions to the growing popularity of Nasserism. They began to invoke the symbols of Nasserism and proclaim their solidarity with the Egyptian president. Thus, the *zuʿama*' did not so much prevent the radicalization of their community as contain it within certain boundaries.

Some established politicians, such as Saeb Salam in Beirut or Rashid Karamé in Tripoli, proved more successful than others in manipulating Nasserism and posing as communal leaders standing for the rights of an oppressed Sunni community in a system working for the benefit of the Maronites. Other established politicians, however, did not fare so well. The already-mentioned example of Sami al-Sulh is often invoked to underline the limits on how far patrons could go in opposing the tide of opinion in an increasingly politicized community.[14] By failing to identify himself with Nasserism at a time when it was becoming the ideology of the street, Sami al-Sulh irremediably lost his influence in the Sunni community, and his political career came to an end. Conversely, by manipulating the symbols associated with Arab nationalism and a variety of leftist ideologies, relative newcomers were able to defeat better known politicians in the elections of 1972 (see below). Only by claiming for themselves the slogans of Nasserism and pan-Arabism were many patrons able to maintain control over their clienteles.[15]

From this evidence, one may draw two opposite conclusions. On the one hand, one may emphasize the ability of skillful patron-politicians to manipulate modern, progressive ideologies in such a way as to deprive these ideologies of their revolutionary potential. However, it seems more accurate to note that, in the long run, the use of radical slogans for political advantage can turn into a dangerous game. Over time, the patron's rhetoric may merely increase the political awareness of his clients. The population at large may become increasingly aware of the discrepancy between the patrons' proclamations and their deeds. Lower-class grievances may become more precisely formulated and less easily contained by the traditional leadership.

This is roughly what happened within Beirut's Sunni community. The watershed may have been the 1958 crisis. From then on, the Sunni notables and the Sunni popular classes began to drift away from each other.[16] The humiliation of Arab armies at the hands of Israel in 1967 and the resulting radicalization of the Sunni middle classes, particularly the students and the intelligentsia, put additional stress on the Sunni elite, whose power base was undermined by the rapid development of a variety of leftist movements allied with Palestinian groups. The educated middle classes, furthermore, were not the only ones to become increasingly alienated from the traditional Sunni leadership, as indicated by the flurry of strikes by industrial workers in the early 1970s.[17] Against this background, the Sunni *zu'ama'* found it increasingly difficult to preserve the status quo, from which they derived considerable material and symbolic benefits, while appearing to be sensitive to the wishes and aspirations of a community that had been radicalized and that was now putting increasing pressures on them to adopt more forceful positions on both domestic and foreign policy issues.

The tensions that resulted from these developments eventually provoked the collapse of the clientelist system of control in Muslim West Beirut in 1975–76 (Johnson 1986). Of course, the Palestinian presence contributed to this breakdown, since it accentuated the radicalization of the Sunni poor and further drove them away from their traditional leaders, and since it was the Sunni leadership's inability to restrain its Maronite coalition partners on this particular issue that made it lose control over the streets (Salibi 1976; Petran 1987). Nevertheless, the strains between the Sunni *zu'ama'* and their clienteles antedated by about fifteen years the emergence of Lebanon as the main Palestinian base, following the PLO's eviction from Jordan in September 1970.

Overall, although the history of the Lebanese Sunni community supports the proposition that patronage networks weaken the potential for radicalism among the lower classes, it also suggests that clientelist structures may be eroded by rapid socioeconomic and political change, and that they may reveal themselves to be an increasingly precarious bulwark against disorder. Under stress, patron-client arrangements may break down, as political developments among Lebanon's Sunnis in the mid-1970s demonstrate. When the Kata'ib militia began to shell the commercial center of Beirut in September 1975, the Sunni leadership lost control of its client populations. Clashes spread throughout the city. With the army unable to step in and prevent further fighting, the local *qabadayat* took it upon themselves to defend their quarters against outside aggressions. As Michael Johnson notes:

> Such clashes mobilized the Sunni sub-proletariat and *menu peuple*, and helped to establish the strongarm men as local leaders independent of the [*zu'ama'*]. If the latter had had some difficulty in controlling their clienteles since the early 1970's, the civil war now made such control impossible. Criminal gangs and local militias—many with Palestinian support and training—were able to operate at will, and violence, looting, and smuggling increased. It is important to emphasize that there was considerable overlap between the 'leftist' militias and criminal gangs. Although some

groups were more principled than others, it was extremely difficult to impose discipline on young, sub-proletarian militiamen,
many of whom were fighting as little more than mercenaries who
saw the small salaries paid them by their leaders as an extremely
attractive alternative to unemployment, especially when their
wages could be supplemented by a share in the spoils of war.
(Johnson 1986, 182)

The Maronite community experienced a phenomenon somewhat similar to the progressive estrangement of the Sunni masses from their traditional
leadership. During the 1960s and early 1970s, large segments of East Beirut's
Maronite population began to reject the traditional "politics of za'imship."
With the expansion of political consciousness and the changes in outlook generated by modernization, many among the Maronite lower and middle classes
began to consider the old Maronite notables as out of step with the times and
as constituting an obstacle to the country's social and economic development.
Such individuals often turned to the Phalange, which partly accounts for the
growth of this party during the 1960s. Significantly, while the leadership of the
Kata'ib remained solidly upper middle class, the rank-and-file members in the
early 1970s were drawn predominantly from the middle, lower middle, and
working classes.[18] The war created a totally new situation and, from 1976
onward, substantial segments of the Maronite electorate became disenchanted
with the Kata'ib as well. It is these groups and individuals who came to swell
the ranks of Bashir Gemayel's Lebanese Forces.[19]

Finally, the case of Lebanon's Shiite community shows that clientelist
structures of political control can fail to cope with the political consequences
of rapid urbanization. Largely as a result of the commercialization and mech-
anization of agriculture in the south and the Bekaa, Shiites started to migrate
in large numbers to Beirut in the 1960s (Nasr, 1985; Norton, 1987). In the
1970s, as the population of the south found itself caught in the middle of
fighting between Palestinian forces and the Israeli army, Shiite peasants were
forced off their land in ever-increasing numbers and swelled the ranks of the
proletariat and lumpenproletariat in the capital's shantytowns and suburbs.

Consequently, in the short span of two decades, the Shiites were turned
from a predominantly rural into a predominantly urban community. By 1975,
more than 60 percent of the rural population of the south had migrated,
mostly to Beirut, as a consequence of the deterioration of the living conditions
in the countryside (Nasr 1985, 11).[20] Unfortunately, the clientelist system in
Beirut proved unable to assimilate the constant flow of Shiite rural migrants,
largely as a result of a key provision in the electoral law according to which
one votes not where one lives, but in the constituency of one's birthplace.

Under such circumstance, no Beiruti *za'im* would perform services for a constituency that was in no position to reciprocate through its vote. This phenomenon turned out to be crucial. The electoral law, written to tie individuals to the patrons of their villages, thwarted the development of Beiruti clientelist structures capable of absorbing the flow of rural migrants that accompanied Lebanon's progressive transformation from a "Republic of villages" into a "city-state," to use Albert Hourani's terminology. Significantly, in the mid-1970s, although Beirut contained more than 50 percent of the country's total population, the city only had sixteen deputies out of a total of ninety-nine in the last elected Parliament in 1972. The Shiites and the Maronites, whose rates of migration into the capital were the highest during the 1960s and early 1970s, only had one Beirut-based deputy each (Salamé 1988).

The Shiite community was particularly affected. Tens of thousands of Shiite migrants and their descendants were never incorporated into the personal followings of Beiruti patrons. It is true that Rashid Beydoun, a Shiite patron, was able to utilize the 'Amiliyya, a Shiite benevolent association in Beirut, to extend the popular base of his political clientage—in a way very similar to Saeb Salam's use of the Maqased (Khalaf 1987, 100). Beydoun's following, however, remained very limited, and his case quite unique. For the most part, Shiite migrants remained outside the capital's clientelist system. Nor was any alternative structure of political control ever established to deal with the continuously expanding population in the suburbs (Johnson 1986, 184).

For a while, the Shiite migrants in Beirut continued to maintain relatively close political ties with their villages of origin. At election time, the *zu'ama'* of their home districts would provide them with transportation back to their villages, where they would vote for their traditional leaders (Ajami 1986, 70–71). Over time, however, the Shiite migrants, no longer dependent on their home villages for livelihood and security, were progressively cut off from the clientelist chains of these villages. In the process, they finally freed themselves from the grip of the reactionary landed elite and obscurantist clergy that had dominated the community for centuries. Yet as was shown above, the Shiite migrants also remained excluded from the patronage system of the capital. In these conditions, perhaps nothing better describes the process in which these individuals became caught up than Karl Deutsch's concept of "social mobilization," that is, "the process in which [as a result of rapid socioeconomic change] major clusters of old social, economic, and psychological commitments are eroded or broken, and people become available for new patterns of socialization and behavior" (Deutsch 1961, 494).

In the late 1960s and early 1970s, politicized Shiites were attracted to a broad spectrum of political organizations, from the Maronite-dominated

Kata'ib to the primarily Sunni Murabitun. Most of them, however, joined leftist parties, particularly the Lebanese Communist Party (PCL) and the Lebanese Communist Action Organization (OACL). In fact, Abu-Khalil points out that the extent of "Shiite involvement in leftist and communist political parties prompted many Lebanese to use the words *Shi'i* (Shiite) and *Shuyu'i* (communist) interchangeably" (Abu-Khalil 1988, 172).[21] The point is that Beirut's clientelist system of control proved unable to prevent the radicalization of large segments of the Shiite community, as politically active Shiites bent on improving the lot and status of their community began to identify with leftist parties protesting the deep and persisting inequities and socioeconomic cleavages in Lebanese society.

This evidence suggests, inter alia, that individuals, groups, and masses that are not "clientelized" become available for participation in radical politics. After 1968, the alienation of the Shiites from the mainstream of Lebanese political life became even more marked as the state proved unable to prevent Israeli raids in the south. The southern Shiites who settled in Beirut's "misery belt" (the belt of poverty surrounding the southern and eastern fringes of the city) came to the capital with an acute sense of grievance toward a political system that had failed to protect them against foreign depredation, and they turned out to have a radicalizing and disintegrative effect on the capital's politics. Not absorbed by the clientelist system, they organized themselves along lines that were at considerable variance with the predominant forms of the capital's political game. They opted for a more ideological, radical, antisystem and mass-based form of political action, turning predominantly to radical leftist movements and, in parallel, to Imam Sadr's communally based mode of political action. In doing so, they provided support for many of the hypotheses, which Joan Nelson and others have recently sought to refute, concerning the disruptive impact of recent migrants to the city.

Ultimately, the radicalization of the Shiites had momentous consequences on the future of the country. As Johnson (1986, 184) reminds us, "Had it not been for the radicalism and determination of two communities outside the Lebanese clientelist system [the Palestinians and the Shiites], the war might well have been contained within manageable limits." The outbreak of hostilities, it should be remembered, occurred in the southern suburbs, controlled primarily by an alliance of Palestinians and Lebanese leftist movements in which Shiites featured prominently. Somewhat similarly, the predominantly Christian eastern suburbs were inhabited mostly by recently urbanized Maronites who did not quite fit in Beirut's clientelist structure and often resented the politics of patronage associated with the Maronite establishment. Over time, Lebanon became the victim of a growing contradiction between, on

the one hand, socioeconomic trends, which were continuously pushing individuals to flow from the periphery of the country to its capital, and, on the
other hand, a static political system that, because of the electoral law, the insufficient number of deputies representing Beirut, and the prominent role of
patronage networks, was in effect denying recently urbanized migrants in the
capital the right to participate fully in that city's politics (Salamé 1988).

The experience of the Shiites shows that the accumulation in the cities,
or on their peripheries, of masses excluded from patronage networks can have
dire consequences on the political system. Thus, the fall of West Beirut to the
Shiite and Druze militias in February 1984 may be seen as the culmination of
a process that can be traced back to the inability of the clientelist structures of
the capital to assimilate successive waves of Shiite rural migrants. Whereas in
1958 the mostly urban-born, lower- and middle-class Sunnis of Beirut,
Tripoli, and Sidon were largely unsuccessful in their attempt to restructure
Lebanon's polity to their advantage, recently urbanized Shiite and Druze elements in the mid-1980s were able to deny an already weakened Maronite
president control over one-half of the capital.

If one adopts a broader perspective, the evolution of Beirut in the 1980s
is somewhat reminiscent of Ibn Khaldun's theory of desert tribes taking over
the city. By the middle of the decade, groups that for decades had been on the
periphery (both physically and symbolically) of Lebanon's political system
had now forced themselves onto center stage. Whenever fighting would rage
in the suburbs, masses of Shiite refugees would pour into dowtown West
Beirut, break into empty apartments, set up shacks, or squat in stylish movie
theaters or elegant boutiques that had just been looted by other offspring
from Beirut's misery belt (Pintak 1988, 185). In one instance—which took
place during the first phase of the civil war (1975–76) and which is highly significant of the transformation of downtown Beirut from the center of a privileged elite into a refuge for dislocated groups—a formerly exclusive beach
club was overrun by displaced and angry Shiite and Palestinian slum
dwellers, who turned the changing cabins into houses for whole families
(Makdisi 1990, 29). As the civil war dragged on, several attractive neighborhoods in West Beirut were progressively converted into quasi slums, dotted
with uncollected garbage and hastily built and ugly housing units (Makdisi
1990, 77).

In a way, by the mid-1980s, Lebanon's political center had been conquered by its periphery. The dispossessed, those left out from the clientelist
structures and those whom the Lebanese establishment had banished from its
consciousness for so long, were now asserting their presence at the very heart
of the city (Makdisi 1990, 79). Predictably, this spilling of the hinterland into
the capital changed the nature of Beirut's politics. A new political vocabulary,

new political actors, new forms of political behavior, and new ways of defining political issues appeared.

West Beirut again was particularly affected, including the formerly open, urbane, and cosmopolitan middle-class district of Ras-Beirut. This area's physiognomy was radically altered (Khalaf 1987, 261–84). Almost overnight, stylish residential and commercial areas were mutilated. Elegant boutiques now had to coexist with street vendors pushing wooden carts filled with everything from food to smuggled or looted luxury items to low-quality wares (Makdisi 1990, 81–82). The physical transformations that affected the area were inextricably related to the progressive destruction of its pluralistic and liberal character. Thus, the sophisticated political debates waged by a handful of privileged and Westernized Arab intellectuals in the cafés near the campus of the American University of Beirut were replaced by artillery duels by militiamen of rural and lower-class backgrounds. Religious fanaticism progressively superseded intellectual exchange. Disagreements were now settled through shoot-outs between rival militias. Predictably, gun wielders from the refugee camps and the suburban slums had no difficulty prevailing over the original inhabitants of Ras-Beirut. Almost overnight, Hamra Street, which had been the preserve of Beirut's intelligentsia, fell into the hands of young and unkempt militiamen of rural origins, who "would patrol the street in their jeeps clutching their *dushkas* [mountless, recoilless rifles], their bodies covered with an assortment of arms, from pistols in holsters, to daggers in sheaths, to hand grenades jostling on their hips, to the ubiquitous Kalashnikovs" (Makdisi 1990, 80).

As Fouad Ajami puts it in a nutshell, the fall of West Beirut to "Shiʿa squatters and urban newcomers" in February 1984 meant that "the world had been stood on its head: sons of villagers proclaimed their triumph over the city, over its ruins" (Ajami 1986, 204). The rise of fundamentalist groups in West Beirut in the mid-1980s, and the demise of the peaceful sectarian coexistence that had survived there for several years into the civil war, were inextricably related to this influx of rural newcomers. Bourgeois cosmopolitanism and open-mindedness gave way to a new form of religious fanaticism that was often a language through which recently urbanized elements simply vented their frustration and rage at a system that had ignored them for so long (Makdisi 1990, 133–34). They did so not only by ransacking stores and by breaking into abandoned houses and looting them thoroughly, but by turning an entire residential portion of the city into a battlefield on which they competed among themselves, without regard for the lives and properties of the area's original inhabitants, and in an attempt to control wealth that, they had just discovered, could easily be taken away from its rightful owners (Petran 1987, 352).

Overall, therefore, the case of Beirut suggests that while rapid urbanization does not necessarily lead to political unrest, it may well lessen the reluctance of individuals and groups to adopt violent means to achieve political objectives. This is perhaps especially true when, as in Lebanon, the groups that move into the city have been subjected to persecution and massive and forced dislocations. Presumably, indeed, populations that lack long-standing ties to the city will be less reluctant than old urbanites to turn it into a battleground, especially when they arrive there feeling victimized by the sociopolitical order. Thus, for instance, the successive waves of refugees driven to Beirut by clashes in other parts of the country and by successive Israeli air strikes and incursions provided the constantly expanding pool out of which militiamen for groups such as Hizballah could be recruited.

One suspects that behind the intensity and scope of the violence in Beirut in the 1980s lay the fact that the capital was now inhabited by recently urbanized populations that treated the city as a foreign territory to be conquered and exploited. Although there is no empirical study of the background of militia members, there is little doubt that the militiamen who destroyed Beirut for fifteen years were essentially recently urbanized groups and individuals who had come to the city but had failed to develop any particular attachment to it.[22] Beirut in the 1980s, in this context, can rightly be described as a battlefield on which individuals of rural origins used new political instruments (the militias) to compete violently for dominance over the capital—and did not particularly worry that the city itself might be destroyed in the process (Salamé 1988). Urbanization, therefore, contributed substantially to the scope, the intensity, the inextricable nature, and the ferocity of violence in Beirut. Such findings support arguments concerning the potentially destabilizing impact of recent rural migrants.

Patronage Networks and the Aspirant Elite

In the late 1960s and early 1970s, the traditionally impoverished and politically excluded Shiite community was profoundly affected by the return to Lebanon of many of its members who had made fortunes overseas and who now formed a new Shiite bourgeoisie in the country. More generally, largely as a result of the progress of literacy in its ranks, the Shiite community now included a growing number of businessmen, professionals, and civil servants. These individuals expected that their success would open doors that had remained closed to their elders, and they wanted the respectability and social recognition to which they believed their achievements had entitled them (Ajami 1986).

Unfortunately, the economic slowdown in Lebanon in the late 1960s and early 1970s limited the Shiite middle class's prospects for further socioeconomic advancement. Meanwhile, the new Shiite bourgeoisie found it difficult to compete with the better established Sunni and Christian bourgeoisies, which already had cornered the most productive sectors of the economy (Nasr 1985, 11).

Most frustrating to the Shiite nouveaux riches, however, was their continued lack of political power and the social discrimination to which they were still subjected. The Shiite political leadership, and in particular the narrow-minded, reactionary, and neofeudal *zu'ama'* of the south, were unwilling to share their privileged position with newcomers of lower social origins. Other Lebanese, especially well-off ones, always found ways of reminding upwardly mobile Shiites of their poor peasant origins.

Thus, by the mid-1970s the aspiring Shiite elite had been unable to convert its newly acquired and hard-earned education and wealth into social status and political power. It is not surprising that many of these men and women—and, over time, an increasingly larger proportion of them—became attracted to Imam Sadr's Movement of the Deprived (Harakat al-Mahrumin).[23] They were not revolutionaries, but pragmatists and moderates who simply wanted the system to recognize their achievements and grant them a fair share of political power and social recognition (Ajami 1986). It is these individuals, particularly those who had made their fortunes in West Africa and the Gulf, who provided Imam Sadr with the financial resources he needed to organize and recruit a mass following for his movement (Johnson 1986, 172). What needs to be emphasized here is the progressive radicalization of these upwardly mobile Shiites, and the strategy they adopted to press their grievances. By 1978, the establishment's failure to satisfy their demand for membership in the elite, combined with the intransigence of the Maronite leadership and the increasingly violent and sectarian nature of Lebanese politics, had convinced them to use the leverage they had built over the years with the Shiite masses to try, at times violently, to force the political establishment to renegotiate the social pact on which the country was based. In so doing, the new generation of Shiite intellectuals, professionals, and businesspeople showed that patronage systems can fail to prevent disorder when they do not show the flexibility required to absorb the new aspirant elites generated by rapid socioeconomic and political change.

It was not only among the Shiites that Lebanon's clientelist system proved unable to provide a niche for younger and better educated aspirant elites of relatively modest origins. Among the Sunnis, too, the first phase of the civil war provoked the collapse of the clientelist structures in West Beirut and brought new influence to the new generation of leaders that for several years had been waiting, increasingly impatiently, for an opportunity to challenge the traditional *zu'ama'*. From then on, the traditional patrons, the likes of Sa'ib Salam in Beirut and Rashid Karamé in Tripoli, had to coexist with a

new generation of younger and more radical leaders, the Ibrahim Quleilats in
Beirut and the Faruq al-Muqaddams in Tripoli (Ibrahim Quleilat was the
head of the Sunni-dominated militia al-Murabitun, which played a prominent role in the civil war up until the mid-1980s, while Faruq al-Muqaddam
rose to become a major militia leader in Tripoli). It is significant that, in the
parliamentary elections of 1972, Faruq al-Muqaddam had failed to capture
the Sunni seat in Tripoli, while Abdul Hafiz Quleilat, a relative of Ibrahim
Quleilat, had lost the election for a Sunni seat in the third electoral district of
Beirut (Abu-Khalil 1988).

These were not isolated cases. In fact, many of the unsuccessful candidates in the 1972 parliamentary elections, or close relative of theirs, became
militia leaders during the war—a tendency particularly visible among Muslim
and leftist militia leaders (Abu-Khalil 1988, 221–25). In retrospect, the 1960s
and 1970s seem to have witnessed the emergence of a new group of individuals of middle- and lower-middle-class backgrounds who, primarily as a result
of economic growth and the expansion of educational opportunities, came to
satisfy many of the traditional prerequisites for elite status. However, given
the rigidity of Lebanese society and the political and clerical leaderships's
refusal to accept new members of lower social background,[24] these upwardly
mobile individuals found it very difficult to break into the ranks of the establishment.[25] Frustrated in its ambitions, a large segment of this aspirant elite
became a counterelite, that, denied access to the establishment through electoral politics, turned to more violent forms of political action.

Even the Maronite community was affected by the phenomena that
have just been described. In 1975–76, Bashir Gemayel's Lebanese Forces (LF)
rapidly undercut the traditional Maronite *zu'ama'*. Pierre Gemayel, the head
of the Phalange and the father of both Bashir and Amin, was himself over-
shadowed by the meteoric rise of his son to prominence. By 1978, the LF had
either marginalized or eliminated (often physically) the traditional Maronite
warlord-notables and their scions. It is true that the rivalry between Bashir
and the old Maronite *zu'ama'* was largely generational and only partly based
on class, as is shown by the fact that Bashir and many of his closest aides were
from well-to-do families (Raad 1990, 13). Nevertheless, the LF and other
Maronite militias did provide frustrated aspirants to elite membership with
channels for socioeconomic promotion and with the organizational basis
from which to challenge the old Maronite clerical and political establishment.

By the mid-1980s, a decade of ferocious civil war had propelled to the
fore a new brand of Maronite leaders—much younger and usually of lower
social origins than the traditional *zu'ama'* and clerical leaders whom they had
sought to displace over the years. Such men—the Michel A'ouns, Samir Ja'ja's,

and Elie Hubaikas—showed repeatedly that they were not easily convinced to give up any part of their newly found power and influence. Thus, A'oun may well have been opposed to the new militias and warlords produced by the war, but he shared with them a clear hostility to the traditional *zu'ama'*.

Unlike the older elite's knack for bargaining and negotiations, this new Maronite elite displayed a more uncompromising style, reminiscent of the harsh and clannish politics that traditionally had prevailed in Mount Lebanon. The rise of this new elite—whether through the rightist militias (as for Ja'ja' or Hubaika), or through the army (as for General A'oun)—formed the background for the devastating infighting that raged within Beirut's eastern, Christian sector from February 1989 through the summer of 1990. It is also revealing of the class differences between this new elite and the traditional *zu'ama'* that even in the late 1980s, much after he had become one of the most powerful figures in the Maronite community, Michel A'oun—the son of a poor peasant, and someone who grew up in a suburb of Beirut's southern belt—was still the object of much disdain by the old Maronite leadership (Raad 1990, 11–13). Significantly, this phenomenon is reminiscent of the contempt that much of the Shiite establishment still had for Amal's leader, Nabih Berri (Norton 1987, 10). One should add that, as much as both Berri and A'oun were mocked by their respective communities' old leadership, they also largely escaped its control. This phenomenon was illustrated most dramatically in April 1989, when Maronite Patriarch Nasrallah Butros Sfair requested that rival Christian armies fighting for control of the Christian enclave in Lebanon lay down their arms and spare their people. The defiant answer of A'oun came almost immediately: "The Patriarch has no jurisdiction over me."

In the end, the civil war greatly weakened the hold of clientelism over the country. In each of the major sects, bureaucratically organized militias rapidly came to play a dominant role. Meanwhile, the old patron group was turned into the shadow of its former self. Many of its leading members (e.g., Pierre Gemayel, Rashid Karamé, and Camille Chamoun) died in the mid- to late 1980s, while others found it increasingly hard to preserve whatever remained of their power and influence in an increasingly radicalized environment dominated by younger militia leaders.

When Middlemen Become Leaders of Popular Movements: The Qabadayat in the Early Phase of the Civil War

At several junctures, we already have met a key figure in the Lebanese clientelist system: the *qabaday*, a strong-arm man and neighborhood leader who acted as an intermediary between the *za'im* and the urban poor. The *qabaday* performed essential functions for the *za'im*. He recruited his boss's clientele, policed it, mobilized it for mass demonstrations of support or even armed clashes, and made sure that, at elections, clients voted for the *za'im* or for the candidates chosen by the *za'im*. The *qabaday* also helped the *za'im* fragment and divide the electorate. In order to prevent the emergence of horizontal solidarities, he actively discouraged the development of groups based on socioeconomic or class affiliations and encouraged individuals to think of themselves primarily as members of the particular neighborhood in which they lived.

The literature on clientelism has put much emphasis on the stabilizing attributes of such middlemen, but it also has tended to downplay the degree of autonomy that they enjoy, and which, at times, can enable them to play a destabilizing role. In Lebanon, for instance, the *qabadayat*'s violent code of honor, and the ease with which they would get involved in vendettas, blood feuds, and murders, led them to disturb public order on a regular basis (Johnson 1986). Since, in Lebanon's confessional society, *qabadayat* always had been perceived as communal champions, fights between *qabadayat* of different religious affiliations easily degenerated into communal warfare. In such instances, the *zu'ama'* were frequently unwilling to prevent the shedding of blood, let alone capable of doing so.

More importantly, the Lebanese experience suggests that under certain circumstances middlemen may escape the control of their patrons, emerge as autonomous leaders of the street, and challenge the traditional leadership. This is indeed exactly what happened to the *qabadayat* when the Lebanese state finally collapsed, in 1975–76 (Johnson 1986, 106). Two factors contributed to the ability of the *qabadayat* to escape the control of their former patrons. One was the quasi absence of links between the state apparatus and the *qabadayat*, since, when Suleiman Franjieh came to power, in 1970, he purged the Deuxième Bureau and thereby deprived the state of the contacts that had been established in the preceding period with Beirut's *qabaday* underworld (Johnson 1986). In addition, at about the same time, many *qabadayat* began to act as the clients of Palestinian organizations and of the Libyan, Iraqi, Syrian, Saudi, and Egyptian governments. Foreign money introduced a completely new element—and clearly a destabilizing one—into the local patronage dynamics. Libya, Syria, Iraq, and Egypt, in particular, proceeded to wage ideological warfare and settle their accounts with one another on Lebanese territory, using local *qabadayat* to do so. Inevitably, foreign financing reduced the leverage of the Lebanese *zu'ama'* over their *qabadayat*. Gradually, as Lebanon was turned into a pawn in inter-Arab struggles, the *qabadayat* became more autonomous and politicized. By the early 1970s, daily armed clashes opposed *qabadayat* affiliated with different foreign patrons. Scores of *qabadayat* had been transformed from mere brokers between patron and clients into largely autonomous and destabilizing political actors.

Clientelist Networks as a Vehicle for Political Unrest

Scholars who emphasize exclusively the stabilizing features of patron-client networks not only ignore that clients or middlemen in the patron-client structures can escape the control of their patrons, and that urban clientelist structures may fail to absorb aspirant elites and/or the masses of rural migrants, but they also pay insufficient attention to the possibility that, under some circumstances, certain types of patrons may have an incentive to mobilize their clients in destabilizing political activities. Throughout Lebanon's history, for instance, *zu'ama'* have showed little restraint in arming their followers and leading them on the warpath for the sake of limited political advantages or in order to settle personal accounts with one another.

The most dramatic example of this phenomenon was probably the 1958 civil war, which was caused primarily by escalating rivalries, personal grudges, and power struggles among Lebanon's foremost politicians—as a glance at the memoirs of some of the leading participants in the conflict reveals (Kerr 1961). The individual most directly responsible for the war was, of course, President Chamoun himself. In an attempt to expand his power and undermine that of other traditional *zu'ama'*, Chamoun used various political machinations (including a redrawing of the boundaries of electoral districts) to prevent the election of many of his rivals to the Lebanese Parliament during the 1957 parliamentary elections. He then proceeded to declare his intention to succeed himself in the presidency, in violation of the constitution.[26] It was against this background that Chamoun's rivals, in an effort to preserve or restore their own privileged positions, incited their followers to take up arms and rise against the government.

The case of Kamal Jumblatt is probably very representative of the motives of other leading *zu'ama'* during this first civil war, which has been adequately described as "the revolt of the Pashas" (Petran 1987, 50–52). Although Jumblatt and his supporters tried to portray their armed revolt as being exclusively a product of strong disagreements with Chamoun's domestic and foreign policies (especially his earlier acceptance of the Eisenhower Doctrine, which seemed to accentuate the pro-Western drift of Lebanese foreign policy at a time when anti-Western Arab nationalism was on the rise both in the region and in Lebanon), the reality was quite different. Ideology had less to do with Jumblatt's call to arms than his long-standing personal rivalry with Chamoun. Jumblatt's defeat in the 1957 elections had come as a devastating blow to the Druze leader's self-esteem and to his status, both within his community and in the country as a whole (al-Khazen 1988, 180). Jumblatt saw his defeat as a personal insult and a daring challenge by Chamoun. The fact that Chamoun originated from Dayr al-Qamar—a Christian town located at the heart of the Shuf, the Druze stronghold in which Maronites had lived for centuries under the protection, and in sufferance, of the Druze—only intensified Jumblatt's sense of humiliation (al-Khazen 1988, 180). In this context, Jumblatt's armed revolt was first and foremost an effort on the part of the "Lord of Mukhtara" to reestablish his position as the undisputed *za'im* of the Shuf, and an attempt on his part to thwart the growing power and ambitions of a Maronite rival, who merely happened to be the president as well.

Battling pro-Chamoun forces were other traditional politicians defeated during the 1957 elections—prominent among whom were Sa'ib Salam and Abdallah al-Yafi in Beirut, and Rashid Karamé in Tripoli—as well as a new group of younger individuals who became patrons in their own right by establishing their credentials as politicomilitary leaders of the streets. Ma'ruf Sa'ad, a *za'im* of Sidon, and Ibrahim Quleilat, a *qabaday* of Beirut, are two well-known examples of leaders whose popularity rose as a result of the fighting. Furthermore, while the core of the opposition to Chamoun was formed of Sunni, Druze, and Shiite *zu'ama'*, a few prominent Maronite politicians— including future president Suleiman Franjieh, former president Bishara al-Khuri, and Patriarch Paul-Pierre Méouchy—were also actively involved in the uprising (Qubain 1961, 83). With the exception of Méouchy, the motives of these leaders were not basically different from those of their Muslim counterparts: Their influence, too, had been undermined by Chamoun, whose intent to be reelected also meant that the presidency would probably be denied to some other ambitious Christian *za'im* such as themselves.[27] Thus, across the political spectrum and across communities, the conflict was primarily the expression of petty feuds among self-centered and egotistical politicians engaged in a Hobbesian struggle for power.

The *zu'ama'* were quick to draw the lessons from the 1958 conflagration. One was that in the future they might once again be forced to mobilize a large armed following to defend their position. Another was that they could in fact further their power by surrounding themselves with gangs and private militias and by using them to undermine rivals. The 1958 war also showed to aspirant patrons that they could force their way on the political stage and displace better established politicians by playing on the lower class's disaffection from the sociopolitical system. It is not surprising, therefore, that the post-1958 period saw the proliferation of armed groups operating under the loose sponsorship of Lebanese patrons or foreign governments. For years, these groups remained essentially patron-client networks, headed by *zuʿamaʾ* or former *qabadayat* who were able to attract increasing numbers of unemployed young people by offering them a regular job and a salary (Johnson 1986, 105). Eventually, in 1975–76, many of these clientelist structures merged into the National Movement.

As the war dragged on, most of these armed groups gave way to full-fledged militias, which in turn became increasingly bureaucratized and formally organized over time. Yet even as late as the 1980s, many of the groups engaged in the fighting remained essentially loosely organized clientelist networks in which individuals fought in exchange for access to the spoils of war. In both the Sunni and the Shiite communities (particularly among the former), the leaders of these groups were usually of lower-middle-class and lower-class backgrounds, and many were self-styled religious preachers and/or former thugs or *qabadayat* (Abu-Khalil 1985). This new generation of leaders quite often behaved like the old patrons they had often pushed aside. They too offered protection and access to goods and services in exchange for loyalty and a willingness to take up arms and fight. To say the least, however, these new leaders demonstrated little propensity for the politics of compromise and bargaining of pre-civil-war Lebanon. In fact, they had brought the prejudices of the street into the heart of the political process. Instead of controlling the potential for insurgency among the lower classes—as one would expect from most of the literature on clientelism—they constantly worked to exacerbate lower-class radicalism, justifying this radicalism by wrapping popular excesses in the garb of religious language or revolutionary slogans.

Like Lebanon, contemporary Iran has had its share of patronage networks playing a destabilizing role. In the 1940s and early 1950s, for instance, both Royalist and National Front politicians frequently used the services of professional mob leaders, known as *chaqu-kashan* ("cutthroats"), in order to mobilize the population into pro- or antiregime activities.[28] Leading politicians would hire *chaqu-kashan*, and the latter, in turn, would round up their followers by using a mixture of bribery, intimidation, and the manipulation of long-standing commitments and loyalties (Kazemi 1980a, 1).[29] For instance, *chaqu-kashan*—and in particular the owner of a *zurkhaneh*, Shaʿban Jaʿfari, also known as Bimokh ("brainless")—played a key role in organizing the demonstration that toppled Mossadegh and paved the way for the return of the shah in 1953.[30] Similarly, several *chaqu-kashan* were actively involved in the June 1963 uprising (Floor 1981, 93). This, however, was their undoing, as it seems to have convinced Muhammad Reza Shah to crack down on them. In the wake of the uprising, many prominent *chaqu-kashan* were executed, while others were deported to Bandar Abbas.[31] The function of controlling the population became the exclusive preserve of SAVAK, the bureaucracy, and the army—modern agencies that the shah probably thought were much more reliable and effective than the old *chaqu-kashan*-controlled networks that he had used in the past. By the mid-1960s, although *chaqu-kashan* could still be found in the bazaar and in their respective neighborhoods, and although they were still involved in a variety of illicit activities (smuggling, stealing, and running brothels and protection rackets), they no longer played an active role in urban politics (Floor 1981, 93).[32]

Repression by the regime, however, was not the only reason behind the *chaqu-kashan*'s eclipse. Tehran's staggering growth after 1950 brought the Iranian capital into the era of mass politics and considerably decreased the ability of *chaqu-kashan*-led networks to affect decisively political outcomes. The conditions prevailing in Tehran in the late 1970s had little to do with what they had been in the early 1950s, when the capital's population was less than one million. Relying on professional mob leaders to organize support and intimidate opponents had become an inappropriate political strategy in a modern and very politicized city that had grown to more than five million inhabitants. Thus, the pro-shah mercenary mob that played an instrumental role in the 1953 events stands in sharp contrast to the large-scale demonstrations of 1977–79, which expressed genuine political feelings. Although some *chaqu-kashan* were reportedly hired both by pro-Pahlavi elements and by the revolutionary forces, they played only a marginal role (Floor 1981, 94-95).

Although the Iranian revolution was the death toll of *chaqu-kashan* networks, it also provided the backdrop for the development of new clientelist structures in Iran's cities. These new patronage networks, furthermore, played a clearly destabilizing role during the first eighteen months of Ayatollah Khomeini's rule. In fact, the radicalization of the revolution from the return of Khomeini and the formation of the Bazargan government (February 1979) to the self-imposed exile of Bani-Sadr (June 1981) demonstrates that, contrary to claims examined in part 1, certain types of patrons do sometimes use the networks they control to bring about a radical and violent transformation of the existing sociopolitical order.

The crucial element in the radical clerics' ability to eliminate their rivals was the control they rapidly established over the revolutionary committees (*komitehs*), the "Party of God" (Hezbollah), and the Revolutionary Guards, or *pasdaran-e Enqelab* (hereafter referred to as pasdaran). These new revolutionary bodies shared important features. First, they rapidly came to assume many of the functions of government agencies, thereby creating the basis for a period of dual sovereignty that began during the winter of 1978–79, before the shah left Iran, and lasted until the escape of Bani-Sadr in June 1981. Throughout that period, the revolutionary institutions weakened the authority of the successive, legitimate governments of Bakhtiar, Bazargan, and Bani-Sadr and were instrumental in helping the militant clerics and their lay followers gain undisputed control over the state machinery.

A second characteristic of these revolutionary bodies was their informal organization. This was perhaps more true of Hezbollah and the *komitehs* than of the pasdaran, but all these groups were, when they first emerged, loosely organized bodies, which reflected a great degree of grassroots initiative and relied heavily on personal ties between clerics and followers. Thus, while the development of revolutionary structures parallel to those of the state is clearly reminiscent of the Soviet Revolution, the *komitehs*, Hezbollah, and the pasdaran appear to have been much more informally organized, much less subject to central control, and much less disciplined than the Soviets, Lenin's party, and other revolutionary institutions in Russia (Sick 1986, xxv).

In fact, many of the revolutionary groups were at first often little more than patron-client clusters that bound lower-middle- and lower-class militant youth to radical clerics. The latter used these networks to implement decisions and eliminate their rivals. In exchange, the upwardly mobile youth staffing the revolutionary bodies were given access to the privileges and benefits controlled by leading clerics (Bakhash 1990, 59). The logic of this system can be better understood through a separate examination of the *komitehs*, the Hezbollah, and the pasdaran.

In the early days of the revolution, a given *komiteh* usually was affiliated with, and owed allegiance to, one particular religious figure. Especially in provincial cities, each prominent local *'alim* frequently ran his own string of committees. Although this cleric would use the *komitehs* he controlled to enhance his personal authority, the upwardly mobile youths who had found their way into the *komitehs* often benefited from their new clerical patrons' influence by receiving government posts, or official protection for their activities—many of which were pecuniarily rewarding but illegal (Bakhash 1990). Revolutionary organizations and an administration undergoing recurrent purges offered plenty of room for ambitious, yet unqualified, young individuals who had attached themselves to rising clerics.

Along similar lines, Hezbollah was less a party than a label to refer to loosely organized, roving gangs of militant youth informally connected to prominent clerics.[33] Since Hezbollahis (members of Hezbollah) were recruited primarily from the youth living in the slums and poorer districts of the cities, their main motivation for becoming Hezbollahis was often the weekly stipend and other material reward that the clergy offered them in return for participating in revolutionary activities and harassing the radical clerics' opponents (Bakhash 1990; Taheri 1987, 79). In the hands of the militant ulama, the

Hezbollahis turned into a formidable weapon. To no small extent, the radical clerics' political success was due to their ability to use the street crowds and gangs mobilized through Hezbollah to scare their opponents into silence or to push them underground. The Westernized middle class in particular found itself unprepared to cope, both mentally and physically, with such raw violence (Bakhash 1990, 165).

> Originally armed only with kitchen knives, chains, clubs, boxes of matches and cans of acid, [the Hezbollahis] established their reputation by murdering opposition spokesmen, setting fire to the offices of newspapers which criticized the government, and disfiguring unveiled women activists with acid and razors....They became the popular arm of the regime and, by 1981, had succeeded in smashing almost all opposition organizations from liberals to Maoists. (Taheri 1987, 79)

The informal organization of Hezbollah did not diminish its effectiveness. In fact, it may well have lain at the heart of the Hezbollahis' ability to act swiftly. In the words of Hadi Ghoffari, head of Hezbollah in the early 1980s:

> The party of Allah is an ethereal organization. It is everywhere and yet nowhere. It is everywhere because it is nowhere. All I need to do is pick up the telephone and half a million people will be in the streets in less than an hour. (quoted in Taheri 1986, 78)

Finally, in May 1979, the creation of the pasdaran provided the revolutionary youth with yet another channel—in addition to the *komitehs* and the various revolutionary courts, tribunals, and councils—through which to get access to the benefits now controlled by the radical ulama.[34] In return, the pasdaran provided the militant clerics with their own organized armed force, at a time when Khomeini and his supporters still needed to strengthen their grip over the state apparatus (including the army) and civil society. At first, the pasdaran, who were assigned the vaguely defined objective of "protecting the Islamic revolution," operated primarily as the personal bodyguards of individual clerics, as the guardians of the facilities that these clerics controlled, and as yet another tool that the militant ulama could use to intimidate and monitor the activities of their rivals, including the guerrilla organizations, which were heavily armed and therefore still represented an obstacle in the way of Khomeini's ambitions (Hiro 1987, 109–10; Wright 1989, 69).

Thus, whether one looks at the pasdaran, the *komitehs*, or Hezbollah, at the revolutionary courts and tribunals, or at the variety of Islamic councils and associations that appeared in the course of the revolution, the same logic was always at work: In return for political loyalty and support, prominent clerics would provide the members of the revolutionary bodies with protection (including from state institutions and groups controlled by rival clerics), a measure of legal recognition, favors (access to goods, schools for children, licenses and permits, etc.), and positions in the bureaucracy (Bakhash 1990). While the Bazargan and Bani-Sadr governments endeavored to restrain the revolutionary bodies and, in the process, alienated them, the radical clerics exerted a conscious effort to cater to the aspirations and ambitions of their members. In exchange, the revolutionary youth helped the clerics harass, frighten, and discredit their adversaries. By mid-1981, through the use of revolutionary institutions to mobilize large segments of the lower classes against their opponents, Khomeini's associates had consolidated their control over both the state apparatus and civil society. They then proceeded to absorb progressively the revolutionary bodies into the state, and in the process built a "centrally controlled system of national security, patronage, mass mobilization, and propaganda" that was much more effective than the Pahlavi dynasty had ever been in creating contacts between the regime and the population (Farhang 1987, 166). In the course of their integration into the state, the revolutionary institutions became more formally organized. By the mid-1980s, this process of bureaucratization and centralization of power—which involved the transformation of what were initially informal networks into formal state agencies—was almost completed.

Within the clerical establishment itself, patron-client networks played an important part in the radicalization of the Iranian revolution. After 1979, lesser clerics began to use their privileged contacts with the new elite to put aside older and more established clerical leaders. Characteristic of this phenomenon was the rapid ascent of the Friday prayer leaders appointed by Khomeini to all of Iran's main cities. Although many of these individuals were simply middle-rank clerics (*hojjat al-Islam* level), they often immediately challenged the authority of the prestigious religious figures of the cities to which they had been assigned—as was the case, for instance, in Tehran, Tabriz, Mashad, and Isfahan (Bakhash 1990, 145). These Friday prayer leaders, who were instrumental in securing the victory of the Islamic Republic Party against Bani-Sadr, the moderate clergy, and the left, considered themselves totally independent of the government and bound only to Khomeini. As a rule, the personal link to the Imam or to his closest associates proved very rewarding.

> Clerics like Musavi-Ardabili and Mohammadi-Rayshahri were running mosques, preaching in small towns, tending to local

parishes, or teaching in religious seminaries before, almost overnight, they found themselves administering ministries and holding the highest offices in the land. Ali Khamane'i was a middle-rank cleric in the provincial capital of Mashad when the revolutionary upheaval carried him to the presidency and then the supreme leadership of the Islamic Republic. Hashemi-Rafsanjani, another minor cleric involved in the clerical opposition, dealt in real estate in Qom before the revolution made him one of the half-dozen most powerful men in Iran [and the most powerful one by 1990]. Mohtashemi served in a minor capacity in Khomaini's household in Najaf, before the revolution propelled him to an ambassadorship in Damascus, then the influential post of interior minister. (Bakhash 1990, 290)

Finally, the Islamic Republic Party itself (Hezb Jomhuri Islami, referred to hereafter as IRP) was largely built around patron-client ties. While information on the IRP's inner structure and functioning is either missing or unreliable, it seems clear that the party never became the kind of bureaucratic machine that one usually associates with the label "political party"—which implies card-carrying members, internal statuses, and institutional and organizational coherence. Instead, the real backbone of the IRP, created by close associates of Khomeini, remained the personalistic network of the radical clergy, and the following that militant ulama and their lay associates could mobilize not so much through the party itself as through the mosques, the revolutionary bodies, and the street gangs.

More specifically, throughout its existence (1979–87), the IRP was made up of two interlocking networks: a small clique of militant clerics at the leadership level, and a nationwide clientelist structure built around the Friday prayer leaders in the Islamic Republic's main cities. A handful of powerful clerics, most of them former students or long-time associates of Khomeini, would set the party's priorities (presumably following Khomeini's directives). These ulama exercised their authority not so much through the IRP as an organization, but through the nationwide network of Friday-prayer leaders, the mosques, the religious associations, and the revolutionary bodies that continued to form the real chain of authority in 1980s Iran. As Bakhash noted, "In many provincial centers, party, revolutionary organizations, and the mosque were inextricably intertwined. The IRP and the local revolutionary committee shared the same offices. The cleric who was Friday prayer leader was also a member of the party and the head of the revolutionary tribunal" (Bakhash 1990, 145).

Significantly, the IRP was abolished in late 1987. The official reason given by then-president Khamaneʻi and Majlis Speaker Rafsanjani to justify the dissolution of the IRP was that the party had completed its mission of mobilizing the population against "counterrevolutionaries" and "foreign plots." With the revolution now firmly established, the two clerics added, the party no longer was needed; by offering avenues for the expression of political disagreements within the new elite, the party instead threatened the unity of the leadership (Wright 1989, 162). In fact, although the dissolution of the IRP might indeed have been prompted by the leadership's fear that the party might increase elite factionalism, it also reflected the difficulties that formal organizations continued to face, in the late 1980s, in the personal and fluid political context of the Islamic Republic, where much power and authority continued to be transmitted through the informal networks controlled by the clerics. It is also revealing that, even as the regime was dispensing with the IRP, it was either unwilling or unable to disband the Hezbollah and the *komitehs*, even though these were at the time the targets of much hostility from the Iranian population at large.

10

Occupational Networks and Political Conflict: The Iranian Bazaar

> The *bazaaris* are a fanatic lot, highly resistant to change because their locations afford a lucrative monopoly. I could not stop building supermarkets. I wanted a modern country. Moving against the bazaars was typical of the political and social risks I had to take in my drive for modernization.
>
> —Mohammad Reza Pahlavi 1980, 156.

As was shown earlier, in the premodern Middle Eastern city, professional bonds, often reinforced by neighborhood and Sufi ties, operated as a source of cohesion and collective identity among craftsmen and merchants. However, with the increasing integration of the Middle East into the world economy and the resulting decline of handicrafts, the twentieth century has seen the weakening or disappearance of the old networks of artisans and traders. In the wake of the revolutions of the 1950s and 1960s, the traditional *suqs* and bazaars were further marginalized by the creation of large public firms and bureaucracies and by the progress of industrialization. Their share in the economy decreased dramatically both in terms of production and as a percentage of the labor force. In the process, *suqs* and bazaars also lost much of their former cohesion and ability to act as a political force.

Against this background, the Iranian bazaar stands out as a quite unique phenomenon in the post–World War II period. Although Iran, too, experienced the development of modern industry and the emergence of a large bureaucracy and public sector, its bazaar was able to survive as a viable and vibrant social and economic entity and a powerful political force.

This chapter focuses on the networks controlled by the *bazaaris* (a generic term that encompasses craftsmen, merchants, shopkeepers, and many moneylenders) and shows how these networks have sometimes provided the *bazaaris* with key instruments through which to organize and mobilize large segments of the urban population. However, before *bazaari* networks and the conditions under which they have become destabilizing can be examined, it is necessary to provide a brief description of the prerevolutionary Iranian bazaar, which constitutes the highly distinctive environment in which these networks developed.

The Social Role, and the Resiliency and Adaptability, of Iran's Bazaars

The self-contained world of the Iranian bazaar has been a vital social arena, especially for the lower- and lower-middle classes. Through the 1970s, the bazaar remained the location of a host of urban voluntary associations, religious groups and brotherhoods, gymnasiums (*zurkhanehs*), and traditional coffeehouses (*qahvekhanehs*), teahouses (*chaikhanehs*), and restaurants. It is also in the bazaar that rumors and information are circulated and that many of the contacts that cut across kinship and residential solidarities have traditionally been established. The bazaar, therefore, plays a key role in the country's public life—a function that it also owes to its multiple ties to the mosque. As was shown in part 2, the bazaar-mosque connection reaches deep into the country's past. Yet it was strengthened from the 1920s onward, when ulama and *bazaaris* began to suffer from similar forms of cultural alienation from the ruling elite. Both came to fear the corroding effects of Western ideas and lifestyles on the country's Shiite heritage and began to regard themselves as the representatives of an indigenous Iranian urban culture besieged by the alien and hostile forces of Westernization and secularization. This phenomenon not only brought bazaar and mosque closer together, but it also strengthened the bazaar's self-perception and projection of itself as a stronghold of religious orthodoxy and traditional urban lifestyles (Miller 1969a; Ashraf 1988).

After World War II, *bazaaris* and ulama continued to share this basic outlook, and they also remained linked to one another by ties of intermarriage. Furthermore, as late as the 1970s most *bazaaris* still received their education in religious schools. This helps explain why throughout their lives they would show great respect for religious learning, while their regular involvement in religious meetings and celebrations heightened their self-perceptions in religious terms (De Groot 1988). It is not surprising, therefore, that a social scientist conducting research in the bazaar of Tehran in the late 1960s concluded that the religious idiom was still "the basic common denominator in the bazaar" and that it worked "to create crosscutting ties and bonds among *bazaaris* of different guilds and professions" (Thaiss 1971, 193–94).

Yet, as shown for instance in a perceptive study of the bazaar of Qazvin, the manifest religiosity of the Iranian bazaar sometimes had less to do with religious feelings per se or with the use of religion to express social solidarities than with the manipulation of religious credentials for commercial or lifestyle purposes (Rotblat 1972, 183–88). Thus, public displays of piety can help a merchant acquire and maintain a personal reputation for honesty—and therefore a clientele. Religion can also be used to legitimize wealth and social prominence. In a culture that frowns upon public displays of wealth and extravagant lifestyles, it is much easier for a well-to-do merchant to retain his prestige in the community and justify the use of his wealth for personal comfort if he also projects the image of someone who fulfills the religious obligations (charity to the poor, financial support of the ulama and of the religious institutions, and pilgrimage to the holy sites of Mecca, Madina, Kerbala, Najaf, and Mashhad) that are seen as incumbent on those who meet with economic success.

Whatever the sources of its religiosity might be, no one disputes the fact that the Iranian bazaar remained an institution imbued with religion and closely connected to the mosque. From our perspective, this phenomenon is important because, given the continued social influence of the ulama in the postwar period, and given the persisting vitality of religious feelings in the Iranian population, it helps explain why the bazaar survived as a potent social force.

This social prominence, furthermore, could easily be translated into political power. In view of the bazaar-mosque connection that has just been described, and in view of the history of political cooperation between *bazaaris* and ulama in the late nineteenth and early twentieth centuries, it is not surprising that, in the post-World War II period, the bazaar frequently acted in cooperation with the mosque. In fact, beginning in the 1950s the bazaar-mosque alliance was strengthened by cultural, political, and financial factors. Culturally, both the bazaar and the mosque became increasingly concerned about the erosion of traditional Shiite values in the country during the 1960s and 1970s. Politically, the bazaar and the mosque each had to suffer from numerous state attempts to limit their respective spheres of influence. This situation reinforced the mutual feeling that they were natural allies in their conflicts with the Pahlavi state. Finally, on a financial plane, with the growing erosion of the ulama's control over the *awqaf*, the bazaar became the backbone of the religious establishment. Thus, in the 1970s the bazaar provided an estimated 80 percent of the ulama's financial resources (Walton 1980, 276).

In the end, however, the decisive factor that enabled the bazaar to pre-serve its sociopolitical power was its status as a pillar of the Iranian economy. Usually located at the heart of the older sections of the cities and towns of Iran, the bazaar had for centuries been the commercial center of urban Iran. It is there that the traditional manufacturing and handicrafts, money lending, and retail and wholesale activities had been concentrated. Although, under the reigns of Reza Shah and his son, the bazaars lost their position as the undis-puted economic centers of Iran's cities, they adjusted remarkably to a chang-ing economic environment.

To be sure, several factors weakened the hold of the bazaars over the eco-nomic life of Iran, among which were the growth of modern industry, the development of a class of new entrepreneurs who benefited from state patron-age, and the appeal of Western-made goods among large segments of the mid-dle and upper classes. The physical expansion of the cities also reduced the bazaar's relative power by providing new locations for shops outside the bazaars. In some instances as well (e.g., in Shiraz and Kermanshah), particu-larly under Reza Shah, new streets and avenues were created that cut right through the bazaar, destroying its physical integrity (see Ashraf 1988, 550–51).

The bazaars, however, did not disappear. In many cases, an informal division of labor evolved between them and the shops located on the new commercial avenues—with the bazaars remaining the center of traditional handicrafts, from textiles to metalwork, and the new retail businesses special-izing in items such as household appliances and imported products (Bonine 1981, 236; Ashraf 1988, 552). Furthermore, although the Westernized upper and upper-middle classes shopped primarily in the new commercial districts, the bazaar remained the prime shopping area and a vital arena of sociability for the lower- and lower-middle classes. The modern sector itself remained closely tied to the bazaar through economic, social, and kinship bonds. For instance, businesses and modern industries located physically outside the bazaar frequently had agents, storage facilities, and money invested in the bazaar. Similarly, members of the so-called new bourgeoisie, or modern entrepreneurial class, were often related to *bazaaris*, with whom they some-times were also engaged in business ventures. In some cases as well, *bazaaris* opened up modern factories outside the bazaar and used their shops in the bazaar as distribution centers (Salehi 1988, 18).

Not only was the bazaar dominant in retail trade, handicraft produc-tion, and small-scale manufacturing, but a substantial segment of wholesale trade, mass production, banking activities, and foreign trade also continued to pass through channels controlled by *bazaaris*. In the late 1970s the bazaar still controlled about two-thirds of retail trade, between two-thirds and three-quarters of wholesale trade, and at least 30 percent of all imports.[1] In addition, perhaps a majority of import-export businesses were operated by individuals with a *bazaari* background.[2] Through its control over key export items such as carpets, the bazaar also had autonomous access to foreign currencies that were not channeled through the official, state-dominated banking system (Graham 1980, 224).

Finally, and perhaps most importantly, the bazaar's economic, social, and political power also stemmed from the fact that it remained, as late as the 1970s, one of the largest employers in the country. A careful examination of Iran's 1976 National Census of Population and Housing for Tehran Shahrestan, for instance, suggests that at least a third of the capital's employed population in the mid-1970s owed its livelihood, directly or indirectly, to the bazaar. These individuals would be the first to be mobilized through the *bazaari* networks. As will now be shown, these networks extended far beyond the bazaar itself, and their scope goes a long way toward explaining the bazaar's ability to act as a destabilizing political force.

Informal Networks in Tehran's Bazaar

Despite outward appearances of unity, homogeneity, and equality, the Iranian bazaar remained, in the late 1970s, a very stratified community. At the top of the hierarchy were the big merchants (*tujjar*, sing. *tajir*) and the money-lenders (*sarrafs*), who together dominated the *bazaari* community.[3] Below the *tujjar* and the *sarrafs*, the less influential wholesale traders and middle-rank merchants could be found, followed by the smaller shopkeepers and crafts-men, who formed the majority of the *bazaari* community. Below the shop-keepers and independent craftsmen, the lower echelons of the bazaar were represented by wage earners—shop assistants and workshop employees—fol-lowed by those, at the very bottom of the *bazaari* hierarchy, who were engaged in marginal economic activities usually associated with "the informal sector" (carwashers, peddlers, street vendors, hawkers, and the like).

Even within the group of self-employed *bazaaris*, there were sharp social and economic differences—for instance, between the few *tujjar* and *sarrafs* and the many small craftsmen and shopkeepers. While the former usually lived in the city's well-to-do districts, located outside the bazaar area, the latter almost invariably lived around the bazaar and in the poorer neighborhoods of the city (Mobasser 1985, 54). Shopkeepers and craftsmen also tended to be markedly more parochial, socially conservative, and religious than the *tujjar*. As Miller noted in the late 1960s, "The traditional *bazaari* is parochial except insofar as business with other cities, nations, and peoples has broadened his outlook...born, educated, employed, housed, fed, entertained, and dying within the confines of the bazaar, the *bazaaris* not surprisingly look upon out-siders with suspicion, fear, and sometimes disdain" (Miller 1969a, 162). Thus, while the big merchants' exposure and connections to the world outside Iran tended to foster a relatively (by the bazaar's low standards) cosmopolitan and liberal outlook, the majority of the *bazaaris* were characterized by a narrow-minded and traditionalist mentality, largely shaped by the closed-in nature of the world in which they lived. In this context, it is also understandable that the small retail shopkeepers and manufacturers have had much stronger connec-tions to the fundamentalist lower clergy than has been the case for other strata in the bazaar.[4]

To a large extent because of these social and economic divisions, the bazaar never was politically homogeneous. In the late 1940s and early 1950s, a new form of class consciousness even began to alienate employers from employees, and apprentices from masters. As a result, the guilds came under stress, as large numbers of wage-earning *bazaaris* were attracted to socialist ideals, the unions, and the Tudeh (Abrahamian 1968, 202). Even though, fol-lowing the 1953 coup and the shah's crackdown on the unions and the Tudeh, the guild elders were able to reassert their control over shop assistants and workshop employees, politics in the bazaar continued to show great diversity (Abrahamian 1982, 433). Thus, throughout the 1960s and early 1970s the bazaar remained politically divided into at least five groups: (a) those who had no definite political allegiance, (b) those who supported the regime, (c) those who always remained close to the National Front, (d) those who were associ-ated with the moderate higher clergy, and, finally, (e) those who backed the radical lower clergy. There is no empirical study that would enable us to assess the relative strength and composition of each group, but it seems clear that *bazaaris* who supported the regime formed a minority group, limited to guild leaders and wealthy *bazaaris*, especially those who dealt in luxury imports (Parsa 1989, 106–7). Most bazaaris probably belonged to categories (a), (c), and (d), and members of category (e) must have come predominantly from the lower echelons of the bazaar.

These differences in political opinion notwithstanding, most *bazaaris* continued to share a sense of collective identity. What defines a "*bazaari*," in fact, is not only his physical location in the bazaar, but also his membership in a distinct community of like-minded individuals bent on preserving the bazaar's relative independence and autonomy against encroachment by out-side forces. Perhaps more than any other factors, it is this sense of collective identity that has enabled the *bazaaris* to transcend their divisions at critical junctures and that has allowed them to act as a powerful political force. This phenomenon, one should add, has been all the more consequential for Iranian politics because, except for the clergy, other social groups in Iranian society (the new middle class, for instance) usually have failed to develop a similar sense of group identity and solidarity.[5]

To account for the bazaar's ability to preserve a sense of unity despite its obvious internal fragmentation, five related elements have to be taken into consideration. The first is the regime's political crackdown following the 1953 coup. Presumably, had the unions, the Tudeh, and other leftist organizations been allowed to operate in Iran, they would have made it easier for class divisions in the bazaar to translate themselves into political cleavages.

A second factor is the existence of shared economic interests among *bazaaris* of all levels. Indeed, despite the socioeconomic differences underlined earlier between wealthy, well-to-do, and lower-level *bazaaris*, and between wage-earners and self-employed merchants and craftsmen, all *bazaaris* share at least some basic economic interests. For one, they all have a stake in the survival of the bazaar as an institution. As will be shown below, this similarity of interest was highlighted dramatically in the 1970s, when the regime moved to threaten the physical integrity and commercial profitability of the bazaar, and when, in response, the *bazaaris* moved decisively to protect their corporate interests.

Under the shah, two other factors that strengthened cohesion in the bazaar were ecological. One was the physical separateness of the bazaar from the rest of urban society—which reinforced, among both insiders and outsiders, the notion that the bazaar was a distinct entity, an urban enclave. Another element was the proximity of *bazaaris* to one another. While it can provide for friction, proximity also makes it easier for individuals to engage in concerted action on issues of common interest. Through the frequency of contacts that it usually involves, proximity also makes it easier for individuals to develop a sense of intimacy.

The last and perhaps most decisive element that enabled the bazaar to survive as a relatively cohesive social world were the interpersonal bonds that cut across income levels and professions in the bazaar. In addition to their predominantly traditionalist and religious outlook, *bazaaris* remained linked to one another through membership in guilds, religious brotherhoods, gymnasiums, and Sufi houses of worship. Moreover, specific restaurants, coffeehouses, and teahouses served as the informal headquarters for those in given trades or crafts (Bill 1972, 132–33; Miller 1969a, 165). Such meeting places provided ample opportunities not only for the exchange of information and opinions, but also for the survival of a distinct bazaar subculture. This *bazaari* subculture, in turn, was characterized by two features. One was the existence of norms, habits, values, codes of behavior, and rules of conduct specific to the bazaar. For instance, through the 1970s the *bazaaris* tried to maintain traditional forms of conflict resolution based on mediation and arbitration. Such practice was not only less expensive and time consuming than having to resort to the modern courts of law, but it also solidified the social ties that bound the *bazaaris* to one another (Thaiss 1971, 190). The second key constitutive element of the *bazaari* subculture was the existence of dense and overlapping social networks within the bazaar. Since a *bazaari's* entire life revolved around the bazaar, most of his personal networks were bazaar-based, and this phenomenon, too, strengthened both intrabazaar cohesion and the survival of a distinct *bazaari* subculture.

Reinforcing the bazaar's sense of group identity were ties of patronage and mutual help between the various levels of the *bazaari* hierarchy described earlier. For instance, a *tajir* would frequently lend money to smaller shopkeepers and craftsmen. Similarly, the *bazaaris* could easily mobilize in defense of their corporate interests the peddlers, carwashers, and street hawkers who gravitated around the bazaar and owed their meager livelihood to it (Mobasser 1985, 54). The main bazaar mosque, where merchants and guild leaders would meet for the midday and late afternoon/early evening congregational prayers, also offered *bazaaris* opportunities to exchange news and rumors and discuss issues of common interest (Ashraf 1988, 543). Yet what has been referred to as "the most significant institutions for group activities in the bazaar" (Spooner 1971, 171) were the informal religious gatherings known as *hay'at-e senfis*, whose impact on political stability will now be examined in some detail.

The Bazaari *Network and Political Unrest in Urban Iran, 1945–79*

The ulama-led *hay'at-e senfis* provide a perfect illustration of the dual effects—normally stabilizing, but destabilizing under certain conditions—that informal networks can have on the urban political order.[6] Thus, the *hay'at-e senfis* usually had an integrative influence, in that they promoted a sense of solidarity and unity among the *bazaaris*. For instance, *hay'at-e senfi* meetings would frequently become an opportunity for *bazaaris* to devise ways of helping some of their colleagues in financial difficulty (Thaiss 1971, 202). Among shopkeepers and craftsmen selling similar products, the *hay'at-e senfis* reduced the negative social consequences generated by the competition inherent in having a multiplicity of small-scale enterprises specialized in the same goods and located in close proximity to one another. In addition, the *hay'at-e senfis* helped overcome class cleavages by bringing together and creating lines of communication and patronage between the various levels of the *bazaari* hierarchy described earlier. Thus, the *hay'at-e senfis* helped counter the appeal in the bazaar of ideologies of structural conflict, such as Marxism. They also provided an arena where well-to-do merchants could exert some control and influence over younger, more restive, lower-class *bazaaris*. Employers in the bazaar were well aware of these qualities of the *hay'at-e senfis*, and they encouraged their apprentices to join such religious gatherings (Mottahedeh 1985, 347).

These integrative functions notwithstanding, the *hay'at-e senfis* and other bazaar-centered networks always represented a potential problem for the authorities. They were, after all, one of the essential channels through which the *bazaaris* expressed and maintained their sense of collective identity. And it is this sense of distinct identity that so often had led the *bazaaris* to mobilize against the authorities whenever they had felt threatened by the state (due to high taxation, government threats to the autonomy or physical integrity of the bazaar, policies harmful to trade and domestic manufacturing) or by excessive foreign influence in the country. The *hay'at-e senfis*, because of their relative fluidity and informal nature, were also much harder for political authorities to control than more formally organized groups such as the guilds.

Because of the frequency of their meetings (at least once a week),[7] the large number of *bazaaris* they involved, and contacts across networks, these religious circles also conveyed a great deal of political information whose diffusion escaped the control of the government. Writing in the late 1960s, a perceptive observer noted that such informal circles were "one of the most pervasive and rapid means of transmission of political information, ideas, or policies to the bazaar" (Miller 1969a, 164). He estimated at the time that these networks enabled political opinions to be transmitted "within hours" from Tehran's main bazaar to "the mosques, caravansaries, workshops, and teahouses in the remotest corners of the South Tehran bazaar" and "within a day or two" to other Iranian cities or foreign countries.

Furthermore, since they were led by clerics, and since they heightened the *bazaaris'* collective identification in religious terms, the *hay'at-e senfis* strengthened the bazaar's connections with influential religious groups and personalities. They therefore provided a basis for coordination and concerted political action by the ulama and the *bazaaris*. It is, in fact, such informal ties and networks between the bazaar and the mosque that, from the Constitutional Revolution at the turn of the century down to the 1977–79 revolution, have enabled militant ulama and *bazaaris* to cooperate with one another in instigating major protest movements against the authorities.

Finally, through the *hay'at-e senfis*, funds were collected to finance charitable institutions, schools, and hospitals and to provide welfare and relief services to the poor (Thaiss 1971, 202).[8] *Hay'at-e senfis*, therefore, allowed the influence of the *bazaari* community to be felt much beyond the physical boundaries of the bazaar. They enabled the *bazaaris*, who historically have always been heavily involved in civic and political affairs, to reach out to urban society at large, and in particular to the urban poor. By creating a basis for patron-client relations between the *bazaaris* and the urban poor, the *hay'at-e senfis* also provided the bazaar with key instruments through which to mobilize large numbers of individuals in the defense of their interests.

Largely because of these features, the *hay'at-e senfis* and other bazaar-centered networks enabled the *bazaaris* to act as an effective political force throughout the post–World War II period. Thus, the bazaar played a prominent role in the unrest of the late 1940s and early 1950s,[9] in the rise of Mossadegh,[10] in the urban riots of 1963,[11] and, most significantly, during the Islamic revolution. In 1978, in particular, the bazaars repeatedly closed down in support of the revolutionary forces. (They did so at first locally and independently of each other, but, beginning in the summer of 1978, also sometimes on a coordinated, countrywide basis.) The bazaar also organized numerous demonstrations. According to Ashraf and Banuazizi (1985, 25), approximately two-thirds of the demonstrations that occurred during the revolution were arranged by the bazaar-mosque alliance. In addition, wealthy *bazaaris* financed revolutionary groups and activities, established funds to pay the salaries of striking workers and professionals, and provided financial help for the families of the "martyrs" of the revolution.

In the course of the revolution, the *bazaaris* not only made full use of the networks already at their disposal, but also created new ones. Thus, when the police and SAVAK began to hire hooligans and thugs to attack, loot, and burn the shops, stores, and homes of merchants who opposed the regime, *bazaaris* organized groups of students and militant youths to protect their property. Many revolutionary committees (*komitehs*) evolved out of these groups.[12] As seen earlier, these *komitehs*, which the *bazaaris* often placed under the leadership of the clergy, strengthened the alliance between the bazaar and the mosque and provided revolutionary forces with new networks with which to reach out to the urban population at large.

Given our interest in the conditions under which informal networks can be turned into vehicles for political protest, it is important to emphasize that the mobilization of *bazaari* networks against the shah was almost always a defensive movement, in which political, cultural, and moral concerns were often as decisive as economic ones. For instance, while the postwar economic crisis in Iran probably fueled the bazaar's discontent, it is doubtful that material interests alone are what prompted *bazaaris* to become involved either in the Fada'iyan-e Islam, or in support of Mossadegh. A look at the platform of the Fada'iyan makes it clear that the main preoccupations of its members were moral and cultural, not economic (Kazemi 1985). The Fadaʿiyan wanted first and foremost to defend and reassert traditional Islamic values and practices and to fight the Westernization and modernization of Iranian society. In a similar vein, even though the bazaar's support for Mossadegh can be traced back in part to the Iranian leader's nationalist economic program and policies, more decisive was Mossadegh's ability to give *bazaaris* the feeling that his government was receptive to their wishes and aspirations and that it was treating them with the respect due to a group that made a vital contribution to the social and economic life of the country (Ashraf 1988, 549). In addition, Mossadegh's embodiment of Iranian pride and national resistance against foreign imperialism enhanced his popularity with the bazaar.

It is also easy to overemphasize the importance of the early-1960s economic slowdown in accounting for the bazaar's active role in the urban uprising of June 1963. Economic explanations of the bazaar's behavior at that time do not survive a look at the evidence. What triggered the rioting in the bazaar of Tehran and other large cities was the arrest of Khomeini in the early hours of June 5.[13] Clearly, Khomeini can hardly be seen as a spokesman for the material interests of the bazaar. The chord his denunciations of the regime had struck with some *bazaaris* was much more tied to his concern with the "moral decadence" that he argued accompanied the shah's modernizing policies. Like Khomeini, many *bazaaris* were particularly alarmed by the shah's earlier decision to grant the right to vote to women, and to enable non-Muslims to hold local elected office—decisions that violated traditional Shiite values and norms regarding the "rightful" position of women and minorities in society. Ever since the October 1962 Local Councils Law had raised the specter of the enfranchisement of women, *bazaari* circles had provided a welcoming audience for Khomeini's denunciation of women's suffrage as an attack on the family and as an invitation to corruption, prostitution, decadence, and the spread of vices.[14]

The shortcomings of narrow economic explanations of the bazaar's political behavior are also visible in the case of the 1977–79 revolution. One frequently reads, for example, that in the 1960s and 1970s the bazaar's economic position deteriorated markedly because the government favored the modern bourgeoisie tied to the regime at the expense of the petty shopkeepers and artisans.[15] The economic crisis of 1977, it is sometimes added, exacerbated this situation, as *bazaaris* became suddenly faced with dwindling business opportunities.[16]

Firsthand accounts published in the late 1980s, however, have rightly questioned such assumptions. Ashraf, who conducted research in the bazaar of Tehran in the late 1970s, asserts that the complaints that motivated the *bazaaris* to become involved against the regime were less economic than political and cultural (Ashraf 1988). Similarly, Parsa reports that, in personal communications with him, scores of *bazaaris* from Tehran and Tabriz acknowledged having benefited considerably from the oil boom of the early 1970s (Parsa 1989, 319 n. 8). Since the *bazaaris* dominated domestic trade, and since they were heavily involved in export-import businesses, they naturally took advantage of the spectacular increase in public investment and national consumption and of the abundance of petrodollars. As consumer goods from all over the world flowed into Iran, and as new markets suddenly opened up in the country, many *bazaaris* also considerably expanded and diversified their operations.[17]

It is factually wrong, therefore, to say that the bazaar became involved in the revolution because economic trends in the country were threatening to destroy its ability to survive as a viable economic entity. Not only was the bazaar able to adapt to a rapidly changing economic environment, but it even prospered and expanded beyond its traditional boundaries by establishing connections to the modern industrial and commercial sectors and to the informal economy (Ashraf 1988). Although it may have declined in relative terms, it expanded in absolute terms, and although it may have benefited less than other sectors from the economic boom, it benefited considerably nevertheless. In fact, one might say that the *bazaaris* participated in the revolution not because they had been hurt by economic developments, but *despite* the fact that they had benefited considerably from the economic expansion of the 1970s.

So why did the *bazaaris* mobilize against the Pahlavi dynasty in the mid- to late 1970s? Largely because they felt endangered by certain state policies and attitudes and by cultural trends in Iranian society at large. What most alarmed the *bazaaris* was the state's hostility and repeated and increasing encroachments on the bazaar. Throughout the 1960s and 1970s the *bazaaris* had to suffer from numerous and arbitrarily implemented commercial regulations and tax laws (Ashraf 1988, 555). In the mid-1970s, provocations of the *bazaaris* by the state reached unprecedented dimensions. In 1975, the government destroyed a large section of the bazaar of Mashhad in order to create a green space. As Ashraf (1988, 557) notes, this was "a limited but symbolically important measure…[that] cost thousands of petty traders and artisans, who were maltreated, their businesses." Shortly afterward, the government disclosed plans for an eight-lane highway that would cut through the main bazaar in Tehran (Halliday 1979, 220). At about the same time, the newly created Rastakhiz party was forced on the *bazaari* community and began to interfere in its affairs (Abrahamian 1982, 443–44). Most consequential, however, was the so-called antiprofiteering campaign of 1975–76, which was an attempt to blame high rates of inflation on the *bazaaris*, resulting in hundreds of them being molested,[18] fined, jailed, or banned from their hometowns.[19] The antiprofiteering campaign generated much resentment, bitterness, and anger, and it was perhaps the most decisive event catalyzing the mobilization of the *bazaaris* against the regime (Ashraf 1988, 557).

Such evidence suggests that *bazaaris* in 1977–79 engaged in collective action against the state not because the free play of market forces was about to create a society in which they would no longer exist as a powerful economic force, but because the state was interfering with the market in a way that not only damaged their opportunities for profit, but made it difficult for them to operate at all. Important as well was the regime's frequently expressed contempt for the *bazaaris* and their "worm-ridden shops," as the shah once referred to them. The Iranian ruler missed few opportunities to portray the *bazaaris* as a reactionary group opposed to change and constituting an obstacle to the country's socioeconomic modernization. These attacks were offensive to the *bazaaris'* sense of self-worth and fostered their anger at the regime.

Finally, cultural factors, too, contributed greatly to the progressive alienation of the *bazaaris* from the monarchy. Throughout the 1960s and 1970s the differences in the cultural outlook of the *bazaaris* and the elite became increasingly pronounced. Many *bazaaris* resented what they saw as the state's growing disregard for Islamic values and lifestyles, and the unwillingness of the shah to preserve the moral and cultural fabric of Iranian society against foreign cultural penetration.[20]

> Among the more conflict-arousing issues in this sphere were the lifestyles and appearance of the more privileged Westernized classes, particularly the unveiled and often 'provocatively clad' upper-class women, and among other things violation of Islamic codes of behavior in public, un-Islamic or anti-Islamic ideas disseminated by the state-controlled media, non-Islamic contents of the curriculum in modern schools, and the increasing influence and presence of Americans and other Westerners at all levels of the country's economic and social life. (Ashraf 1988, 557)

As the preceding account makes clear, there was nothing inevitable in the eventual clash between the *bazaaris* and Muhammad Reza Shah. The shah's desire to modernize the country did not require him to turn against the bazaar. Political mismanagement, not economic necessity, was the most immediate cause of the confrontation between the *bazaaris* and the regime; had the shah handled the *bazaaris* better, he would have enhanced his regime's chance of survival. The mobilization of the bazaar against the shah was a primarily *defensive* movement, in which political and cultural factors, and not economic ones, played the determining role. It was an attempt by a substantially unified community to demonstrate and reassert its power and influence vis-à-vis a modernizing state whose policies were increasingly perceived as arbitrary, insulting, and harmful to both the material interests of the bazaar and the Islamic nature of Iranian society.

11

Religious Networks and Urban Unrest

Although the renewed relevance of Islam to Middle Eastern politics has received much attention over the last fifteen years, scholars have focused almost exclusively on two aspects of this phenomenon. One has been the political manipulation of Islamic symbols and concepts by both regimes and opposition groups. The other has been the presumed ideological and structural causes of Islamic movements, including the lack of legitimacy of Middle Eastern regimes, rapid modernization and the stresses and tensions it generates, the search for cultural authenticity and meaning, the "exhaustion" of the modern secular state in the Middle East, and a general disillusionment with Western ideologies, values, and ways of life. Much less is known, however, about the groups through which the Islamic revival has expressed itself and through which the Islamic message has been transmitted. While observers have noted repeatedly that one important manifestation of the resurgence of Islam has been the multiplication of informally organized, locally based, and loosely connected networks that are vaguely labeled "Islamic," there has been very little effort to look at these networks, and in particular at their impact on political stability, from a comparative perspective. In an attempt to do so, in this chapter I distinguish between two types of religious networks, the first of which I call "double-edged," and the second "radical-utopian."

Double-Edged Religious Networks

Double-edged religious networks may exert either a stabilizing or a destabilizing influence on the political system, depending upon the circumstances. Under normal conditions, they tend to be stabilizing, in that they provide some of the social, economic, and/or psychological support to absorb tensions associated with rapid socioeconomic change. At other times, however, they can also become powerful vehicles for the mobilization of individuals into oppositional activities. These features can be shown by an examination of five types of double-edged religious networks, two in Egypt and three in Iran.

Religious Networks on Egyptian University Campuses, 1970–81

In the early 1970s, small clubs and circles broadly committed to the study of Islam began to appear on most Egyptian university campuses.[1] The mid-1970s then saw a dramatic increase in the number, activities, and appeal of these groups, which came to be known by the generic term of *jama'at islamiyya* (Islamic groups). By 1977–78, the *jama'at islamiyya* controlled most of the student unions and had grown into a major political force on university campuses.

Two aspects of the *jama'at islamiyya* deserve special attention: their organizational structure and their impact on political stability. On an organizational plane, the *jama'at* remained loosely organized and locally based groups. They had no list of members, no internal status and regulations, and no clearly defined program or ideology, beyond a commitment to broadly defined Islamic causes. Nor is there any evidence that *jama'at* from various universities ever significantly coordinated their activities at the national or even regional level. What is really striking is the speed with which the movement spread throughout the country's universities *despite* the absence of formal organization and nationwide coordination. Out of a multiplicity of small groups of activist students operating at the local level, a national movement developed in the short span of five years, between 1973 and 1978. It was only after the *jama'at* already had gained control of student unions and the national General Confederation of Egyptian Students that the resources of formal organizations were harnessed by the *jama'at* and that some form of national coordination took place among Islamicist students (Kepel 1985, 139–41). The *jama'at*, however, continued to differ in their respective views, goals, and activities, and they never developed into formally organized groups.

An examination of the *jama'at*'s impact on political stability shows that informal networks that are normally stabilizing can nevertheless operate as vehicles of political protest under certain circumstances. The *jama'at* were initially encouraged by the regime, which attempted to use these religious clubs to counter the influence of Nasserism and Marxism in the student body (Kepel 1985, 133–35). This strategy paid off, since by the mid-1970s the left had been marginalized on university campuses. In addition, the *jama'at* played a functional role by providing students with vital goods and services. In fact, their unmatched ability to address the students' needs is precisely what made the *jama'at* so successful. Students unable to buy expensive textbooks were happy to see the *jama'at* photocopy them and sell copies at only a fraction of the books' market prices. Students having difficulty taking notes in overcrowded and noisy amphitheaters were pleased to be able to buy low-cost copies of lecture notes distributed by the *jama'at*. Female students physically harassed on the public transportation system welcomed the *jama'at*'s organization of a special bus line for them. Similarly, when they asked that male and female students sit in separate rows during lectures, the *jama'at* found a receptive audience among female students who felt their physical integrity endangered in packed, mixed-sex lecture halls. Students finding it hard to study in noisy dormitories and unable to pay for expensive private tutoring eagerly joined the study groups and review sessions for examinations that the *jama'at* organized in local mosques or in places that they had asked the university authorities to set aside for prayer.[2]

The most important functions of the *jama'at*, however, may well have been psychological and sociological: to offer a sense of community and belonging to students who only recently had been drawn away from their familiar surroundings and families, and who now found themselves in the impersonal and bewildering environment of a large university in Cairo or in one of the rapidly expanding provincial cities. It is significant, as several observers have noted, that the clubs out of which the *jama'at islamiyya* developed were initially known as *usar*, which literally means "families." The formation of such "families" shows a deliberate effort to recreate ties of intimacy and solidarity and to shelter oneself against isolation and loneliness.[3] Similarly, through their heavy emphasis on moral themes, and especially sexual mores, the *jama'at islamiyya* provided traditionally raised youths with vehicles for the expression of their outrage at the perceived moral permissiveness prevailing on Egyptian university campuses (Davis 1984).

While the *jama'at* supplied large segments of the student community with various mechanisms to facilitate their adjustment to university life, many also eventually became an oppositional force, both on and beyond university campuses. Bolstered by their successes in student elections and having grown into a powerful movement, the *jama'at islamiyya* turned increasingly assertive. They endeavored to prevent "anti-Islamic" behavior and activities on university campuses and began to harass Coptic and secularist students and faculty, frequently resorting to violence and intimidation.

The Islamicist monolith [that the *jama'at islamiyya*] sought to impose on the universities turned those campuses on which they were the dominant force into a kind of *terra islamica* from which they banned, clubs in hand, anything that fell foul of their norms: couples [for instance, those holding hands in public] were physically attacked for violations of upright Islamic morals; films [deemed "indecent" by the *jama'at*] could not be shown; concerts and evening dances could not be held. (Kepel 1985, 151)

Some *jama'at* did not content themselves with attempting to turn universities into "small Islamic enclaves" (Kepel 1985). After Sadat's 1977 trip to Jerusalem and the Camp David Accords in 1978, they also became increasingly critical of Sadat's policies and began to spread their message beyond university premises. They agitated in favor of the application of the *shari'a* (Islamic law), criticized the regime for the peace treaty with Israel, and instigated and participated in some of the most violent incidents of communal strife in the country's history, especially in Minia, Assiut, and Cairo.[4]

The radicalization of some *jama'at islamiyya* after 1978 eventually forced the regime to crack down on them. Indiscriminate repression by the state, however, turned the *jama'at* into one of the main sources of opposition to the regime (Kepel 1985, 149). It also strengthened the ties between the *jama'at* and small radical underground organizations, driving many of the formers' members into the ranks of the latter. In Upper Egypt, for instance, Jihad appears to have developed out of the *jama'at islamiyya* (Kepel 1985, 205). Significantly as well, one of the factors that appear to have motivated Khalid Islambuli to kill Sadat on 6 October 1981 was the fact that, a month earlier, his brother, a leader of the *jama'at islamiyya* of the university of Assiut, had been beaten up following his arrest during the government's crackdown on the opposition (Kepel 1985, 129–30).

Of course, the threat posed by the *jama'at* ought not to be exaggerated. Throughout the 1970s, political activists—Islamists and others—remained a tiny minority on university campuses (Abdalla 1985, 232). Furthermore, the *jama'at*'s attempt to extend their appeal beyond university campuses met with only limited success. Consequently, when the state cracked down on them, they found themselves politically isolated, and, following Sadat's assassination, the regime found it relatively easy to destroy the *jama'at*'s infrastructure and force their members underground. For at least four years, not much was heard from the *jama'at*, even in their strongholds of Upper Egypt.

These limits notwithstanding, the *jama'at islamiyya* were responsible for much of the turbulence of the 1979–81 period. Their experience shows that networks that at first emerge to facilitate the adjustment of individuals to their environment, that successfully fulfill all sorts of stabilizing functions, and that for a while may even be co-opted by the state, can nevertheless under certain conditions escape government control, become alienated from the regime, be radicalized, and clash with authorities. The very same resources that enable these networks to meet their members' needs can then be harnessed against the state.

In the second half of the 1980s, recovering from a period of decline and passivity, the *jama'at islamiyya* scored impressive successes in elections to student unions and faculty clubs (Springborg 1989, 226–27). They often used this new power to force the university authorities to concede to many of their demands, such as sexually segregated seating, the creation of prayer sites on university premises, and the cancellation of plays, concerts, student dances, and other activities fundamentalists deem decadent and frivolous. The most militant *jama'at* were even implicated in several incidents of communal violence or antiregime activities. During the spring and fall of 1986, in particular, Islamicist students fought repeatedly with security forces on campuses throughout Upper Egypt, contributing to what Springborg described as "the most widespread religiously inspired violence to affect Egypt since the summer of 1981" (1989, 217). A few years later, in December 1989, Islamic militant students in Assiut confronted the police with guns, chains, knives, and gasoline bombs during clashes that left forty wounded and more than three hundred in jail.[5] Such incidents demonstrated once again that, while the *jama'at* lacked the resources and the following to effectively challenge the state, they nevertheless offered a minority of committed activists the channels through which to express violently their frustrations at the system.

Finally, as many of their former members have moved into the professions and other positions of influence in Egyptian society, the influence of the *jama'at islamiyya* is now felt much beyond universities. By the late 1980s, individuals whose first political experiences were gained in the *jama'at* under Sadat formed an influential constituency in several professional syndicates, in scores of voluntary Islamic associations, in local government agencies, and in the Muslim Brotherhood.[6] It is too early to assess the political significance of this phenomenon, but two different analyses can be made. On the one hand, one may interpret the presence of former *jama'at* members in many powerful institutions as a sign that the movement has been co-opted by the Egyptian establishment and that its revolutionary potential has been deflected. On the other hand, one might argue that the *jama'at* have infiltrated and established power bases in so many of the country's key institutions and groups that they have laid the foundation for an Islamic takeover of the country. Should the economic situation in Egypt continue to deteriorate, and should moderate Islamic militants succeed in convincing a majority of Egyptians that an Islamic order would better meet the population's needs, the *jama'at*'s old-boy network might become more threatening to the regime.

Voluntary Islamic Associations in Mubarak's Egypt

The campus-based *jama'at islamiyya* should not be confused with another type of voluntary Islamic associations known by the same name but existing throughout Egyptian society at large. These associations, whose number rose sharply in the 1980s, are essentially self-help groups that developed out of grassroots attempts to cope with the harsh socioeconomic environment in which the Egyptian urban population has to live. Some of these groups go so far as to provide their members with most of their basic material needs. The majority, however, have more modest goals and aim only at solving specific problems. For example, to deal with the housing crisis, individuals will pool their resources to buy or rent flats—and to do so they will create an "Islamic" association among them.

Side by side with these *jama'at,* Islamic charitable associations (*al-jam'iyyat al-khayriyya al-islamiyya*) were created, thanks to the contributions of wealthy individuals with Islamic convictions. Many of these "Islamo-capitalists" had made their fortunes by taking advantage of the policy of economic liberalization initiated by Sadat. By the 1980s, they were found at the head of "Islamic" investment banks and companies with interests abroad, particularly in the Gulf.[7] While they have pressed for a gradual extension of the *shari'a* and are dedicated to turning Egypt into a country with greater respect for Islamic values and norms, they refuse recourse to violence. Instead, they have tried to convince Egyptians that "Islam is the way" by building a variety of educational and health care facilities—hospitals, clinics, day-care centers, schools, and so on—that mix the teachings of Islam with a remarkable ability to deliver high-quality social services for which they charge only nominal fees. As an observer puts it, "Islamist primary schools offer children not only religious indoctrination but a rigorous education superior to that available from badly overcrowded public schools. Islamist medical clinics, well-staffed and outfitted with the latest medical equipment, contrast starkly with state-run hospitals with their low sanitation standards and long delays" (Sadowski 1987, 45). In many instances, these philanthropic associations were built around private (*ahli*) mosques.[8] To this private mosque-charitable association nucleus were often progressively attached a whole variety of educational and social institutions engaged in community work and relief services.

Although the 1980s saw no significant example of *jama'at* or *jam'iyyat* involved in destabilizing political activities, these networks, and the variety of formally organized groups and institutions that have evolved out of them, can be described as "double-edged." On the one hand, they so far have helped keep the country stable by fulfilling a variety of vital functions that the overextended, understaffed, underequipped, inefficiently managed, and underfinanced state-controlled educational and welfare systems set up by Nasser can no longer fulfill. Significantly, both Islamic self-help groups and charitable associations developed with the approval of the authorities, and sometimes with their explicit endorsement. Should Islamic associations develop into a danger for the government, the latter could always step in and either take control of them or limit their operations. At any time, the state can also impose regulations that will make life difficult for the Islamic banks and investment companies that bankroll the Islamic movement. This is, in fact, exactly what it did in 1987 and 1988 (see Roussillon 1988, 28–37). The very structure of the movement formed by the *jama'at* and *jam'iyyat*—its many-headed and fragmented character, as well as its reliance on outside patrons whom the government can influence or even control—plays into the hands of the regime (Springborg 1989, 232).

In any event, many of those who finance Islamic associations are not always politically active. When they are, they tend to be associated not with the extremist fringes of the Islamic movement, but with the legalist Muslim Brotherhood, which has developed a stake in Egypt's polity and economy and whose leaders emphasize gradualism, dialogue with the state and mainstream opposition parties, and conversion to the Islamic movement not through violence, but through persuasion and personal example.

Finally, there is no evidence of substantial coordination among Islamic voluntary associations or between them and the Islamic movement's other branches, especially the more radical ones. It seems farfetched to assume that Islamic self-help and philanthropic groups, the Muslim Brotherhood, popular *imams*, the Islamic investment banks, companies, schools, clinics, and social institutions, the campus-based *jama'at*, and the radical underground Islamic networks all secretly share the same goal and form a single-minded movement dedicated to the overthrow of the regime. On the contrary, there is evidence of considerable organizational fragmentation and disagreements on tactics and goals (Springborg 1989, 222–23). Thus, the possibility that the various Islamic associations might be integrated into a nationwide movement susceptible of posing a threat to the government appears remote at best.

On the other hand, the *jama'at* and *jam'iyyat* could play a destabilizing role. These associations, many of which have now developed into bureaucratically organized institutions, control considerable resources that lie outside direct government control, and have developed a parallel economy and a parallel welfare system. The fact that the individuals who operate these institutions are proving themselves to be much better than the authorities at delivering high–quality services—a fact that they are quick to advertise—could in the long run undermine the legitimacy of the state, erode the population's commitment to the survival of the secular political order, and pave the way for a tacit popular endorsement of a takeover by nonradical Islamic forces (Sadowski 1987; Springborg 1989). Along different lines, if the government continues to purse belt-tightening policies that result in popular discontent, the infrastructure provided by the networks of voluntary Islamic associations could be mobilized against the state, possibly in a temporary alliance with the Muslim Brotherhood and more radical Islamic elements. It is important here to remember that both the 1977 popular uprising and the police riots of 1986 had heavy Islamic undertones, and that the issues that triggered them were in both cases economic. Should Mubarak be forced to limit his commitment to political liberalization in order to impose austerity policies, there might be a coalescence against the regime of individuals and groups that so far have been working within the system because they believe that the state can be reformed from within and that Egyptian society can be "Islamized" through peaceful means. Figure 6 describes the connections between the different categories of Islamic networks, as well as the contacts between these networks and more formally and bureaucratically organized groups and institutions: professional associations, the Muslim Brotherhood (and, therefore, Parliament), local government agencies, and political parties. The barriers between Islamic networks and the organizations that either bankroll the various wings of the Islamic movement ("Islamic" investment companies and banks) or are a direct expression of it ("Islamic" schools, clinics, day-care centers, and so on) are becoming thinner every day.

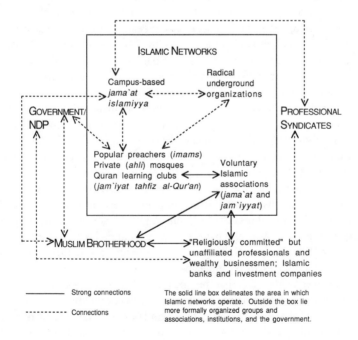

Figure 6.   Islamic Networks in Egypt

Religious Gatherings, the Urban Poor, and the Iranian Revolution

If one now leaves Egypt to look at Iran under the rule of Muhammad Reza Shah, the first example of double-edged religious network that comes to mind is represented by the Shiite religious groups known as *hay'ats*. Less structured and more recent than the *hay'at-e senfis* of the bazaar, these associations began to multiply among the urban poor in both the squatter settlements and the poor sections of Iran's cities in the late 1960s. Led by a lower-ranking cleric, the *hay'ats* met in members' homes, not in the mosque. They were of relatively small size—typically around thirty people—and were formed on the basis of regional or ethnic origin, neighborly contacts, or place of work.[9] Roy Mottahedeh has provided us with a description of a typical meeting of a *hay'at* among the urban poor.

> [It] would begin with members reading verses from the Koran in sequence, while the mullah corrected their pronunciation; or, in the case of a *hay'at* of nearly illiterate members, the mullah would recite himself the Koran in Arabic. Then the mullah would preach, and, finally, he would open the meeting to questions....Then came the *rowzeh*: the events of Hosain's martyrdom were recited by the clergyman, after which all stood and for ten to fifteen minutes beat their breasts in a rhythm to fit an elegiac poem. (Mottahedeh 1985, 350–51)[10]

Only a minority of the urban poor belonged to *hay'ats*, which met on an irregular basis. Yet these networks were politically significant in at least three respects. First, they were the only voluntary associations independent of the government found among the urban poor in Iran prior to the revolution, and some of their members were extremely attached to them.[11] Second, *hay'ats* created lines of communication and feelings of solidarity between clerics and the urban poor, as well as among the urban poor themselves, since *hay'ats* from different parts of the city were connected to one another (Kazemi 1980a, 63). Finally, *hay'at* members looked up to the cleric who led the discussion, and probably saw him, in part, as a patron—the more so since the networks of mosques and *hay'ats* were meshed, and both sometimes served to distribute food, clothes, and other vital items to the needy. *Hay'ats* and mosques, therefore, formed the backbone of a clientelist structure in which the ulama provided psychological and social support and welfare services. In return, the clerics could expect a certain degree of respect and political loyalty on the part of Iran's urban masses (Kazemi 1980b, 259).

Until about 1978, the *hay'ats* of the poor remained largely irrelevant to Iranian politics. If anything, they played a stabilizing role, providing the urban poor with a much-needed sense of community. As one young squatter in Tehran declared, "Nothing brings us together more than the love for Imam Hosain. My personal view is that these *hay'ats* have a positive aspect in uniting us and keeping us informed about each other's affairs" (Kazemi 1980a, 63). In a city such as Tehran, where in the mid-1970s over 50 percent of the population were migrants, *hay'ats* offered spiritual guidance in what must have seemed a baffling environment to recently urbanized Iranians, many of whom originated from small communities (Mottahedeh 1985, 348). It is significant that most of the questions addressed to clerics who led the discussions in *hay'ats* were about what constituted proper Islamic behavior, what was pure or impure, and how one could protect oneself against the new material and sexual temptations to which one was inevitably exposed in the city (Mottahedeh 1985, 350–51).

These stabilizing functions notwithstanding, there is also evidence that when revolutionary activities gathered momentum in the late summer and fall of 1978, militant clerics were able to use the *hay'ats* to mobilize against the government large segments of the poor who until then had remained politically passive.[12] Ever since the late 1960s, cassettes containing sermons of preachers critical of the regime had been played during *hay'at* meetings (Mottahedeh 1985, 351). In 1978 this phenomenon took on a new dimension, as messages of Khomeini in Paris were transmitted by telephone to Tehran, where they were rerecorded and distributed throughout the country, especially in the largest urban centers.[13] Tapes containing the ayatollah's virulent denunciations of the shah were avidly listened to in many *hay'ats*, and they helped draw substantial segments of the poor to the demonstrations of late 1978 and early 1979 (Mottahedeh 1985, 356). Thus, by fostering group solidarity, disseminating information, and creating lines of communication between militant clerics and the poor, *hay'ats*, which acted in coordination with the nationwide network of mosques, played a significant role in the revolutionary process.

It is, in fact, by using mosques, *hay'ats*, as well as various rituals such as funeral processions, passion plays, and religious sermons, that the merchant-clerical alliance turned into a popular upheaval a movement of protest that for several months had been limited to the intelligentsia, the *bazaaris*, and the radical clerics. Thus, although the urban poor were latecomers to the revolutionary process (they did not become involved to any extent before the late summer and early fall of 1978, and it was only in the last few months of 1978 that they played a significant role), their contribution to the final success of the movement nevertheless cannot be ignored.[14] It is not sure that the opposition forces would have triumphed at all had they not succeeded in mobilizing precisely those elements who were not active from the start. After all, it was the involvement of virtually all segments of the population in mostly peaceful demonstrations against the regime that gave the Iranian revolution its most dramatic aspect and made it very difficult for the government to fight.

There is some evidence, furthermore, that the urban poor constituted a majority of those who lost their lives during the demonstrations and anti-regime activities of 1978. According to one estimate, "Nearly 95 percent of those gunned down in the streets of Iran in 1978 were teenagers from urban slums" (Farhang 1987, 164). If this is true (the percentage does seem high, and the author does not indicate his source of information), the poor provided the revolution not only with its foot soldiers, but with its martyrs as well. Motta-hedeh, speaking of the urban poor, notes:

> Of the angry, they were the angriest. They created neither the strategy nor the ideology of the revolution, and their opposition alone would never have cowed the regime. But they contributed the gigantic numbers before which the will of the government and the army collapsed. The mullahs, who had telephones, knew whom to contact to bring out the masses without telephones; many of those who marched came as members of their *hay'ats.* And many felt that they had internalized the fearless spirit of Hosain. (Mottahedeh 1985, 356)

The poor, however, did not start the Islamic revolution; the intelligentsia did. In turning from the poor to the intelligentsia, we can observe again some networks' dual effects on political stability.

The Religious Networks of the Iranian Intelligentsia

The development of religious circles within the Iranian intelligentsia goes back to the 1960s, when rapid social change and the deepening of West-ern influence in the country made many educated Iranians feel a growing sense of cultural alienation. While the majority of these intellectuals did not question the desirability of some form of modernization—many, such as Mehdi Bazargan, who would become the first prime minister of the Islamic Republic, were Western-trained scientists—they refused the premise that modernization had to amount to Westernization and secularization. They believed that the country had become a victim of what the Iranian writer Al-e Ahmad called "*gharbzadegi,*" "Westoxification" or "West-stricken-ness" (see Mottahedeh 1985, 296). By the mid-1970s, such feelings of cultural alienation had become so prevalent among educated Iranians that Najmabadi (1987a) speaks of a "paradigmatic shift" to describe the transformations that the Iranian intelligentsia as a whole experienced during the 1960s and 1970s. Whereas earlier generations of Iranian intellectuals had been concerned primarily with finding ways to modernize the country, many educated Iranians in the 1960s and 1970s became obsessed with maintaining the moral and cultural fabric of Iranian society. The search for progress had given way to a quest for authenticity and roots; the preoccupation with overcoming backwardness had been replaced with a fear of moral decay and the loss of cultural identity. Accordingly, moral and cultural standards, not material achievements, had become most Iranian intellectuals' basis for assessing social, economic, and political developments in the country. The West was no longer seen as a model to be emulated, but as a force responsible for the cultural and moral degeneration of Iranian society (Najmabadi 1987b, 203).

Since Shiism is such a large component of Iran's indigenous culture, the "paradigmatic shift" described by Najmabadi led to a rediscovery of Shiism by Iranian intellectuals, which in turn was the driving force behind the multiplication of Shiite associations on campuses, in high schools, and in the private homes of intellectuals. Similar networks were soon formed by Iranian students abroad. At first, most of these religious circles were formed for the purpose of praying and exchanging views on religion, and they did not preoccupy themselves with explicitly political issues. To the extent that they played a political role, it was a stabilizing one in at least two respects. First, one of these associations' primary goals was to thwart the spread of Marxism among the educated youth. As in the case of the campus-based *jama'at islamiyya* in Egypt, it was this objective that ensured the government's protection of many of these groups in their early stages (Bayat 1987, 68–69). Second, one suspects that these associations must have facilitated the intellectual, social, and psychological adjustment of many university students who were recent migrants to large cities and/or from clerical-bazaar petty bourgeois backgrounds.[15] Indeed, not only did religious circles offer such students membership in a community of like-minded individuals and opportunities for socializing and discussing issues of common interest, but they also propagated a view of the world that was activist and future-oriented—therefore addressing these students' longing for sociopolitical change—yet phrased in the familiar idiom of Islam, in which these students had been socialized, and which therefore provided them with a much-needed sense of continuity with their past. Such characteristics explain the appeal to the educated youth of the ideas of Shari'ati, whose writings provided the substance for so many of the discussions in high school and university Islamic circles in the 1960s and 1970s.

> [Shari'ati's] ideas had an emotional power which derived above
> all from the fact that they appeared at once authentically Islamic

and authentically modern. To young people whose education had disoriented them with half-understood Western ideas, he restored confidence in their own culture and their own religion. He, more than anyone, popularized the idea that in fighting for Islam one was not demanding a return to obscurantism but working towards genuine national liberation and enlightenment. (Mortimer 1982, 341)

Initially, Shari'ati's popularity came from the lectures he delivered in Tehran at the Hosseiniyeh Ershad, a sort of club for the diffusion of a reformulated and modernized understanding of Shiite Islam. The Hosseiniyeh Ershad became so popular that it inspired the formation of similar associations and meeting places elsewhere in the country. Tehran's original Hosseiniyeh Ershad had been established only in 1965 (Shari'ati joined it in 1967). Yet by 1974 "there were 322 Hosseiniyeh-type centers in Tehran, 305 in Khuzestan and 731 in Azerbaijan" (Arjomand 1984b, 216).

Parallel to the development of lay Islamic networks within the intelligentsia itself, contacts between religiously inclined intellectuals and a new generation of "progressive" clerics increased regularly throughout the 1960s and 1970s. These younger ulama often had been educated in modern high schools, and some even pursed their studies at universities while attending the religious seminaries (Mottahedeh 1985; Ashraf 1990, 118). Unlike their elders, they were familiar with Western disciplines and interested in the problems of the modern world. In order to survive, they thought, the clergy needed to present to the youth and the intelligentsia a more enlightened, activist, and inspiring version of Shiism that explicitly addressed the country's contemporary social, cultural, and political problems (Akhavi 1980, 117–20). In an effort to reach out to the lay intelligentsia, they began to publish a few journals and anthologies dealing with the issues facing the country (Ashraf 1990, 120).

Many intellectuals, frustrated by the regime's growing authoritarianism and by its perceived subservience to the United States and close ties to Israel, and deeply disturbed by what they saw as the excessive Westernization of the country, welcomed and even encouraged such reformist tendencies among the ulama.[16] In fact, religious-minded nationalist liberals, especially Mehdi Bazargan, played a pioneering role in trying to make Shiism and the Shiite religious institutions more relevant to the aspirations of the modern intelligentsia. Together with such "progressive" clerics as Taleqani, Beheshti, and Mottahari, they established, in the early 1960s, informal "Islamic associations" (*Anjomanha'ye Islami*) that were the first clear organizational manifestations of the then-still-incipient ulama-intelligentsia alliance (Akhavi 1980; Milani 1988, 143). In the 1960s and early 1970s, as such associations multiplied, some Iranian intellectuals also established contacts with Khomeini in Najaf, while Khomeini and pro-Khomeini forces in Iran endeavored to build ties to Iranian students abroad, especially the Moslem Student Association in the United States (Milani 1988, 144).

Even though the lay and clerical Islamic networks that have just been described fulfilled politically and socially integrative functions, they nevertheless made two essential contributions to Khomeini's ability to overthrow the Pahlavi dynasty. First, and most importantly, they enhanced the receptiveness of high school and university students to the propaganda of the radical ulama and thereby paved the way for the alliance between the militant clergy and a segment of the young intelligentsia.[17] They may even help explain the intelligentsia's acceptance of the clerical leadership of the revolution (Arjomand 1988, 97). Second, there is also evidence that, in 1977–79, the revolution's leaders used these clerical and lay networks in order to mobilize the educated youth against the regime (Bayat 1987, 68-69).[18] The significance of these factors becomes evident when one remembers that the young intelligentsia was among the first forces to mobilize against the shah and that it provided the revolution with many of its rank-and-file members.

While the analysis so far has been limited to certain types of religious associations—the *hay'ats* of the poor, Islamic networks among intellectuals, and militant ulama-lay activists networks—the prerevolutionary Shiite establishment as a whole can be thought of as a double-edged "network of networks." This can be shown through an examination of the informal organization of the religious institution under Muhammad Reza Shah, and of the sudden transformation of its role from being system-supportive to being system-challenging.

Religious Networks and the Pahlavi State:
From Accommodation to Confrontation

Until the 1977–79 revolution, at least, the Shiite establishment remained decentralized and built around a series of loosely connected groups and places of worship and religious learning: mosques, shrines, *madrasehs* (seminaries), *hay'ats*, religious associations in schools, universities, offices, and factories, and Hosseiniyehs and *taqiyehs* (religious centers for debating and propagating the faith).[19] Statistics on this network in the mid-1970s vary greatly, but some of the most reliable figures include some 200 seminaries, 1,200 shrines, and between 20,000 and 80,000 mosques—including at least a quarter in urban centers.[20] In Tehran alone, there were in the mid-1970s some 164 registered permanent *taqiyehs* and an estimated 12,300 *hay'ats*.[21]

This network was operated by some 180,000 clerics (Keddie 1983a). At the top of the clerical hierarchy were a few "grand ayatollahs" (*ayatollah al-ʿozma*).[22] In 1975, it was usually acknowledged that there existed six such ayatollahs: Kho'i and Khomeini in Najaf, Golpayegani, Shariatmadari, and Marashi-Najafi in Qom, and Khonsari in Tehran (Fischer 1980, 88).[23] Immediately below the grand ayatollahs were about a hundred ayatollahs (literally, "sign of God," an honorific title conferred upon senior professional ulama, who studied religious law and taught the seminary students).[24] Another important group was formed by about five thousand *hojjat al-Islam* (proof of Islam), middle-rank clerics whose primary role was to interpret and transmit the opinions and teachings of the more senior clerics. Also included in the religious network, or gravitating around it, were some eleven to thirteen thousand theology students (*tollab*, sing. *talabeh*), more than six thousand of whom studied in Qom alone, some six hundred thousand *asyad* (plural of *sayyid*, i.e., a descendant of the family of the Prophet),[25] and thousands of shrine attendants.[26] Webs of personal contacts and networks of reciprocal exchange connected these various individuals not only to one another, but also to virtually all strata of Iranian society.

The networks formed around the senior ayatollahs were of particular significance. Ayatollahs who developed substantial followings were (and still are) known as *marajiʿ-i taqlid* (sing. *marjaʿ-i taqlid*), or "sources of imitation." Because of the personalized link between these ayatollahs and their respective followings of *muqallids*,[27] the religious establishment in Iran, until the revolution at least, was essentially a collection of loosely connected networks led by prominent *marajiʿ-i taqlid*. The fluid and informal nature of an institution built around such personal links needs to be emphasized. Scholars have highlighted the independence of the clergy from the state, but they have rarely paid enough attention to the substantial autonomy that each *marjaʿ* enjoyed vis-à-vis the rest of the religious establishment. As will now be shown, the respective networks formed by each source of imitation and his following were organizationally, financially, and ideologically independent of one another.

On an organizational plane, the *marjaʿ*'s position did not spring from his occupation of a formal office that might have been awarded to him by a bureaucratically organized religious institution. Instead, this position flowed first and foremost from the deference and loyalty that the *marjaʿ* would receive from all those who recognized his opinions as authoritative. Typically, Milani (1988) tells us, the network of a *marjaʿ* would consist of the *marjaʿ* himself, "a few hundred of his close associates, usually former students, who in turn [would] administer a large network of mosques, *taqiyehs*, and *hosseiniyehs*, each of which [would have] a considerable following of its own" (154). As in the case of lesser *mujtahids*, the bond between the *marjaʿ* and his *muqallids* was a purely personal one. In theory at least, it was based exclusively on the *muqallid*'s respect for the learning and scholarly achievements of the *marja*ᶜ and on his agreement with the *marja*ᶜ's interpretation of the law. By the same token, *muqallids* could shift their allegiance from one *marja*ᶜ to another. As a result, the whole structure of Shiism was in constant flux (Mallat 1988, 27).

Among *maraji*ᶜ and *mujtahids* themselves, a great deal of informality prevailed. For example, once an individual had reached the level of *mujtahid,* the question of who was an *ayatollah* or a *marja*ᶜ*-i taqlid* was decided only by the informal consensus of those who exerted influence in the affairs of the religious community. Such individuals consisted primarily of *maraji*ᶜ, *ayatollahs,* and other leading *mujtahids.* Some very prominent *bazaari* merchants or famous religious propagandists who were not *mujtahids* could also play a role, albeit a less determining one. The point to be underlined is that status and position in the religious elite were conferred not by appointment or decree, but through the consensus of the community's most prominent members. The same was true of the position of *marja*ᶜ*-i mutlaq,* conferred upon the one leading *marja*ᶜ at any time.[28] Significantly, after the death of Ayatollah Borujirdi (in 1961), the "office" of *marja*ᶜ*-i mutlaq* remained vacant because no consensus could be reached on which ayatollah was the most learned. (The word *office,* as applied to the supreme *marja*ᶜ, is poorly suited to describe a position that once again implies considerable power and influence but is not acquired through formal appointment and does not involve clearly formulated and written rights and duties.)

It is also revealing that, in the late 1940s and early 1950s, Borujirdi, who frowned upon political activism on the part of the ulama, could not "defrock" or exclude from the religious establishment militant clerics such as Ayatollah Kashani and other lesser clerics. Borujirdi was no Shiite pope. All he could do was manifest his discontent through largely symbolic measures (such as not inviting Kashani to stay overnight during one of his visits to Qom). Concretely, however, Borujirdi had no effective means of preventing Kashani from driving large numbers of religiously minded people into the National Front between 1950 and 1952 (Mottahedeh 1985, 131). An even more striking example is that of Ayatollah Burqaᶜi, the "red Ayatollah," who openly pronounced himself in favor of the program of the Tudeh in the 1950s. In this case as well, Borujirdi's ability to enforce sanctions was strictly limited. The *marja*ᶜ*-i taqlid* did exile Burqaᶜi from Qom. But exile did not mean excommunication, and Burqaᶜi remained a full-fledged ayatollah all of his life.

Sources of imitation remained ideologically autonomous as well, since *maraji*ᶜ were "accountable to no one except God" (Milani 1988, 154). While all the followers of a particular *marja*ᶜ had to accept unconditionally his legal pronouncements or transfer their allegiance to another source of imitation, the *marjaʿ* himself enjoyed total freedom of interpretation of the religious texts. This intellectual freedom is precisely what enabled Khomeini to build his theory of the *vilayat-e faqih* (the rule of the jurisconsult), which is clearly antithetical to traditional Shiite thought. The *marajiʿ*'s ideological autonomy also explains why the social base of a given *marjaʿ* tended to be rooted in particular constituencies. For example, in the early months of the revolution, Shariatmadari was widely regarded as a spokesman for the moderate ulama, for the middle and upper ranks of the bazaar, and, more generally, for those moderate social forces who did not call for a rejection of the monarchy but, inter alia, called for limiting the shah's power by implementing the 1906 Constitution. Khomeini's main power base, by contrast, was initially located in the lower and middle clergy, in the lower echelons of the bazaar, and among the *tollab*.

Finally, the autonomy of the *marajiʿ* was not only organizational and ideological, but financial as well, since each *marjaʿ* had his own nationwide network of representatives who acted as his personal agents and levied the religious dues known as *sahm-i imam*, or "share of the [Hidden] Imam."[29] Thus, each source of imitation received financial support directly from his followers; as Fischer notes, "funds are a way the Muslim public votes for *marajiʿ-i taqlid*" (1980, 88). Having received the *sahm-i imam*, the *marjaʿ* would then act very much as a patron, by redistributing it in the form of financial support for seminary students and poor mullahs, for the upkeep and operating of seminaries and mosques, and for charitable causes and the support of the poor and orphans.

Despite the extremely decentralized nature of the *marjaʿ* system, informal processes held the religious institution together and provided for cooperation and coordination among rival *marjaʿ* networks. *Marajiʿ* and other leading *mujtahids* frequently met with one another. In addition, there was a frequent flow of second-rank aides from one *marjaʿ* to another, which ensured some degree of communication between *marajiʿ*. The fact that most religious students (*tollab*) received funds from several if not all *marajiʿ* also reinforced the unity of the religious establishment, by creating multiple and overlapping loyalties to leading religious figures. Cohesiveness was further strengthened by the links of intermarriage and common ancestry between members of the ulama elite in general (Akhavi 1980, 66–67; Fischer 1980, 88–91).

However, the greatest homogenizing factor within the ulama elite may well have been the shared formative experiences associated with living for several years in the unique and self-contained world of the seminaries of Qom, Mashhad, and Najaf.[30] At an age when personalities are formed, several years spent in a *madrasa* , studying theology and Islamic law according to medieval pedagogical methods, developed a similarity in outlook and ways of approaching problems. By deciding to become a *talabeh*, which literally means "seeker," one had also joined the closed-in, self-contained social world of those who devoted their entire lives to the quest for religious knowledge. Within this group, those clever enough to reach the upper levels of the *madrasa* curriculum could feel that, together, they formed a small elite that, through intelligence and hard work, had reached an approximation of the most precious goal in life, reserved for the select few: the knowledge of God's laws (Mottahedeh 1985, 108–9). But even among those who never became *mujtahids*, the shared burden of coping with the austere and rough environment of the seminaries had promoted a certain solidarity.[31] Even mullahs who became anticlerical activists would often evoke with some nostalgia the sense of camaraderie they had felt during their seminary years.[32] Moreover, the friendships and personal loyalties to former teachers woven during the years spent in the seminaries were strong and long-lasting. They also cut across national borders to form transnational networks that brought together members of the Shiite world of scholarship.

Thus, the shared experiences of seminary training and the sense of distinct collective identity they promoted, the friendships among former students, the devotion to old teachers, the commitment to religious learning, and the uniformity of dress code were all powerful unifying forces among clerics. Significant as well were a series of informal devices, practices, and beliefs, specifically sanctioned by Shiite texts and deliberately used by Iranian ulama both to maintain some form of unity in their ranks and to make it difficult for outsiders to understand the inner workings of the religious establishment. "Mutually protective silence," for instance, when combined with the practice of *tanfiyeh* (to refrain from making any move at times of turmoil or factional disputes), has historically tended to lessen strife among Shiite clerics, although often at the cost of lengthening factional rivalries (Schahgaldian 1989, 27–31). These features explain the ulama's ability to overcome divisions in their ranks whenever they were faced with important threats to their power. This phenomenon, in turn, is largely what enabled them to seize power and, more importantly, to consolidate their rule in the face of several serious domestic and external challenges to their authority between 1981 and 1983.[33] (Figure 7 summarizes the workings of the religious institution prior to the 1977–79 revolution.)

Inextricably related to the religious establishment's amorphous organization under Muhammad Reza Shah was the informal foundation of its power in Iranian society at large. By the early 1940s, in the wake of Reza Shah's reforms, state and religion had already become "disembedded" (Arjomand 1981b, 1988). As a result, the ulama's influence had come to lie first and foremost in the strength of their relations with the population. These relations

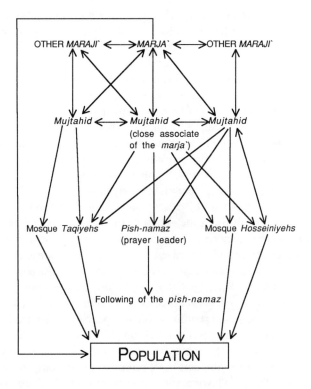

Figure 7. A Marja'‘'s Network

were fluid, and their fluctuations reflected essentially the evolution of social, economic, and political conditions in the country. This feature, for instance, explains the marked increase in the social standing of the ulama between 1941 and 1958, since large segments of the population continued to look upon activist clerics as the natural standard-bearers and defenders of the political and cultural integrity of a nation that, at the time, was suffering from recurrent foreign attempts to control its political life and economic resources (Akhavi 1980). Similarly, the enhanced status of the ulama in the population during the 1960s and 1970s flowed in part from the skill a militant faction among them showed in capitalizing on widely held grievances against the shah, in particular his perceived sellout of the country to the West. More generally, throughout the post–World War II period, the ulama derived much of their power from their ability to embody popular concerns and aspirations, present themselves as the spokesmen for the population at large, and pose as the protectors and guarantors of the integrity of an embattled nation.[34] In this respect, the continuity with the political role of the ulama in nineteenth-century Iran is unmistakable (Algar 1972, 255).

As we shift our attention from the informal channels through which the ulama continued to exercise their power under Muhammad Reza Shah to an examination of the clerics' political behavior, the ability of certain religious networks to shift their role from being system-supportive to being system-challenging is once again apparent. Until the early 1960s, at least, Muhammad Reza Shah and most of the Shiite *mujtahids* endeavored to remain on good terms with one another. Although relations deteriorated steadily afterward, only during 1978 was the possibility of an accommodation between the regime and the religious establishment definitely lost.

Throughout the 1940s and 1950s, the senior ayatollahs, and in particular Borujirdi, refrained from using the networks under their control against the state. On the contrary, they repeatedly threw their weight behind the regime. This peaceful coexistence and mutual support between the state and the clergy rested primarily on a tacit exchange between the shah and Borujirdi. On the one hand, Muhammad Reza Shah refrained from encroaching on clerical vested interests (such as control over religious endowments) and even allowed a certain revival of ulama power. For instance, he repealed the ban that his father had imposed on the pilgrimage and on passion plays held outside the confines of mosques. He also tolerated a certain involvement of the clergy in public matters, as was shown by his willingness to let prominent *mujtahids* issue religious pronouncements (*fatvas*) in favor of the nationalization of oil and on matters of public morality (Akhavi 1980, 61–63). In 1955, the Iranian monarch even went as far as tolerating the clergy's public campaign against the Bahais and persecution of them. Most important, perhaps, was the shah's display of respect for Shiism and its leaders, backed up by concrete measures such as the decision to increase the time devoted to religious instruction in secular schools and his willingness to enforce the various prohibitions associated with the month of Ramadan. The shah also repeatedly engaged in public acts intended to demonstrate his (fake or real) consideration and esteem for Borujirdi—for example, by personally paying his respects to the *marjaʿ-i mutlaq* in Qom (Mottahedeh 1985, 237).

In exchange for the shah's willingness to accommodate the clergy, Ayatollah Borujirdi provided support for the regime in more ways than one. In February 1949 he convened a large conference in Qom, during which he condemned political activism by ulama. From then on, the majority of the ulama—and virtually the entirety of the ulama elite—refrained from interfering in politics, implicitly supporting the status quo. As Mottahedeh notes, throughout Borujirdi's lifetime, and "in spite of a great deal of pressure from the [*tollab*] who were swept up in the causes of the fifties, Borujirdi kept silent on political issues and sometimes silenced those who talked too much" (Mottahedeh 1985, 237).

There were, to be sure, a few exceptions to this peaceful coexistence of the ulama and the state, particularly in the late 1940s and early 1950s. The cases of Ayatollah Burqaʿi and of those lower-ranking ulama grouped around Ayatollah Kashani already have been mentioned. In addition, between 1951 and 1953 the majority of the ulama in the Majlis (Parliament) regularly lent their support to Mossadegh. The scope and political significance of ulama activism, however, should not be exaggerated. Support for Burqaʿi remained insignificant (Akhavi 1980, 66). As for the clerical supporters of Dr. Mossadegh, many proved unreliable political allies. In fact, the fall of the Iranian prime minister in 1953 was greatly facilitated by a withdrawal of support by Kashani and like-minded clerics. Those religious networks that played a destabilizing role during the 1940s and 1950s lay for the most part outside the religious establishment, or on its periphery.[35]

Following the death of Ayatollah Borujirdi in 1961, the relationship between the regime and the religious establishment entered a period marked by greater tensions. Despite widespread and increasing ulama resentment of the shah's modernizing policies, however, most clerics, including all the grand ayatollahs except Khomeini, refrained from an open confrontation with the state. This attitude continued well into the Islamic revolution. During the early phase of political mobilization against the shah, throughout 1977 and even during the first few months of 1978, the majority of the ulama remained inactive. Even after the publication, at the instigation of the government, of an article defaming Khomeini in the leading daily *Etella'at*, in January 1978, the high ulama, including the three sources of imitation in Qom,[36] remained cautious in their attitude toward the regime: "They expressed their indignation at the article; they strongly criticized its authors. But they urged the students to protest peacefully, and they assured them they were doing what was necessary in taking up the issue with the authorities in Tehran. It was the religious students who pressed their leaders for a stronger stand" (Bakhash 1984b, 178). Throughout the spring and the summer of 1978, the senior clerics consistently tried to prevent the politicization of religious ceremonies. Although they criticized the regime, especially when it used violence to deal with demonstrators and strikers, they refrained from condemning the shah and from advocating the overthrow of the monarchy. They repeatedly appealed for calm and condemned the use of violence by protesters.[37]

By mid-1978, however, the majority of the ulama had become involved against the monarchy. Their ultimate conversion from political passivity and tolerance of the regime to active opposition to it was largely a product of three circumstantial factors: the sheer revolutionary momentum, the government's mishandling of the uprising, and the relentless pressures that Khomeini and his clerical followers exerted on the rest of the religious establishment to force it to become active in the opposition movement. As in the case of the *bazaaris,* therefore, the eventual confrontation between the ulama and the regime was far from being inevitable. Nevertheless, the mobilization of the mosque network against the state in 1978–79 was greatly facilitated by two structural trends that had been at work in Iran for at least two decades: the attempt by a modernizing state to reduce the power and the autonomy of the ulama, and moral and cultural changes in the country. In other words, the ulama's political behavior in 1978–79, like the *bazaaris'*, was shaped by a consideration of both their material interests and of broad cultural and moral issues.

Pressures on the ulama had been building up for at least five decades. Since the reforms of Reza Shah, they had lost their control over the educational and judicial systems and had been deprived of their privileged access to, and partnership with, the political elite (Arjomand 1988). In the 1960s, the land reform,[38] the creation of the Literacy Corps,[39] the local election bill,[40] the reduction of the number of *madaris* and mosques, and the growing interference by the state in the administration of religious institutions had limited even further the ulama's independence and prerogatives.[41] From the early 1970s onward, however, pressure on the ulama intensified sharply. The shah's creation of a Religious Corps (Sipah-i Din) and a group of Religious Propagandists (Muravvijin-i Din), established to spread among the Iranian masses the state's own version of Shiism, threatened to deprive the ulama of the last prerogatives they had managed to retain: their status as guardians of the faith, and their historic monopoly over the interpretation and diffusion of religion.[42] By establishing these two state-controlled agencies and assigning them many of the ideological and social service functions that traditionally had been the preserve of the ulama, the shah threatened to deal a fatal blow to the future of the religious establishment.[43] Other policies contributed to the ulama's perception of being engaged in a deadly struggle for collective survival, including the torture and assassination of two prominent clerics by SAVAK,[44] the arrest of scores of other ulama during the 1970s, the destruction of the *madaris* in Mashhad to create a green belt around the shrine, and the army's attack on the Fayziyyeh seminary in 1975 (Fischer 1980, 120–23). Fischer summed it up: "The atmosphere of Qom in 1975 was one of siege and courageous hostility to a state perceived to be the stronger, but morally corrupt, opponent" (Fischer 1980, viii).

In the end, however, the state's frontal attack against the clergy and their vested interests was perhaps less decisive than moral and cultural issues in provoking the ultimate conversion of the majority of the ulama to the revolutionary cause. By the mid-1970s, the ulama felt engaged in a desperate struggle for the survival of the last vestiges of a religious culture besieged by a state that was seen as forcing modernization and Westernization on the country. First, there was the regime's increasing downplaying of Iran's Shiite identity and its growing emphasis on the country's pre-Islamic roots and history.[45] More significantly, throughout the 1960s and 1970s the majority of the ulama became increasingly horrified by what they perceived to be the growing moral corruption and decadence produced by the shah's modernization program, and by increasing Western (especially American) influences in the country. Thus, Iran's rapid modernization in the 1960s and 1970s went hand in hand with a marked increase in petty crimes (theft, mugging, robberies, and the like) and with a rise in social problems such as suicide, alcoholism, and prostitution. Drawing on a speech made after the revolution by Ayatollah Khomeini's influential son, Ahmad, Ervand Abrahamian has suggested that it was this "moral laxity," more than any other factor, that led the majority of the clerics, who had remained silent until 1976–77, to slowly join the radical, lower clergy in its campaign against the shah.

> According to Ahmad Khomeini, what...led [the majority of] clerics to break their silence was...the shock of seeing 'moral decadence' flaunted in the streets and the double shock of finding that the authorities were unwilling, if not incapable, of cleaning up the 'social filth'. Having no channels through which they could communicate [their] grievances to the political system, they reluctantly joined the antiregime clergy to mount the final assault against the shah. (Abrahamian 1980, 26)

Revealing as well is the moral and cultural content of many of the demands put forward by the moderate, leading clerics throughout 1978. For instance, the demands addressed to the government by Mashhad clerics on 29 August 1978 included "the elimination of centers of immorality," "return to the Islamic calendar," "correspondence between the national culture, the Quran, and the ordinances of the Imams," "cabinet members to be of Shiite faith," "dismissal of Bahais from official and semiofficial positions," "all rules passed by parliament to correspond to the principles of Shiite Islam," and "the abolition of anti-Islamic laws" (Parsa 1989, 204). While these demands are more than cultural, since greater deference to religion would have entailed the restoration of the rights and prerogatives of the ulama, they nevertheless point to the clerics' concern with the preservation of traditional Shiite values and codes of behavior, especially with respect to women and members of the religious minorities.

Finally, a look at what the ulama did in the 1980s can give us some further indication of what their motives were in overthrowing the monarchy. Clearly, during its first decade, the Islamic Republic put the "moral purification" of Iranian society, the reversal of the Westernization process, and the strict enforcement of Islamic values, morality, and codes of behavior at the top of its list of policy objectives. In fact, when Khomeini died, on 3 June 1989, the Islamization of Iranian society stood as the most undeniable achievement of the regime he had created.[46]

The Iranian revolution, therefore, was to a large extent a product of the ulama's fear that whatever remained of the Islamic character of Iranian society was irremediably threatened by the spread of alien influences and moral corruption and that the shah was not willing to do anything to stem these trends. As in earlier instances when ulama-led networks became vehicles of opposition to the state, cultural and moral questions, inextricably linked to the issue of foreign influence in the country, were very prominent forces in causing religious networks to become vehicles for political mobilization against the regime.

Radical-Utopian Networks

The double-edged networks that have been examined so far differ greatly from a second category of religious networks, which I call "radical-utopian." Unlike double-edged networks, radical utopian ones *always* have a destabilizing impact on the sociopolitical system, since they essentially represent conspiracies organized by small groups of committed activists. Yet, like their double-edged counterparts, they draw much of their appeal from their ability to provide individuals poorly integrated into modern society with alternative channels for membership into a tightly knit community. To their members, these networks also constitute instruments toward the realization of a millenarian dream, and for the making of a pure religiopolitical order, in which injustice and foreign domination will have no place. These features can be found in four examples of radical-utopian networks: the radical Islamic underground in Sadat's Egypt, the Fada'iyan-i Islam in 1940s and 1950s Iran, the Khomeini network under the shah, and fundamentalist Shiite and Sunni groups in Lebanon in the 1980s.

The Islamic Radical Underground in Sadat's Egypt

The official support that Sadat gave to the *jama'at islamiyya* in the early 1970s was part of a broader strategy that involved the manipulation of religious symbols and groups in order to bolster the regime's legitimacy. By the mid-1970s, however, it was already clear that the Egyptian president could not fully control the forces that he had unleashed only a few years earlier. Radical Islamic groups began to confront the regime.[47] The following discussion emphasizes the informal organization of these networks and suggests that their success was due to their ability to offer a new sense of security to young, dislocated individuals who emerged from their experience with modern urban society feeling betrayed and unfulfilled.

Radical Islamic groups in Egypt developed out of small cells, made up of a few individuals usually grouped around a more prominent or charismatic leader referred to as *amir* (commander).[48] Such units first emerged in Nasser's prisons, among Muslim Brothers[49] influenced by the militant writings of Sayyid Qutb.[50] After Sadat began to release them from jail, in the early 1970s, former members of the Muslim Brotherhood created similar cells throughout Egypt. The loose structure of these groups, as well as the sense of brotherhood and solidarity that they provided for their members, is well expressed in some of the words used to refer to them: *usar, 'anaqid,* or *majmu'at. Usar,* as mentioned earlier, means "families." *'Anaqid* literally means "clusters"; it comes from a root that signifies a close association or embrace between two individuals, or between individuals and a doctrine or a religion. As for *majmu'at,* which in this particular instance can be translated as "groups," it comes from the same root as *jama'at,* which conveys the idea of community and togetherness.

These informally organized associations developed in an ad hoc, unplanned, and largely uncoordinated fashion. To recruit new members, they relied on religious ties, friendship, kinship, and other personal contacts. Typically the leaders began with close relatives and friends (often from prison days), and those in turn enlisted relatives and trusted friends. In the case of the Takfir wa'l-Hijra (Excommunication and Hegira),[51] the founder of the group started by gathering his first disciples and by moving from one locality to another, trying to spread the group's message and enlarge the movement by bringing handfuls of individuals into it at a time (Kepel 1985, 76). Also important in the strategy of some groups was the identification of potential recruits by observing worshipers in local mosques. Discreet contacts established in mosques located in neighborhoods where members of a given group were already well established was often one of the main channels for bringing new members into that same group.[52] Significant also of the personalized nature of the entire radical Islamic movement, the leaders of the major groups of the 1970s almost all knew and interacted with one another. As figure 8 indicates, they were mutually related through ties of kinship and friendship, and through common regional roots (Springborg 1989, 238).

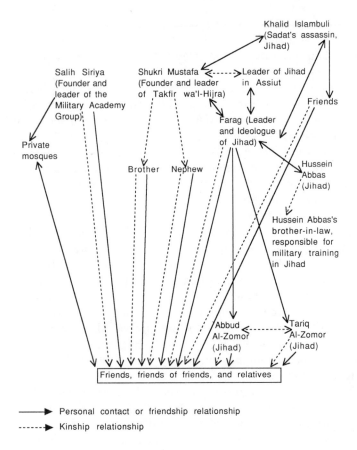

Figure 8. Some Networks in Egypt's Radical Islamic Underground in the 1970s

Derived from: Ibrahim 1982, Kepel 1985, Dekmejian 1985, Ansari 1986, Springborg 1989.

The intense personalism that sustained radical Islamic groups in their early stages did not diminish over time, and none of these groups ever evolved into an "organization" in the formal and technical sense. It is significant that Shukri Mustafa, the leader of the Takfir wa'l-Hijra, continued to insist on an oath of personal allegiance (*bay'a*) for new recruits. Similarly, even in the late 1970s, Jihad (Holy War, the group that assassinated Sadat) seems to have been little more than a label put by observers and members alike on semiautonomous and self-contained units (Dekmejian 1985, 98–99). The Cairo branch of Jihad, Kepel tells us, "was composed of five or six groups (*majmu'at*), each of which had its own *amir*. The *amirs* met weekly to work out general strategy [but] each *amir* seems to have retained some degree of autonomy" (Kepel 1985, 206).

One way to identify the forces that led to the multiplication of radical Islamic groups in Egypt is to look at the social basis of these groups. We know that, throughout the 1970s, members of radical Islamic groups were primarily young, educated, and achievement-oriented individuals (typically, university students or recent graduates in the sciences, aged twenty to twenty-five), with provincial and largely traditional backgrounds, and with poor prospects of ever finding a job commensurate with their aspirations and education.[53] These individuals usually lived in substandard housing in the newer, poor, and over-crowded districts located on the peripheries of the big cities, especially Cairo. As Kepel points out, "these people [were] marginal in every sense of the word, to begin with in their physical location in a middle ground that is no longer the countryside from which they came, but not yet the city, whose heartland they do not penetrate" (Kepel 1985, 217–18).[54]

Against this background, a credible hypothesis, advanced by several authors and touched upon earlier, is that radical Islamic groups provided young, uprooted provincials, who had failed to find a niche in the large city to which they had moved only recently, with ways to express their frustration at the system and with the social integration and sense of group membership for which they longed.[55] According to this analysis, radical Islamic groups became a source of comfort and reassurance for individuals who might otherwise have suffered from loneliness and disorientation and who, having been raised in traditional ways, were probably shocked by the consumerism and the perceived moral laxity prevailing in the megalopolis. Joining radical Islamic groups became a way for young provincials to recreate a sense of community and identity, and to lessen what Festinger called the "cognitive dissonance" between reality and the norms in which these individuals had been raised. One might even suggest that the initial force behind the development of many radical Islamic groups in Egypt was less a desire by their members to overthrow the regime, than an attempt to satisfy some vital psychosociological needs. The destabilizing functions that these networks rapidly came to assume may have been only a by-product of the ideology that held these groups together, and according to which fighting the "pagan state" was the only means to bring about an Islamic order in Egypt.

There is evidence to support these hypotheses. For instance, three concepts that all the radical Islamic ideologies of the 1970s have in common are *tawhid,* or unity (of individual and God, individual and society, and religion and state), solidarity (e.g., the need to restore the solidarity of *al-umma al-islamiyya* , the Islamic community of believers), and *shumul,* a term used to refer to the comprehensive character and integrated nature of Islam (Etienne

1987; Davis 1984). Such concepts do seem to reflect a preoccupation with social disintegration and fragmentation (Davis 1984, 146). It is also significant that Islamic militants often refer to their primary organizational unit as *al-usra*, or "the family." As Davis suggests, "By forming cells in major urban centers and in provincial capitals, Islamic groups seek to reconstruct the corporate unity of traditional rural life. The 'Islamic family' thus provides a sense of identity and protection within what is perceived to be a hostile and capricious environment" (Davis 1984, 144). Membership in radical Islamic groups, and the psychological support these groups offer, may also explain why radical Islamic militants appear not to be alienated, anomic, or mentally disturbed (Ibrahim 1982; Kepel 1985). It also may account for the fact that, during their trials, many Islamic radicals impressed observers with their calm, even relative serenity, and with the inner logic of their arguments and the strength of their convictions.

Among all the radical groups of the 1970s, the Takfir wa'l-Hijra perhaps best demonstrates that radical Islamic networks can be destabilizing at the macrolevel while fulfilling vital integrative functions at the microlevel. On the one hand, the Takfir wa'l-Hijra challenged the Egyptian state and the prevailing sociopolitical order in several respects. It first admonished its members to separate themselves, both spiritually and physically, from Egyptian society, which was condemned as having reverted to a state of unbelief (*jahiliyya*). The strategy of withdrawal made it incumbent upon the group's members to refuse conscription or employment in the bureaucracy and, more generally, to deny any form of legitimacy and allegiance to the "infidel" state.[56] More directly threatening to the authorities, however, was the group's ideology, according to which the phase of separation from society would eventually be followed, after the group had gained sufficient strength, by an assault on the state, as a prelude to the revolutionary transformation of society along Islamic lines.

While the Takfir wa'l-Hijra had a gradualist strategy, its margin for maneuver was considerably reduced after an aborted coup by another radical Islamic group, the Islamic Liberation Organization (*al-munazzamat al-tahrir al-islami*), better known as the "Military Academy" group. Following the crackdown on the Islamic Liberation Organization, the security forces began to arrest members of the Takfir wa'l-Hijra. Takfir wa'l-Hijra subsequently came into open confrontation with the regime, when its members kidnapped and later killed a former minister of religious affairs.[57] In the wake of this assassination, the government ruthlessly repressed Takfir wa'l-Hijra, executing Shukri Mustafa and five other leaders and imprisoning dozens of members.[58]

Although it eventually clashed with the regime, the Takfir wa'l-Hijra operated as a stabilizing force in the life of its own members. It provided them with membership in a much-improved society, a miniature of the perfect, genuinely Islamic society it aimed to establish. It was a world in which, for instance, in sharp contrast with the current situation in Egypt, marriage at an early age was possible, and housing was readily available.[59] Shukri Mustafa would arrange marriages between members of the group, which would then provide the new couple with a place to live. Mustafa ensured the continued supply of cash needed to finance this system by sending some of the group's male members to the Gulf countries. Upon their return to Egypt, these individuals would be provided with a bride (if they had not left one behind) and housing, and other members of the Takfir wa'l-Hijra would replace them as migrant workers to Saudi Arabia and the smaller oil-rich states (Kepel 1985, 70–102).

To a large extent, the Takfir wa'l-Hijra enabled its members to live a communal life, based on the simple and attractive ideology of a return to the "Golden Age of Islam." To segments of the youth who felt alienated, their dreams of upward social mobility smashed, and their hopes in modernity's ability to deliver destroyed, the Takfir wa'l-Hijra appeared as an attractive exit from contemporary Egyptian society and its problems. That the group provided such an escape from reality explains why the regime and many observers initially saw it, too optimistically as it turned out, as "absorbing discontent and channeling dissent in a 'positive' way" (Sivan 1985, 87).[60]

The Fada'iyan-e Islam, 1945–55

In the late 1940s and early 1950s, Iran experienced a wave of terrorist activities perpetrated by a small group known as the Fada'iyan-e Islam (often translated as "the Devotees of Islam," but literally "those who sacrifice themselves for Islam," or "the martyrs of Islam"). Although we still know more about the ideology of this group than about its internal structure and modes of operation, there is little doubt that, from the time of its creation in 1945 by a *talabeh* (seminarian) operating under the pseudonym of Navvab Safavi,[61] until its banning by the government in November 1955, the Devotees of Islam never developed into an organization, but instead remained an informally organized brotherhood of fanatical Shiite activists bound to one another by intensely personal ties (Kazemi 1984, 169).

> The [Fada'iyan's] organizational set-up...consisted of a series of horizontally connected cells....New members were entrusted to the care of a more senior one, who was responsible for testing them and before long assigning them to specific tasks, which varied according to each member's abilities. The most common one was observation—keeping an eye on one's friends, relatives and

neighbors to make sure that they did not transgress the rules of Islam. A woman who did not wear the veil would be admonished. A young man who liked drinking beer would be encouraged to return to the right path. Evil-doers in the neighborhood would be identified and exposed, so that believers would ostracize them. Shops belonging to non-Muslims would be marked and boycotted. But above all, a new member had to attend as many religious ceremonies as possible; he had to be seen to be an exemplary Muslim. (Taheri 1987, 59–60)

A central characteristic of the Fada'iyan was its ability to combine highly disruptive activities, at the level of society as a whole, with a vital integrative and supportive role with respect to its own members. To be sure, it is the Devotees of Islam's actions as a terrorist group that have received the most attention from scholars. And there is no denying that the Fada'iyan, who advocated the physical elimination of "the enemies of Islam," engaged in numerous acts of violence between 1945 and 1955. Secular politicians and writers were favorite targets of the group. In less than a decade, the Fada'iyan assassinated more than a dozen individuals, among them a prominent anti-clerical historian,[62] two prime ministers,[63] and a former education minister and president of the Tehran University law faculty.[64] Fada'iyan members also engineered assassination attempts against the shah, Mossadegh, Hossein Fatemi (a well-known Tehran publisher, parliamentarian, and former deputy prime minister under Mossadegh), prime minister Hossein Ala,[65] Tehran's military governor, and other high officials. Through these and similar actions, the Devotees of Islam succeeded in creating a climate of political terror and in frightening secular intellectuals and politicians.

The Fada'iyan, however, was more than simply a "terrorist" society, as some have labeled it. To understand the social and psychological needs the group also answered, one has to remember the general sociopolitical context in which it emerged. In the late 1940s and early 1950s, Iran experienced an economic recession, considerable political turmoil, and the repeated interference of outside powers in its internal affairs. The country was in the midst of rapid socioeconomic and political change. Traditional norms, values, and patterns of behavior were being eroded. Prominent among those affected by these developments were the illiterate or semiliterate lower echelons of the bazaar. These small shopkeepers, store attendants, apprentices, footboys, and peddlers are those most immediately and directly hurt by economic crises, and they tend to be somewhat parochial, suspicious of the outside world, concerned with moral and cultural norms, and traditional in their interpretation of Islam. It is not surprising that they also constituted the rank and file of the

Fadaʿiyan, whose ideology emphasized the need to uphold Islamic standards of morality and to fight the rampant "moral corruption" brought about by modernization and the "excessive" presence of foreigners in Iran.[66] Significant of the Fadaʿiyan's religious traditionalism and of their preoccupation with moral and cultural decay is the four-point program that they are said to have submitted to Mossadegh at the very beginning of his tenure as prime minister. This program involved "(1) making veiling mandatory, (2) dismissing female employees from government offices, (3) banning alcohol, and (4) making participation in congregational prayers mandatory for all government employees" (Yazdi 1990, 299).

Thus, the Fadaʿiyan's violence can be seen as a desperate attempt to fight what its members perceived to be the "impure" forces of modernity and of the "infidel" West, which were making rapid headway in Iran's largest urban centers,[67] and which were threatening to create a world in which there would no longer be any room for the values and ways of life associated with lower- and lower-middle-class *bazaaris*. As a temporary substitute for the establishment of an Islamic order in Iran, which was the Fadaʿiyan's ultimate goal, the Devotees of Islam also provided membership in a tightly knit community of individuals who shared the same outlook on life and the same firm belief that a return to the "Golden Age of Islam" represented the only chance of personal and collective survival. To tradition-minded youth in the urban lower classes, who were the Devotees of Islam's primary constituency, the Fadaʿiyan's ideology was attractive mainly because it was easy to understand and consonant with a traditional upbringing and deeply held religious values, and because it most directly addressed their concerns and aspirations, which were primarily cultural and moral. At a time when many lower-class *bazaaris* felt their lives to be increasingly beset by disorder and by material and psychic insecurity, the Fadaʿiyan's ideology seemed to hold the promise of restoring the perceived coherence of the past.

Hindsight suggests that three factors allowed the Devotees of Islam to play in the late 1940s and early 1950s a role disproportionate to their numerical strength[68]: the group's willingness to use violence, its alliance with Ayatollah Kashani,[69] and the weakness of the state. In April 1951, however, Kashani broke with the Fadaʿiyan, and the government finally cracked down on the group. Two months later, the Fadaʿiyan's top leaders, including Safavi, were under arrest (Kazemi 1984, 165). Most of them, and Safavi himself, were subsequently executed, and the Fadaʿiyan was officially banned in November 1955 after the abortive attempt on Prime Minister Hosein Ala's life. The Iranian population at large watched the crushing of the Fadaʿiyan by the state with feelings ranging from indifference to satisfaction.

By the mid-1950s, the group had been virtually destroyed, although some of its more junior members succeeded in escaping police detection and reportedly continued to operate underground (Kazemi 1984, 166). That these individuals may have succeeded in keeping the flame alive is indicated by the activities of the shadowy Hezb-e Millal-e Islami (literally, "Islamic Nations Party," but once again closer to a violent underground brotherhood than a terrorist organization in the formal and technical sense). Some of the members of this new group, which was responsible for the assassination of Prime Minister Hassan Ali Mansur in 1965, may well have been former members of the Fadaʿiyan, and there may even have been other links between the Fadaʿiyan and the Hezb-e Millal-e Islami that have not yet been identified (Kazemi 1984, 167). One should also remember that when the Islamic Republic was established, some of its most influential leaders claimed to have been longtime members of the Fadaʿiyan,[70] and that various groups appeared, posing as the heirs of the movement.[71] Sources published in Iran after the revolution suggest that Khomeini himself might have maintained close ties with former members of the Devotees of Islam, well after the group's repression by the state. In the absence of definite evidence, it is hard to assess either the validity of such claims or the extent to which the Fadaʿiyan survived the authorities' crackdown on it. What seems clear, however, is that whether or not the Fadaʿiyan network was really destroyed in the mid-1950s, individuals who might or might not have been former members of the Fadaʿiyan, but who were in either case committed to the group's objectives and methods, used the Fadaʿiyan label to give both legitimacy and meaning to their actions.

The Khomeini Network, 1961–79

In the 1960s, Khomeini picked up where the Fadaʿiyan left off. Throughout Borujirdi's tenure as *marjaʿ-i mutlaq*, no prominent cleric, including Khomeini, had dared come out openly against Muhammad Reza Shah. Borujirdi's death and the shah's reforms of the early 1960s offered Khomeini a golden opportunity to speak out against the government. Then one of several leading ayatollahs, but by no means the most prominent, Khomeini began to gather around himself a group of dedicated former students who shared in his criticism of the erosion of the place of religion and clerics in Iranian society. It was this incipient network that led the short-lived but violent uprising that, in June 1963, shook several major Iranian cities, including Tehran, Qom, Isfahan, Mashhad, and Shiraz.

A look at the declarations of Khomeini around this period, from his attack against the Local Councils Law (1962) to his denunciation of the Status of Forces Agreement (1964), makes it clear that broad moral and cultural issues were what mattered most to him and his followers.[72] More specifically, Khomeini was most concerned about three interrelated sets of problems.

The first was what he saw as the "moral corruption" and "cultural decay" generated by the shah's policies (Tabari 1983). In order to counter these trends, he emphasized the necessity of restoring the subordinate place that Shiism assigns to women and minorities in an Islamic society. He also stressed the need to uphold Islamic codes of dress and behavior in public—repeatedly lashing out against the "decadent" lifestyle and public behavior of the Westernized classes.

A second of Khomeini's major grievances was the regime's perceived subservience to the United States and Israel. He thought this subservience to be so pronounced as to imply the shah's complicity in a foreign plot, presided over by the U.S. and Israeli governments, the Jews, and the Bahais, acting in Iran as agents of the Jews and Israel (Bakhash 1990, 26–30). Khomeini was particularly incensed by the 1964 decision to offer full diplomatic immunity to American military personnel and their dependents in Iran—significantly known in Iran as the "Capitulations Agreement"—which he saw as a sellout to the United States and an insult to Iran's dignity (Bill 1988, 156–60). It was, in fact, his scathing denunciation of the regime for having accepted such a major abandonment of sovereignty that convinced the shah to exile the ayatollah.

The third major source of Khomeini's bitterness at the regime was the shah's deliberate effort to curb the social role and standing of the clergy through his secularizing and modernizing policies (Tabari 1983, 68). Khomeini was also deeply offended by the shah's repeated insults and public humiliation of the ulama, as when the Iranian monarch portrayed the clerical opposition to his "White Revolution" as the "black reaction," or when he referred to the clerics as "the lice-ridden mollas," and to the ulama and the religious students as "parasites."[73]

As such grievances make clear, Khomeini and the militant ulama grouped around him were primarily concerned with the preservation of the cultural and moral foundations of the traditional order. They wanted first and foremost to preserve the Islamic character of Iranian society, under a state that would publicly acknowledge the contribution of clerics and religion to a healthy society and try to uphold the social status of the ulama as the official guardians of the Shiite traditions (Tabari 1983; Floor 1983). This does not mean that material interests had no bearing on the militant clerics' political behavior. Clearly, when Khomeini was grieving the deterioration of the social prestige of the ulama and looked back with nostalgia to the days when rulers heeded the clergy's advice, he also mourned the clergy's lost prerogatives and sociopolitical power. Nevertheless, as Tabari has shown, it is significant of the primacy of cultural and moral determinants that Khomeini neither protested nor agitated against the land reform or the first phases of its implementation (even though other clerics did, including grand ayatollahs Marashi Najafi, Golpayegani, and Khonsari). Had Khomeini and his closest associates been motivated primarily by the material interests of the clergy, then the land reform should have been the focus of their criticism of government policies (since religious endowments were to be subject to the reform). By contrast, when the issue of women's suffrage and the right of minorities to run for office came up through the local election bill, Khomeini's negative reaction was immediate (Tabari 1983, 66–67).

In the wake of the ulama-led June 1963 uprising, many of Khomeini's followers kept in close contact with one another by participating in small clandestine associations known as Hay'at-e Mo'talefeh-ye Islami, or "unified Islamic groups."[74] These associations, whose functioning might have been overseen by Khomeini himself, are said, for instance, to have provided the infrastructure for the distribution, in Tehran and Isfahan, of some forty thousand pamphlets containing Khomeini's denunciation of the Status of Forces Agreement in 1964. There might also have been links between the Hay'at-e Mo'talefeh-ye Islami, former members of the Fada'iyan, and the Hezb-e Millal-e Islami (Mozaffari 1988, 91-95). Thus, clandestine groups broadly sympathetic to Khomeini's message remained active in the few years immediately following the 1963 uprising. While these groups were by and large dismantled after 1965, activities by pro-Khomeini forces did not stop. From then on, however, they were carried out by limited if dedicated circles of ulama faithful to Khomeini's cause and working largely independently from one another at the local level. It is these networks that deserve our attention.

The June 1963 uprising increased the determination of Khomeini's supporters and brought new recruits, especially from among the newer generation of ulama and religious students, to the incipient Khomeini network (Milani 1988, 98). After the shah sent him into exile, in 1964, "Khomeini left behind clerics in Tehran, Qom, and other provincial cities who were either committed to him personally or who broadly shared his political aims" (Bakhash 1990, 40). The overwhelming majority were middle-rank ulama (*hojjat-i Islam* level). Some taught in the seminaries, particularly in Qom. Many, in any event, were from among the ten thousand or so seminary students whom Khomeini is estimated to have taught during the forty years he lived in Qom. It is out of this core group that emerged not only the central core of Khomeini's post-1964 network, but also many of the key leaders of the Islamic Republic in the 1980s.[75]

In the 1960s and early 1970s, the social base of the Khomeini network remained very limited, lying primarily in the largest urban centers, especially Qom, among *tollab* and segments of the lower and middle echelons of the bazaar. Within the religious establishment itself, the militant ulama were still isolated and scorned as "political clerics"—a pejorative label used against them (Ashraf 1990, 120). Throughout the 1960s and 1970s, the grand ayatollahs remained distrustful of Khomeini and reluctant to become involved in politics. After Khomeini developed his theory of the *vilayat-i faqih* in a series of lectures given at Najaf in 1971, the overwhelming majority of the prominent ayatollahs went out of their way to dissociate themselves from his militant views on Islam and on the leading role that Shiite clerics should play in politics and government. Most of the theology teachers in religious schools and seminaries also continued to oppose Khomeini (Ashraf and Banuazizi 1985, 26).

Despite its isolation, the Khomeini network was able to survive, largely because of the intensely personal commitments uniting Khomeini and his followers. Khomeini supporters in Iran, spread throughout the country, remained in communication with each other even though they continued to operate independently. They made a deliberate effort to travel widely inside Iran in order to broaden their networks (Parsa 1989, 205). Through their preaching in Tehran, provincial cities, and smaller towns, militant clerics kept Khomeini's name and ideas alive in Iran (even though Khomeini's popularity remained very limited until 1977). While constrained by their vulnerability to government repression, these clerics missed few opportunities to voice their grievances against the regime and capitalize on the population's growing alienation from the state. Their criticisms continued to focus on issues of public morality, corruption involving individuals related to the regime, the destruction of indigenous Shiite values by foreign influences, and the shah's "selling out" of the country to foreign (particularly U.S.) interests.

Predictably, many of these pro-Khomeini clerics were arrested. Some died in prison, which increased their fame and gave them an aura of "martyrs in the path of Islam." Others were sent to remote localities. Ironically, as Shaul Bakhash has noted, "exile to isolated provincial towns only allowed these clerics to spread their teaching further afield. The 1970s found Mahdavi-Kani teaching and preaching in Bukan; Ali Khamane'i in Iranshahr; Montazeri in Tabas, Khalkhal, and Saqqez; [and] Ali Tehrani in Saqqez" (Bakhash 1990, 43). All these individuals would subsequently occupy leading positions in the Islamic Republic.

From his exile in the Iraqi city of Najaf in 1965–78, Khomeini continued to expand the circle of his students and disciples through his teaching and scholarship. Meanwhile, he built very valuable lines of communication with Iran and other parts of the Shiite world, especially southern Lebanon, by receiving pilgrims, visitors to the holy shrines, and devoted followers (Algar 1972, 249). As *marja'-i taqlid*, Khomeini also continued to be entitled to his *sahm-i Imam*, which, according to Bakhash, was collected by Khomeini loyalists throughout Iran and then forwarded to Khomeini's brother, Morteza Pasandideh, in Qom (Bakhash 1990, 40).[76] These very substantial financial resources enabled him to spread his ideas, fund opposition movements, and support his followers. Finally, the ayatollah also remained in close contact with religiously committed intellectuals opposed to the shah, such as Bazargan and his Freedom Movement associates, who provided him with a link to the new middle class. Beginning in the early 1970s, Khomeini also intensified and solidified his contacts with activist Iranian student leaders in Europe and the United States, including Bani-Sadr and Shamran, who eventually became, respectively, the first president and the first minister of defense of the Islamic Republic.[77]

When, in 1976–77, Khomeini decided that the conditions were ripe for a confrontation with the regime, the Khomeini network was ready to be activated. A tightly knit group of militant clerics around Ayatollah Mottahari, acting in Tehran as the representative of Khomeini (who sent his directives from Najaf and then Paris), played a key role in the initial phase of the revolution (Taheri 1986). As revolutionary activities gathered momentum, the Khomeini network fulfilled three key functions.

First, it constantly encouraged the movement and widened it. Militant ulama played a critical role in spreading unrest and insurrections throughout the provincial towns. Typically, a local cleric or nonclerical political activist would arouse crowds in a village or small town. Confrontations with the security forces would ensue and increase support for the movement. Demonstrations and clashes would then spread to other localities and eventually to the provincial center or other large cities. Throughout 1978, many radical ulama moved almost incessantly from one village or town to another, preaching and trying to muster support for the revolutionary movement (Bakhash 1984b).

Second, Khomeini's clerical followers persistently attempted to force the hand of the high ulama, arguing that compromise and moderation were self-defeating strategies. Such pressures from the radical clerics played a decisive role, given the overwhelming evidence to show the unwillingness of most of the senior ulama to become involved against the regime. Eventually, the militant ulama succeeded in convincing the clerical establishment to side against the monarchy, which in turn was critical to the success of the revolution because it made the resources of the religious institution as a whole available to Khomeini and his associates.

Finally, and most importantly, the Khomeini network gave shape and meaning to a spontaneous and highly decentralized movement whose only purpose initially was to provide Iranians from all walks of life with an opportunity to vent their long-accumulated anger at the regime and the person of the shah. Progressively, the Khomeini network helped weave together scores of locally based uprisings into a national insurrection (Bakhash 1984b). In this context, Khomeini's greatest contribution to the revolution was to provide it with a charismatic leader around whom many of the networks described earlier coalesced. Thus, the revolutionary coalition of 1977–79 can be conceptualized as a series of interlocking networks that, combined, provided much of the "organizational" backbone of a mass movement. The key network was that of the radical clerics. Revolving around it, however, were other informal groups and alliances that came to play an essential role in the mobilization of the population: bazaar-centered associations, the religious circles of the intelligentsia, the ulama-intelligentsia networks, and, from the fall of 1978 onward, the multiplicity of networks organized around the religious institution as a whole. While it is clear that the revolution was carried out primarily by these networks, precisely how each of them operated and how coordination among them was effected is not yet known.

Eventually, the coming together of the Khomeini network and the state apparatus strengthened them both. On the one hand, shared control of the government, and the experience of facing together the challenge posed by the domestic opposition and the war with Iraq, created new common interests and enhanced group feelings among members of the Khomeini network. On the other hand, the strong ideological and personal ties between former students and associates of Khomeini made coordination and centralization of power easier to achieve, after these individuals were catapulted from secondary religious positions in Iran's provincial cities and towns to key government positions in the capital. Similar backgrounds, shared prison experiences, and close and long-standing personal ties among radical clerics, for instance, meant that these clerics were "well aware of one another's personality traits, private weaknesses, ambitions, and ties to trusted colleagues...[which gave] key members of the network ample opportunity for developing various mechanisms for self-preservation and at the same time [made] personal or factional rivalries among them more manageable" (Schahgaldian 1989, 26).

Religious Networks in the Lebanese Sunni and Shiite Communities in the 1980s

Khomeini's network was transnational, as are all those controlled by *mujtahids* who attended the religious academies of Najaf and Qom. For several centuries before the Iranian revolution, ties to former teachers, friendship, kinship, and shared seminary experiences had connected Shiite clerics in Iran, southern Iraq, and southern Lebanon. After the establishment of the Islamic Republic, these networks were activated in an attempt to export

Khomeini's brand of Shiite fundamentalism to targeted areas of the Arab world. One manifestation of this phenomenon was the creation in late 1982 of the "Party of God," or Hizballah , in Lebanon.

In many respects, the Baathist takeover in Iraq in July 1968 had paved the way for the emergence of Hizballah. In the early 1970s, concerned with the militancy of some leading ulama in Najaf and with the possible spread of radical Shiite ideas, the Baathist regime began to deport scores of foreign clerics living in Najaf, some of whom had been affiliated with the underground Shiite party al-Daʿwa. As a result, several dozens of Lebanese Shiite clerics, many of whom had studied under the activist ayatollahs Muhsin al-Hakim and Muhammad Baqir al-Sadr, returned to Lebanon. There, in an effort to propagate the views in which they had been indoctrinated, some of them created Shiite educational centers modeled after the religious academies of Najaf. These religious institutions came to complement the work that had been launched a few years earlier by Muhammad Hussein Fadlallah, a then little-known *mujtahid*. In 1966, Fadlallah, a graduate from the academy of Najaf, returned to his parents' ancestral home, Lebanon, where he settled in al-Nabʿa, a quarter of East Beirut inhabited predominantly by recent Shiite migrants from the south and the Bekaa.[78] To provide support for these urban poor, Fadlallah established a variety of philanthropic associations combining religious instruction and the dispensing of welfare and relief services (Shapira 1988, 116–17).

Against this background, when Hizballah was created under the sponsorship of a contingent of Iranian Revolutionary Guards sent to the Bekaa in 1982, there already existed a rudimentary infrastructure of loosely connected Shiite militant clerics and institutions around which Hizballah could be organized. What needs to be emphasized here is the loose structure and intense personalism that characterized Hizballah, in its early stages at least.

Although, as the 1980s wore on, Hizballah became increasingly organized—primarily at the instigation of its Iranian patrons, who wanted to make it easier for Tehran to control the movement—Hizballah never became a party in any conventional sense. For instance, it never issued membership cards. The "members" of Hizballah remained merely those who identified with the general philosophy of the movement, those who, as a calling and a way of life, chose to "support God."[79] A Hizballah leader put it succinctly: "Every Muslim is automatically a member of Hizballah, thus it is impossible to list our membership" (Kramer 1990, 133–34). For the more doctrinaire "members" and Iranian sponsors of Hizballah, in fact, there were only two "parties" in Lebanon in the 1980s: the Party of God and the Devil's Party (Kramer 1990, 133).

The informal structure of Hizballah is also reflected in the fact that the movement was not divided into branches and offices with specific responsibilities. In the mid-1980s, "members of the Party of Allah [were] free to organize themselves in whatever way they deem[ed] best. Some [were] members of circles that [would meet] once or twice a week for Quranic studies and discussions. Others [would] create clandestine terrorist cells to eliminate the enemies of the faith. Still others belong[ed] to fairly large militia groups" (Taheri 1987, 122). Even Fadlallah denied being Hizballah's leader, a denial that can only be understood against "historical forms of *Usuli* Shiism which make a 'party' an oddity....Fadlallah [did] not need Hizballah, because a close association with this or any other party means formally a reduction of his followers by as many *muqallids* who do not adhere to a party" (Mallat 1988, 27–28).

Throughout the 1980s, the primary "organizational" infrastructure of Hizballah remained the personal followings of individual shaykhs, the mosques, and the network of Hosseiniyehs and Quranic study circles that militant clerics influenced by Iran developed in Lebanon in the late 1970s and early 1980s (Pintak 1988, 255). Even as late as 1990, Hizballah was still essentially an umbrella for various groups, most of which antedated Hizballah, but became part of it in 1982–83. These groups included al-Jihad al-Islami (Islamic Jihad), al-Amal al-Islami (Islamic Amal), Tajammuʿ al-ʿUlamaʾ al-Muslimin (the Rally of Muslim Clergymen),[80] al-Daʿwa al-Islamiyya (the Islamic Call, which had been created in the early 1970s as a branch of the Iraqi movement bearing the same name), and the Association of Muslim Students.[81] Despite their loose association under the Hizballah label, each of these groups remained eager to preserve its autonomy—a feature that largely reflects the concern of individual clerics not to undermine their power base by merging the followings they controlled into a larger organization.

Hizballah's intense personalism is yet another characteristic that made it closer to a network than an organization in the usual sense. Even though the movement eventually developed its own newspaper and radio station, it initially spread through personal contacts. In a few instances, as in the case of the extended Musawi family, kinship and clannish ties were primary channels for recruitment into the movement. In general, however, especially in the larger urban centers, Shiite clerics inspired by the Iranian revolution would bring their respective circles of disciples into Hizballah. These clerics themselves would usually recognize the authority and follow the religious pronouncements of clerics senior to them (Kramer 1990, 134). The most prominent Lebanese *mujtahids*, in turn, had ties to Iraqi and Iranian clerics, whom they often had met in the hallways and courts of the Najaf seminaries. They also tended to recognize the spiritual authority of Fadlallah, who himself, until Khomeini's death in 1989, was heavily influenced by the rulings and opinions of the "Supreme Guide" in Tehran. Fadlallah's own charisma and the appeal of his sermons and writings were a major factor in drawing many individuals to Hizballah. Those who considered themselves members of Hizballah were often only those who identified with Fadlallah's line (Taheri 1987, 122).

The same personalism applied to lower-ranking ulama operating at the local level under the Hizballah umbrella. These clerics' role was often limited to providing broad spiritual guidance, and legitimation of acts of violence. The loose nature of their authority over their followers is reflected in the fact that they may not even have known in advance of some of the suicidal bombings and kidnappings committed by their followers. As Kramer points out in his description of many of the Hizballah cells in the suburbs of Beirut and in South Lebanon,

> what Najaf's alumni have done is essentially to replicate the structure of religious authority that characterizes the Shiite academy. The relationship of master to disciple, of the initiated to the novice, has been reproduced in many Najafs—in Qom, Tehran, South Beirut, South Lebanon, and wherever there are activist ulama. They teach, preach, and indoctrinate the same set of ideas that so influenced them in Najaf, recreating with their followers the same bonds of absolute spiritual dependence that tied them to their own teachers. In this manner, they have built dedicated followings. What are often called Shiite extremist or terrorist 'organizations' are in fact men of religion in the circle of their disciples. It is the disciples, fired by the vision elaborated by the man of religion, who take action, with the certain acquiescence and possible foreknowledge of their inspirational leader. Some of these radical circles are quite small, but a few have grown to such size that the contact between the man of religion and the disciple is mediated by lesser clerics and functionaries. (Kramer 1987, 45)

The lack of formal structure and the intense personalism that have been shown to be characteristic of Hizballah are qualities that were shared in the 1980s by a variety of smaller and less known religiopolitical groups, both in the Shiite and in the Sunni communities. These groups, too, tended to be based in particular localities or neighborhoods and to be led by young, charismatic religious leaders (often referred to by the word *amir*), who would organize and arm their followers to spread their radical understanding of the faith.[82] Unofficial spokesmen for these groups, too, were often busy repudiating the label of "party" to describe their movement, insisting that the notion of a party is foreign and even antithetical to Islam, since it implies divisions in the community of the faithful. These groups did not have central committees, head offices, and secretariats. Their name, like Hizballah's, was often little

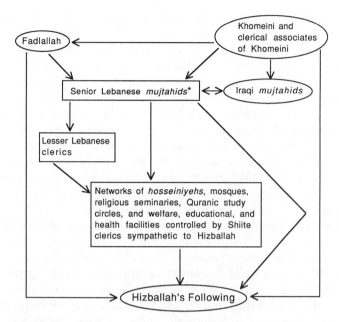

Figure 9. Organization of Hizballah (Lebanon) in the 1980s

*This group would include Abbas al-Musawi, Subhi al-Tufayli, Muhammad Yazbek, Ibrahim al-Amin, Ismail al-Khaliq, and Hassan Nasrallah. All of these men graduated from the religious academies of Najaf and/or Qom in the 1960s or 1970s.
Arrows indicate means of influence, not lines of authority.
Derived from: Taheri 1987; Kramer 1987, 1990; Shapira 1988; Mallat 1988.

more than a label that followers and observers alike would invoke to account for specific acts (often of violence) by "members" of the group. Belonging to such groups did not imply membership in a tightly organized, structured, and disciplined organization, endowed with written statuses regulating the operation of each of the group's branches. It did not even always need to involve participation in the group's meetings. Rather, it implied a state of mind, a general affinity with the group's ideology—or rather the ideology that is ascribed to the group, whether or not the group really exists—and a propensity to follow the pronouncements of the religious "leader" of the group. As one of the leaders of Amal once replied when asked about the Shiite radical groups of the late 1980s in Lebanon: "I have all the intelligence resources of our organization at my disposal. I know the [religious leaders], I have an extensive network of contacts, relatives, and acquaintances to draw on, and even I have no idea who some of these groups are" (quoted in Pintak 1988, 9–10).

Such loosely connected cells—not formally organized entities—became the mediating structures of Islamic fundamentalism in Lebanon in the 1980s, and their proliferation was largely responsible for the high degree of fluidity in Lebanon's Muslim community at the time. Members would shift from one group to another with considerable ease, depending on political conditions, on the changing charismatic and ideological appeal of the clerics heading these groups, and on which groups happened to benefit most from financial and organizational support from foreign governments. Groups that had just merged with one another would suddenly fragment again, and their constituent cells would begin to fight with one another.[83] Not only were alliances between groups short-lived, but the groups themselves were the objects of frequent fissions, fusions, disappearances, and re-formations. "The joke about the left-leaning, Israeli-backed, pro-Syrian, Islamic fundamentalist Christian militiaman was only just beyond the realm of the possible" (Pintak 1988, 9). Thus, the Lebanese Muslim community of the 1980s reminds one of Geertz's description of North African reality as "an ad hoc constellation of miniature systems of power, a cloud of unstable micropolitics, which compete, ally, gather strength, and, very soon overextended, fragment again" (Geertz 1971, 20). Sectarian affiliations, in this context, had ceased to provide a perspective from which one could understand the ongoing turmoil. As Norton notes, "The confessional labels, while certainly not devoid of political meaning, tend to obscure underlying bases for social solidarity which are much more personal, intimate, and impenetrable. The result is an unstable pattern of social fragmentation that divides and subdivides the sect. In this setting, there is a fluid or ephemeral quality to political affiliations" (1988, 44).

Thus, the evolution of the Lebanese Sunni and Shiite communities in the 1980s provides yet another illustration of the wide popular appeal that radical-utopian religious networks can exert, especially at times of societal crisis and social disintegration. As in Iran in the 1970s, small, intensely personal groups based on religious ties and loyalties proved to be highly effective ways of channeling people's energies in destabilizing political activities. In fact, these groups proved much more successful in generating a social movement endowed with a large popular base and with a radical program of social change than any of the secular, self-professed "revolutionary" political parties that appeared in Lebanese politics throughout the 1940s–1970s period. They, especially Hizballah, were able to inflict substantial setbacks to the better organized Amal militia, the Syrian forces in Lebanon, and the Israeli-backed South Lebanon Army. Most significantly, through their suicide bombings and constant harassment, they were able to force the Israeli and multinational forces out of Lebanon—a remarkable achievement if one considers the discrepancy between the resources of Hizballah and those of the Israeli and American governments (Kramer 1990).

As we turn to an examination of the conditions that facilitated the development of the Lebanese networks that have been examined, three factors deserve particular attention. One, the success of the Iranian revolution, was external. Without the logistic, financial, organizational, and military support of the Iranian government, Hizballah could neither have recruited so many members nor been as effective. While Hizballah's religious ideology did galvanize individuals, just as decisive in convincing many to join were the stipends that Hizballah militiamen received and the pensions dispensed by the movement's leaders to the families of those "martyred in the path of God" (Norton 1987, 102). In addition, monetary grants from Iran provided for the improvement or expansion of educational, welfare, and health facilities (religious and vocational schools and institutes, clinics, hospitals, orphanages, etc.), which also contributed greatly to the popularity of the movement and to its ability to expand so rapidly (Shapira 1988).

The second factor that paved the way for the sudden mushrooming of religiopolitical groups was the growing foreign involvement in the internal affairs of Lebanon. The Israeli invasion of Lebanon in the summer of 1982, and the subsequent assignment of a "multinational" (in fact, Western) peacekeeping force to Beirut, were important milestones. Indeed, the perceived encroachment of "Zionist" and "imperialist" forces radicalized large numbers of Lebanese Muslims and led them to join small fundamentalist movements, whose fiery rhetoric and militancy provided both an outlet for long-accumulated frustrations and suffering and a blueprint for fighting "the infidels." For many Sunni fundamentalist movements in the north, the Syrian presence in the Bekaa and around Tripoli was also crucial. In this context, militant clerics, especially among the Shiites, could rationalize violence, presenting it as a religious duty and as an act of self-defense to free Lebanon from "perverting" alien influences and foreign attempts to dominate the country (Kramer 1990).

Finally, the success of religiopolitical networks was also due to their ability to reintegrate into a new community individuals who for so many years had been displaced, dispossessed, and victimized. Through their activities, these groups provided traumatized and uprooted populations with a measure of empowerment and an added sense of self-respect, pride, and superiority—especially toward the West.[84] They also offered a bright vision of the future—the hope that, in the pure Islamic polity that they were working to bring about, Lebanon would be freed of Christian domination and foreign interferences, and that war and chaos would give way to peace and justice for all. In this respect, at least, these groups resemble the radical Islamic cells in Sadat's Egypt or the Fada'iyan under the shah: While having an undeniably destabilizing effect on the larger political system, they nevertheless acted as social and psychological stabilizers in the lives of their own members.

When looking at radical-utopian networks, therefore, the observer is faced less with "terrorist organizations," as these networks are often mistakenly called, than with secret brotherhoods of individuals brought and kept together by intensely personal ties and by an unfailing devotion to a militant, fundamentalist version of Islam. Accordingly, the overt hostility that members of such groups express toward the political system and their surrounding environment is mirrored only by the equally high degree of solidarity and sense of community they feel among themselves. Therefore, not only do radical-utopian groups offer their members an opportunity to fight for the "re-creation" of an Islamic order, but, pending the advent of this ideal society, they also give alienated individuals a chance to experience membership in microcommunities that provide a refuge from the perceived chaos and incoherence of life. In all these groups, the very same ideology that encourages and legitimizes violent actions toward the outside world is also that which binds the group's members so closely to one another. This phenomenon is strongly reminiscent of a characteristic feature of the traditional Middle Eastern city: the existence of strong, narrowly based *'asabiyat* which encourage solidarity at the group level and yet provide for a high degree of factionalism at the level of the city and the political system as a whole.

Conclusion

As we complete our journey into the social and political life of several Middle Eastern cities over several centuries, it is time to summarize this study's main implications, which can be grouped under five separate headings:

1. The changing features of urban networks in the Middle East and their continuing relevance to the region's politics

2. The ability of these groups to function as effective vehicles for collective resistance to the authorities

3. The conditions under which informal networks can change their role from being system-supportive to being system-challenging

4. The independent impact of Islam on contemporary forms of urban violence in the Middle East

5. The relationship between rapid urbanization and political unrest.

1. Middle Eastern Urban Informal Networks in Historical Perspective

In the twentieth century, and especially since World War II, one of the most important changes in the role played by informal networks in Middle Eastern urban politics has been the end of these networks' ability to operate as the main links binding the elite to the masses. As long as cities remained of modest size, and as long as the population in them was not too politicized, networks based on patronage, religion, and residential, kinship, or occupational ties could compensate for the weakness of formal institutions and provide for social and political order. The late-twentieth-century urban landscape, however, constitutes a radically different environment. Over the last forty years especially, the ever-increasing size of Middle Eastern cities, and the complexity and magnitude of the infrastructural, economic, political, and social problems arising in their midst, have made the political management of these cities much more difficult. Furthermore, late-twentieth-century cities are becoming increasingly politicized. In the cities one finds the most politically conscious and vocal strata in society—intelligentsia, students, industrial workers—and large reservoirs of groups that usually are not politically active but may, in times of crisis, become involved in destabilizing political activities: the slum and shanty-town dwellers and the populations of the lower-income, inner-city quarters. In the cities, too, Middle Easterners are most easily exposed to the problems that beset their societies, including cultural alienation, economic crisis, the gaps between the haves and the have-nots, and the stifling atmosphere generated by repressive regimes.

In this context, one better understands why it is dangerous for any government to rely on informal contacts and networks as the main instruments of political management—a strategy that in most countries no longer constitutes an option anyway. Thus, drawing on Albert Hourani's work, this study suggested that one of the flaws of what for long passed as "the Lebanese model" was precisely to believe that a modern city (admittedly in a particularly volatile environment) could be managed essentially as in the past, by relying on informal ties, networks, and loyalties. Along similar lines, chapter 9 underlined the futility of the shah's belated and desperate attempt to mobilize support for his regime by hiring *chaqu-kashan* in the last days of 1978. Largely because of Tehran's phenomenal growth in the 1960s and 1970s, the monarchy could no longer be saved, as it had been in 1953, by relying on professional mob leaders. To maintain political control over their cities in the late twentieth-century, Middle Eastern governments have no choice but to engage in institution building, à la Samuel Huntington (1968). Political chaos may well be the only alternative to the institutionalization of power.

However, the fact that informal networks no longer are sufficient to bind elite and masses does not mean that they have become irrelevant to Middle Eastern politics. On the contrary, it was established in the preceding chapters that the particular forms that networks assume, and their relations to the central authorities, often exert a major influence on political outcomes. It was shown, for instance, that a focus on informal networks enables one to better understand processes as varied as the Iranian revolution and its aftermath, the breakdown of political order in Beirut in 1975 and the civil war that followed it, or the survival of political order despite the accumulation of staggering socioeconomic and infrastructural problems in a city such as Cairo. More generally, numerous examples were given to show that while rapid socioeconomic and political change erodes some networks,[1] it also strengthens others,[2] and leads to the emergence of new ones.³ Such findings underline the inadequacy of the "traditional-modern" dichotomy, since they suggest that informal groups based on primary relationships and affinities can be extremely effective in meeting individual and collective needs in contemporary urban societies.

At the same time, although informal groups as a whole have remained up to this day important channels for political participation in Middle Eastern cities, the politically most salient types of networks have differed greatly from one city to another. For instance, as shown in part 3, until the mid-1970s, at least, clientelist ties remained essential to Beiruti politics, but were far less significant in Cairo or, for that matter, in Tehran. By contrast, no network comparable to that built around Tehran's bazaar was operative either in the Khan al-Khalili *suq* in Cairo or in the commercial areas of downtown Beirut. Moreover, in each city the relative importance of religious, clientelist, and residential networks has changed dramatically over time. One may contrast, for instance, the erosion of patron-client networks in Beirut in the early to mid-1970s with the progressive emergence of clientelist-like structures between the clergy and the urban poor in Tehran from the late 1960s onward. Similarly, one might compare the relative decline of patronage networks and the increasing prominence of small, locally based fundamentalist religious groups in the Lebanese Sunni community throughout the 1980s. Thus, in the process of describing the evolution of informal networks over time, this study also documented the changing nature of political loyalties in three Middle Eastern countries, and it identified the major forces—in particular the centralization of power by modernizing authoritarian states, foreign penetration, urbanization, and the expansion of higher education—that have been responsible for transforming the structures that Middle Easterners have used to participate in politics, ranging from the most informal types of associations to quite formally organized groups.

2. Informal Networks and Collective Resistance

This book has provided much evidence to suggest that while informal networks usually have a stabilizing influence on the urban sociopolitical order, they can also function as powerful bases for the mobilization of individuals into destabilizing political activities. In this respect, Egypt, Iran, and Lebanon are certainly not isolated cases. In almost every other Middle Eastern country, for instance, the Islamic movement consists primarily of a conglomeration of personalistic groups. Even though they are informally organized and loosely interconnected, these networks have nevertheless been the source of some of the most important challenges to the bureaucratic-authoritarian Middle Eastern state in recent years.[4]

Similarly, following Iraq's invasion of Kuwait on 2 August 1990, the infrastructure of the Kuwaiti resistance to the Iraqi occupation grew out of the *diwaniyyas* (small informal gatherings of men who meet on a regular basis in a member's home in order to socialize, play cards, and discuss issues of common interests). Also active in the resistance were various Islamic and pan-Arab secular associations that since 1986 had pushed for the restoration of the Parliament dissolved by the Emir. This network played a key role not only in offering services that the defunct Kuwaiti government could no longer deliver (such as trash collection, distribution of food, and health services), but also in supporting civil disobedience and organizing resistance to Iraqi rule.[5] It was soon complemented by scores of new popular committees, formed by young Kuwaitis eager to rid their country of Saddam Hussein's tyranny (Ghabra 1991).

Two even more striking examples of the ability of informal associations to provide effective instruments for political resistance are Morocco's struggle for independence from France, and the Palestinian uprising, or *intifada*, in the territories occupied by Israel since the 1967 war. During the 1940s and early 1950s, Morocco's fight for national liberation was led by the Istiqlal (Independence) party. This party, however, relied heavily on tribal-trading networks to provide the nationalist movement with the mass support that the merchant bourgeoisie leading the Istiqlal could not deliver.[6] These networks, in turn, had been formed in the interwar period, when wealthy Swasa wholesalers (i.e., wholesalers originally from the Sous region in southern Morocco) began to help fellow tribesmen who had migrated to the cities of the north set up their own businesses as retailers (Waterbury 1972a, 63–65). In doing so, Swasa wholesalers contributed to the emergence of a nationwide system of tribal-grocers/patron-client networks. After 1953, it was this informal structure that provided the organizational backbone of the urban resistance to French colonial rule. More specifically, the patron-client networks controlled by the Swasa businessmen were instrumental in expanding the Moroccan nationalist movement from its originally limited bourgeois base to include large segments of the urban lower middle and working classes, and even some shantytown dwellers.

> [The Swasa retailers] proved important to the Istiqlal as it sought to penetrate the urban areas and organize the working class and the unemployed. The retailers were ideally situated to promote this task for fairly obvious reasons. First, their tribal-commercial information networks, within and among cities, provided an effective grapevine for the movement of political information and

'intelligence' as well as the movement of personnel. This communication network, so intimately a part of the legitimate commercial activities of the *Swasa*, was not readily accessible to French surveillance. Secondly, the retailers came in daily contact with workers, slum dwellers, the lower middle classes of the *medinas*, and the European population. Their shops could serve as informal party headquarters, refuge for nationalists hiding from the police, intelligence posts and sometimes arms cache. After the French exiled the Moroccan Sultan in 1953, because of his close links with the *Istiqlal*, a number of *Swasa* helped organize the armed urban resistance groups. (Waterbury 1972b, 245–46)

More recently, the Palestinian uprising in the West Bank and Gaza Strip has demonstrated perhaps better than any other example that a multiplicity of informally organized groups can be woven together into a powerful, broadly based social movement directed against the authorities. Although our knowledge of the structure of the *intifada* is still limited, and although formal groups and institutions (universities, research and technical centers, unions, etc.) have played a key role in sustaining the movement, the backbone of the uprising nevertheless appears to have been provided by loosely organized associations. This statement applies both to the Islamic activists, whose infrastructure has been built around the mosque and a host of charitable societies, and to the secularists, who have skillfully used the networks of contacts and ties that they established during the 1970s and 1980s with the refugee camps and key sectors of the population (the youth, students, professionals, workers, and women).[7] Throughout the uprising, formal organizations, such as Fatah and other PLO-affiliated groups, have themselves relied heavily on informal networks—the variety of sport, charitable, vocational, social, and cultural associations and self-help groups that they established in the preceding two decades—to make their influence felt.[8] By establishing lines of communication and control over resources, such clubs, groups, and associations provided the infrastructure that made the organization of the resistance possible. Fatah's *shabiba* (youth) movement, outlawed in March 1988 is a good example.

[This] informally organized [movement]...consisted of a loose network throughout the West Bank, Gaza, and East Jerusalem, whose members, while not formally affiliated, were certainly sympathetic to Arafat and the PLO. While *shabiba* activities did include communal self-help projects and aid to the elderly, there is little doubt that the organization provided middle and lower cadres of the *intifada* who relayed messages from the leadership, distributed leaflets, organized demonstrations, and the like. (Peretz 1990, 76)

More importantly perhaps, several authors have emphasized the key role played by loosely organized, ad hoc committees and local self-help groups that appeared *during* the uprising. These grassroots associations not only managed essential aspects of the *intifada* (organizing street demonstrations and strikes, assisting with the injured, etc.), but also made it possible for the population to cope with the new situation created by the violence, the curfews, the repression, and the disorganization of public services. Thus, they often took charge of such basic functions as trash disposal, public safety, the patrolling of streets and neighborhoods, the mediation of disputes, and the distribution of scarce foodstuffs. They also promoted local agricultural self-help projects, and in response to the Israeli authorities' repeated closing down of schools, they set up alternative classes for children.[9] In other words, informally organized groups and committees provided the local Palestinian population with the counterinstitutions that made possible resistance to the occupying forces, and they go a long way toward explaining the remarkable ability of the *intifada* to sustain itself over such a long period of time, despite the repression, the shortages, and the inhospitable conditions of life under siege and curfew conditions.

The ability of informal networks to operate as channels for political dissent is of course not limited to the Middle East. Similar phenomena can be documented in environments as different as nineteenth-century France, or Latin America in the 1970s and 1980s. For instance, working-class networks contributed to the development of class conflict in the French city of Toulouse in the nineteenth century (Aminzade 1977, 1979). In the course of Toulouse's rapid growth and industrialization, the city's new working class created social clubs, mutual aid societies, and a variety of small, informal friendship groups that met in cafés, taverns, cabarets, and dance halls. Although these groups were initially formed merely to provide for sociability and mutual help, they rapidly acquired political overtones by enabling working-class Toulousains to develop a sense of collective identity and a better appreciation of their shared interests—and of how these interests differed from those of the social strata (the aristocracy and the clergy) that traditionally had controlled them. Eventually these groups proved instrumental in the ability of Toulouse's workers to "break the chains of dependency" (Aminzade 1977) and move the city's politics from patronage to class politics in less than forty years.

In a similar vein, the informal circles known as *chambrées* played an instrumental role in the politicization of the French Mediterranean department of the Var during the first half of the nineteenth century. These *chambrées* consisted essentially of "groups of men created for the purpose of meeting together after work, amusing themselves together, playing cards and talking, etc." (Agulhon 1982, 133). They met regularly in the shop, workshop, or individual home of one of their members, in cabarets or, in the case of the unmarried youth working in industry, in dormitories. Agulhon argues that the proliferation of *chambrées* created a climate very conducive to the politicization and slow radicalization of the lower classes of the small towns of the Var. In this instance, therefore, informal networks did not serve directly as vehicles for political protest, but they nevertheless played an essential role in converting individuals to much more radical ideas than the ones they had traditionally held. By resocializing a traditionally quiescent and legitimist population into the new democratic ideas, *chambrées* lay the essential groundwork for the eventual rise of republicanism in the Var.

In turning to Latin America, one also notices that several of the sociopolitical movements directed against existing regimes in the 1970s and 1980s drew much of their strength from the mobilization of small, informally organized associations among the urban poor, especially the grassroots activist Catholic groups known as CEBs (from the Spanish *comunidades eclesiales de base*, i.e., "Christian base communities").[10] Originally, the CEBs were not created for political purposes. They simply emerged to provide arenas for sociability and mutual support and to foster a sense of community. People from the same neighborhood and social background would meet to discuss the Bible and common problems, exchange ideas, help one another, and pool their resources to reach common goals.[11] Over time, however, CEBs often have developed into groups that have challenged the authorities, especially in countries such as Nicaragua, Brazil, Chile, and El Salvador.[12] Thus, for instance, the CEBs played an instrumental role in mobilizing thousands of Nicaraguans in the Sandinista revolution. In the late 1960s, sporadic clashes began to take place between the authorities and the militant clergy and activist youth working at the local level through CEBs. This conflict culminated in the late 1970s, when clerical and lay activists involved in CEBs moved into open and direct support of the Sandinista Front of National Liberation (FSLN). The support of such individuals and of the CEBs, Dodson argues, "was clearly a valuable resource to the FSLN, which found the work of organizing people in the insurrection [against Somoza] to be much easier in the areas where CEBs were firmly rooted. These institutions of religious inspiration were, in short, effective vehicles of grassroots political action in the revolutionary setting of the popular insurrection....Indeed the CEBs provided intelligence, communication links, food, safe houses, medical aid, and combatants" (Dodson 1986, 86, 93).

Mexico City presents us with yet another situation in which a multiplicity of small, informally organized associations joined together to form a powerful, if amorphous, urban popular movement. By the early 1980s, this grassroots movement had become an influential force in the politics of the Mexican capital, and its power at that time rivaled that of the formally organized groups that have traditionally dominated Mexican politics (i.e., the bureaucracy, the ruling party, the Church, and opposition political parties). The backbone of this popular movement was the multitude of neighborhood groups whose number in the preceding twenty years had grown as fast as Mexico City itself, and which originally had emerged from the collective efforts of the poor to pressure the state to legalize property titles and to secure access to basic goods and services.[13] As elsewhere, these groups usually had worked in close cooperation with the authorities, not against them. They had provided instruments through which the state had been able to demobilize local communities and co-opt their leaders.

By the early 1980s, however, the urban popular movement no longer shied away from confronting the authorities. Thus, in the 1980s, federations of popular associations in Mexico City organized resistance to cuts in food, transportation, and education subsidies. They also opposed state attempts to evict and/or relocate by force low-income tenants, particularly after the earthquake of 1985 (Annis 1988, 140; Eckstein 1990). Although these associations were loosely organized and coordinated their actions only on an informal basis, they proved very effective in bringing pressure to bear on the government and in wresting concessions from it. Susan Eckstein even sees them as "a manifestation of the breakdown of state hegemony" (1990, 169).

In the late 1980s, these associations were led by a popular figure, known as "Superbarrio," a Robin Hood–like, good-humored folk hero who also came off as a shrewd and politically astute individual (Annis 1988, 142). Superbarrio embodies the dynamism of the urban popular movement in Mexico City. He has become not only a symbol, but also a constant reminder of the new political assertiveness of the poor, who, through the informal associations in which they participate, have not hesitated to confront the bureaucracy and its local representatives.

In the constantly changing Mexican urban movement, individual organizations rise and die and new organizations rise, phoenix-like, from their ashes. What is more permanent is a still-amorphous but nonetheless very real bartering structure through which the poor can independently engage the state....Certainly social movements that rise in cities are nothing new on Latin America's landscape. But, on the other hand, the tendency to respond 'plus ça change, plus c'est la même chose' may cause us to overlook something that is genuinely new: the *scale* of mobilization among the urban poor, the *magnitude* of social energy that it has captured, and the *certainty* that the poor will increasingly be negotiating on their own behalf. (Annis 1988, 142–43)

In light of the evidence that has been presented in this section, students of urbanization in the Third World should not overestimate the integrative qualities of urban networks, and they might wish to reassess the prevailing consensus concerning the stabilizing role that informal groups play among the urban poor. Ad hoc associations that reduce individual and societal stress by providing marginalized, alienated, or victimized populations with access to resources and sources of social solidarity can also operate as very effective structures for political mobilization against a regime. As mentioned earlier, this is especially true in authoritarian political contexts, where co-opted or repressed formal organizations do not constitute an option to express dissatisfaction with the government.

At a time when there is much talk about the dynamism of civil society and its reassertion in relation to the state in Eastern Europe, Latin America, Asia, Africa, and the Middle East, it is important to note that informal associations often are the primary vehicles of this new grassroots political dynamism. It is often through such associations that individuals shelter themselves against the possibility of true totalitarian control. Although the present study concentrated on rather dramatic outbursts, such as riots, popular uprisings, political assassinations, and large-scale demonstrations, the potential contribution of informal networks to civil society's resistance to the hegemonic ambitions of the modern state presumably is not limited to such spectacular events. For instance, it would be fascinating to explore how subordinated social groups have used informally organized groups to engage in the kind of low intensity, "everyday forms of resistance" that James Scott (1985) has studied in another context. Similarly, ideologies of resistance to the authorities are often progressively elaborated or diffused in the kinds of networks that this study has examined. Thus, the study of the "infrapolitics" of subordinated populations (Scott 1990) cannot limit itself to the analysis of how critiques of power and the established order are elaborated. It also needs to describe how a clandestine organizational life, usually built around informal netwoks, allows this ideological insubordination to gain widespread acceptance. In Iran, for instance, the myriad of *hay'ats* and Shiite associations on university campuses, high schools, factories, and offices were instrumental in the development and transmission of some of the themes—including the critique of Westernization and loss of cultural identity, and the notions of moral corruption and cultural decadence—that Khomeini subsequently wove into a revolutionary ideology of delegitimation of the Pahlavi state. Networks may be facilitating the social acceptance of radical ideologies contesting the legitimacy of the existing sociopolitical order in many parts of the Third World at this very moment. But when exactly do they shift their role from being system-supportive to being system-challenging?

3. When Networks Become Destabilizing

One generalization consistent with the political histories of Egypt, Iran, and Lebanon over several centuries is that networks can be most disruptive when the following three conditions are met.

1. The networks are under the influence of a counterelite, which has access to far-ranging resources, independent of those controlled by the state.

2. This counterelite feels threatened by hostile forces, which it sees as being directly or indirectly associated with the authorities.

3. The counterelite benefits from a weak,[14] suddenly weakened,[15] or indecisive[16] central authority.

While the weakness or breakdown of the state has provided highly favorable conditions for informal networks to play a destabilizing role in many of the cases that this study examined, the first two conditions above deserve particular attention.

Counterelites and Resources

The counterelites we encountered consisted either of prominent individuals (e.g., the leaders of the *ashraf* in eighteenth-century Egypt, Syrian notables in the nineteenth century, *mujtahids* in nineteenth-century Iran, and *zu'ama'* in Lebanon) or of communities endowed with a sense of collective identity and solidarity (e.g., *bazaaris* and ulama in Iran since the mid-nineteenth century, *zu'ar, ahdath, 'ayyarun,* and *futuwwat* in historical times). The fact that notables or patrons can at times lead movements of popular protest deserves particular emphasis, given the widespread perception that patronage systems always uphold established power structures. From the evidence that has been presented, two major reasons account for the occasional willingness of patrons to use the networks they command in destabilizing ways.

First, in the Middle East as elsewhere, there is only so much that patrons can do to contain the radicalism of their followings without risking the loss of their power bases. One should therefore expect that at times they will be unwilling to take steps to prevent rioting by their clients. As patrons find themselves in a situation where opposing their followers' urge to rebel will meet with failure and lead to the erosion of their influence, they might simply condone a popular uprising and either follow their clients into it or even assume the full leadership of the uprising themselves, in an attempt to capitalize on a popular cause. As we saw, this if-you-can't-beat-'em-join-'em reasoning helps explain events as diverse as the involvement of some prominent ulama in the uprising against the French in Cairo in 1798 and the radical rhetoric adopted by many a Sunni patron faced with a radicalized street in 1950s and 1960s Lebanon.

Second, patrons may incite their followings into rioting simply to demonstrate their power to their rivals or to the central authorities. After all, politicians seek clients largely because a dedicated following provides them with a certain leverage toward competitors and the government. Therefore, a patron should be expected to rouse his clients, from time to time, into destabilizing political activities, either to show his opponents what good weapons he controls or to protect himself against attempts to undercut him on his turf (Gellner 1962). The 1958 uprising in Lebanon constitutes a dramatic illustration of this phenomenon. Similarly, the political mobilization of the *bazaaris* and the ulama in Iran in 1977–79 was essentially a display of force by two communities faced with Muhammad Reza Shah's frontal assault on them.

In these as in other instances, the decisive factor that enabled counterelites to mobilize effectively against the state was the *resources* at their disposal. In turn, three types of resources were shown to be particularly useful. The first two were financial and organizational independence from the government, which have always been important, whether one looks at the *bazaaris* and the ulama in Iran, the *zu'ama'* in Lebanon, or notables in historical times. In some cases, the resources financing networks have come from the outside. In Lebanon, for example, cash transfers from foreign countries were shown to be decisive in enabling *qabadayat*, street gangs, and fundamentalist groups and militias (especially Hizballah), to act as disruptive forces in the 1970s and 1980s. Most often, however, the resources that have enabled networks to confront the state have been generated by domestic processes of rapid socioeconomic change. For instance, as was explained earlier, the shah's attack against the *bazaaris* and the ulama was all the more ill-conceived because it came at a time when both communities were proceeding from a much stronger base than was available to them a few decades earlier. The *bazaaris* had benefited considerably, in material terms, from the economic growth of the 1970s. Religious networks, too, were strengthened by modernization. For example, the expansion of modern communications and transportation made possible the centralization of religious taxes by the source of imitation in Qom, and increased the number of pilgrims to religious shrines.[17] In addition, the oil boom and economic expansion enlarged the flow of resources from prosperous *bazaaris* to the ulama, which in turn increased the latter's independence from the government and compensated for the state's increasing interference in the management of religious institutions.

The third kind of resource that has been as vital to the counterelites' political power as their financial and organizational autonomy is a variable much harder to determine, namely, social influence. Social influence itself is largely a factor of the counterelites' control over extensive social networks. Thus, in Iran the bazaar's and the mosque's ties to most of Iran's urban classes proved decisive in these two communities' ability to turn a middle-class movement of protest into a popular upheaval. By contrast, what Egyptian radical Islamicists in the 1970s lacked was precisely the type of wide-ranging networks of social relations established by the radical ulama and *bazaaris* in Iran. As a result, they were unable to penetrate deeply into Egyptian society and found themselves politically isolated. Their presence, for the most part, remained limited to the university system and, to a lesser extent, to the new, substandard quarters located on the periphery of Egypt's metropolis, especially Cairo's poverty belt.[18]

Embattled Individuals, Groups, and Communities

In almost all the instances examined in this book, the perception of being under threat from hostile forces, and the feeling that the authorities were unable or unwilling to do anything about it, were critical factors in the readiness of patrons or cohesive communities to use the networks under their control against the state. Thus, most of the cases of unrest analyzed in this book were primarily defensive movements by individuals and groups who believed that their very existence, values, and ways of life were under siege from inimical forces. If one concentrates on the 1970s, it is noteworthy that the sense of being a beleaguered community was a critical factor in inducing the political mobilization of both the Maronites in Lebanon and the *bazaaris* and militant ulama in Iran. In these two cases, the potential for concerted political action inherent in communities that have maintained a certain homogeneity and sense of solidarity manifested itself most clearly when these communities felt increasingly provoked and harassed by hostile forces: a modernizing state that encroached on the traditional prerogatives of the ulama and *bazaaris* in Iran, and the Palestinians and an increasingly radicalized Muslim community in Lebanon.

More generally, the diffuse sense of threat, which has provided the catalyst for the mobilization of networks into destabilizing political activities, has been of two main types. One has been the potential or actual undermining of the material interests and sociopolitical influence of powerful, well established communities or individuals. It was often in reaction to this perceived challenge to their vested material interests that the counterelites used their networks against what they saw as the aggressor: the government, foreign powers, or rival communities and notables. Examples here would include the active role played by some ulama in the uprising against the French in Cairo in 1798,[19] the encouragement of sectarian violence by some notables in the mid-nineteenth century in cities of Palestine and Syria,[20] the involvement of the *bazaaris* in Iranian popular protest movements in the late nineteenth century and at the turn of the twentieth century,[21] the 1958 uprising in Lebanon,[22] the extremist political behavior of the Maronite community in 1975–76,[23] and the mobilization of the *bazaaris*[24] and the *ulama*[25] against the Pahlavi dynasty in 1977–79.

Culture, and in particular true religiosity, has been the second dimension of the perceived threat that often has driven counterelites to use their networks in a destabilizing fashion. For instance, most of the instances of unrest that were just mentioned also contained very heavy cultural-religious components. In 1798, many Egyptian ulama feared the religious and moral consequences of the encroachment of the "French infidels" on their society. Similar concerns played a role in the communal riots of the mid-nineteeth century in the Ottoman Empire, in the *mujtahids'* leadership of popular urban protest movements in nineteenth-century Iran, and in the ulama's and the *bazaaris'* decision to turn against the shah in 1977–79. In the same manner, in Lebanon in 1975–76 it was the feeling that they were fighting for the survival of Christianity in the Levant that convinced many Maronites to go along with their leadership's decision to escalate the conflict, wield the threat of partition, and destroy the downtown areas of Beirut.

Finally, while there are important differences between the Fada'iyan in Iran in the late 1940s and early 1950s, and the university-based *jama'at* and the radical Islamic movements of the 1970s and 1980s in Egypt, all these groups shared two essential features. One was their preoccupation with religious-moral themes and their insistence on upholding rigidly Islamic prescriptions regarding the subordinate position of women and religious minorities in society, the ban on alcohol, and "proper" Islamic behavior (which involved, in particular, the refusal to mix sexes in public places and strict dress codes for women outside the home). The second common attribute of these groups was that they were all formed to fight the forces (foreign penetration, Westernization, the modernizing state) and the individuals (religious minorities, secular intellectuals, secular-modernizing leaders) that they saw as responsible for the undermining of these sacred religious-cultural norms. What all these groups bemoaned first and foremost was the moral "depravity," "corruption," and "decadence" that they saw besetting their societies. They all equated Westernization with moral decay, the spread of social vices, and "sexual promiscuity and indecency," and saw the spread of Western lifestyles as a deadly threat to the cultural fabric and integrity of their society. In other words, the main common denominator of these groups was the cultural-religious motives that drove them. It is significant that the primary targets of the Fada'iyan were prominent secularist writers and politicians. Similarly, in Cairo, a militantly secular magazine editor was the victim of an attempted assassination by the radical Islamic group *al-Najun min al-Nar*, or "the Saved from the Inferno," in 1987, and a vocal critic of the creeping Islamization of Egyptian life, Faraq Foda, was killed by Islamic Jihad outside his office in June 1992. More generally, much of the violence generated by radical Islamic groups and by the university-based *jama'at* in Egypt has been directed against Copts, against nighclubs, bars, and cabarets, against perceived violations of Islamic norms of behavior and dress in public, against secularist faculty and students, against the consumption of alcohol, and against activities on university campuses, such as dances, plays, and concerts, that the *jama'at* label "un-Islamic." Thus, the perception of a threat to a sacred core of religious beliefs has been, either alone or in combination with other factors, one of the most consistent and essential forces that has prompted informal networks to play a destabilizing role. By emphasizing the use of Islam as a language to express political, economic, and social grievances, much of the recent literature on Islamic fundamentalism may run the risk of dismissing too easily the role that altruistic religiosity has played in the turmoil that has gripped the Middle East over the last two decades.

Cultural, moral, and religious concerns, inextricably meshed with the issue of foreign influence, were observed to be particularly influential factors in Iran. In chapter 10 it was shown that, from the 1940s through the 1970s, the bazaar's mobilization against the state was consistently affected by many *bazaaris'* resentment of the state's unwillingness to stop the erosion of traditional Shiite values, norms, and codes of behavior (especially for women). The intelligentsia's cultural critique of Westernization and the loss of identity also paved the way for its alliance with militant clerics, while the bulk of the religious establishment decided to throw its lot in with the radical clergy largely because of its fear of moral laxity and corruption. Most importantly, as emphasized in chapter 11, Khomeini's concerns were always primarily cultural and moral. Overall, therefore, the Iranians' general preoccupation with broadly defined cultural and moral issues in the 1970s was one of the most decisive factors in facilitating the emergence of a broad revolutionary alliance.

By emphasizing moral issues, Khomeini achieved several objectives. First, he was able to weave together the myriad of networks whose single most important common denominator was the concern with such problems. In doing so, he reached millions of people who were particularly receptive to a political discourse phrased in moral terms, because they themselves were experiencing the moral and existential dilemmas of individuals caught in the midst of a dislocating process of rapid socioeconomic change. Personal identity crises and a desire for self-purification could be seen as parts of a larger process of national redemption involving the revitalization of old cultural forms. By the same token, feelings of guilt based on an individual's own moral failings could be blamed on the West. Thus, by making people's personal dignity and integrity dependent upon the integrity of Iran, which itself was said to be best preserved by fighting Western influence in the country, Khomeini formulated a new definition of nationalism, based on a fierce animosity toward the West, with which the masses of hitherto apolitical, primarily lower- and lower-middle-class Iranians could identify.

Second, by defining the problems confronting Iran in moral and cultural terms, Khomeini justified the clergy's involvement in politics, since clerics could legitimately be said to be in the best position to speak about issues of morality in a country portrayed as a Muslim nation threatened by infidels. After the establishment of the Islamic Republic, the struggle for "moral purification" even came to provide the radical clerics with new modes of political control and repression. For instance, between 1979 and 1981 the fundamentalists' crackdown on the universities, which were strongholds of the left and the Islamic left, was portrayed as a necessary measure to eradicate Western cultural hegemony (Milani 1988, 294–95). By presenting political authority in the Islamic Republic as sacred, and by making obedience to the new laws of the land a religious duty, radical clerics have articulated a new language that entirely redefines the basis of political legitimacy (Arjomand 1988, 181–83).

4. The Impact of Islam: How Unique is the Middle East?

Few of the phenomena that this book describes can be said to be culturally specific to the Middle East, including the continued relevance of informal groups to urban politics, or these networks' ability to serve as vehicles for political protest. As shown earlier, similar facts can be documented in other parts of the Third World. It is undeniable, however, that Islam has had an independent impact on some of the characteristics and behavior of most of the networks we examined.

First, through the social ties built around mosques, preachers, and

Islamic associations, Islam offers a ready-made basis for recruitment, proselitization, and clandestine activities. Since regimes cannot repress or crack down on this network without undermining their legitimacy, Islamic groups and institutions provide potential opponents of a regime with a zone of autonomy from state control, which they can use to organize against the authorities. This zone of autonomy is all the more extensive in that, through its vast network of institutions, through the prevalence of Islamic symbolism in the daily life of the population, and through its emotional hold over the people, Islam penetrates Middle Eastern societies in a way that has no equivalent, for instance, in contemporary Western societies. In such an environment, most networks take on a religious coloring or dimension, even when they emerge to address needs, problems, and aspirations that have little to do with religion per se (the voluntary and charitable Islamic associations in Egypt today constitute a clear example of this phenomenon).

Second, as was discussed in the preceding section, a recurrent feature of most of the protest movements described in this study is the perception of a lethal danger to the Islamic nature of indigenous society, arising from an all-out attack on Islam by foreign powers, often seen as acting in cooperation the country's leaders or with members of the local religious minorities (Christians, Jews, or Bahais). Repeatedly, networks (as well as more formally organized entities) have been mobilized to fight religiopolitical battles against the threat of cultural "pollution" or "poisoning" from the outside. Islam, therefore, can function as an independent variable that, even though it rarely operates alone, may drive networks to act in destabilizing ways. (This is *always* true in instances where religious networks have been disruptive, and often true of cases when patron-client or bazaar-based networks have becomes vehicles for political dissent.) As one thinks back on the various cases of urban unrest described in this study, it becomes clear that, if religion were not a variable, there would be few examples of destabilizing networks left.

Third, as exemplified again by the Iranian revolution, Islam has sometimes provided the ready-made ideology that has been able to unify a multiplicity of informal networks—even, once again, when these groups originally appeared as a result of concerns and forces that are neither religious nor specific to Arab-Muslim culture (e.g., the quest for identity and cultural authenticity, the resentment of foreign domination and Western cultural influences, the search for individual and collective empowerment, and the failure of the Third World state's modernizing ideologies and projects). Seen in this light, the broadly defined "Islamic" ideologies that flourished in the 1970s and 1980s can be seen, in part, as devices to build broadly based political coalitions cutting across networks and traditional socioeconomic and political cleavages. In Lebanon, for instance, the manipulation of Shiite symbols and rituals, and the emphasis on a

distinctively Shiite identity, enabled both Musa al-Sadr and Hizballah's ideo-
logues to bridge some of the gaps between the uprooted Shiites living in the suburbs of Beirut and the Shiite villagers of the south, and between the quiestist,
subdued Shiite peasants of the Jabal ʿAmil and the "wild and assertive [Shiite]
clansmen" in the Bekaa (Ajami 1986, 127). Similarly in Iran, the reference to an
all-encompassing Shiite discourse and utopia enabled Khomeini to build a revolutionary alliance including large segments of constituencies as disparate as the
ulama, the *bazaaris,* the intelligentsia, and the urban poor.

One final manifestation of the independent impact of Islam has been
the forms assumed by some networks and their modes of operation. In particular, it is hard to avoid the impression that Islamic history facilitated the
emergence of what I called "radical-utopian networks." When one looks at the
Fadaʿiyan-e Islam, at the Takfir waʾl-Hijra, and at some of the more militant
and violent *jamaʿat islamiyya* on Egyptian university campuses, one feels that
these groups' basic strategy and ultimate goals were largely modeled after
those of the Prophet Muhammad himself, as he was trying to build the Islamic
community.

Similarities between such groups and Muhammad's original community can be observed at several levels (not coincidentally, for these groups have
sought to legitimize their behavior with appeals to the example of the
Prophet). One is the use of kinship, friendship, and other personal ties and
loyalties to bring new members into the movement. Another is the reliance on
small, highly personal, and secretive cells. Both of these features closely resemble the strategy followed by Muhammad himself to integrate and consolidate
the early Islamic community.[26] At one level, of course, these resemblances
simply reflect the fact that, for radical-utopian networks, informal organization is a matter of survival (it hampers detection by the authorities). To the
extent that the struggle between modernizing authoritarian rulers and the
Islamicists consists of an unequal fight between a powerful state and a few
dedicated individuals who have the odds against them, Islamic militants may
have no choice but to operate in a clandestine fashion and rely on the mobilization of already-formed bonds (religion, kinship, friendship, and neighborly ties). Furthermore, recruitment through personal contacts and secretive
cell organization are characteristics that also describe such varied and non-
Muslim organizations as the Red Brigades, the Freemasons, and Peru's Shin-
ing Path. In the Middle East, however, such informal organization is no longer
merely a matter of political survival, and it does not simply reflect the absence
of organizational alternatives; it is also the reproduction, either deliberate or
unconscious, of a culturally and historically sanctioned pattern, endowed with
the greatest legitimacy of all: that of having been used by the Prophet himself.
Because this pattern is both sacred and rooted in people's minds, it confers

added legitimacy on informal modes of organization. It is significant that, in an effort to legitimize their own actions, the leaders of Islamic radical groups themselves often make explicit references to Muhammad's dependence on small groups and personal ties to spread the faith. This was, for instance, a frequent theme in Safavi's few writings (Taheri 1987, 52).

Most important is what one might call the *hijra* paradigm, and the Islamic search for utopia. *Hijra*, perhaps the single most important event in early Islamic history, refers to the flight of Muhammad and his followers from Mecca to Medina in 622. In Mecca, the leading families' opposition to Muhammad's teachings greatly constrained the Prophet's activities. In the much more receptive environment of Medina, Muhammad was able to operate freely, which made it possible for him to expand the size of his incipient Islamic community and create a strong esprit de corps among his followers. Eventually, from this strengthened power base the Prophet was able to defeat the Meccans. Soon afterward, he converted many Arabian tribes to Islam, which in turn provided the basis for the rapid and dramatic expansion of the new religion beyond Arabia.

Because Muslims are fully aware of the contribution of *hijra* to the triumph and expansion of Islam, there is much room for political entrepreneurs to admonish the faithful to practice *hijra* themselves, that is, to withdraw from a world denounced as corrupt and to find refuge in microcommunities, patterned after Muhammad's at the time of his *hijra*. The Takfir wa'l-Hijra (the name is revealing), the Fada'iyan, and the more radical *jama'at islamiyya* represent, to some extent at least, contemporary manifestations of this phenomenon. For instance, the summer camps that the *jama'at islamiyya* organized in the early 1970s have been rightly described as "micro-cosmic experiments in Islamicist utopia, past and future.…[They] were meant to be a model of the future Islamic society that the young Islamicists intended to build on the ruins of the jahiliyya [the corrupt society]" (Kepel 1985, 139). Islam, in other words, provides a readily available mythicohistorical frame of reference that individuals can draw on to build certain types of networks. This frame of reference, furthermore, tends to enhance the destabilizing potential of these networks, since their ultimate goal is, following the precedent created by Muhammad's conquest of Mecca, to regroup the faithful, resocialize them, indoctrinate them, and enable them to move against the state, defeat it, and "reestablish" a "true" and "pure" Islamic society. Such were the explicitly stated objectives of both the Fada'iyan and the Takfir wa'l-Hijra. Similarly, in the 1980s a Sunni radical thinker in Tripoli (Lebanon) could admonish his followers to establish a miniature countersociety patterned after Muhammad's small group of followers in Mecca and to proceed to use this countersociety, as Muhammad did, to fight both the pagan society all around it and the state (Sivan 1985, 85–86).

Radical-utopian Islamic networks, therefore, are at once arenas of communal life for their members and centers of opposition to the authorities. They also are simultaneously past- and future-oriented. They are past-oriented because they draw much of their inspiration from the state of the Islamic community during the Golden Age of Islam—the period of Muhammad and the first four Caliphs for the Sunnis, and of Muhammad and Ali for the Shiites. They represent a deliberate effort by individuals to legitimize a political project by appropriating sacred history, by manipulating the system of cultural representations that make up collective memory, and by using the language of roots, authenticity, and purity. At the same time, however, radical-utopian networks are also future-oriented, because their objective is less to turn the clock back to the seventh century than to use the idealized image of the early Islamic community as a blueprint to build an Islamic utopia in the late twentieth century. The countersociety that they build is not only the vanguard of dedicated Muslims that will overthrow the present, corrupt order; it is also a model for the society of the future (Sivan 1985, 85).

5. Rapid Urbanization and Political Stability

As we shift our attention from culture to socioeconomic processes, it becomes possible to assess the extent to which rapid urbanization has been responsible for the unrest that has shaken Iranian, Lebanese, and Egyptian cities in the last five decades. One remembers, here, that this study began as a challenge to some of the basic tenets of the extensive literature on Third World urbanization of the 1970s and early 1980s. As shown in part 1, three related, core propositions of this literature were that (a) rapid urbanization does not appear to be an overly destabilizing process in the Third World, (b) the urban poor in particular do not constitute a major danger to the authorities, and (c) one of the major factors explaining (a) and (b) is that informal networks play a stabilizing role in the process of urbanization.

Against this background, this study can be seen as a contribution to an incipient revisionist perspective on Third World urbanization (see also Eckstein 1990). Indeed, the preceding chapters have documented many instances in which rapid urbanization, informal networks, and the urban poor have been destabilizing forces. Some of these findings can be summarized here, by contrasting figure 10—which captures the reasoning of those who see networks as a bulwark against the destabilizing effects of rapid urbanization (see also part 1)—and figure 11, which is based on the recent political histories of Egypt, Lebanon, and Iran and which captures some of the connections, highlighted in the preceding chapters, between urbanization, networks, and urban

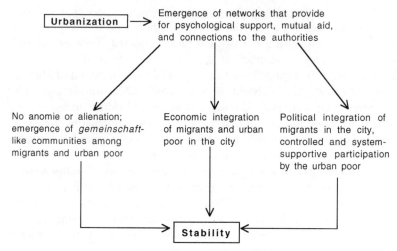

Figure 10.   Informal Networks as Stabilizing Agents

unrest. (Indicated between parentheses are the countries and groups to which a given connection applies particularly.)

Three types of connections in figure 11 deserve particular attention:

1. Those linking urbanization to unrest through heightened religiosity and/or the heightened political salience of religious affiliations and loyalties

2. Those linking urbanization to unrest through the multiplication of double-edged or radical-utopian religious networks

3. Those linking urbanization through the availability of a pool of urban poor who can be mobilized for destabilizing purposes.

Before we look in some detail at each of these connections, it should be clear that the claim made here is not that rapid urbanization has been the main force behind the unrest that has taken place in the three countries that formed the focus of this book. Instead, the argument is only that urbanization has been one of several factors—albeit a very significant one—that has contributed these countries' turmoil. As shown throughout this book, for instance, Westernization and the expansion of educational opportunities have been two other particularly powerful forces that have shaped the environment out of which political protest movements have emerged. In some instances, these and other trends even have been more decisive than urbanization in

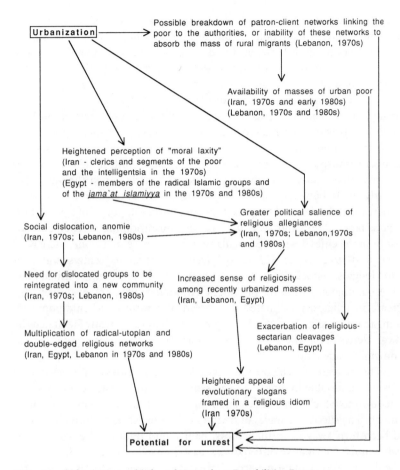

Figure 11. Urbanization and Informal Networks as Destabilizing Forces

fueling unrest. Overall, however, urbanization has clearly had an independent impact, as the following discussion will now make clear. In other words, the role of the city has not been limited to providing an arena in which some of the disruptive forces that beset contemporary Middle Eastern society can play themselves out. The city itself has fostered unrest.

Urbanization, Religiosity, and the Heightened Political Salience of Religious Networks and Affiliations

In all three countries, there has been a definite connection between rapid urbanization and increased religiosity. Increased religiosity, in turn, has sometimes contributed to political unrest, especially in Iran and Lebanon.

The connection between rapid urbanization and popular protest through the medium of increased religiosity was particularly visible in Tehran and Iran's other largest urban centers. Several observers have suggested that recent migrants and their offspring displayed a much greater respect for religion and the ulama than villagers.[27] Significantly, a survey carried out in 1974 in a poor district of Tehran discovered that the recently urbanized poor living in that area found it more necessary to have a mosque than a sewer system, schools, or transportation services (Kazemi 1980a, 79). Most indicative of the increased vitality of religion in Iran's major urban centers in the late 1960s and early 1970s, however, was the staggering growth of religious associations, the increase in the demand for preachers, and the development of a market for religious tapes (Arjomand 1988, 91–93). The mushrooming of religious associations in the cities deserves particular emphasis. In Tehran alone, there were in the mid-1970s some 322 Hosseiniyeh-type religious centers and over 12,300 religious associations, most of which brought together the urban poor and recent migrants from the provinces (Arjomand 1988, 92). Eventually this increase in religiosity facilitated the spread of a form of Islamic populism among lower-class groups of rural origins, which in turn greatly facilitated the radical clerics' task when they tried to mobilize the urban poor behind Khomeini's leadership.

The increase in religiosity observable in Iran's cities in the 1960s and 1970s was undoubtedly linked to the sense of cultural malaise and societal breakdown to which very sudden and rapid rates of urbanization contributed so much. The successive waves of migration into the cities of individuals who had been torn away from their roots, habits, and traditional environments created much "normative disturbance," as Arjomand puts it (1988, 112), and this collective disorientation, particularly visible among the lower classes, created a longing for a new system of cultural representations that might enable so many of these displaced individuals to make sense of the new world in which they lived. The Pahlavi system, disconnected as it was from the society in which it developed, could not fill this demand for a new moral and mental map of the universe. This is where Khomeini and his radical colleagues stepped in and proved so successful when they turned a thirteen-century-old ideology into a powerful mobilizing myth (Arjomand 1988).

In the very different context of Lebanon, urbanization appears to have contributed to political violence through its exacerbation of existing sectarian-religious cleavages in society. There is indeed evidence to suggest that, in the 1960s and 1970s, Beirut's rapid growth strengthened sectarian affiliations and loyalties at the expense of kinship and home-based ties.[28] This phenomenon partly reflects the fact that, in the city, relatives are likely to be in much fewer numbers than in the village, and the same holds true for individuals sharing a similar regional background. As a result, "migrants are...forced to rely more than others on members of their own religious or ethnic community. Of the traditional allegiances of family, community, and region, community is the least apt to be weakened by the move [to the city] and [therefore] takes on a decisive role in the new milieu" (Fawaz 1983, 6). In other words, since the sect presents the advantage of mobilizing a larger base than kinship or home-ties groups, sectarian organizations and networks were particularly well suited to the integration of large numbers of migrants with diverse family and regional backgrounds into meaningful political entities. At the same time, sectarian identities provided migrants with an intermediary reference group for identification, somewhere between the family, which loomed so large in the village, and a "Lebanese nation," which for these migrants was but an abstraction to which they could not relate.

There clearly seems to be a causal link between the increased political vitality of sectarian affiliations and the exacerbation of confessional tensions in the capital. Khuri (1975) was overly optimistic when he proposed that the growing sect-identification fostered by urbanization was "a stage between family and national allegiance." The shift of the basis of factional conflict from the family (in the village) to the sect (in the city) did not represent any progress toward national integration and the emergence of a widely shared civic consciousness. It only indicated that empathy, a term dear to Daniel Lerner (1958), was being shifted from one's kin to one's sect fellows. A particular form of "primordial" allegiance was simply transformed into another. In the end, far from promoting a sense of national identity, the heightened political relevance of sectarian loyalties merely increased the distance between groups and exacerbated the already deeply fragmented character of Lebanese society.

Against this background, urbanization can be seen as one of the forces that counteracted the progress that had been made in the preceding decades toward greater integration between religious groups, the strengthening of nonconfessional identities in the country, and the progress of secularization.[29] By the same token, it may have been one of the reasons why a conflict that initially was not sectarian rapidly came to assume a sectarian dimension, which in turn became increasingly pronounced over time.[30]

It is instructive to compare the Iranian and Lebanese experiences to the Egyptian one. In Egypt, too, there is some evidence that sectarian affiliations may take on an increased relevance in the urban environment.[31] In Egypt, however, heightened sectarian consciousness cannot translate itself into urban unrest or communal violence as easily as it can in Lebanon, for three essential and related reasons.

First, Egypt's political system and dominant political tradition have consciously endeavored to keep politics and religion separate. Not only is there no institutionalization of religious differences in Egypt, but there has been a constant and deliberate effort at the elite level to downplay the political significance of these differences.[32] Second, despite numerous incidents of communal violence in the last twenty years, especially in Upper Egypt, the Muslim-Christian cleavage is by no means as pronounced in Egypt as it is in Lebanon. This is due both to the tradition, just mentioned, of keeping politics and religion separate, and to the fact that the Egyptian population, which prides itself on being one of the Arab world's most cosmopolitan, has consciously shunned sectarian dogma. Finally, the Egyptian central authorities, whose coercive power is well developed (unlike in 1970s Lebanon), would never permit autonomous bodies to take the law into their own hands. In fact, in 1979–80, President Sadat repeatedly made specific references to the Lebanese case, indicating that such a situation would not be tolerated in Egypt. Similarly, Mubarak has intervened decisively and successfully whenever he has felt that public displays of religiosity, or the use of religion for political purposes, has posed a threat to the unity of Egypt's society.

Comparing now Egypt with Iran, there is evidence too that, in Egypt as well, recently urbanized masses display a greater degree of religiosity than other segments of the population. Yet unlike in Iran, it is not radical Islam, but what some have called "popular Islam," that in Egypt was the main beneficiary of rapid urbanization in the 1970s and 1980s. The reasons for this phenomenon are easy to understand. Popular preachers, for instance, unlike Islamic radicals, speak a language that the masses of the poor, illiterate Egyptian rural migrants can understand. Similarly, through the services they dispense, the voluntary Islamic associations (*jama'at* and *jam'iyyat*) have been able to attract large numbers of migrants, because the latter's primary concern is to make ends meet. Finally, the various popular religious practices, rituals, and ceremonies that are associated with the tombs of saints (such as Sayyida Zeinab in Cairo) and the belief in superstitions and miracles may also be strengthened by the constant flow into the city of rural migrants seeking security and a sense of community. There is, in fact, some evidence that celebrations of *mawlids* (saints' birthdays), *zar* (exorcism) ceremonies, and other manifestations of popular practices and beliefs underwent a certain revival in the early 1980s.[33] What these various forms of Islam have in common is either their apolitical character or their ability to provide recent migrants with sources of support and ways to relieve psychological tensions. In both cases, they do not pose a major threat to the authorities.[34] In the absence of the unique conditions that in Iran made the fusion of various Islamic networks against the Pahlavi dynasty possible,[35] the increase in religiosity brought about by the rapid growth of Cairo and other cities was unlikely, by itself, to result in a major danger to the authorities.

Before turning to the link between urbanization and the multiplication of radical or double-edged Islamic networks, one should add that urbanization sometimes involves the transfer to the cities of (religious) hostilities and grievances that were developed in another context. As different as they are, Egypt and Lebanon provide in this respect an interesting basis for comparison. From the late 1970s onward, the constant flow into Beirut of populations that had been neglected for decades by the government, and that furthermore had recently been victimized and forcibly displaced by members of other sects or by Israeli raids in the south, brought to the heart of the Lebanese capital animosities that resulted in heightened sectarian tensions and pronounced anti-Israeli and anti-Western feelings. It is in this environment that religious fundamentalism began to grow. The sheer size of Beirut compounded the destabilizing impact of this phenomenon, since it had created an environment in which sects had been able to develop their own institutions, and in which the coexistence of many such sects and institutions increased the possibility of inter-sect conflict.

Somewhat similarly, one of the major reasons why migrations from Upper Egypt to Cairo have often fueled communal unrest in the Egyptian capital is that migrants have often brought with them the religious prejudices and feuds that have long characterized the relatively poor and underdeveloped villages of Upper Egypt (Ayubi 1991, 164–65). Significant in this respect were the communal clashes that took place in June 1981 in Zawiyya al-Hamra, in the northeastern part of Cairo. These events, which were the bloodiest incidents of communal conflict in Egypt in many decades, were preceded by the arrival into the neighborhood of rural migrants from the Minia province in Upper Egypt. Their immediate cause, however, was the government's forced relocation into the neighborhood of slum dwellers from two other districts of the city that had been targeted for an urban renewal project (Ansari 1986, 225–26). Significantly, therefore, the explosion was precipitated by two factors—forced dislocation (of the slum dwellers, who had resisted their earlier eviction and felt very bitter about their relocation) and grievance transfer (from Minia to Cairo)—which were also at work, although in a different context, in the environment of Beirut. While in Beirut it was the issue of the Palestinian presence in the country that provided the spark for the initial outbreak of hostility (e.g., the ʿAin al-Rummaneh massacre), in Zawiyya al-Hamra it was simply the extreme conditions of overcrowdedness and dreadful sanitation and housing conditions.

In Cairo as in Beirut, furthermore, the initial outbreak of violence (caused by a dispute between Copts and Muslims over a piece of land) was able to degenerate into large-scale fighting primarily because religious institutions and networks that had developed beforehand (the *jama'at* in particular) were able to step in the fray, mobilize their followers, exploit religious prejudices, and fuel the fire (Ansari 1986, 227–28).

Urbanization and the Multiplication of Double-Edged and Radical-Utopian Religious Networks

In all three countries, urbanization has led to the multiplication of both double-edged and radical-utopian religious networks. As was shown earlier, these groups have often played a very destabilizing role, because while they provide for social integration at the microlevel, they also are frequently based on alternative visions of society and the world, and therefore present a direct challenge to the existing order. This is almost always true of radical-utopian networks, but it is often true of double-edged networks as well. The *hay'ats*, for instance, provided channels through which Khomeini and the radical clerics were able to spread their militant and at first marginal views. When radical-utopian or double-edged networks are linked to counterelites that have their own grievances toward the state and have access to independent resources (as was the case in Iran but not in Egypt), their destabilizing potential is greatly enhanced.

There are at least six plausible connections between rapid urbanization and the multiplication of double-edged and radical-utopian religious networks. The first runs from urbanization through social dislocation, the need for dislocated groups to be reintegrated into a new community, and the resulting appearance of networks that do offer this new sense of community (e.g., the radical Islamic networks in Egypt, or the *hay'ats* in Iran). Second, it is in the city that are often most visible some of the practices that can be considered deviant from a strict, traditionalist Islamist perspective (such as sexual promiscuity, conspicuous consumption, lavish lifestyles, corruption, and "improper" or "undecent" behavior or dress for women).[36] This perceived moral laxity contributed to the development of radical-utopian and double-edged Islamic networks, whose preoccupation with sexual mores and issues of morality was noted earlier. Third, since the city remains the place where innovation, creativity, eccentricity, and unconventionality flourish, it is more likely to encourage the emergence of networks driven by marginal, unorthodox, or radical ideas (Fischer 1984, 216). Fourth, megalopolises also provide individuals with potential anonymity, a factor that facilitates underground activities.

However, the two most important factors in explaining the ability of the city to promote the emergence of double-edged and radical-marginal networks are probably sheer population size and density. As Claude Fischer notes, "Urban concentration affects the minority, the unconventional, and the deviant most. The average citizen can find comradeship almost anywhere; but the more unusual people are, the larger the population they require to find their like" (1984, 224–25). The city, in other words, provides the "critical mass" or "markets" that radical ideologies and groups need to develop, be sustained, and affect the wider environment (Fischer 1984, 228–29). If only one person in a thousand is potentially attracted to a marginal ideology, then no group based on such an ideology is likely to form in small villages. A few radical groups might form in large towns and small cities, but they will not be able to attract many members and are unlikely to have a major impact on politics. In cities of several million people, however, one can imagine the creation of radical informal networks capable of attracting hundreds of individuals and of exerting a major destabilizing influence on the politics of that city. Thus, the increase in urban density and in the absolute size of cities can result in the multiplication of radical networks that otherwise would not appear. Much of the evidence presented in the section of this book dealing with the contemporary period could clearly be read in such stochastic terms.

One should add that such a line of reasoning leads one to predict that, with the growth of cities, radical-utopian networks will continue to flourish, all the more so in conditions of widespread economic crisis and austerity. It does not mean that these networks will ever be able to pose a real challenge to authorities whose coercive power is well developed. What it does mean is that they will keep Islamic utopias alive, that they will persist in their attacks against practices, individuals, and places that they look upon as heretical, and that they will continue to clash on a regular basis with the authorities. The model here may be Egypt in the early 1990s, where the radical Islamic movement suffers from great structural weaknesses (internal fragmentation, the debilitating effects of repeated crackdowns by the authorities, a leadership that has been executed by the government or that languishes in jail, a population that has no appetite for religious dogma and sees radical Islamic militants as fanatics and criminals), but where it nevertheless remains alive and can draw on a readily available pool of new recruits in the ever-expanding new and poor districts of Cairo's periphery.

The Destabilizing Potential of the Urban Poor

There are several aspects of the Egyptian and Iranian experiences that at first seem to support the notion that the urban poor do not constitute an overly destabilizing force. For instance, despite the dramatic growth of Cairo and provincial cities in Egypt over the last thirty years, despite continuing high rates of migration into the capital, and despite the fact that most of Egypt's urban population can be characterized as poor, there has been no clear trend toward large-scale unrest in the country. In addition, the violence that Egypt has experienced has rarely posed a real challenge to the regime. It has been predominantly localized and transient, and either has revolved around bread-and-butter issues (and therefore has been diffused through the distribution of economic rewards) or has been communal (and therefore not directly aimed at the government). More importantly from our perspective, the key partici-pants in incidents of political unrest in Egypt since 1968 have not been anomic masses or uprooted slum and shantytown dwellers confused by rapid socioe-conomic change, but high school and university students[37] and industrial workers.[38] In particular, in Egypt as elsewhere, Islamic radicalism has been not a movement of the downtrodden masses, but a phenomenon largely confined to the educated youth of lower-middle- and middle-class backgrounds.

Although the cases of Iran and Lebanon lend themselves to more nuanced conclusions, they do support the contention that the poor and recent migrants are unlikely to initiate antiregime activities. In Iran, the Fada'iyan drew most of its members not from recent migrants, but from the pool of lower-class urbanites whose lives revolved around the bazaar. More signifi-cantly, in 1977–79 the core of the revolutionary coalition was formed not of uprooted migrants, but of older and better established communities, well inte-grated into the life of the city: the bazaar and the mosque. The migrants to Tehran and other cities became involved only in the revolution's last phase. There is even evidence to indicate that recent migrants were among the groups least inclined to act collectively against the government (Parsa 1989, 5).

The case of Lebanon is somewhat different, in that recently urbanized, lower-class elements there played an active role in the hostilities early on, and their militancy and political assertiveness increased over time. Yet even in Lebanon, the first "round" of the civil war (1974–76) was dominated by the Maronites, who, despite their relatively new presence in Beirut, can be described more adequately as a cohesive community than as unanchored masses.

Thus, in both Lebanon and Iran, the actors who mobilized first and asserted themselves most powerfully and effectively in the political arena were not individuals and groups that had been displaced and whose way of life had been disrupted, but those communities that had best preserved their sociocul-tural identities, cohesion, internal solidarity, and sense of unity and purpose despite rapid modernization: the Maronite community in Lebanon, and the radical clerics and *bazaaris* in Iran. Both examples support Oberschall's con-tention that "it is…the groups least disintegrated that mobilize most rapidly and most effectively to promote their corporate interests" (Oberschall 1973, 123).

In Lebanon, the Maronite community had maintained a sense of collective identity and a substantial degree of internal unity not only at a time of rapid socioeconomic change, but also as both the Sunni and the Shiite populations were drifting away from their traditional leaderships. Similarly, in Tehran and other major Iranian cities, the core of the revolutionary coalition was formed by the strongholds of traditional urban life in the country, the bazaar and the mosque. The Iranian bazaar community was able to preserve its cohesion and sociocultural integrity throughout the postwar period. As for the religious community, despite continuing divisions in its ranks, it was able to act with a substantial degree of unity once revolutionary activities gathered momentum. The essential point is the following: In Lebanon as in Iran, contrary to what both Marxist and modernization theories would lead one to expect, the key actors in the initial phase of mobilization were neither classes nor dislocated and unanchored masses, but cohesive communities and groups.

While the experiences of Egypt, Iran, and Lebanon support the contention that recent migrants do not *by themselves* constitute a destabilizing force and are unlikely to *initiate* antiregime activities, Iran and Lebanon also present us with instances in which large segments of the urban poor (many of whom were migrants) rapidly became mobilized by radical forces. In both countries, the poor made an essential contribution to the demise of the old political order and to the subsequent radicalization of political life. Even in Egypt, large segments of the urban poor joined the "food riots" of January 1977, and they could do so again in similar circumstances of acute crisis.

In Iran, the broad, mass-based demonstrations of late 1978 and early 1979 would not have been possible had it not been for the urban poor's participation in them. In this context, it is important to remember that it was urbanization that prompted the remarkable growth of the *mostaz'afin*, the "disinherited," "dispossessed," and "oppressed" whom Khomeini and his associates claimed to represent. Significantly, the largest concentrations of poor migrants were in the southern sections of Tehran, which is also where some of the largest demonstrations against the shah took place in late 1978 and early 1979 (Kazemi 1980b, 262).[39] More generally, as shown in the Introduction, many among the poor were recent migrants to the capital. While mobilization of these recent migrants was late, partial, and incomplete, the rapid urbanization that preceded the Iranian upheaval nevertheless provided the revolution with a reservoir of lower-class individuals, often underemployed or unemployed, large segments of whom were mobilized by the clerics in the last few months of 1978. Although these individuals provided neither the inspiration nor the leadership of the revolution, they were its foot soldiers and martyrs, and it is they who gave the movement its power.

Recently urbanized masses not only made a critical contribution to the overthrow of the shah, but, as shown earlier, their role in the radicalization of the revolution after the return of Khomeini was even more pronounced. It was the *mostaz'afin* who rapidly became the revolution's most loyal supporters, and it they who contributed most decisively to the radical clerics' ability to eliminate their enemies during the postrevolutionary struggle for power. And they did so largely out of the feeling of empowerment that the radical clerics gave them, and out of the belief that, for the first time, decision makers truly cared about their fate.

Somewhat similarly, this book shows how the accumulation in Beirut of masses that were not absorbed by the capital's patron-client networks contributed greatly to the outbreak of conflict. It is significant that the breakdown of order first took place in the suburbs, which were inhabited primarily by recently urbanized Shiites and Maronites (in addition to lower-class Palestinians). Over time, such elements came to play a growing and clearly destabilizing role in Beirut's politics, while the older, more established Beiruti Sunni and Greek Orthodox communities were increasingly marginalized and proved unable to prevent the destruction of "their" city by newcomers to it. By the mid-1980s, West Beirut, the traditional home of the urbane, cosmopolitan Sunni community, had fallen under the control of Shiite and Druze militiamen of rural origins, filled with anger, intolerant of other sectarian groups, and often bent on looting and destruction. While much of the bitterness and destabilizing impact of these groups should be ascribed to phenomena that have little to do with urbanization per se (one need only think of the violence, displacements, and trauma to which their members were subjected throughout the war), urbanization nevertheless contributed to the violence in Beirut and other Lebanese cities by providing radical forces with a pool of young, assertive slum dwellers, squatters, and other recent migrants. From the mid-1970s onward, militias and street gangs (several of them generously financed by foreign governments) came to provide large segments of the hitherto politically passive or "controlled" populations with channels for upward social mobility. The worsening of the country's economic situation, the control exercised by the militias over the new economic opportunities created by the war (pirate ports, smuggling, trafficking, illegal imports), and the large scale dislocations to which increasing numbers of individuals became subjected, swelled the ranks of the militias.

Both Lebanon's and Iran's recent experiences demonstrate that lower classes can become a reservoir of violence that radical counterelites can tap in a bid for power. They also suggest that a return to the status quo ante may become an illusive task, once large segments among the poor have become politically active and begin to benefit, even if in modest or primarily symbolic ways, from the prevailing unrest (as in 1979–84 Iran, where Khomeini and his lieutenants proved expert at communicating with the masses of the urban poor, at catering to their emotions and aspirations, and at providing them with a new sense of self-worth and empowerment).[40] Thus, the survival of the Islamic Republic between 1981 and 1984, despite growing disillusionment about the course of the revolution, owed a great deal to the new regime's popularity among the urban poor and lower middle classes, composed primarily of individuals who had become politically active during the revolution and who had now been given a stake in the survival of the new order (Hiro 1987, 3). This base of support goes a long way toward explaining why, after 1983–84, the Islamic Republic faced no serious internal challenge. One of the political constraints that now bears on the heirs to Khomeini's mantle is that the *mostaz'afin*, who owe everything to the revolution and their clerical benefactors, will not easily be convinced to relinquish any parcel of their newly found feelings of power and influence. Similarly, in Lebanon, one of the tasks now confronting the Hrawi government is to facilitate the transition to peaceful occupations of the thousands of illiterate or semiliterate young militiamen who know little else than fighting, and who, for fifteen years, owed their livelihood to "the war economy."

Such findings do question the new conventional wisdom regarding the quiescent nature of the political participation of the urban poor in developing countries. While such populations may not be destabilizing by themselves, and while they are unlikely to initiate large-scale antiregime activities, they can nevertheless be radicalized once political unrest already has become widespread. A society already in crisis may turn formerly subdued or controlled populations into highly disruptive forces that either play a major role in perpetuating unrest (as in Lebanon) or provide much of the social base for militant regimes (as in Iran). These conclusions should be kept in mind when one considers scenarios for the future of Third World cities in the next few decades. Given continuing high rates of urbanization and the ever-increasing tensions generated by strained and debt-ridden economies, the kinds of destabilizing phenomena described in this book will become much more prevalent in the future.

Notes

Introduction

1. See *World Bank*, 1984, p. 67, table 4.3.

2. It is revealing to look at Joan Nelson's 1979 book and at Henry Bienen's 1984 article, which are perhaps the best two syntheses of works carried out in the 1960s and 1970s in the field of urban politics in the Third World. Henry Bienen's review of the literature could draw on only seven pieces with a Middle Eastern focus, all of which in fact dealt exclusively with Egypt or Turkey. Moreover, only one study (Karpat 1976) had urban politics as its primary focus.

Nelson's book reflects a similar imbalance. The book is remarkable in its scope: Some four hundred studies were consulted, and their results are clearly presented and summarized in what is the most comprehensive synthesis in the field. Yet Nelson's references on the Middle East can be mentioned in only a few lines: Lapidus 1969; a series of dated works on Turkish migrants (Sewell 1964; Suzuki 1966; Kiray 1970; Makofsky and Ergil 1972; Karpat 1976); three other works on Turkey (Landau 1974; Özbudun 1976 and 1980); a 1959 article on rural-to-urban migrations in Iraq (Phillips 1959); and Abu-Lughod 1969, Petersen 1971, and Geiser 1977 on migrants in Cairo.

To say the least, this is not much, especially if one considers the abundance of references to Latin America, Africa, and Asia (in that order). Furthermore, as in the case of Henry Bienen's article, most of the studies on the Middle East that Nelson consulted are only very indirectly concerned with urban politics and the issue of political stability. Instead, they are often written by sociologists concerned with documenting the "urban villagers" thesis.

3. Patron-client relations "represent a special kind of personal exchange, one where two individuals of different socioeconomic status enter into a relationship in which the individual of higher status uses his influence and resources to provide protection and benefits for the person of lower status, the

latter reciprocating by offering his personal services, loyalty, and general support" (Rassam 1977, 158).

4. Three particularly helpful reviews of the literature on this subject are Nelson 1979 and 1987, and Bienen 1984.

5. See, for instance, Dessouki 1982, 23; Khoury 1983a, 227; and Taheri 1988, 253–54.

6. See, however, Brown 1976; Brown et al. 1986; and Saqqaf 1987.

7. See, for example, the chapters on Cairo in Waterbury 1978; Richards and Waterbury 1990, 263–99.

8. See, for instance, Karpat 1976; Waterbury 1978; and Kazemi 1980a.

9. See, however, the works of Abu-Lughod on Cairo, Karpat on Turkey, Kazemi on Iran, and Khalaf on Lebanon.

10. The best presentation of this argument can be found in Bill and Springborg 1990, 85–136.

11. See, for example, Bill (1972, 1975) and Zonis (1971) on *dowrehs* in Iran; Springborg (1975, 1982) on *shillas* in Egypt; Nakhleh (1976) on the *nawadi* and *jam'iyyat* in Bahrain; and Ghabra (1991) on *diwaniyyas* and other associational groups in Kuwait.

12. See, for instance, the strike of Helwan steel workers in August–September 1971, the rioting by Shubra al-Khayma workers in March–April 1972 and by industrial workers in Cairo in January 1975, the strikes of textile workers in Mahalla al-Kubra in March 1975 and August 1976, and the strike of public transportation workers in Cairo in September 1976. Workers were also active in the street demonstrations ("the food riots") of January 1977 in Cairo, Alexandria, and other cities.

13. For details, see Springborg 1989; Bianchi 1989b; Ayubi 1991.

14. Khouri-Dagher 1985, 53.

15. See Iran's *National Census of Population and Housing* for 1956, 1966, and 1976.

16. The figure for the 1965–80 period is taken from Richards and Waterbury 1990, 266 table 10.2. The authors emphasize that their calculation method underestimates the share of rural-to-urban migrations in urban growth. For the other figures, see Osman 1987, 66.

Chapter 1

1. See, for instance, Hanna Arendt's (1951) study of the rise of totalitarianism and William Kornhauser's (1959) theory of the "mass society."

2. There is an economic side to this "theory of the disruptive migrants," as Joan Nelson calls it. Migrants are alleged to arrive in the city with high expectations, which are further raised by the display of wealth and affluent lifestyles in their new environment. Soon, however, the migrants' hopes of a decent standard of living give way to the reality of low wages, high unemployment, inadequate housing, and other economic deprivations. In this context, migrants become increasingly frustrated and disappointed, and they become a pool of disaffected individuals who can easily be mobilized by radical movements.

3. See Lewis 1961, and, for a summary and criticism of his views, Nelson 1979, 129–30.

4. See Tilly 1970; Hahn and Feagin 1973, 126–27.

5. See Cornelius 1975 on Mexico; Perlman 1976 on Rio; Karpat 1976 on Turkey; Dietz and Moore 1979 on Peru; and Nelson 1979 and Bienen 1984 for two comprehensive reviews and analyses of the literature.

6. See, for instance, Farsoun 1988, 225–26, on the Arab world.

7. A similar process has been at work elsewhere in the Third World. See De Soto 1988 on Peru.

8. Nelson 1979, 1987; Bienen 1984.

9. For examples in a Middle Eastern context (Turkey), see Karpat 1976, 231–32; Suzuki 1966; Sewell 1964.

10. Networks based on primordial ties and loyalties can also serve as avenues for the economic promotion of a given ethnic or religious group. Abner Cohen, for instance, showed how the Hausa community in Nigeria was able to capitalize on such informal networks to dominate the long-distance trade between the savanna and the forest belt (Cohen 1969, 1974). Cohen also notes that the mobilization of ethnic ties and solidarities helps explain the economic success of Lebanese and Syrian communities in West Africa, and of

Chinese communities in parts of the Far East and South East Asia (1969, 191). In a similar vein, John Waterbury (1972a) has documented how the Swasa of Morocco were able to use tribal-based networks to gain control over much of the retail trade in the northern cities of Morocco, especially Casablanca, in the relatively short span of some twenty-five years (1920–45).

11. For a perfect illustration, in a Middle Eastern country, of the type of phenomena that Bienen describes here, see Karpat 1976, 43–44, 134–35.

12. As a broker between a patron and a local community, the *cacique* resembles the Lebanese *qabaday*. There are, however, at least two essential differences between *caciques* and *qabadayat*. First, up to the 1970s at least, the clientele of the *qabaday* was not usually made up primarily of recent migrants to urban areas. Second, unlike the *cacique*, who operates in an ethnically and religiously homogeneous society, the *qabaday* was often perceived as a communal champion. In part 3 the two figures will be further compared and contrasted, particularly from the perspective of their respective impact on urban political stability.

13. See, for example, Cornelius 1977, 347–48.

14. See, for instance, Dietz and Moore 1979 on the poor in Peru, and Karpat 1976 on the *Gecekondus* in Turkey.

Chapter 2

1. See the discussion in Bill and Springborg 1990, 90–91.

Chapter 3

1. Although the weakness of formally organized groups and the absence of municipal institutions differentiate the historic Middle Eastern city from its counterparts in late medieval Europe, these two features are hardly specific to the Middle East. Chinese cities, for instance, also lacked formal institutions during much of their existence (Hourani 1970, 15–16).

2. One thinks here in particular of the ulama, with the control that they *as a group* developed over a variety of educational and judicial institutions, charitable foundations, and especially the religious endowments (*awqaf*), which became an important source of corporate ulama wealth (see Keddie 1972b, 2–3). The guilds as well, while loosely organized at first, did become more structured and permanent over time, especially under the Ottomans

(Issawi 1982, 120). (For evidence of the substantial degree of internal structure displayed by Middle Eastern guilds, see Qudsi—translated in McChesney 1988—on Syria in the nineteenth century; Marcus 1989, esp. pp. 52 and 175 on Aleppo in the eighteenth century; Raymond 1973–74, on Cairo in the eighteenth century; Hopkins 1974, 430, on Tunis.)

A list of urban groups endowed with some corporate features should also include the janissaries (members of the local Ottoman garrisons) and the *ashraf* (descendants of the Prophet) in Aleppo and Damascus in the eighteenth century, as well as the young men's clubs and associations known as *futuwwat* (*javanmardi* in Persia) between the middle of the tenth and the middle of the twelfth centuries. (On the *futuwwat* and related groups, see Hodgson 1974, 66, 108, 125–31; Cahen 1958, 1959a, 1959b. On the *ashraf* and the janissaries as semicorporate groupings in Syrian cities during the late Ottoman period, see Bodman 1963; Meriwether 1981; Marcus 1989.)

3. See Baer 1964, 1970, on Egypt, Syria, and Turkey; Floor 1975, and Ashraf 1970 on Iran; and the more general comments in Hourani 1970, 14–15; Moore 1974, 216.

4. Organizational weakness was not limited to political groups and institutions, but included economic ones as well. Thus, Charles Issawi notes that "in the medieval period, guilds, banks, and shipping convoys were less structured than their European counterparts" (Issawi 1982, 172). Elsewhere, Issawi speaks of "the capacity among Europeans to build larger, more complex, and more durable economic structures than the Middle Easterners built" (Issawi 1981, 120).

5. Issawi 1982, 170; Hodgson 1974, 106.

6. See, however, Cigar's 1981 piece on the development of an urban bourgeoisie in precolonial Morocco.

7. For comments along the same lines, see Cahen 1958, 229; Hodgson 1974, 63, 108; Staffa 1977, 3.

8. The discussion in this paragraph draws heavily on Hodgson 1974, 66–108; Bill and Springborg 1990, 47–48.

9. One thinks here of the "factions" in Byzantine history, for example.

10. See Hourani 1968; Khoury 1983b; Shoshan 1986.

11. Interestingly, given this study's concern with the impact of urbanization on city politics, Lapidus notes that the *zu'ar* were particularly strong in those quarters of Damascus that lay outside the city walls and contained a

population of rural background that had not been assimilated by the city (Lapidus 1984, 154).

12. On the Sufi orders and their significance, see Hodgson 1974, 201–54.

13. These individuals were variously referred to as *ʿarifs, amins,* or *muqaddams.* On the role of the *ʿarifs* under the Mamluks, see Lapidus 1984, 98–99.

14. It is the Ottomans who, in their attempt to govern without having to resort to a centralized administration, made the most efficient use of professional solidarities (and, as we shall see, of neighborhood solidarities). The Ottomans promoted a system of guilds, which they used for purposes of tax collection and control of the population. They also devolved on the guilds tasks such as water supply, urban transport, and street cleaning (for evidence on eighteenth-century Cairo, see Raymond 1973–74). In Safavid and Qajar Iran, too, the shah used guild leaders (*kadkhudas*) and guild elders (*rish safids*) to perform tax collecting and other administrative and economic functions.

15. See, for instance, Meriwether 1981, 38, and Marcus 1989, 315, on Aleppo in the eighteenth century.

16. In the Arab world, the role of heads of quarters reached its highest level under the Ottomans. See, for instance, Staffa 1977, 268, on the broad powers vested in the *shaykh al-hara* in Cairo.

17. See Cahen 1958, 1959a, 1959b, 1960, 1965; Hodgson 1974; Sabari 1981; Lapidus 1984.

18. It is difficult to establish a precise genealogy linking the *ʿayyarun* and the *lutis* (but see Floor 1971, 113; Fathi 1979, 59–60, n. 20). What is clear, however, is that the *ʿayyarun* and the *lutis* resemble one another in several respects, including the existence of similar ideals and values, and a common association with the *zurkhaneh* (gymnasium).

19. In Qajar Persia, the word *luti* could also refer to entertainers, such as acrobats, actors, and dancers (Floor 1971, 103–7).

20. In Qajar Persia, many members of the rich merchant class, and even some princes, were attracted by the ideals of the *lutis* and became *lutis* themselves (Floor 1971, 112).

21. *Lutis* were also distinguished by their distinct costume and carefully cultivated outward appearance (described in Arasteh 1961a, 48) and by their reputation for wit, repartee, and banter (Fathi 1979, 58).

22. Arasteh 1961a, 51; Fathi 1979, 58.

23. Fathi 1979, 59; Floor 1971, 112.

24. This phenomenon is clearly reminiscent of some young men's clubs' attempts to act as urban militias in the cities of Iraq and Syria between the ninth and the twelfth centuries (Cahen 1958, 1959a, 1959b).

Chapter 4

1. The *zurkhaneh* played a particularly important role in the *luti*'s life. It was there that the *luti* could best show some of the qualities that were expected from him, such as physical strength and endurance. See Arasteh 1961a, 1961b; Floor 1971, 1981.

2. One can distinguish between "good *lutis*" and "bad *lutis*" (in which case the word *awbash* may be substituted), "good *futuwwat*" and "bad *futuwwat*" (*baltagi*, literally "thug" or "tough"), *zu'ar* representing the interests and aspirations of the population of their respective quarters, and *zu'ar* composed of criminal elements that preyed on the local population (Floor 1971, 112–13; El-Messiri 1978, 70). It is more likely, however, that the same groups could either help or harm the population of their respective quarters, depending on their moods and on the circumstances.

3. See Cahen 1965 on the *'ayyarun* in Abbassid Baghdad; El-Messiri 1978, 28–29, on the *zu'ar, shuttar,* and *'usab* in medieval Cairo; Mardam-Bey 1982 on the role of the *zorbas* in popular uprisings in eighteenth-century Damascus; and De Groot 1983 and Fathi 1979 on the contribution of the *lutis* to urban unrest in nineteenth-century Iran.

4. Here, one thinks, for example, of the clashes between Sunni and Shiite quarters in medieval Baghdad, or between *Ni'mati* and *Haydari* quarters in late nineteenth-century Iran.

5. As in the case of taxation deemed excessive, large-scale abuses of power by local officials, or lack of essential food items, such as bread.

6. For further documentation, see Raymond 1973–74 on popular uprisings in eighteenth-century Cairo; Shoshan 1980 on grain riots in Cairo during the fourteenth and fifteenth centuries; Lapidus 1984 on Cairo, Aleppo, and Damascus under the Mamluks; De Groot 1983 on urban disturbances in nineteenth-century Iran; and Burke 1986, 1988, on what he calls an "Islamic moral economy."

7. The Constitutional Revolution, for instance, started when two prominent ayatollahs (Ayatollahs Bihbihani and Tabataba'i) took refuge in the shrine of Shah Abd al-Azim, in the south of Tehran, to protest against what they considered to be the government's oppressive policies. Similarly, the traditionalist clerical opposition to constitutionalism, which developed from 1907 onward under the leadership of Fazlallah Nuri, started when Shaykh Fazlallah took refuge in this same Abd al-Azim shrine in the evening of 20 June 1907.

8. See Marsot 1972, 153; Burke 1988.

9. Prior to the modern period, it is only in late-eighteenth- and early-nineteenth-century Egypt, nineteenth-century Iran, and early-twentieth-century Turkey that one reads about significant examples of ulama taking part in uprisings against the authorities.

10. They often shared the economic and political interests of the elite, to which they were sometimes tied through familial (intermarriage) and other social bonds. For historical documentation of the high ulama's political timidity, tendency to defer to the established authorities, and unwillingness to assume a direct role in political decision making, see Crecelius 1972, Baer 1977, 234; Raymond 1985, 83–84.

11. Among the lesser ulama, it was perhaps the seminary students who rebelled most often against the authorities. In Iran, they continued to do so through the 1970s (see part 3). In Egypt, they were particularly active in the forty years preceding Muhammad Ali's rise to power (Baer 1977, 218–19).

12. Lapidus 1984, 144, has emphasized the generally defensive character of such movements in Damascus, Aleppo, and Cairo under the Mamluks, and notes that they "were always protective in nature and never designed to advance new claims."

13. A large number of butchers resided in al-Husayniyya.

14. Such close connections between brotherhoods, guilds, and quarters were not unique to eighteenth-century Cairo. They also existed in other Ottoman cities, where, as in Cairo, they seem to have greatly enhanced the ability of the local population to challenge the authorities. See, for instance, Mardam-Bey 1982 on the Maydan and Salihiya quarters in eighteenth-century Damascus.

15. The translations are drawn from Lapidus 1984 and Baer 1977.

16. See, for instance, Floor 1971, 117, on Qajar Iran.

17. See, for instance, Bodman 1963, 57–64, 100–102.

18. Prisoners would be liberated. Sabari 1981, 74, gives specific examples about Baghdad in the Abbassid period.

19. These incidents, as is well known, were fueled by Europe's increasing political, religious, and commercial presence and influence in the Ottoman Empire, and by the various advantages and privileges that the Ottoman authorities had granted to Christians as a result of European pressures (see, for instance, Ma'oz 1968).

20. Cahen 1958, 1960.

21. For evidence on Tripoli and Aleppo, see Ma'oz 1968, 6–8. On the *yerliyyan*'s contribution to popular uprisings in eighteenth-century Damascus, see Mardam-Bey 1982. The prominent political role of the *ashraf* in Aleppo is quite exceptional. For a discussion, see Raymond 1985, 86–88.

22. The following discussion draws on Hourani 1970, 19; Khoury 1983b, 3.

23. Notables usually act as intermediaries between the authorities and the population, and their ability to deliver goods and services to their clients depends on their cooperating with the government, which normally controls, directly or indirectly, the resources available to the notables. It follows that, unless they have independent access to resources, notables will not generally challenge the authorities.

24. The leader of the *ashraf*, i.e., those individuals with recognized claims to being descendants of the Prophet through the male line.

25. *Iltizams* were state-owned lands and properties that the Ottoman rulers had turned into tax concessions.

26. See also Raymond 1985, 85.

27. Two such ulama were Shaykh Ahmad al-Dardir, the Maliki Mufti and Shaykh of the Sa'idis (students from Upper Egypt) at al-Azhar, and Sayyid Badr al-Maqdisi, who belonged to a famous family of *ashraf* and who had established close ties to the people of al-Husayniyya, where he resided.

One anecdote may suffice to illustrate the destabilizing role that such patrons could play at times. After a group of people came to complain to Shaykh Ahmad al-Dardir that a Mamluk Bey had plundered the house of the head of the Bayyumi order (Marsot 1972, 161), and after the inhabitants of al-Husayniyya had already engaged in rioting, Dardir found it appropriate to further stir them up, as he addressed them in the following terms: "Tomorrow, we will assemble the inhabitants of the suburbs, the quarters, Bulaq, and Old Cairo, and I shall ride with you, and we will loot their houses [the Mamluk ruling elite's] as they have looted ours. Either we shall gain victory or die as martyrs" (quoted in Baer 1977, 229).

28. See Raymond 1973–74, 419; Baer 1977, 218–19.

29. For details, see Ma'oz 1968 and Hourani 1968.

Chapter 5

1. This is shown, for instance, by the substantial revival of the ulama's influence in public affairs after 1941, despite Reza Shah's earlier secularizing policies.

2. See, for example, Crecelius 1972, 1980; Marsot 1968, 1972.

3. Crecelius 1972, 187; Marsot 1968, 279.

4. For details, see De Jong 1978.

5. For instance, there was no formal procedure to determine who was a *mujtahid*. Instead, one's position in the hierarchy rested on the informal consensus of those learned in religious matters.

6. Following the pronouncements of a dead *mujtahid* was forbidden.

7. *Muqallids* literally refers to "those who practice *taqlid* (imitation)."

8. In the nineteenth century, as today, such an assessment relied a great deal on general guidelines and personal preference. No specific rules describing how a believer should select a mujtahid were ever established (Algar 1969, 9–10).

9. For evidence of connections between the *lutis* and Hajji Sayyid Muhammad Baqir, the powerful religious figure who dominated the life of Isfahan in the first half of the nineteenth century, see Algar 1969, 109–12.

10. See also Lambton 1987, 218.

11. See Algar 1969; Hairi 1977.

12. Marsot 1968, 267.

13. Raymond 1973–74, 529–44; Baer 1964, 7–10.

14. See Raymond 1973–74, 421–24. Raymond, incidentally, gives a description of Cairo's *tujjar* that resembles in some respects the image we have

of the *tujjar* in Iran at the end of the nineteenth century. They formed a very wealthy and homogeneous group, whose members were united by shared economic interests and blood ties. As their Iranian counterparts, they were also engaged in long-distance trade.

15. Hourani 1968, 50.

16. For further documentation, see Raymond 1973–74, 426–29.

17. Gabriel Baer has argued that, as a result of these and other processes, there were no longer guilds in Egypt by the turn of the twentieth century. See, however, Goldberg 1986, 47–49, 80–92, for a recent and interesting reappraisal of the question.

18. On these developments, see Abu-Lughod 1973, 101–2.

19. See Algar 1969, 131–36; Lambton 1970, 261.

20. Lambton 1987, 301 n. 1.

21. Algar 1969, 174–78; Keddie 1981a, 58–61.

22. See Keddie 1966a; Algar 1969, 205–21; Lambton 1987, 223–76.

23. On the *anjumans,* see also Arjomand 1988, 38–39.

24. See, for instance, Nadim 1979, 1985, on Cairo.

25. For instance, the work of Joseph (1978c, 1982, 1983) on Beirut, of El-Messiri (1977, 1978, 1988), of Hoodfar (1988), and of Singerman (1993) on Cairo, and of Bauer (1985) on Tehran all points to the importance of neighborhood-based ties and networks for excluded, impoverished, and relatively marginal groups, especially lower-class women.

Chapter 6

1. For instance, local dignitaries in eighteenth- and nineteenth-century Ottoman cities, *bazaaris* and ulama in nineteenth-century Iran, heads of the *ashraf* and the Sufi orders, and prominent merchants and guild and neighborhood leaders in the late eighteenth and early nineteenth centuries in Egypt.

2. An exception, here, would be the *ashraf* and the janissaries in Aleppo in the eighteenth and early nineteenth centuries, in that both groups did put forward new claims to a greater share of political power in the city.

3. Instances that clearly fit that pattern include the role of the notables during the disturbances in the Syrian provinces in the eighteenth and nine-

teenth centuries, and that of the ulama and *bazaaris* in the protest movements in Iran in the late nineteenth and early twentieth centuries.

Chapter 7

1. The interested reader can consult the outstanding syntheses of Salibi 1965, 1988; Hourani 1946, 1966, 1976, 1986.

2. "In Sunni Beirut, this consisted of a fez (*tarbush*), moustache, a cloth belt (*zunnar*) with a dagger and pistol pushed into it, a short cane, and a pair of baggy trousers (*sirwal*) drawn in tight below the knee and weighted with pebbles" (Johnson 1986, 20).

3. The association's full name was The Beirut Islamic Society of Benevolent Intentions (*jam'iyya al-maqasid al-khayriyya al-islamiyya fi bayrut*).

4. As Johnson (1986, 15) has noted, the Maqasid's founding fathers appear to have been concerned about Christian ascendancy in trade, and to have linked the Sunnis' ability to keep up with the educational promotion of the community. Over time, however, the *Maqasid* widened considerably its range of activities to include a variety of welfare as well as purely educational services.

5. It is true that there were always links between Mount Lebanon and Jabal 'Amil, between the port of Tripoli and 'Akkar, or between Jabal 'Amil and the coastal city of Tyre. Nevertheless, until the nineteenth century, at least, the five areas distinguished in the text remained distinct from one another.

6. Albert Hourani (1976) was the first to point to the crucial importance of the opposition between the mountain and the city in Lebanese politics. See also Picard 1988, 19–24.

7. While Muslims formed the most important segment of *ahl al-sahil*, the "ideologies of the cities" were not specifically Muslim ideologies. The Greek Orthodox and, to a lesser extent, the Greek Catholic populations of the coast also participated in them.

8. For details, see for instance Hourani 1966; Salibi 1965; Hudson 1968.

9. The National Pact became the cornerstone of the postindependence Lebanese political system. It consisted of an unwritten agreement between Bishara al-Khouri and Riad al-Sulh, the leaders of the Maronite and Sunni communities at the time. Through this covenant, the Sunni community

acknowledged the Maronites' predominant position in the country and recognized the existing borders of Lebanon as a sovereign and independent state, thereby abandoning the idea of reintegrating Lebanon into a broader Syrian entity. In exchange, the Maronites recognized the "Arab character" of Lebanon and committed themselves not to seek European protection and interference in the affairs of Lebanon.

Chapter Eight

1. Literally Hezb-e Tudeh-e Iran, or Party of the Iranian Masses, Iran's communist party.

2. According to Abrahamian, for instance, only about two thousand individuals participated in the procession, which, in 1905, took refuge (*bast*) in the Abdul Azim shrine in southern Tehran and thereby started the Constitutional Revolution (Abrahamian 1968, 185).

3. See Abrahamian 1968; 1982, 347–71.

4. The purpose of these unions was not to represent the interests of labor, but rather to bind the working class to the regime through the selective distribution of incentives, rewards, and punishments. Unions shied away from political issues and remained concerned exclusively with wages, bonuses, and working conditions. They also suffered from extreme fragmentation, as most of them were confined to individual factories (Halliday 1979, 203–7).

5. See Goldberg 1986; Beinin 1987, 1988; Beinin and Lockman 1988. Unions contributed greatly to the atmosphere of social and political upheaval in the country at the time. They came to play a particularly disruptive role in the transportation sector (one thinks in particular of the powerful Cairo Tramway Workers Union) and in the textile industry, especially in the factories of Shubra (a northern suburb of Cairo) and in Ramlah (near Alexandria), where they attracted several thousand workers (Goldberg 1986; Beinin and Lockman 1988).

6. For details, see Abdalla 1985, 119–37; Bianchi 1986; Beinin 1989.

7. *PPS* stands for Parti Populaire Syrien, the French name by which the Syrian Social Nationalist Party is better known.

8. On the PPS, see Yamak 1966a, 1966b.

9. There is evidence of organized labor groups operating in Lebanon as early as the beginning of the century. On the trade union movement under the

French mandate, see Couland 1970. In the 1950s, unions were active around the Port of Beirut, the refinery of the Iraq Petroleum Company in Tripoli, among tobacco workers, and in the banking and the railroad sectors (Stauffer 1952, 84–85).

10. The labor movement remained imbued with confessional and regional loyalties. In addition, well into the 1960s, craft unions and house unions continued to outnumber industry unions by a margin of about two to one (see Khalaf 1968, 120, tables 2 and 3). Inevitably, the large number of house unions continued to feed paternalistic relations between employers and employees, while few unions were able to cooperate with one another (Khalaf 1968, 130–36). As a result, national federations remained weak, and not until 1970 was a General Confederation of Lebanese Trade Unions created. Even then, government, factory owners, and union leaders often cooperated closely with one another to contain labor militancy and keep workers in ignorance of their rights. Much of the rising labor militancy of the early 1970s, in fact, reflected a strong desire on the part of the rank and file to reform the union movement, make it more democratic, more representative of workers' interests, and more assertive vis-à-vis employers (Petran 1987, 131–33).

11. For specific examples involving the lawyers', bank employees', and teachers' unions, see Messarra 1988, 19–20.

12. See, for instance, Snider 1984 on the Lebanese Forces.

13. Clément and Paul 1984, 24; Entelis 1987, 23.

14. Ironically, for a party that purports to be leftist and future-oriented, patron-client ties and family prestige often have been more important than ideology or programmatic appeal in ensuring whatever success the party has had. For instance, the party's secretary-general, Khalid Muhyi al-Din, hardly owes his prominent local position in the Qalyubiyya district to his ideology or national stature. More important to his Qalyubiyya followers have been his personality, his patronage, and his family connections (G. Krämer 1987–88, 289).

15. See Hendriks 1987; Roussillon 1987–88; Springborg 1989; Makram-Ebeid 1989.

16. As in the case of spontaneous popular uprisings (e.g., in January 1977 and February 1986) or of rioting by students (e.g., in 1968, 1972–73) and industrial workers (e.g., in 1968, 1971–72, 1975–77, and on a regular basis since 1984).

17. See Qubain 1961 and Hottinger 1961.

18. The Baʿath, for instance, played an instrumental role in sparking the uprising in Tripoli, while the communists were active in some of Beirut's quarters, especially Museitbe. As the crisis wore on, however, the alliance between Communists and Baʿathists broke apart (largely because of developments in Damascus), and soon the two parties began fighting each other (Hottinger 1961, 138).

19. Even within more formally organized entities such as the Lebanese Forces, the PSP, Amal, and the LCP, the civil war witnessed a tendency toward devastating power struggles and the formation of coteries, cliques, and groups based on narrow bases of solidarity.

Chapter 9

1. See, for example, the essays in Binder 1966b and Salem 1973. An important dissenting voice was Hudson 1968.

2. Significantly, not only were most members of the Lebanese Parliament unaffiliated with any political party, but most parties were parties in name only. They had no clear program or ideology, and very little internal structure. They were primarily instruments that prominent families used to organize their clienteles. It is revealing that, in the 1940s, followers of the National Bloc and of the Constitutional Union (or Destour) were simply referred to as "Khourys" or "Eddés," after the names of their respective leaders (Suleiman 1967, 269). Similarly, the National Liberal Party and the Progressive Socialist Party remained very closely identified with, respectively, Camille Chamoun and Kamal Jumblatt.

3. The monarchy's belated attempt to create, in 1975, a single mobilization party, Rastakhiz (Resurgence), ended up in total failure. To many Iranians, in fact, Rastakhiz's rapid demise only offered further proof that the state was essentially a superstructure floating above society, but without any substantial link to it.

4. Such as Sayyid Gallal, described by Springborg (1975).

5. In the early to mid-1970s, Jumblatt was able to mobilize large segments of the Sunni community. He even received significant support from progressive Shiites and Christians alienated from their community leaderships (al-Khazen 1988, 195; Petran 1987, 154).

6. Najah Wakim, a Greek Orthodox candidate to the parliamentary elections of 1972, won one of the seats allocated to his community in Beirut,

thanks to the support of the Sunni electorate, while few Greek Orthodox voted for him (Petran 1987, 125; Khalaf 1985, 92).

7. Although religious animosity was inextricably meshed with real or perceived class inequalities, religion was a centrifugal force of its own.

8. A key stage in this strategy was when the Kata'ib brought the war from the suburbs, to which clashes had been limited until then, into the heart of the Lebanese capital. The Kata'ib shelled downtown Beirut and eventually left the commercial area almost completely destroyed. Salibi has rightly emphasized the irony inherent in this high point of the first phase of civil war, by noting that "the party which, since its foundation in 1936, had dedicated itself to the preservation of Lebanon, seemed now bent on the reduction of the Lebanese capital to ashes" (Salibi 1976, 126).

9. An implicit element of the 1943 Pact was that Lebanon's Muslim population would not try to use the help of its fellow Muslims in neighboring states to enhance its power position within the Lebanese entity.

10. See, for instance, Purcell 1981, 209–10 on Mexico.

11. Johnson 1986, 155; Petran 1987, 58–59.

12. Sarkis, however, would be elected in 1976.

13. Along somewhat similar lines, in Iran, rapid urbanization accentuated the limits of the shah's patrimonial policies. The capital, especially, with its rapidly increasing population and its concentration of politically aware and active groups (the new middle class, the *bazaaris*, the intelligentsia, and the students) constituted an area where the shah's politics of co-optation and repression proved antiquated and inadequate. A population of five million people—most of it below age twenty-five, and a large segment of it literate and politically conscious—could hardly be denied indefinitely some form of political participation.

14. Hottinger 1966, 96; Johnson 1986, 50.

15. Owen 1976b; Johnson 1986, 131.

16. See Khalaf 1976, 444; Farouk-Sluglett and Sluglett 1982, 62.

17. Khalidi 1979; Petran 1987, 119–41.

18. Entelis 1974, 112–13; Stoakes 1975, 216.

19. Norton 1987, 129; Cobban 1985, 219.

20. The percentage of Shiites living in urban areas had increased from about 10 percent in the late 1940s to 63 percent in 1974 (Nasr 1985, 10–11).

21. Substantial numbers also flowed to Imam Musa al-Sadr's Movement of the Disinherited, although it was not until 1978 that Amal rose to a position of prominence.

22. For some evidence on the rural migrants' lesser attachment to the city than to their respective villages of origin and sects, see Khuri 1975. Statistics on the growth of the Lebanese capital in the last three decades make it inevitable that newcomers and their children formed a majority of Beirut's population in the 1970s and 1980s (see the Introduction).

23. Initially, Imam Sadr intended his Harakat al-Mahrumin to be open to all of Lebanon's "disinherited," not to the Shiites alone; and in its early years, indeed, the movement was able to appeal to a significant number of Christians.

24. In fact, in the early 1970s, much of the political strategy of the traditional *zu'ama'* and their sons aimed at preventing "upstarts" from building a clientele for themselves.

25. To be sure, the 1960s and early 1970s saw an overall broadening of elite recruitment, a relatively high rate of turnover of deputies to the Parliament, and a tendency for the elite to draw on younger and more educated elements than in the past (Khalaf 1987, 121–22). Yet elite members continued to be drawn, to an overwhelming extent, from the same notable families (Khalaf 1987, chap. 6). In fact, in the parliaments of 1964, 1968, and 1972, the proportion of sons who simply inherited their seats from their fathers was not only surprisingly high (about 20 percent), but higher than it had been in the 1943 Parliament (Khalaf 1987, 138). Similarly, almost half the deputies in the same three parliaments belonged to families with a history of parliamentary representation (Khalaf 1987, 138–39).

26. In order to be elected for a second term, Chamoun needed a constitutional amendment, which required a two-thirds majority in Parliament—hence his decision to rig the 1957 elections.

27. Méouchy's opposition to Chamoun stemmed primarily from the patriarch's fear that, by aligning Lebanon far too closely with the West, and by illegally excluding Muslim opposition leaders from participation in the political process, Chamoun was violating the covenant on which the Lebanese political system was based, thereby endangering sectarian harmony and, therefore, the position and security of the Maronites in the country. See Frankel 1976a, 1976b for details.

28. *Chaqu-kashan* were the heirs of the *lutis*, which part 2 examined.

242   *Urban Unrest in the Middle East*

The *lutis*, who had kept a low profile during Reza Shah's reign, reemerged in the 1940s, at which point they came to be referred to as *chaqu-kashan*.

29. Although most political factions used *chaqu-kashan*, mobs, Cottam tells us, "were most frequently purchased by rightist and royalist politicians." Thus, Cottam sees *chaqu-kashan* in this period playing a key role in translating the unskilled workers' "vague loyalty to the shah" into "overt political support" (Cottam 1979, 37–38).

30. To reward Sha'ban Ja'fari for his services, the shah had a luxurious sport palace built for him. See Floor 1981, 93.

31. I am indebted to Ahmad Ashraf for providing me with this information.

32. By eliminating the *chaqu-kashan* as a political force, the shah may have deprived himself of popular leaders whom he could have used to prop up his regime in 1977–78. It is perhaps significant that one of the very first individuals to be executed by the new regime was a certain Hossein Faroutan, a *chaqu-kashan* accused of having organized antirevolutionary bands in the last few months of the Pahlavi dynasty (Ahmad Ashraf, personal communication). This incident would seem to indicate that many revolutionaries believed that *chaqu-kashan* still represented a potential danger because of their ability to organize and mobilize segments of the lumpenproletariat.

It is doubtful, however, that the shah could have saved himself and his regime by manipulating *chaqu-kashan* networks. In any event, although the regime did hire a few *chaqu-kashan* to attempt to reverse the course of events in the last few months of 1978, this policy not only failed to attain its desired objectives, but even proved counterproductive, since the violence, destruction, and looting perpetrated by hooligans and thugs hired by SAVAK and the police had the effect of further alienating large segments of the population, especially the *bazaaris*, from the regime (Parsa 1989, 115–19, 225–30).

33. The term *Hezbollahis* was also used by Khomeini and militant clerics simply to describe their supporters.

34. There is much disagreement among scholars as to who was a typical member of the pasdaran in the early to mid-1980s. At a conference on revolutionary Iran organized by Princeton University in April 1987, Ahmad Ashraf suggested that the pasdaran were recruited primarily from among the educated youth who, often inspired by the ideas of Ali Shari'ati, had been active in the antishah demonstrations during 1977–78. Both Bakhash (1984a) and Hiro (1987), however, emphasize the lower-class or lower-middle-class backgrounds of the youth staffing the pasdaran. According to Hiro, "A typical rev-

olutionary guard came from a lower-middle-class or poor urban family, and was totally dedicated to Khomeini and the Islamic revolution" (1987, 110). Similarly, Bakhash argues that tens of thousands of lower-class young men, unemployed or underemployed and living in the slums and poorer districts of the cities, found much needed work in the pasdaran (1984a, 244). In the second edition of his book, he also notes that most pasdaran commanders "rose from humble and poor backgrounds" (Bakhash 1990, 290). Cottam, for his part, refers to "one revolutionary leader [who] described the composition of the revolutionary guards contingents he knew as 10 percent city thugs, 60 percent poor youths who needed a job, and 30 percent ideologically dedicated youth" (Cottam 1988, 192). Overall, the pasdarans seem to have recruited from a broader social base than the *komitehs* and Hezbollah. By contrast in particular with the *Hezbollahis*—the overwhelming majority of whom were definitely of lower-class and lumpenproletarian origins—the guards appear to have been able to attract large numbers of educated youth.

Chapter 10

1. Halliday 1979, 220; Graham 1980, 224; Abrahamian 1982, 433.

2. Ahmad Ashraf, personal communication.

3. In fact, *tujjar* and *sarrafs* often were the same individuals (Mobasser 1985, 52).

4. Significantly, after they took control of the Iranian revolution, the radical fundamentalist clerics often praised the shopkeepers, while being highly critical of the big merchants, who by and large had supported Ayatollah Shariatmadari between 1979 and 1983 (Ashraf 1983).

5. See, for instance, Zonis (1971) on the lack of cooperation and widespread distrust among members of the political elite, and Arjomand 1988, 108–14, on how the shah's policies were able to keep the new middle class divided, atomized, and therefore incapable of acting as a "class for itself."

6. For a description of a typical meeting of a *hay'at-e senfi*, see Thaiss 1972, 353–56.

7. See Mottahedeh 1985, 347; Thaiss 1971, 201; Thaiss 1972, 353.

8. The *hay'at-e senfis* controlled considerable resources, as shown by this anecdote: "At a *hay'at* I attended on the anniversary of the death of the Sixth Imam, a group of *bazaaris* and others were asked by a religious leader to help build a school where the ulama could control the teaching of religious

doctrine. Within half an hour, someone had donated 1,800 meters of land, another had contributed all the bricks necessary, another all the plaster, another lime, and several offered to share the cost of steel girders and beams. It was then proclaimed to the group that more than 400,000 tomans (about $53,500) [written in 1971] had been pledged" (Thaiss 1971, 202–3).

9. From the mid-1940s to the mid-1950s, the bazaar provided much of the support for two religious groups closely tied to the militant Ayatollah Kashani: the Mojahedin Islam Society (nominally headed by the preacher Shams Qanatabadi), and the much more radical Fadaʿiyan-e Islam of Navvab Safavi. The Fadaʿiyan, in particular, recruited mostly among illiterate or semi-literate lower- or lower-middle-class _bazaari_ youth (Kazemi 1984, 168). Significantly perhaps, Muhammad Mehdi Abd-e Khodaʿi, the fifteen-year-old member of the Fadaʿiyan who, in February 1952, attempted to assassinate a National Front Majlis deputy (Hossein Fatemi), was a minor attendant in a small hardware store, while the man who attempted to murder prime minister Hossein Ala in November 1955 was a small shopkeeper (Kazemi 1984, 166). It also seems that a few _bazaari_ merchants provided the Fadaʿiyan with much of its financial resources, and that pressure from the bazaar played an important role in securing the release from prison of Tahmasabi (prime minister Razmara's assassin) and the Imami brothers (the assassins of prominent secular historian Ahmad Kasravi).

10. Throughout the 1945–53 period, the bazaar revealed itself to be one of the main sources of support of Mossadegh, the charismatic, nationalist politician who was a bitter foe of the shah and became Iran's prime minister between 1951 and 1953. In Tehran and other cities, the bazaar repeatedly shut down to support Iran's nationalist leader. Most spectacularly, when Mossadegh resigned in July 1952, the bazaar was actively involved in the unfolding nationalist uprising in the capital and other major cities (Ashraf 1988, 548; Parsa 1989, 96). Drawing on Iranian sources published after the revolution, Ashraf writes that "of a total of thirty five demonstrators who were arrested in Tehran during [that] uprising, twenty five were petty traders, craftsmen, apprentices, and footboys, four were drivers, two journalists, one white-collar worker, one student, and one unskilled worker....It is likely that, of a total 235 people killed and injured...,the majority were middle and lower _bazaari_ members" (Ashraf 1988, 548). Following Mossadegh's arrest, _bazaaris_ continued to strike in his support, despite heavy government repression.

11. Scattered and limited evidence indicates that lower _bazaaris_ formed the majority of the participants in the insurrection of June 1963. In Tehran and Tabriz, according to Ahmad Ashraf (who relies on a variety of Iranian,

European, and American sources), "tens of thousands of lower *bazaari* elements participated in [the] demonstrations, [and] approximately 200 to 300 demonstrators, many of whom came from the masses of the lower *bazaaris* (apprentices and footboys) were killed in clashes with the security forces" (Ashraf 1988, 550).

There are some striking similarities in the bazaar's political role in 1951–53 and in 1963. In both cases, the bazaar as a whole shut down repeatedly, either in support of Mossadegh or to protest against the shah's policies. In both instances, too, strikes and riots in the bazaars started the major uprisings in the capital and in the largest provincial cities, with the unrest spreading only subsequently to other areas of the cities (Abrahamian 1968, 205–6).

12. Ashraf and Banuazizi 1985, 15; Parsa 1989, 115–19.

13. Algar 1972, 248; Bakhash 1990, 30.

14. See Tabari 1983; Bakhash 1984a, 24–28; Arjomand 1988, 85.

15. See, for instance, Balta and Rulleau 1979, 169; Milani 1988, 116.

16. See, for example, Bakhash 1984a, 13.

17. Parsa 1989, 101; Salehi 1988, 13.

18. "Price squads" formed under the auspices of the Rastakhiz party were sent to force the *bazaaris* to sell at prices set by the government.

19. See Taheri 1978, 98–101; Halliday 1979, 220; Graham 1980, 224; Abrahamian 1982, 498; Bashiriyeh 1984, 103; Ashraf 1988, 557; Parsa 1989, 103–5.

20. Vahid Nowshirvani, who is extremely familiar with the world of Iran's bazaar, confirmed this to me in several telephone interviews conducted in 1988.

Chapter 11

1. On the genesis of these groups, see El Guindi 1981; Kepel 1985, 129–41; Abdalla 1985, 226; Bianchi 1989b, 194–95.

2. On these and other services provided by the *jama'at*, see in particular Kepel 1985, 142–46; Bianchi 1989b, 194–95.

3. For hypotheses along these lines, see Davis 1984.

4. Kepel 1985, 156–71; Bianchi 1989b, 196–97.

5. Alan Cowell, *The New York Times*, Section A, p. 7, col. 1, 13 December 1989.

6. See Hendriks 1987, 27; Sadowski 1987, 37; Springborg 1989, 229; Bianchi 1989a, 1989b.

7. On Islamic investment companies, their links to the Islamic movement, and their conflict with the state in the 1980s, see Roussillon 1988; Springborg 1989, 47–61; and Ayubi 1991, chap. 8.

8. Until the mid-1980s, there were, in Egypt as in many other Middle Eastern countries, two kinds of mosques: public (*hukumi*) and private (*ahli*) mosques. Private mosques were largely independent of government control. In these *ahli* mosques, the preacher was chosen by the individual who owned the mosque (often the one who had the mosque built, or his descendants). The prayer leader (*imam*), however, was usually much more important than the owner of the mosque, as shown by the fact that a private mosque would often be known by the name of its preacher and be referred to as "the mosque of Shaykh X" (Gaffney 1987, 47).

The 1970s saw the doubling of the number of *ahli* mosques in the country, from about twenty thousand in 1970 to about forty thousand in 1981 (Ansari 1986, 218). The number and popularity of popular *imams* increased accordingly. In the late 1970s, several of these clerics made national reputations for themselves, some of them by engaging in polemics with the government. Concerned with the autonomy displayed by private mosques and their preachers, the interior minister announced in the summer of 1985 that the Ministry of Awqaf henceforth would exert direct control over all the *ahli* mosques. Immediately afterward, large numbers of *ahli* mosques, particularly those serving as a focus for the activities of Islamic militants, were invested with *imams* appointed by the state. They became, in theory, *hukumi* mosques. In practice, however, the Ministry of Religious Endowments lacked the resources to exert direct and effective control over the formerly private mosques, especially because in the preceding decades al-Azhar had not produced enough graduates to provide an *imam* to each of the forty thousand or so private mosques (Springborg 1989, 242; Ansari 1986, 218). In this context, many mosques continued to operate outside direct government control in the early 1990s.

9. Kazemi 1980a, 63; Mottahedeh 1985, 350.

10. Hosain was the Prophet Muhammad's grandson, who was martyred at Kerbala in the seventh century and whose life is central to Shiite theology. See Fischer 1980, 13–21, and Ajami 1986, 139–42, on what Fischer called "the Kerbala paradigm."

11. See Kazemi 1980a, 63; Mottahedeh 1985, 355–56.

12. Kazemi 1980b, 259; Mottahedeh 1985, 356.

13. Zonis 1983, 592–93; Taheri 1987, 213.

14. Kazemi 1980a; Ashraf and Banuazizi 1985, 25.

15. As Bashiriyeh notes, "Shariʿati, Al-e Ahmad, and Bani-Sadr were all sons of provincial clerics closely associated with the bazaar" (1984, 75).

16. In a famous lecture given in 1962, for example, Mehdi Bazargan had called upon the ulama to break their isolation and involve themselves more actively in public affairs. (By late 1979, Bazargan probably regretted having done so, and wished that the ulama would now return to their mosques and seminaries.)

17. It is ironic that the writings of Shariʿati, who was very anticlerical and sought to break the ulama's power on Shiite thought, convinced many young intellectuals to participate in a movement that resulted in clerical rule in Iran.

18. Needless to say, the networks that have been described mobilized only *segments* of the educated youth. Many others became involved through the leftist and Islamo-leftist underground movements of the 1970s and, albeit to a lesser extent, through the National Front and the Tudeh, both of which were revived during the revolutionary process. Much of the youth's participation in the revolutionary events also took place on an unorganized, spontaneous basis.

19. Literally, *hosseiniyehs* are places for the celebration of the martyrdom of Imam Hosain.

20. See Halliday 1979, 19; Balta and Rulleau 1979, 152; Akhavi 1980, 187; Schahgaldian 1989, 22.

21. Milani 1988, 193; Arjomand 1981b, 312.

22. *Ayatollah al-ʿozma* literally means "greatest signs of God."

23. In late 1991, there were five grand ayatollahs: Golpayegani, Khoʾi, Tabatabaʿi Qomi, Montazeri, and Araki (Ahmad Ashraf 1990 and personal communications; Schahgaldian 1989, 22 n. 32).

24. Schahgaldian estimates the number of ayatollahs in the late 1980s at some two hundred (1989, 22). Under the Islamic Republic, many ayatollahs' functions have come to include the day-to-day management of government branches.

25. *Mollas, tollab,* and *asyad* are, of course, overlapping categories.

26. Abrahamian 1980, 24; Akhavi 1980, 187; Fischer 1980, 79. Green (1984, 156) puts the number of shrine attendants in Tehran alone at some five thousand.

27. As shown earlier, ever since the nineteenth century, Shiites seeking guidance and advice on what is permissible or forbidden by religious law would usually follow the opinions of a living *mujtahid,* that is, a cleric whose learning entitles him to interpret Islamic law. A *mujtahid's* followers are known as *muqallids,* i.e., those who practice *taqlid* (imitation).

28. Writing only a few years after the death of Ayatollah Borujirdi, Binder made the following observations on the procedure that until then had governed the choice of the *marjaʿ-i mutlaq:* "It would seem that a relatively small group of some thirty or forty persons, most of whom reside at Qom, perform the function of the College of Cardinals by acknowledging the leadership to someone. To the insiders, these are known as *raʾis tarash* (sculptors of the head) or *marjiʿ dorostkun* (creators of the following). This group is partially comprised of *Ayatullahzadegan,* or the descendants of once famous and learned *mujtahids,* and partially of the leading teachers at Qom. Certain merchants are important, as is the influential Ayatollah Behbahani in Teheran, and a small group of *muballighin,* or propagandists, who are not *mujtahids* but preachers" (Binder 1965, 134).

29. The *sahm-i imam* represents one-half of the *khums,* itself one-fifth of annual income that Muslims, especially wealthy ones, are expected to contribute to the religious authorities.

30. See Mottahedeh 1985; Fischer 1980, chaps. 2 and 3; Kazemi 1988, 29; Schahgaldian 1989, 25–26.

31. This is how a former theology student in Najaf remembers the place between the two world wars: "I came to Najaf when it was a city of disease and poverty, with pale faces, ragged clothes, and crumbling houses filled with insects and scorpions, where the streets were narrow and filthy, the beggars at every door and corner, the drinking water carried from far away on donkeys and sold like bread and gas. Most Najaf resources consisted of trusts, charities, and fifths (*akhmas*) coming from outside and from visitors and mourners who reached the valley of peace from various points of the world" (quoted in Mallat 1988, 18).

32. See the cases of, respectively, Ahmad Kasravi and Jalal Al-e Ahmad, in Mottahedeh 1985, 109, 289.

33. Milani 1988, 307; Schahgaldian 1989.

34. This ability, again, varied over time according to particular domestic and international circumstances, state policies, and clerical leadership.

35. Most prominent here was the case of the Fadaʿiyan-e Islam, which will be examined later.

36. Grand Ayatollahs Najafi Marashi, Golpayegani, and Shariatmadari.

37. Bakhash 1984b, 181; Parsa 1989, 201–5.

38. Since the land reform was applied to religious endowments, it deprived the clergy of much-needed resources that until then had been the main source of financial support for the upkeep of mosques, seminaries, shrines, and clerics.

39. The Literacy Corps was an institution through which young graduates of Iran's high schools and universities were sent to the countryside to teach children basic literacy skills. Bakhash notes, "From the point of view of the ulama, the Literacy Corps threatened to spread the seeds of secularism from the cities to the villages, and challenged the role of the mollas…as village teachers" (1990, 25).

40. See chapter 10.

41. Akhavi 1980, 129–43; Bill 1982, 25.

42. Akhavi 1980, 138–40; Fischer 1980, 120–21; Milani 1988, 118.

43. The Religious Corps's mission was to propagate an ideology that emphasized the compatibility, and indeed the complementary nature, of religion and the modernization undertaken under the banner of the shah's "White Revolution" (Akhavi 1980, 139). As for the Religious Propagandists, they were to engage in a variety of religious, health, educational, development, and social activities that often overlapped considerably—especially in the rural areas, where they were supposed to concentrate their actions—with those activities through which the ulama had been able to preserve a modicum of power and influence (Akhavi 1980, 140–41; Mortimer 1982, 319–20).

44. Ayatollah Saʿidi in 1970 and Ayatollah Ghoffari in 1975.

45. The 1971 Persepolis celebrations and the replacement of the Islamic calendar with an imperial one are two examples of such policies.

46. For a description of some of the specific government policies and decisions aimed at the islamization of Iranian society, see, for instance, Milani 1988, 308–9.

47. The genesis and activities of these groups have been well documented. See, inter alia, Ibrahim 1982; Kepel 1985; Sivan 1985; Dekmejian 1985, chap. 6. For the decade of the 1980s, see Springborg 1989, 215–45; Bianchi 1989b, 199–204.

48. *Amir* often has a religious connotation, as in *amir al-mu'minin*, commander of the faithful.

49. The Muslim Brotherhood was outlawed in 1954, after the new regime blamed it for a failed attempt on Nasser's life. Thereafter, it went underground, where it managed to survive despite successive crackdowns by the state.

50. A Muslim thinker executed in Cairo in 1966, whose writings have served as a source of inspiration for the current generation of Islamic radicals throughout the Sunni world.

51. Takfir wa'l-Hijra is a name that was given to the group by outside observers. The group's real name was *jama'at al-muslimin* (the Society of Muslims).

52. See Ibrahim 1982, 128; Dekmejian 1985, 95; Ansari 1986, 216–18; Kepel 1985, 206.

53. See Ibrahim 1980; Davis 1984; Kepel 1985; Ansari 1986.

54. On the Jihad group in particular, see Kepel 1985, 217–18; Ansari 1986, 221. The background of arrested members of the "Video Group"—an offshoot of Jihad that in the mid-1980s made a name for itself by engaging in acts of arson against video stores dealing in "decadent" films—points to a somewhat different profile, in which the traditional urban working class is much more heavily represented (see Springborg 1989, 214). This may indicate that radical Islamic groups are diversifying their social base and are now reaching out to more "traditional urbanites" types.

55. Davis 1984; Kepel 1985; Sivan 1985.

56. Kepel 1985, 84; Sivan 1985, 86; Davis 1984, 155.

57. Dr. Husain al-Dhahabi, one of Egypt's top ulama at the time.

58. For details, see Kepel 1985, 91–102; Ibrahim 1982, 134–35; Dekmejian 1985, 96.

59. In contemporary Egypt, young people often have to postpone marriage because they do not have the money to rent a place to start their household.

60. It is too early to assess the significance of the upsurge in the activities of radical Islamic groups in the second half of the 1980s (Gordon 1990; Springborg 1989, 215–45; Ayubi 1991). While the arrest of hundreds of members from the Islamic underground in 1987, 1988, and 1989 suggests that the authorities felt a renewed sense of danger, it remains unlikely that radical Islamicists can pose a real threat to the regime—except to the extent that they have been able to infiltrate the military. In fact, the acts by which the Islamic radicals manifested themselves between 1986 and 1990—sectarian violence, and assassination attempts on U.S. and Israeli diplomatic personnel, on prominent secular journalists, and on former government officials known for their hunting down of Islamic militants—may have been spectacular, but they remained sporadic and limited in scale. The violence of these acts, well publicized by the government, may also increase the average Egyptian's dislike of the radicals and their methods, and strengthen public support for a government crackdown on the Islamic underground. More importantly, such violence "can be interpreted as the desperate acts of the weak" and as "evidence of the relatively peripheral nature of Islamic radicalism" (Springborg 1989, 218) under a government that has displayed great skill at isolating and discrediting the extremist Islamic groups through its control of the media and by allowing the more moderate wings of the Islamic movement to participate in the political process and develop a stake in the health of the Egyptian economy.

61. His real name was Sayyid Mojtaba Mir-Lowhi. The pseudonym refers to the Safavid dynasty, which made Shiism the state religion of Iran in the early sixteenth century.

62. Ahmad Kasravi (in March 1946).

63. Abdul-Hosein Hazhir (in November 1949) and Haj-Ali Razmara (in March 1951).

64. Hamid Zanganeh (in March 1951).

65. In November 1955.

66. Kazemi 1984, 168; Ferdows 1983, 242; Taheri 1987, 58.

67. The membership of the Fadaʿiyan was overwhelmingly urban, and concentrated in the largest cities, especially Tehran and Mashhad (Kazemi 1984, 168).

68. The Fadaʿiyan consistently failed to extend its appeal beyond the lower- and lower-middle-class youth from the bazaar. Kazemi, relying on estimates by Adele Ferdows, argues that "at its height, the organization had [no more than] between 20 and 25,000 members in Tehran, and between 12 and

15,000 members in other cities, notably Mashhad" (Kazemi 1984, 168). An indication of the Fadaʿiyan's numerical strength is that no more than five hundred individuals, and perhaps as few as one hundred, protested against Safavi's arrest in June 1951, and they failed to secure his release (Kazemi 1984, 165, 168).

69. Ayatollah Kashani used the Devotees to expand his influence and, in return, he provided them with some clout and protection.

70. This, for instance, was the case of Sadeq Khalkhali (the "hanging judge"), Assadullah Lavejardi (the "butcher of Tehran"), and Habiballah Asghar-Owladi (who became commerce minister in 1981).

71. On these groups, see Richards 1985, 76–80. For a more recent and comprehensive review of the activities of the Fadaʿiyan under the Islamic Republic, see Schahgaldian 1989, 65–68.

72. Tabari 1983; Bakhash 1990, 24–38.

73. Algar 1972, 247; Bakhash 1990, 28.

74. Mozaffari 1988, 91; Milani 1988, 99; Arjomand 1988, 95.

75. Bakhash 1984b, 181; Schahgaldian 1989, 26

76. Before he died, Borujirdi had launched several key reforms (see Algar 1972, 243–44). First, he had reorganized Qom's theological seminary (*hawzat al-ʿilmi*) and turned it into a center for the propagation of Shiism in Iran and abroad. He also had centralized the collection of *zakat* and *khums* in Qom, and restructured on a more effective basis the whole system governing the collection and distribution of religious taxes. Ironically, as several observers have noted, these achievements by the politically quietist Borujirdi eventually benefited the radical Ayatollah Khomeini and his militant followers, who were able to use the Qom-centered network of tax collection and communication to diffuse Khomeini's message in Iran during the ayatollah's exile in Najaf.

77. Bakhash 1990, 39–40; Mallat 1988, 12.

78. Fadlallah was born in Najaf in 1935, while his father was a seminary student there. He belonged to a prestigious family of religious scholars in southern Lebanon (Shapira 1988, 116; Kramer 1990, 138).

79. The name Hizballah is drawn from a Quranic verse: "And verily the party of God is sure to triumph" (Kramer 1987, 131).

80. The Rally of Muslim Clergymen, whose main goal was to increase

political cooperation between the Sunni and Shiite branches of the Lebanese Muslim community, included both Sunni and Shiite clerics.

81. See Deeb 1986, 18; Taheri 1987, 124–25; Shapira 1988, 124–28.

82. Deeb 1986; Abu-Khalil 1985, 38–41.

83. See, for instance, the case of the Islamic Unification Movement (Harakat al-tawhid al-islami), led by Shaykh Shaʿban and described by Seurat 1985 and Deeb 1986, 7–10.

84. The display of power over the West was expressed through the Western countries' inability to put an end to kidnappings and suicidal bombings, and to retrieve their hostages.

Conclusion

1. See, for instance, the decreasing density, scope, and political relevance of neighborhood-based networks in most contemporary Middle Eastern cities, the quasi demise, except in Iran, of the networks based on the old crafts and trade, or the breakdown of the traditional patterns of political mobilization associated with *chaqu-kashan*-led networks in Iran.

2. See, for instance, chapters 10 and 11 on how modernization and economic expansion in Iran strengthened the religious and *bazaari* networks.

3. See, for instance, chapter 11 on the mushrooming of Islamic voluntary associations in Egypt in the 1980s.

4. In Tunisia, for instance, the Islamic Tendency Movement (better known by the acronym of its French name, MTI), developed in the early 1970s out of informally gathered "circles" or "seminars" (*halaq*, sing. *halqa*). *Halaq* were held first in mosques, but subsequently throughout society, and particularly on university campuses. By mobilizing individuals through *halaq*, the MTI became, in less than a decade, the most powerful opposition movement since the country's independence. By the late 1970s, it had evolved into a parallel society, and the counterculture that it propagated fueled repeated clashes with the authorities (Hermassi 1984; Waltz 1986, 656). Informally organized networks had generated a sociopolitical movement that was threatening a regime often held by observers to be a model of stability and legitimacy in the Middle East.

5. As in the case of the Iranian revolution, informal networks relied on modern technology to organize Kuwaiti political resistance. Thus, reminiscent

of Khomeini's use of tape-recorded messages and sermons to spread his message throughout Iran, the Kuwaiti underground disseminated directives through a network of faxes, photocopies, and computers (Ghabra 1991, 199).

6. For a detailed discussion, see Waterbury 1972a, 1972b; Geertz 1979, 163–64.

7. Peretz 1990, 43; Miller 1989, 74.

8. See Johnson et al. 1989, 38; Stork 1989, 71–72; Peretz 1990, 76 and 96.

9. See Cantarow 1989, 91; Stork 1989, 71; Miller 1989, 74–75; Vitullo 1989, 49; Peretz 1990, 75, 90.

10. For a succinct presentation of these groups, see Levine 1986a, 827.

11. Like the *hay'ats*, the CEBs developed from the late 1960s onward as a result of two trends. The first was the emergence of a new generation of militant priests and lay Catholics trying to make religion more relevant to the concerns and aspirations of the poor, in order to rejuvenate the church and reverse the trend toward its loss of influence. The second trend was the increasing demand for religion, as poor people and clerical and lay activists turned to religion for inspiration and guidance in confronting their problems.

There are at least three additional similarities between the CEBs and the *hay'ats*. First, various Christian base communities are indirectly linked to one another through their common relation to an established church endowed with considerable material resources and symbolic power. Second, CEBs originally developed independently of the religious hierarchy, which was very reluctant to confront the authorities. Finally, as in the case of the *hay'ats*, whose main activities were centered around the reading and discussion of the Quran and Shiite traditions, exposure to the Bible and commenting on its teachings represent the core of the activities of CEBs (see Levine 1986c, 10). One important difference between *hay'ats* and Christian base communities, however, is that while the former constitute an exclusively urban phenomenon, the latter are by no means restricted to the cities (on Nicaragua, see Dodson 1986; on Brazil, see Bruneau 1986).

12. For evidence, and an analysis of the reasons that led CEBs to clash with the state, see Levine 1986c, 10–15; Levine 1986a, 823–28; Bruneau 1986, 110.

13. Cornelius 1975; Eckstein 1977; Annis 1988, 137.

14. For instance, as shown in part 2, urban popular disturbances in

nineteenth-century Iran were greatly facilitated by the weakness of the Qajars' authority outside the capital, the loose control of provincial governors over local society and politics, and these governors' lack of support from, and indeed conflict with, the Qajar dynasty. Similarly, the relative weakness of the Lebanese state in 1958 was also an important factor in the ability of the insurgent *zu'ama'* to bring the country into its first civil war (see chapter 9). Finally, the still-fragile nature of Muhammad Reza Shah's power in Iran in the late 1940s and early 1950s was shown to have been one of the reasons for the Fada'iyan's ability to act as a destabilizing force in Iranian society and politics for so many years.

15. Historical instances here would include unrest in mid-nineteenth-century Cairo, which was made possible, in part, by an increase in factionalism in the ranks of the Mamluk elite and the weakening of central authority in the provinces of the Ottoman Empire in the eighteenth and early to mid-nineteenth centuries, which provided local groups and powerful individuals with an opportunity to challenge the city authorities.

16. Here, the best example is the 1977–79 revolution in Iran. As many scholars have noted, the shah's indecisive character, cancer, and diminishing determination, combined with the pressures he was under from his chief foreign patron, the United States, resulted in hesitations, confusion, lack of resolve, vacillations, and inconsistent and contradictory policies that emboldened and further alienated the Iranian opposition. See, for instance, Zonis 1991.

17. Algar 1972, 243–44; Halliday 1979, 19.

18. Unlike in Tehran, where the bazaar and the mosque, those strongholds of traditional urban life in the Iranian capital, provided the leadership of the revolutionary movement, the older, medieval quarters of Cairo appear to have remained untouched by Islamic radicalism (for evidence on Jihad, see Kepel 1985, 217–18; Ansari 1986, 221).

19. As shown in part 2, they feared that the establishment of a new, French-controlled order might weaken their prominent position in society.

20. As shown in part 2, the notables resented the erosion of their power brought about by Ottoman reformation (the *tanzimat*), European penetration and the increasing prominence of Western consuls and local members of the religious minorities. By condoning violence, they hoped to reassert their position as the natural intermediaries between the population and the authorities.

21. *Bazaaris* were hurt by the increasingly inefficient, arbitrary, and despotic nature of Qajar rule. See part 2.

22. *Zuʿamaʾ* opposed to Chamoun essentially engaged in a show of force to reassert their power positions. See chapter 9.

23. The Maronites saw the National Movement's call for deconfessionalization and the alliances formed between Lebanese Muslim groups and the Palestinians as a direct challenge to the privileged status of their community in Lebanon. See chapter 9.

24. The *bazaaris* resented the extent to which their operations were being hurt by the state's increasing interventions in their affairs (e.g., the tax regulations and commercial laws passed in the 1960s and 1970s, the attempt to impose the Rastakhiz party on the bazaar in the mid-1970s, and, especially, the 1975–76 antiprofiteering campaign). See chapter 10.

25. The ulama resented the state's attempt to deprive them of their few remaining prerogatives and privileges. See chapter 11.

26. See Bill and Springborg 1990, 139-51.

27. Khosrokhavar 1980; Mottahedeh 1985, 352; Arjomand 1988, 96.

28. Fuad Khuri illustrated the shift from family to sect politics in his study of two suburbs of Beirut, Shiyah and Ghobeiri, in the late 1960s (Khuri 1972, 1975). Khuri observed a strengthening of sectarian identities as a result of the process of urbanization, and he noted that sect-based networks and institutions had come to perform, in pre-civil-war Beirut, many of the political functions that, back in the village had been carried out by the family.

Salim Nasr's 1979 study of the transformation of "traditional" ties in Beirut supports Khuri's conclusion that the growth of the Lebanese capital was accompanied by a strengthening of confessional affiliations and a weakening of family and regional ties. Nasr acknowledges that, in addition to the sect, other groups based on primordial ties played the role of "adjustment structures" and provided for social, economic, and psychological support in the process of urbanization. He points out, however, that such groups (e.g., the extended family) were not able to resist the impact of socioeconomic differentiation. Accordingly, they tended to disappear among second-generation urban dwellers.

One of the facts underlined by Nasr is the decreasing rates of preferential weddings with the patrilinear cousin, which suggests a weakening of family ties. Nasr also notes that this phenomenon was more pronounced among families that had been living in the urban setting for a longer period of time. It should be clear, however, that the weakening of family and regional ties need not mean their demise. Thus, in their study of Hamra, Khalaf and Kongstad

(1973) showed that choice of residence, visiting habits, and voluntary associations were all sustained by family and village ties. Similarly, in her study of Borj Hammoud, Suad Joseph (1982) emphasized the continued importance of family ties in that neighborhood of Beirut.

29. Dubar and Nasr 1976; Smock and Smock 1975; Harik 1980; Nasr 1988, 19; Salibi 1988, 196.

30. Other explanations would include the misguided policies of the sectarian leaderships, which tried to increase popular support by appealing to religious feelings and emotions; the social salience of religious loyalties, despite the progress of secularization; and, most importantly perhaps, the fact that the basic structures mediating between the individual and the political system remained essentially confessional (Salibi 1988, 196). Because of this latter factor, the advances realized at the social level toward the integration of religious groups had few political consequences. In other words, while Lebanese *society* may have become more integrated and secular, Lebanon's *polity* remained largely sect-based.

31. Fernea 1969; Rugh 1978, 384–85.

32. This perhaps explains why, in the early 1970s, Sadat's use of religion to bolster his personal legitimacy provoked such an outcry in some Egyptian political circles, or why, in the mid-1980s, many prominent Wafd party members decided to leave their party after it contracted a political alliance with the Muslim Brotherhood in the Parliamentary election of 1984.

33. Hourani 1983, 227; Kupferschmidt 1987, 413.

34. On the *jama'at* and *jam'iyyat*, however, see the scenario developed in the second half of the section devoted to these networks.

35. These conditions included the Shiite clergy's autonomy and independent power, Khomeini's charisma and shrewd leadership of the revolution, the shah's misguided policies in the early to mid-1970s, and his mishandling of the uprising in 1977–78, the widespread hatred of the shah and his regime, the bazaar-mosque connection, and the new middle class' abdication to the will of the radical clergy.

36. One needs only think here of the infamous Road of the Pyramids in Cairo, which, to many of Egypt's Islamic radicals, was the epitome of the immorality generated by Sadat's *infitah* policies (Ayubi 1991, 75).

37. As during the student demonstrations of 1968 and the tumultuous student riots of 1972–73.

38. A look at the chronology shows the frequency of labor unrest in Egypt in the early to mid-1970s: the strike of Helwan steel workers in August–September 1971, the rioting by Shubra al-Khayma workers in March–April 1972 and by industrial workers in Cairo in January 1975, the strikes of textile workers in Mahalla al-Kubra in March 1975 and August 1976, and the strike of public transportation workers in Cairo in September 1976. Workers were also active in the "food riots" of January 1977 in Cairo, Alexandria, Assiut, and other cities.

39. Note the contrast with the 1953 uprising that brought down Mossadegh's government, during which the slums of Teheran were quiet. In fact, those segments of the slums that became involved in the 1953 events did so on the side of the royalists (Abrahamian 1968, 207). In 1977–79, of course, some strata among the poor migrants proved more easily mobilized than others. Kazemi, for instance, argues that the nonsquatting poor migrants and unskilled migrant factory workers eventually became mobilized in large numbers against the regime, while "mobilization of the squatters was at best incomplete" (Kazemi 1980b, 271).

40. The same could be said of the radical, charismatic young preachers who played a role in the radicalization of politics in the Lebanese Muslim community in the 1980s (see chapter 11).

Appendix

Data on Urban Growth
in the Middle East

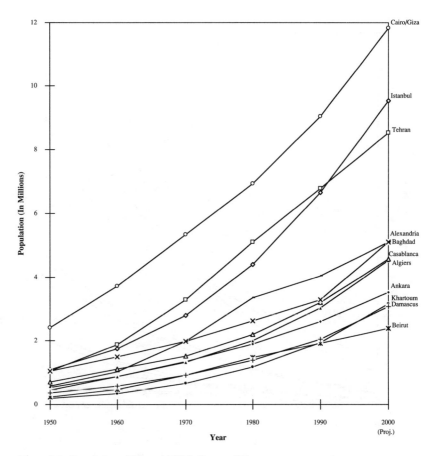

Figure A.1 Population of Selected Middle Eastern Cities

Source: Department of International Economic and Social Affairs, United Nations (U.N.), *Prospects of World Urbanization, 1990* (New York: U.N. 1991)

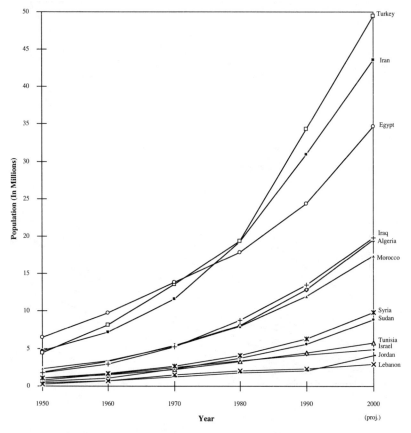

Figure A.2 Urban Population in Selected Middle Eastern Countries

Source: Department of International Economic and Social Affairs, United Nations (U.N.), *Prospects of World Urbanization, 1990* (New York: U.N. 1991)

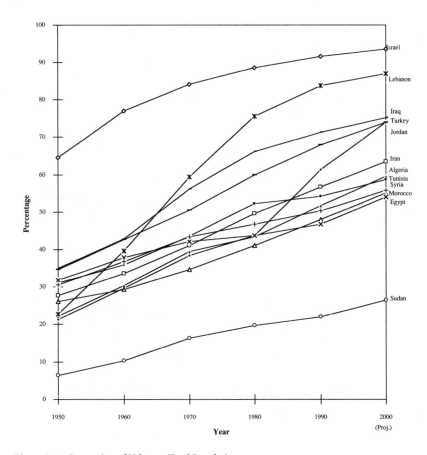

Figure A.3 Proportion of Urban to Total Population

Source: Department of International Economic and Social Affairs, United Nations (U.N.),
Prospects of World Urbanization, 1990 (New York: U.N. 1991)

Bibliography

Abdalla, Ahmed. 1985. *The Student Movement and National Politics in Egypt, 1923–1973.* London: Al Saqi Books.

Abrahamian, Ervand. 1968. "The Crowd in Iranian Politics 1905–1953." *Past and Present* 41:184–210.

———. 1980. "Structural Causes of the Iranian Revolution." *MERIP Reports* No. 87 (May): 21–26.

———. 1981. "The Strengths and Weaknesses of the Labor Movement in Iran, 1941–1953." In *Modern Iran.* See Bonine and Keddie 1981.

———. 1982. *Iran between Two Revolutions.* Princeton, N.J.: Princeton University Press.

Abu-Khalil, Asʿad. 1985. "Druze, Sunni, and Shiite Political Leadership in Present-Day Lebanon." *Arab Studies Quarterly* 7 (4): 28–58.

———. 1987. "Inter- and Intra-Confessional Conflict." *Journal of Arab Affairs* 6 (Spring): 11–17.

———. 1988. "The Politics of Sectarian Ethnicity: Segmentation in Lebanese Society." Ph.D. diss., Georgetown University.

Abu-Lughod, Janet. 1969. "Varieties of Urban Experience: Contrast, Co-existence, and Coalescence in Cairo." In *Middle Eastern Cities.* See Lapidus 1969a.

———. 1971. *Cairo: 1,001 Years of the City Victorious.* Princeton, N.J.: Princeton University Press.

———. 1973. "Cairo: Perspectives and Prospects." In *From Madina to Metropolis.* See Brown 1973.

———. 1987. "The Islamic City—Historic Myth, Islamic Essence, and Contemporary Relevance." *International Journal of Middle East Studies* 19 (May): 155–176.

Agulhon, Maurice. 1982. *The Republic in the Village: The People of the Var from the French Revolution to the Second Republic.* Cambridge: Cambridge University Press. First published in French in 1970.

Ajami, Fouad. 1986. *The Vanished Imam: Musa al Sadr and the Shia of Lebanon.* Ithaca, N.Y. and London: Cornell University Press.

Akhavi, Shahrough. 1980. *Religion and Politics in Contemporary Iran: Clergy-State Relations in the Pahlavi Period.* Albany: State University of New York Press.

———. 1987. "Elite Factionalism in the Islamic Republic of Iran." *Middle East Journal* 41 (Spring): 181–201.

Algar, Hamid. 1969. *Religion and State in Iran, 1785–1906: The Role of the Ulama in the Qajar Period.* Berkeley and Los Angeles: University of California Press.

———. 1972. "The Oppositional Role of the Ulama in Twentieth-Century Iran." In *Scholars, Saints, and Sufis.* See Keddie 1972d.

———. 1981. *Islam and Revolution: Writings and Declarations of Imam Khomeini.* Berkeley, Calif.: Mizan Press.

Aminzade, Ronald. 1977. "Breaking the Chains of Dependency: From Patronage to Class Politics, Toulouse, France, 1830–1872." *Journal of Urban History* (August): 485–506.

———. 1979. "The Transformation of Social Solidarities in Nineteenth-Century Toulouse." In *Consciousness and Class Experience in Nineteenth-Century Europe,* edited by John Merriman, 85–105. New York: Homes & Meier.

Annis, Sheldon. 1988. "What Is Not the Same about the Urban Poor: The Case of Mexico City." In *Strengthening the Poor: What Have We Learned?*, edited by John P. Lewis, 133–48. New Brunswick, N.J.: Transaction Books.

Ansari, Hamied. 1986. *Egypt: The Stalled Society.* Albany: State University of New York Press.

Antoun, Richard T., and Mary E. Hegland, eds. 1987. *Religious Resurgence: Contemporary Cases in Islam, Christianity, and Judaism.* Syracuse, N.Y.: Syracuse University Press.

Arasteh, Reza. 1961a. "The Character, Organization, and Social Role of the Lutis (Javan-Mardan) in the Traditional Iranian Society of the Nineteenth Century." *Journal of the Economic and Social History of the Orient* 4:47–52.

———. 1961b. "The Social Role of the Zurkhana (House of Strength) in Iranian Urban Communities during the Nineteenth Century." *Der Islam* 37:256–59.

Arendt, Hanna. 1951. *The Origins of Totalitarianism.* New York: Harcourt.

Arjomand, Said Amir. 1981a. "The Ulama's Traditionalist Opposition to Parliamentarism: 1907–1909." *Middle Eastern Studies* 17 (April): 174–90.

———. 1981b. "Shi'ite Islam and the Revolution in Iran." *Government and Opposition* 16 (Summer): 293–316.

———, ed. 1984a. *From Nationalism to Revolutionary Islam.* Albany: State University of New York Press.

———. 1984b. "Traditionalism in Twentieth-Century Iran." In *From Nationalism to Revolutionary Islam.* See Arjomand 1984a.

———. 1988. *The Turban for the Crown: The Islamic Revolution in Iran.* New York: Oxford University Press.

Ashraf, Ahmad. 1970. "Historical Obstacles to the Development of a Bourgeoisie in Iran." In *Studies in the Economic History of the Middle East.* See Cook 1970.

———. 1981. "The Roots of Emerging Dual Class Structure in Nineteenth-Century Iran." *Iranian Studies* 14 (1–2): 5–27.

———. 1983. "Bazaar and Mosque in Iran's Revolution." *MERIP Reports* No. 113 (March–April): 16–18.

———. 1988. "Bazaar-Mosque Alliance: The Social Basis of Revolts and Revolutions." *Politics, Culture, and Society* 1 (Summer): 538–67.

———. 1990. "Theocracy and Charisma: New Men of Power in Iran." *International Journal of Politics, Culture, and Society* 4 (1): 113–52.

Ashraf, Ahmad, and Ali Banuazizi. 1985. "The State, Classes, and Modes of Mobilization in the Iranian Revolution." *State, Culture, and Society* 1 (Spring): 3–40.

Ashraf, Ahmad, and H. Hekmat. 1981. "Merchants and Artisans and the Developmental Processes of Nineteenth-Century Iran." In *The Islamic Middle East: 700–1900, Studies in Economic and Social History,* edited by A. Udovitch, 725–50. Princeton, N.J.: Princeton University Press.

Ayubi, Nazih. 1982–83. "The Politics of Militant Islamic Movements in the Middle East." *Journal of International Affairs* 36 (Fall–Winter): 271–83.

———. 1991. *Political Islam: Religion and Politics in the Arab World.* New York: Routledge.

Baer, Gabriel. 1964. *Egyptian Guilds in Modern Times.* Jerusalem: Israel Oriental Society.

———. 1968. "Social Change in Egypt: 1800–1914." In *Political and Social Change in Modern Egypt.* See Holt 1968.

———. 1970. "Guilds in Middle Eastern History." In *Studies in the Economic History of the Middle East.* See Cook 1970.

———. 1977. "Popular Revolt in Ottoman Cairo." *Der Islam* 54 (2): 213–42.

———. 1984. "Islam and Politics in Modern Middle Eastern History." In *Islam and Politics in the Modern Middle East,* edited by Metin Heper and Raphael Israeli, 11–28. New York: St. Martin's Press.

Bakhash, Shaul. 1978. *Iran: Monarchy, Bureaucracy, and Reform under the Qajars: 1858–1896.* London: Ithaca Press.

———. 1984a. *The Reign of the Ayatollahs: Iran and the Islamic Revolution.* New York: Basic Books.

———. 1984b. "Sermons, Revolutionary Pamphleteering and Mobilisation: Iran, 1978." In *From Nationalism to Revolutionary Islam.* See Arjomand 1984a.

———. 1990. *The Reign of the Ayatollahs.* 2d ed. New York: Basic Books.

Balta, Paul, and Claudine Rulleau. 1979. *L'Iran Insurgé.* Paris: Sindbad.

Barakat, Halim. 1977. *Lebanon in Strife: Student Preludes to the Civil War.* Austin and London: University of Texas Press.

Barbir, Karl K. 1980. *Ottoman Rule in Damascus, 1708–1758.* Princeton, N.J.: Princeton University Press.

Bashiriyeh, Hossein. 1984. *The State and Revolution in Iran, 1962–1982.* New York: St. Martin's Press.

Batatu, Hanna. 1978. *The Old Social Classes and the Revolutionary Movements of Iraq.* Princeton, N.J.: Princeton University Press, 1978.

———. 1981. "Some Observations on the Social Roots of Syria's Ruling, Military Group and the Causes for Its Dominance." *Middle East Journal* 35 (Summer): 331–44.

————. 1984. "The Egyptian, Syrian, and Iraqi Revolutions: Some Observations on their Underlying Causes and Social Character." Washington, D.C.: Center for Contemporary Arab Studies, Georgetown University.

Bauer, Janet. 1985. "Demographic Change, Women and the Family in a Migrant Neighborhood of Tehran." In *Women and the Family in Iran*, edited by Asghar Fathi, 158–86. Leiden: E. J. Brill.

Bayat, Mangol. 1980. "Islam in Pahlavi and Post-Pahlavi Iran: A Cultural Revolution?" In *Islam and Development*. See Esposito 1980.

————. 1987. "Mahmud Taleqani and the Iranian Revolution." In *Shi'ism, Resistance, and Revolution*, edited by Martin Kramer, 67–94. Boulder, Colo.: Westview Press.

Beinin, Joel. 1987. "The Communist Movement and National Political Discourse in Nasirist Egypt." *Middle East Journal* 41 (Autumn): 568–84.

————. 1988. "Islam, Marxism, and the Shubra al-Khayma Textile Workers: Muslim Brothers and Communists in the Egyptian Trade Union Movement." In *Islam, Politics, and Social Movements*. See Burke and Lapidus 1988.

————. 1989. "Labor, Capital, and the State in Nasserist Egypt, 1952–1961." *International Journal of Middle East Studies* 21 (February): 71–90.

Beinin, Joel, and Zachary Lockman. 1988. *Workers on the Nile*. Princeton, N.J.: Princeton University Press.

Beyhum, Nabil. 1989. "L'Organisation de la vie quotidienne d'un quartier de Beyrouth-Ouest: Habitants, commercants, et miliciens." *Maghreb-Machrek*, No. 125: 100–116.

Bianchi, Robert. 1986. "The Corporatization of the Egyptian Labor Movement." *Middle East Journal* 40 (Summer): 429–44.

————. 1989a. "Islam and Democracy in Egypt." *Current History* 88 (February): 93–104.

————. 1989b. *Unruly Corporatism: Associational Life in Twentieth-Century Egypt*. New York: Oxford University Press.

Bienen, Henry. 1984. "Urbanization and Third World Stability." *World Development* 12 (July): 661–91.

Bill, James A. 1972. *The Politics of Iran: Groups, Classes, and Modernization*. Columbus, Ohio: Charles E. Merrill.

————. 1973. "The Plasticity of Informal Politics: The Case of Iran." *Middle East Journal* 27 (Spring): 131–51.

————. 1975. "The Patterns of Elite Politics in Iran." In *Political Elites in the Middle East*, edited by George Lenczowski, 17–40. Washington, D.C.: American Enterprise for Public Policy Research.

————. 1982. "Power and Religion in Revolutionary Iran." *Middle East Journal* 1 (Winter): 22–47.

Bill, James A., and Robert Springborg. 1990. *Politics in the Middle East*. Glenview, Ill.: Scott, Foresman.

Binder, Leonard. 1965. "The Proofs of Islam: Religion and Politics in Iran." In *Arabic and Islamic Studies in Honor of Hamilton A. R. Gibb*, edited by George Makdisi, 118–40. Cambridge: Harvard University Press.

————. 1966a. "Political Change in Lebanon." In *Politics in Lebanon*. See Binder 1966b.

————, ed. 1966b. *Politics in Lebanon*. New York: Wiley.

Bodman, Herbert L. 1963. *Political Factions in Aleppo, 1760–1826*. Chapel Hill: University of North Carolina Press.

Boissevain, Jeremy. 1973. *Friends of Friends*. London: Basil Blackwell.

Bonine, Michael E. 1977. "From Uruk to Casablanca: Perspectives on the Urban Experiences of the Middle East." *Journal of Urban History* 3 (February): 141–80.

————. 1981. "Shops and Shopkeepers: Dynamics of an Iranian Provincial Bazaar." In *Modern Iran*. See Bonine and Keddie 1981.

————. 1983. "Cities of the Middle East and North Africa." In *Cities of the World: World Regional Urban Development*, edited by Stanley D. Brunn and Jack F. Williams, 282–324. New York: Harper & Row.

Bonine, Michael E., and Nikki R. Keddie, eds. 1981. *Modern Iran: The Dialectics of Continuity and Change*. Albany: State University of New York Press.

Brown, Kenneth. 1976. *People of Salé: Tradition and Change in a Moroccan City, 1830–1930*. Cambridge: Harvard University Press.

Brown, Kenneth, Michèle Jolé, Peter Sluglett, and Sami Zubaida, eds. 1986. *Middle Eastern Cities in Comparative Perspective*. London: Ithaca Press.

Brown, Kenneth, and Claude Liauzu, eds. 1988. *Etat, Ville, et Mouvements Sociaux au Maghreb et au Moyen-Orient/Urban Crises and Social Movements in the Middle East.* Paris: L'Harmattan.

Brown, L. C., ed. 1973. *From Madina to Metropolis.* Princeton, N.J.: Princeton University Press.

Browne, E. G. 1910. *The Persian Revolution of 1905–1909.* Cambridge: Cambridge University Press.

Bruneau, Thomas C. 1986. "Brazil: The Catholic Church and Basic Christian Communities." In *Religion and Political Conflict in Latin America.* See Levine 1986b.

Buccianti, Alexandre. 1984. "Les Elections législatives en Egypte." *Maghreb-Machrek*, No. 106 (October–December): 54–74.

Buheiry, Marwan. 1987. *Beirut's Role in the Political Economy of the French Mandate.* Papers on Lebanon No. 4. Oxford: Centre for Lebanese Studies.

Burke, Edmund, III. 1986. "Understanding Arab Protest Movements." *Arab Studies Quarterly* 8 (4): 333–45.

———. 1988. "Toward a History of Urban Collective Action in the Middle East: Continuities and Change, 1750–1980." In see Brown and Liauzu, 1988.

Burke, Edmund, III, and Ira M. Lapidus. 1988. *Islam, Politics, and Social Movements.* Berkeley: University of California Press.

Cahen, Claude. 1958. "Mouvements populaires et autonomisme urbain dans l'Asie Musulmane du Moyen Age, I." *Arabica* 5:225–50.

———. 1959a. "Mouvements populaires et autonomisme urbain dans l'Asie Musulmane du Moyen Age, II." *Arabica* 6 (January): 25–56.

———. 1959b. "Mouvements populaires et autonomisme urbain dans l'Asie Musulmane du Moyen Age (Fin)." *Arabica* 6 (September): 233–65.

———. 1960. "Ahdath." In *The Encyclopaedia of Islam, New Edition* 1:256. Leiden: E. J. Brill.

———. 1965. "Futuwwa." In *The Encyclopaedia of Islam, New Edition* 2:961–65. Leiden: E. J. Brill.

———. 1970. "Y a-t-il eu des corporations professionnelles dans le monde Musulman classique?" In *The Islamic City.* See Hourani and Stern 1970.

Calhoun, Craig Jackson. 1983. "The Radicalism of Tradition: Community Strength or Venerable Disguise and Borrowed Language?" *American Journal of Sociology* 88 (March): 886–914.

Cantarow, Ellen. 1989. "Beita." In *Intifada*. See Lockman and Beinin 1989.

Chevallier, Dominique. 1968. "Western Development and Eastern Crisis in the Mid-Nineteenth Century: Syria Confronted with the European Economy." In *Beginnings of Modernization*. See Polk and Chambers 1968.

Cigar, Norman. 1981. "Socio-Economic Structures and the Development of an Urban Bourgeoisie in Pre-Colonial Morocco." *Maghreb Review* No. 5: 55–76.

Clément, Jean-Francois, and Jim Paul. 1984. "Trade Unions and Moroccan Politics." *MERIP Reports* 14 (October): 19–24.

Cobban, Helena. 1985. *The Making of Modern Lebanon*. Boulder, Colo.: Westview Press.

Cohen, Abner. 1969. *Custom and Politics in Urban Africa: A Study of Hausa Migrants in Yoruba Towns*. Berkeley and Los Angeles: University of California Press.

———. 1974. *Two-Dimensional Man: An Essay on the Anthropology of Power and Symbolism in Complex Society*. London: Routledge & Kegan Paul.

Cook, Michael, ed. 1970. *Studies in the Economic History of the Middle East*. London: Oxford University Press.

Cooper, Mark N. 1982. *The Transformation of Egypt*. Baltimore: John Hopkins University Press.

Cornelius, Wayne A. 1969. "Urbanization as an Agent in Latin American Political Instability: The Case of Mexico." *American Political Science Review* 63 (September): 833–57.

———. 1975. *Politics and the Migrant Poor in Mexico City*. Stanford, Calif.: Stanford University Press.

———. 1977. "Leaders, Followers, and Official Patrons in Urban Mexico." In *Friends, Followers, and Factions: A Reader in Political Clientelism*. See Schmidt et al. 1977.

Cottam, Richard. 1979. *Nationalism in Iran*. Pittsburgh: University of Pittsburgh Press.

———. 1988. *Iran and the United States: A Cold War Case Study.* Pittsburgh: University of Pittsburgh Press.

Couland, Jacques. 1970. *Le Mouvement syndical au Liban,* 1919–1946. Paris: Editions Sociales.

Crecelius, Daniel. 1972. "Nonideological Responses of the Egyptian Ulama to Modernization." In *Scholars, Saints, and Sufis.* See Keddie 1972d.

———. 1980. "The Course of Secularization in Modern Egypt." In *Islam and Development.* See Esposito 1980.

Curtis, Michael, ed. 1981. *Religion and Politics in the Middle East.* Boulder, Colo.: Westview Press.

Davis, Eric. 1984. "Ideology, Social Class, and Islamic Radicalism in Modern Egypt." In *From Nationalism to Revolutionary Islam.* See Arjomand 1984a.

Dawisha, A. and I. W. Zartman, eds. 1988. *Beyond Coercion: The Durability of the Arab State.* London: Croom Helm.

Deeb, Marius. 1986. *Militant Islamic Movements in Lebanon: Origins, Social Basis, and Ideology.* Occasional Papers Series. Washington, D.C.: Center for Contemporary Arab Studies.

De Groot, Joanna. 1983. "Mullas and Merchants: The Basis of Religious Politics in nineteenth-Century Iran." *Mashriq* (Proceedings of the Eastern Mediterranean Seminar, University of Manchester, England, 1979–1982) 11–36.

———. 1988. "The Formation and Re-formation of Popular Political Movements in Iran." In see Brown and Liauzu, eds. 1988.

De Jong, Fred. 1978. *Turuq and Turuq-linked Institutions in Nineteenth Century Egypt: A Historical Study in the Organizational Dimensions of Islamic Mysticism.* Leiden: E. J. Brill.

———. 1983. "Aspects of the Political Involvement of Sufi Orders in Twentieth Century Egypt (1907–1970)—an Exploratory Stock-Taking." In *Islam, Nationalism, and Radicalism in Egypt and the Sudan,* edited by Gabriel R. Warburg and Uri M. Kupferschmidt, 183–212. New York: Praeger.

Dekmejian, Hrair. 1985. *Islam in Revolution.* Syracuse, N.Y.: Syracuse University Press.

De Planhol, Xavier. 1959. *The World of Islam.* Ithaca, N.Y.: Cornell University Press.

De Soto, Hernando. 1988. *The Other Path.* New York: Harper & Row.

Dessouki, Ali E. Hillal. 1981. "The Resurgence of Islamic Organizations in Egypt: An Interpretation." In *Islam and Power,* edited by A. Cudsi and Ali Dessouki, 107–18. Baltimore: Johns Hopkins University Press.

———. 1982. "The Islamic Resurgence: Sources, Dynamics, and Implications." In *Islamic Resurgence in the Arab World,* edited by Ali E. Hillal Dessouki, 3–31. New York: Praeger.

Deutsch, Karl W. 1961. "Social Mobilization and Political Development." *American Political Science Review* 55 (September): 493–514.

Dietz, Henry A., and Richard J. Moore. 1979. *Political Participation in a Non-Electoral Setting: The Urban Poor in Lima, Peru.* Athens, Ohio: Center for International Studies, Ohio University.

Dodson, Michael. 1986. "Nicaragua: The Struggle for the Church." In *Religion and Political Conflict in Latin America.* See Levine 1986b.

Dubar, Claude, and Salim Nasr. 1976. *Les Classes sociales au Liban.* Paris: Fondation Nationale des Sciences Politiques.

Durkheim, Emile. 1949. *The Division of Labor in Society.* Glencoe, Ill.: Free Press.

Eckstein, Susan. 1977. *The Poverty of Revolution: The State and Urban Poor in Mexico.* Princeton, N.J.: Princeton University Press.

———. 1990. "Urbanization Revisited: Inner-City Slum of Hope and Squatter Settlement of Despair." *World Development* 18 (2): 165–81.

Eickelman, Dale F. 1981. *The Middle East: An Anthropological Approach.* Englewood Cliffs, N.J.: Prentice-Hall.

———. 1987. "Changing Perceptions of State Authority: Morocco, Egypt and Oman." In *The Foundations of the Arab State,* edited by Ghassan Salamé, 177–203. London: Croom Helm.

Eisenstadt, S. N. 1973. "Post-traditional Societies and the Continuity and Reconstruction of Tradition." *Daedalus* 102 (Winter): 1–27.

Eisenstadt, S. N., and R. Lemarchand, eds. 1981. *Political Clientelism, Patronage, and Development.* Beverley Hills, Calif.: Sage Publications.

El Guindi, Fadwa. 1981. "Veiling Infitah with Muslim Ethic: Egypt's Contemporary Islamic Movement." *Social Problems* 28 (April): 465–85.

El-Messiri, Sawsan. 1977. "The Changing Role of the Futuwwa in the Social Structure of Cairo." In *Patrons and Clients in Mediterranean Societies.* See E. Gellner and J. Waterbury.

———. 1978. *Ibn al-Balad: A Concept of Egyptian Identity.* Leiden: E. J. Brill.

El Sayed, Mustapha K. 1988. "Professional Associations and National Integration in the Arab World, with Special Reference to Lawyers Associations." In *Beyond Coercion.* See Dawisha and Zartman 1988.

Enayat, Hamid. 1983. "Revolution in Iran 1979: Religion as Political Ideology." In *Revolutionary Theory and Political Reality,* edited by Noel O'Sullivan, 191–206. New York: St. Martin's Press.

Entelis, John P. 1974. *Pluralism and Party Transformation in Lebanon: al-Kata'ib, 1936–1970.* Leiden: E. J. Brill.

———. 1981. "Ethnic Conflict and the Reemergence of Radical Christian Nationalism in Lebanon." In *Religion and Politics in the Middle East.* See Curtis 1981.

———. 1987. "Politics and Culture in Morocco." Ann Arbor: Center for Political Studies, Institute for Social Research, University of Michigan.

Esposito, John L., ed. 1980. *Islam and Development: Religion and Sociopolitical Change.* Syracuse, N.Y.: Syracuse University Press.

———. 1984. *Islam and Politics.* Syracuse, N.Y.: Syracuse University Press.

Etienne, Bruno. 1987. *L'Islamisme radical.* Paris: Hachette.

Farhang, Mansur. 1987. "How the Clergy Gained Power in Iran." In *The Islamic Impulse,* edited by Barbara F. Stowasser, 157–74. London: Croom Helm.

Farhi, Farideh. 1990. *States and Urban-based Revolutions: Iran and Nicaragua.* Urbana and Chicago: University of Illinois Press.

Farouk-Sluglett, M., and P. Sluglett. 1982. "Aspects of the Changing Nature of Lebanese Confessional Politics: *Al-Murabitun,* 1958–1979." *Peuples Méditerranéens* No. 20: 59–73.

Farsoun, Samih K. 1988. "Class Structure and Social Change in the Arab World: 1995." In *The Next Arab Decade,* edited by Hisham Sharabi, 221–37. Boulder: Westview Press.

Fathi, Asghar. 1979. "The Role of the 'Rebels' in the Constitutional Movement in Iran." *International Journal of Middle East Studies* 10 (February): 55–66.

————. 1980. "Preachers as Substitues for Mass Media: The Case of Iran, 1905–1909." In *Toward a Modern Iran: Studies in Thought, Politics, and Society,* edited by Elie Kedourie and Sylvia G. Haim, 169–84. London: Frank Cass.

Fawaz, Leila T. 1983. *Merchants and Migrants in Nineteenth-Century Beirut.* Cambridge: Harvard University Press.

Ferdows, Amir. 1983. "Khomeini and Fadayan's Society and Politics." *International Journal of Middle East Studies* 15:241–57.

Fernea, Robert. 1969. In "Discussion" In *Middle Eastern Cities.* See Lapidus 1969a.

Fischer, Claude S. 1982. *To Dwell among Friends: Personal Networks in Town and City.* Chicago: University of Chicago Press.

————. 1984. *The Urban Experience.* New York: Harcourt Brace Jovanovich.

Fischer, Claude S., Robert Max Jackson, C. Ann Stueve, Kathleen Gerson, and Lynne McCallister Jones (wtih Mark Boldassare). 1977. *Networks and Places: Social Relations in the Urban Setting.* New York: Free Press.

Fischer, Michael M. J. 1980. *Iran: From Religious Dispute to Revolution.* Cambridge: Harvard University Press.

————. 1982. "Islam and the Revolt of the Petit[e] Bourgeoisie." *Daedalus* III (Winter): 101–25.

Floor, William. 1971. "The Lutis—A Social Phenomenon in Qajar Persia: A Reappraisal." *Die Welt des Islams* 13:103–20.

————. 1975. "The Guilds in Iran: An Overview from the Earliest Beginnings till 1972." *Zeitschrift der Deutschen Mörgenländischen Gesellschaft* 125:99–116.

————. 1976. "The Merchants (tujjar) in Qajar Iran." *Zeitschrift der Deutschen Mörgenländischen Gesellschaft* 126.

————. 1981. "The Political Role of the Lutis in Iran." In *Modern Iran.* See Bonine and Keddie 1981.

————. 1983. "The Revolutionary Character of the Ulama: Wishful Thinking or Reality?" In *Religion and Politics in Iran.* See Keddie 1983b.

————. 1984. "Guilds and Futuvvat in Iran." *Zeitschrift der Deutschen Mörgenländischen Gesellschaft* 134 (1):106–14.

Gaffney, Patrick D. 1987. "The Local Preacher and Islamic Resurgence in Upper Egypt: An Anthropological Perspective." In *Religious Resurgence*. See Antoun and Hegland 1987.

Geertz, Clifford. 1963. *Old Societies and New States*. New York: Free Press.

———. 1971. "In Search of North Africa." *New York Review of Books* 22 April: 20–23.

———. 1979. "Suq: The Bazaar Economy in Sefrou." In *Meaning and Order in Moroccan Society: Three Essays in Cultural Analysis*, edited by Clifford Geertz, Hildred Geertz, and Laurence Rosen, 123–244. Cambridge: Cambridge University Press.

Geiser, Peter. 1977. "Some Differential Factors Affecting Population Movement: The Nubian Case." *Human Organization* 26 (Fall).

Gellner, Ernest. 1962. "Patterns of Rural Rebellion in Morocco: Tribes as Minorities." *Archives Européennes de sociologie* 3:297–311.

Gellner, Ernest, and J. Waterbury, eds. 1977. *Patrons and Clients in Mediterranean Societies*. London: Duckworth.

Ghabra, Shafeeq. 1991. "Voluntary Associations in Kuwait: The Foundation of a New System?" *Middle East Journal* 45 (Spring): 199–215.

Gilsenan, Michael. 1973. *Saint and Sufi in Modern Egypt: An Essay in the Sociology of Religion*. Oxford: Clarendon Press.

———. 1982. *Recognizing Islam: Religion and Society in the Modern Arab World*. New York: Pantheon Books.

Goitein, S. D. 1966. *Studies in Islamic History and Institutions*. Leiden: E. J. Brill.

———. 1969. "Cairo: An Islamic City in the Light of the Geniza Documents." In *Middle Eastern Cities*. See Lapidus 1969a.

———. 1983. *A Mediterranean Society: The Jewish Communities of the Arab World as Portrayed in the Documents of the Cairo Geniza*. Vol. 4, *Daily Life*. Berkeley and Los Angeles: University of California Press.

Goldberg, Ellis. 1986. *Tinker, Tailor, and Textile Worker: Class and Politics in Egypt, 1930–1952*. Berkeley and Los Angeles: University of California Press.

———. 1988. "Muslim Union Politics in Egypt: Two Cases." In *Islam, Politics, and Social Movements*. See Burke and Lapidus 1988.

Gordon, Joel. 1990. "Political Opposition in Egypt." *Current History* 89 (February): 65–80.

Graham, Robert. 1980. *Iran: The Illusion of Power.* New York: St. Martin's Press.

Green, Jerrold D. 1982. *Revolution in Iran: The Politics of Countermobilization.* New York: Praeger.

———. 1984. "Countermobilization as a Revolutionary Form." *Comparative Politics* 16 (January): 153–69.

Gubser, Peter. 1973. "The Zuʿamaʾ of Zahlah: The Current Situation in a Lebanese Town." *Middle East Journal* 27 (Spring): 73–90.

Haddad, Wadi D. 1985. *Lebanon: The Politics of Revolving Doors.* New York: Praeger.

Haddad, Yvonne Y. 1987. "Islamic 'Awakening' in Egypt." *Arab Studies Quarterly* 9 (3):234–59.

Hahn, Harlan, and Joe R. Feagin. 1973. "Perspectives on Collective Violence: A Critical Review." In *Ghetto Revolts: The Politics of Violence in American Cities,* edited by Joe R. Feagin and Harlan Hahn, 125–55. New York: Macmillan.

Hairi, Abdul-Hadi. 1977. *Shiʾism and Constitutionalism in Iran.* Leiden: E. J. Brill.

Hakim, Besim Selim. 1986. *Arabic-Islamic Cities: Building and Planning Principles.* London and New York: KPI.

Halliday, Fred. 1974. *Arabia without Sultans.* New York: Penguin Books.

———. 1979. *Iran: Dictatorship and Development.* New York: Penguin Books.

Hanf, Theodor. 1988. "Homo Oeconomicus–Homo Communitaris: Crosscutting Loyalties in a Deeply Divided Society: The Case of Trade Unions in Lebanon." In *Ethnicity, Pluralism, and the State in the Middle East,* edited by M. Esman and I. Rabinovitch, 173–84. Ithaca, N.Y.: Cornell University Press.

Harik, Iliya. 1973. "The Single Party as a Subordinate Movement: The Case of Egypt." *World Politics* 26 (October): 80–105.

———. 1980. "Voting Participation and Political Integration in Lebanon, 1943–1974." *Middle Eastern Studies* 16 (January): 27–48.

————. 1985. "The Economic and Social Factors in the Lebanese Crisis." In *Arab Society: Social Science Perspective*, edited by Saad Eddin Ibrahim and Nicholas Hopkins, 412–31. Cairo: American University of Cairo Press.

Hegland, Mary E. 1983. "Two Images of Husain: Accommodation and Revolution in an Iranian Village." In *Religion and Politics in Iran*. See Keddie 1983b.

————. 1987a. "Conclusion: Religious Resurgence in Today's World: Refuge from Dislocation and Anomie or Enablement for Change?" In 233–56.

————. 1987b. "Introduction." *Religious Resurgence*. See Antoun and Hegland 1987.

————. 1987c. "Islamic Revival or Political and Cultural Revolution?" In see Antoun and Hegland 1987, 194–219.

Hendriks, Bertus. 1987. "Egypt's New Political Map." *Middle East Report* 17 (July–August): 23–30.

Hermassi, Elbaki. 1981. *The Third World Reassessed*. Berkeley and Los Angeles: University of California Press.

————. 1984. "La Société Tunisienne au miroir Islamiste." *Maghreb-Machrek* 103:39–56.

Hinnebusch, Raymond A. 1985. *Egyptian Politics under Sadat: The Post-populist Development of an Authoritarian-Modernizing State*. Cambridge: Cambridge University Press.

————. 1988a. "Authoritarian Power under Pressure: Comparative Patterns of Persistence and Change in 'Post-populist' Egypt and Syria." Unpublished paper.

————. 1988b. "Political Parties in the Arab State: Libya, Syria, Egypt." In *Beyond Coercion*. See Dawisha and Zartman 1988.

Hiro, Dilip. 1987. *Iran under the Ayatollahs*. New York: Routledge & Kegan Paul.

Hobsbawm, E. J. 1959. *Primitive Rebels: Studies in Archaic Forms of Social Movements in the Nineteenth and Twentieth Centuries*. Manchester, England: Manchester University Press.

Hodgson, Marshall G. S. 1974. *The Venture of Islam: Conscience and History in a World Civilization*. Vol. 2, *The Expansion of Islam in the Middle Periods*. Chicago: University of Chicago Press.

Hoodfar, Homa. 1988. "Survival Strategies among Lower-Income Households in Newly Urbanized Neighborhoods of Cairo." Ph.D. diss. Department of Anthropology, Kent University.

Hopkins, Nicholas S. 1974. "Traditional Tunis and Its Transformations." *Annals of the New York Academy of Sciences* 220:427–40.

Hottinger, Arnold. 1961. "Zuʿamaʾ and Parties in the Lebanese Crisis of 1958." *Middle East Journal* 15 (Spring): 127–40.

———. 1966. "Zuʿamaʾ in Historical Perspective." In *Politics in Lebanon*. See Binder 1966b.

Hourani, Albert H. 1946. *Syria and Lebanon: A Political Essay*. London: Oxford University Press.

———. 1966. "Lebanon: The Development of a Political Society." In *Politics in Lebanon*. See Binder 1966b.

———. 1968. "Ottoman Reform and the Politics of Notables." In *Beginnings of Modernization*. See Polk and Chambers 1968.

———. 1970. "The Islamic City in the Light of Recent Research." In *The Islamic City*. See Hourani and Stern 1970.

———. 1976. "Ideologies of the Mountain and the City." In *Essays on the Crisis in Lebanon*. See Owen 1976a.

———. 1981. *The Emergence of the Modern Middle East*. Berkeley and Los Angeles: University of California Press.

———. 1983. "Conclusion." In *Islam in the Political Process*, edited by James P. Piscatori, 226–34. Cambridge: Cambridge University Press.

———. 1986. *Political Society in Lebanon: A Historical Introduction*. Cambridge: Center for International Studies, Massachusetts Institute of Technology, and Oxford: Center for Lebanese Studies.

———. 1988. "Visions of Lebanon." In *Toward A Viable Lebanon*, edited by Halim Barakat, 3–11. London: Croom Helm.

———. 1992. *A History of the Arab Peoples*. New York: Warner Books.

Hourani, Albert H., and S. N. Stern, eds. 1970. *The Islamic City*. Philadelphia: University of Pennsylvania Press.

Hourcade, Bernard. 1988. "Conseillisme, classes sociales et espace urbain: Les squatters du sud de Téhéran, 1978–1981." In see Brown and Liauzu, eds. 1988.

Hudson, Michael C. 1968. *The Precarious Republic: Political Modernization in Lebanon.* New York: Random House.

———. 1976. "The Lebanese Crisis: The Limits of Consociational Democracy." *Journal of Palestine Studies* 5 (Spring–Summer): 109–22.

———. 1977. *Arab Politics: The Search for Legitimacy.* New Haven: Yale University Press.

———. 1980. "Islam and Political Development." In *Islam and Development.* See Esposito 1980.

Huntington, Samuel P. 1968. *Political Order in Changing Societies.* New Haven and London: Yale University Press.

Hussain, Asaf. 1985. *Islamic Iran.* New York: St. Martin's Press.

Ibrahim, Saad Eddin. 1980. "Anatomy of Egypt's Militant Groups: Methodological Notes and Preliminary Findings." *International Journal of Middle East Studies* 12 (December): 423–53.

———. 1982. "Islamic Militancy as a Social Movement: The Case of Two Groups in Egypt." In *Islamic Resurgence in the Arab World,* edited by Ali E. Hillal Dessouki, 117–37. New York: Praeger.

Ilbert, Robert. 1982. "La Ville Islamique: Réalité et Abstraction." *Les Cahiers de la recherche architecturale* No. 10–11 (April): 6–13.

Issawi, Charles. 1981. *The Arab World's Legacy.* Princeton, N.J.: Darwin Press.

———. 1982. *An Economic History of the Middle East and North Africa.* New York: Columbia University Press.

Johnson, Michael. 1986. *Class and Client in Beirut: The Sunni Muslim Community and the Lebanese State: 1840–1985.* London: Ithaca Press.

Johnson, Penny, Lee O'Brien, and Joost Hillermann. 1989. "The West Bank Rises Up." In *Intifada.* See Lockman and Beinin 1989.

Joseph, Suad. 1978a. "Muslim-Christian Conflict in Lebanon: A Perspective on the Evolution of Sectarianism." In *Muslim-Christian Conflicts: Economic, Political, and Social Origins,* edited by Suad Joseph and Barbara L. K. Pillsbury, 62–97. Boulder, Colo.: Westview Press.

———. 1978b. "Muslim-Christian Conflicts: A Theoretical Perspective." In *Muslim-Christian Conflicts: Economic, Political, and Social Origins,* edited by Suad Joseph and Barbara L. K. Pillsbury, 1–60. Boulder, Colo.: Westview Press.

————. 1978c. "Women and the Neighborhood Street in Borj Hammoud, Lebanon." In *Women in the Muslim World*, edited by Lois Beck and Nikki Keddie, 541–57. Cambridge: Harvard University Press.

————. 1982. "Family as Security and Bondage: A Political Strategy of the Lebanese Urban Working Class." In *Toward a Political Economy of Urbanization in Third World Countries*, edited by Helen I. Safa, 151–71. Delhi: Oxford University Press.

————. 1983. "Working-Class Women's Networks in a Sectarian State: a Political Paradox." *American Ethnologist* 10 (February): 1: 1–22.

Karpat, Kemal H. 1976. *The Gecekondu: Rural Migration and Urbanization.* Cambridge: Cambridge University Press.

Kazemi, Farhad. 1973. *Social Mobilization and Domestic Violence in Iran, 1946–1968.* Ph.D diss., University of Michigan.

————. 1980a. *Poverty and Revolution in Iran: The Migrant Poor, Urban Marginality, and Politics.* New York and London: New York University Press.

————. 1980b. "Urban Migrants and the Revolution." *Iranian Studies* 13 (1–4): 257–277.

————. 1984. "The Fada'iyan-e Islam: Fanaticism, Politics and Terror." In *From Nationalism to Revolutionary Islam.* See Arjomand 1984a.

————. 1985. "State and Society in the Ideology of the Devotees of Islam." *State, Culture, and Society* 1 (Spring): 118–35.

————. 1988. *Politics and Culture in Iran.* Ann Arbor: Institute for Social Research, University of Michigan.

Keddie, Nikki R. 1966a. "The Origin of the Religious-Radical Alliance in Iran." *Past and Present* 34 (July): 70–80.

————. 1966b. *Religion and Rebellion in Iran: The Tobacco Protest of 1891–1892.* London: Frank Cass.

————. 1972a. "The Economic History of Iran, 1800–1914, and Its Political Impact: An Overview." *Iranian Studies* (Spring–Summer): 58–78.

————. 1972b. "Introduction." In *Scholars, Saints, and Sufis.* See Keddie 1972d.

————. 1972c. "The Roots of Ulama Power in Modern Iran." In *Scholars, Saints, and Sufis.* See Keddie 1972d.

———, ed. 1972d. *Scholars, Saints, and Sufis: Muslim Religious Institutions since 1500.* Berkeley and Los Angeles: University of California Press.

———. 1977. "Iran, 1797–1941." In *Commoners, Climbers, and Notables: A Sampler of Studies on Social Ranking in the Middle East,* edited by C. A. O. Van Nieuwenhuijze, 122–39. Leiden: E. J. Brill.

———. 1981a. *Roots of Revolution: An Interpretive History of Modern Iran.* New Haven and London: Yale University Press.

———. 1981b. "Socioeconomic Changes in the Middle East Since 1800: A Comparative Analysis." In *The Islamic Middle East, 700–1900: Studies in Economic and Social History,* edited by A. L. Udovitch, 761–84. Princeton, N.J.: The Darwin Press.

———. 1983a. "Introduction." In *Religion and Politics in Iran.* See Keddie 1983b.

———, ed. 1983b. *Religion and Politics in Iran: Shi'ism from Quietism to Revolution,* edited by Nikki R. Keddie, 1–18. New Haven and London: Yale University Press.

Kepel, Gilles. 1985. *The Prophet and Pharaoh: Muslim Extremism in Egypt.* London: Al Saqi Books.

———. 1986. "Les Groupes Islamiques en Egypte: Flux et reflux, 1981–1986." *Politique étrangère* 51 (2): 429–46.

Kerr, Malcolm H. 1961. "Lebanese Views on the 1958 Crisis." *Middle East Journal* 15 (Spring): 211–17.

Khalaf, Samir. 1968. "Lebanese Labor Unions: Some Comparative Structural Features." *Middle East Economic Papers,* 111–38.

———. 1979. *Persistence and Change in Nineteenth-Century Lebanon: A Sociological Essay.* Beirut: American University of Beirut and Syracuse University Press.

———. 1985. "Social Structure and Urban Planning in Lebanon." In *Property, Social Structure, and Law in the Modern Middle East,* 213–35. Albany: State University of New York Press.

———. 1987. *Lebanon's Predicament.* New York: Columbia University Press.

———. 1988a. "On Entrapment and Escalation of Violence." In "A Symposium on Lebanon." *American-Arab Affairs,* No. 24 (Spring): 14–18.

———. 1988b. "Ideologies of Enmity in Lebanon." *Middle East Insight* 6 (Summer): 3–17.

Khalaf, Samir, and G. Denoeux. 1988. "Urban Networks and Political Conflict in Lebanon." In *Lebanon: A History of Conflict and Consensus*, edited by Nadim Shehadi and Dana H. Mills, 181–200. London: I. B. Tauris.

Khalaf, Samir, and Per Kongstad. 1973. "Urbanization and Urbanism in Beirut: Some Preliminary Results." In *From Madina to Metropolis*. See Brown 1973.

Khalaf, Tawfiq. 1976. "The Phalange and the Maronite Community." In *Essays on the Crisis in Lebanon*. See Owen 1976a.

Khalidi, Tarif. 1981. "Shaykh Ahmad ʿArif al-Zayn and Al-ʿIrfan." In *Intellectual Life in the Arab East, 1890–1939*, edited by Marwan R. Buheiry, 110–24. Beirut: American University of Beirut.

Khalidi, Walid. 1979. *Conflict and Violence in Lebanon: Confrontation in the Middle East*. Cambridge: Center for International Affairs, Harvard University.

al-Khazen, Farid. 1988. "Kamal Jumblatt, the Uncrowned Druze Prince of the Left." *Middle Eastern Studies* 24 (April): 178–205.

Khosrokhavar, Farhad. 1979. "Le Comité dans la révolution Iranienne, cas d'une ville moyenne: Hamadan." *Peuples Méditerranéens* No. 9 (October–December): 85–100.

———. 1980. "Hassan K., paysan dépaysanné parle de la révolution Iranienne." *Peuples Méditerranéens* (April–June): 3–30.

Khouri-Dagher, Nadia. 1985. "La Survie quotidienne au Caire." *Maghreb-Machrek* No. 110 (October–December): 56–71.

Khoury, Philip S. 1983a. "Islamic Revivalism and the Crisis of the Secular State in the Arab World." In *Arab Resources: The Transformation of a Society*, edited by Ibrahim Ibrahim, 213–36. London: Croom Helm.

———. 1983b. *Urban Notables and Arab Nationalism: The Politics of Damascus, 1860–1920*. Cambridge: Cambridge University Press.

———. 1987. *Syria and the French Mandate: The Politics of Arab Nationalism, 1920–1945*. Princeton, N.J.: Princeton University Press.

———. 1988. "A Reinterpretation of the Origins and Aims of the Great Syrian Revolt, 1925–1927." In *Arab Civilization: Challenges and Responses*, edited by Georges Atiyeh and Ibrahim Oweiss, 241–69. Albany: State University of New York Press.

Khuri, Fuad I. 1972. "Sectarian Loyalty among Rural Migrants in Two Lebanese Suburbs." In *Rural Politics and Social Change in the Middle East*, edited by Richard Antoun and Iliya Harik, 198–209. Bloomington and London: Indiana University Press.

———. 1975. *From Village to Suburb: Order and Change in Greater Beirut.* Chicago: University of Chicago Press.

———. 1980. "Urbanization and City Management in the Middle East." In *The Changing Middle Eastern City*, edited by H. A. Rivlin and K. Helmer, 1–15. Binghamton: State University of New York.

———. 1981. "The Social Dynamics of the 1975–1977 War in Lebanon." *Armed Forces and Society* 7 (Spring): 383–408

———. 1987a. "Ideological Constants and Urban Living." In *The Middle East City*. See Saqqaf 1987.

———. 1987b. "The Ulama: A Comparative Study of Sunni and Shi'a Religious Officials." *Middle Eastern Studies* 23 (July): 291–312.

Kiray, Mubeccal. 1970. "Squatter Housing: Fast Depeasantization and Slow Workerization in Turkey." Paper presented at the Seventh World Congress of Sociology, Varna.

Kornhauser, William. 1959. *The Politics of Mass Society.* Glencoe, Ill.: Free Press.

Krämer, Gudrun. 1987–188. "The Change of Paradigm: Political Pluralism in Contemporary Egypt." *Peuples Méditerranéens* No. 41–42 (October–March): 283–301.

Kramer, Martin. 1987. "The Structure of Shi'ite Terrorism." In *Contemporary Trends in World Terrorism*, edited by Anat Kurz, 43–52. New York: Praeger.

———. 1990. "The Moral Logic of Hizballah." In *Origins of Terrorism*, edited by Walter Reich, 131–57. Cambridge: Cambridge University Press.

Kupferschmidt, Uri M. 1987. "Reformist and Militant Islam in Urban and Rural Egypt." *Middle Eastern Studies* 23 (October): 403–18.

Lambton, Ann K. S. 1970. "The Persian Ulama and Constitutional Reform." In *Le Shi'isme Imamite*, edited by Ann Lambton, 245–69. Paris: Presses Universitaires de France.

———. 1987. *Qajar Persia: Eleven Studies.* London: I. B. Tauris.

————. 1988. *Continuity and Change in Medieval Persia: Aspects of Administrative, Economic, and Social History, 11–14th Centuries.* Albany, N.Y.: Bibliotheca Persica.

Landau, Jacob. 1974. *Radical Politics in Modern Turkey.* Leiden: E. J. Brill.

Lapidus, Ira M., ed. 1969a. *Middle Eastern Cities.* Berkeley: University of California Press.

————. 1969b. "Muslim Cities and Islamic Societies." In *Middle Eastern Cities.* See Lapidus 1969a.

————. 1973a. "The Evolution of Muslim Urban Society." *Comparative Studies in Society and History* 15 (January): 21–50.

————. 1973b. "Traditional Muslim Cities: Structure and Change." In *From Madina to Metropolis.* See Brown 1973.

————. 1983. *Contemporary Islamic Movements in Historical Perspective.* Berkeley and Los Angeles: University of California Press.

————. 1984. *Muslim Cities in the Later Middle Ages.* Cambridge: Cambridge University Press.

Laroui, Abdallah. 1976. *The Crisis of the Arab Intellectual: Traditionalism or Historicism?* Berkeley and Los Angeles: University of California Press.

Lazarus-Yafeh, Hava. 1983. "Muhammad Mutawalli al-Sha'rawi a Portrait of a Contemporary 'Alim in Egypt." In *Islam, Nationalism, and Radicalism in Egypt and the Sudan,* edited by Gabriel R. Warburg and Uri M. Kupferschmidt, 281–98. New York: Praeger.

Legrain, Jean-Francois. 1986. "Islamistes et lutte nationale Palestinienne dans les territoires occupés par Israel." *Revue Francaise de science politique* 36 (April): 227–47.

Lemarchand, René, and Keith Legg. 1972. "Political Clientelism and Development: A Preliminary Analysis." *Comparative Politics* 4 (January): 149–78.

Lerner, Daniel. 1958. *The Passing of Traditional Society: Modernizing the Middle East.* New York: Free Press.

Le Tourneau, Roger. 1949. *Fez avant le protectorat: Etude économique et sociale d'une ville de L'Occident Musulman.* Casablanca: Société Marocaine de Librairie et d'Edition.

————. 1957. *Les Villes Musulmanes de L'Afrique du Nord.* Alger: La Maison des Livres.

————. 1961. *Fez in the Age of the Marinides.* Translated from the French by Besse Alberta Clement. Norman: University of Oklahoma Press.

Levine, Daniel H. 1986a. "Is Religion Being Politicized? And Other Pressing Questions Latin America Poses." *Political Studies* 19 (4): 825–31.

————1986b. *Religion and Political Conflict in Latin America.* Chapel Hill: University of North Carolina Press.

1986c. "Religion, the Poor, and Politics in Latin America Today." In *Religion and Political Conflict in Latin America.* See Levine 1986b.

Lewis, Bernard. 1937. "The Islamic Guilds." *Economic History Review* No. 3: 20–37.

Lewis, Oscar. 1961. *The Children of Sanchez.* New York: Random House.

Liauzu, Claude. 1986. "Sociétés urbaines et mouvements sociaux: Etat des recherches en langue Anglaise sur le 'Middle East.'" *Maghreb-Machrek* No. 111: 24–56.

————. 1987. "Etat, ville, et mouvements sociaux au Maghreb et au Moyen-Orient." *Maghreb-Machrek* No. 115 (January–February): 53–70.

Liauzu, Claude, Gilbert Meynier, Maria Sgroï-Dufresne, and Pierre Signoles. 1985. *Enjeux urbains au Maghreb.* Paris: L'Harmattan.

Lijphart, Arend. 1969. "Consociational Democracy." *World Politics* 21 (January): 207–25.

Limbert, John W. 1987. *Iran: At War with History.* Boulder, Colo.: Westview Press.

Lockman, Z., and J. Beinin, eds. 1989. *Intifada: The Palestinian Uprising against Israeli Occupation.* Boston: South End Press.

Makdisi, Jean Said. 1990. *Beirut Fragments: A War Memoir.* New York: Persea Books.

Makofsky, David, and Dogu Ergil. 1972. "The Social Basis of Conservatism and Radicalism in Turkish Shantytown Workers." Paper presented at the Middle East Studies Association Annual Conference.

Makram-Ebeid, Mona. 1989. "Political Opposition in Egypt: Democratic Myth or Reality?" *Middle East Journal* 43 (Summer): 423–36.

Maksoud, Clovis. 1966. "Lebanon and Arab Nationalism." In *Politics in Lebanon.* See Binder 1966b.

Mallat, Chibli. 1988. *Shi'i Thought from the South of Lebanon* Papers on Lebanon No. 7. Oxford: Center for Lebanese Studies.

Ma'oz, Moshe. 1968. *Ottoman Reform in Syria and Palestine, 1840–1861: The Impact of the Tanzimat on Politics and Society.* Oxford: Clarendon Press.

Marcus, Abraham. 1989. *The Middle East on the Eve of Modernity: Aleppo in the Eighteenth Century.* New York: Columbia University Press.

Mardam-Bey, Farouk. 1982. "Tensions sociales et réalités urbaines à Damas au 18e siècle." In *La Ville Arabe Dans L'Islam*, edited by A. Boudhiba and D. Chevallier, 117–36. Paris: C.E.R.E.S.– C.N.R.S.

Mardin, Serif. 1969. "Power, Civil Society, and Culture in the Ottoman Empire." *Contemporary Studies in Society and History* 11 (June): 258–81.

———. 1978. "Youth and Violence in Turkey." *European Journal of Sociology* 19 (2): 229–54.

———. 1987. "Culture and Religion towards the Year 2000." Unpublished paper.

Margulies, Ronnie, and Ergin Yildizoglu. 1984. "Trade Unions and Turkey's Working Class." *MERIP Reports* 14 (February): 15–31.

Marsot, Afaf Lutfi Al-Sayyid. 1968. "The Role of the Ulama in Egypt during the Early Nineteenth Century." In *Political and Social Change in Modern Egypt.* See Holt 1968.

———. 1972. "The Ulama of Cairo in the Eighteenth and Nineteenth Centuries." In *Scholars, Saints, and Sufis.* See Keddie 1972d.

Martin, V. A. 1987. "Shaikh Fazlallah Nuri and the Iranian Revolution, 1905–1909." *Middle Eastern Studies* 23 (January): 39–53.

Massignon, Louis. 1935. "Sinf." In *Encyclopaedia of Islam.* Leiden: E. J. Brill.

McChesney, R. D., trans. 1988. "Ilyas Qudsi on the Craft Organizations of Damascus in the Late Nineteenth Century." In *A Way Prepared: Essays on Islamic Culture in Honor of Richard Bayly Winder*, edited by Farhad Kazemi and R.D. McChesney, 80–106. New York: New York University Press.

McDowall, David. 1983. *Lebanon: A Conflict of Minorities.* Minority Rights Group Report No. 61. New York: Minority Rights Group.

Meriwether, Margaret Lee. 1981. "The Notable Families of Aleppo, 1770–1830: Networks and Social Structure." Ph.D. diss. University of Pennsylvania, Philadelphia.

Messarra, Antoine N. 1988. *The Challenge of Coexistence*. Papers on Lebanon. Oxford, England: Centre for Lebanese Studies.

Migdal, Joel. S. 1987. "Strong States, Weak States: Power and Accommodation." In *Understanding Political Development*. See Weiner and Huntington 1987.

Milani, Mohsen M. 1988. *The Making of Iran's Islamic Revolution : From Monarchy to Islamic Republic*. Boulder and London: Westview Press.

Miller, Aaron David. 1989. "Palestinians and the Intifada: One Year Later." *Current History* 88 (February): 73–107.

Miller, William Green. 1969a. "Political Organization in Iran: From Dowreh to Political Party (Part 1)." *Middle East Journal* 23 (Spring–Summer): 159–67.

———. 1969b. "Political Organization in Iran: From Dowreh to Political Party (Part 2)." *Middle East Journal* 23 (Spring–Summer): 343–50.

Mitchell, J. Clyde. 1969. "The Concept and Use of Social Networks." In *Social Networks in Urban Situations: Analyses of Personal Relationships in Central African Towns*, edited by J. C. Mitchell, 1–50. Manchester, England: Manchester University Press.

Mitchell, Richard P. 1969. *The Society of the Muslim Brothers*. London: Oxford University Press.

Mobasser, Soussan. 1985. "Le Bazaar de Téhéran." *Economie et Humanisme* No. 286 (November–December): 49–61.

Moore, Clement Henry. 1974. "Authoritarian Politics in an Unincorporated Society." *Comparative Politics* 6 (January): 193–218.

Mortimer, Edward. 1982. *Faith and Power: The Politics of Islam*. New York: Vintage Books.

Mottahedeh, Roy P. 1980. *Loyalty and Leadership in an Early Islamic Society*. Princeton, N.J.: Princeton University Press.

———. 1985. *The Mantle of the Prophet*. New York: Simon & Schuster.

Mourim, Khosrow. 1987. "La Prière du Vendredi: Théatre, salle de classes, et conférence." In *Téhéran: Au dessous du volcan" (special issue)*. Autrement No. 27: 60–68.

Mozaffari, Mehid. 1988. "La Violence Shi'ite contemporaine: Evolution politique." *Maghreb Review* 13 (1–2): 84–96.

Munson, Henry. 1986. "The Social Base of Islamic Militancy in Morocco." *Middle East Journal* 40 (Spring): 267–84.

———. 1988. *Islam and Revolution in the Middle East.* New Haven: Yale University Press.

Naba'a, Roger, and Souheil al Kache. 1982. "Récits Eclatés d'une révolution manquée." *Peuples Méditerranéens* No. 20 (July–September): 139–66.

Nadim, Nawal al-Messiri. 1979. "The Concept of the Hara: A Historical and Sociological Study of al-Sukkariyya." *Annales Islamologiques* (Cairo: Institut Francais d'Archéologie Orientale du Caire) 15:313–348.

———. 1985. "Family Relationships in a 'Harah' in Cairo." In *Arab Society: Social Science Perspectives*, edited by Saad Eddin Ibrahim and Nicholas Hopkins, 212–22. Cairo: American University in Cairo Press.

Nagata, Judith. 1987. "Indices of the Islamic Resurgence in Malaysia: The Medium and the Message." In *Religious Resurgence.* See Antoun and Hegland 1987.

Najmabadi, Afsaneh. 1987a. "Depoliticization of a Rentier State: The Case of Pahlavi Iran." In *The Rentier State*, edited by Hazem Beblawi and Giacomo Luciani, 211–27. London: Croom Helm, and New York: Methuen.

———. 1987b. "Iran's Turn to Islam: From Modernism to a Moral Order." *Middle East Journal* 41 (Spring): 202–17.

Nakhleh, Emile. 1976. *Bahrain: Political Development in a Modernizing Society.* Lexington, Mass.: Lexington Books.

Nasr, Salim. 1979. "Les Formes de regroupement traditionnel (familles, confessions, communautés régionales) dans la société de Beyrouth." In *L'Espace social de la ville Arabe*, edited by Dominique Chevallier, 145–93. Paris: G. P. Maisonneuve et Larose.

———. 1982. "Formations sociales traditionnelles et sociétés urbaines du Proche Orient: Beyrouth, Damas, Bagdad." In *La Ville Arabe dans l'Islam*, edited by A. Boudhiba and Dominique Chevallier, 357–81. Paris: C.E.R.E.S.–C.N.R.S.

———. 1985. "Roots of the Shi'a Movement." *MERIP Reports* 15 (June): 10–16.

———. 1988. "A New Approach to the Conflict: The Social Dynamics of an Internal War." In *A Symposium on Lebanon Arab-American Affairs* (Summer): 19–21.

———. 1990. "Lebanon's War: Is the End in Sight?" *Middle East Report* No. 162: 5–8.

Nelson, Joan M. 1969. *Migrants, Urban Poverty, and Instability in Developing Nations.* New York: AMS Press.

———. 1979. *Access to Power: Politics and the Urban Poor in Developing Nations.* Princeton, N.J.: Princeton University Press.

———. "Political Participation." In *Understanding Political Development.* See Weiner and Huntington.

Norton, Augustus Richard. 1987. *Amal and the Shi'a: Struggle for the Soul of Lebanon.* Austin: University of Texas.

———. 1988. "Lebanon: Conflict without End?" *Middle East Insight* 6 (Summer): 43–49.

Oberschall, Anthony. 1973. *Social Conflict and Social Movements.* Englewood Cliffs, N.J.: Prentice-Hall.

Osman, Osman M. 1987. "Population Movement and Urbanization in the Arab World." In *The Middle East City.* See Saqqaf 1987.

Owen, Roger. 1976a. *Essays on the Crisis in Lebanon.* London: Ithaca Press.

———. 1976b. "The Political Economy of the Grand Liban, 1920–1970." In *Essays on the Crisis in Lebanon.* See Owen 1976a.

Özbudun, Ergun. 1976. *Social Change and Political Participation in Turkey.* Princeton, N.J.: Princeton University Press.

———. 1980. "Turkey." In *Electoral Politics in the Middle East: Issues, Voters, and Elites,* edited by Jacob M. Landau, Ergun Özbudun, and Frank Tachau, 107–44. London: Croom Helm.

Pahlavi, Mohammad Reza. 1980. *Answer to History.* New York: Stein & Day.

Park, Robert E. 1925. "The City: Suggestions for the Investigation of Human Behavior in the Urban Environment." In *The City,* edited by Robert E. Park, 1–46. Chicago: University of Chicago Press.

Parsa, Misagh. 1989. *Social Origins of the Iranian Revolution.* New Brunswick, N.J.: Rutgers University Press.

Paul, Jim. 1984. "States of Emergency: The Riots in Tunisia and Morocco." *MERIP Reports* 14 (October): 3–6.

Peretz, Don. 1990. *Intifada: The Palestinian Uprising.* Boulder, Colo., Westview Press.

Perlman, Janice. 1976. *The Myth of Marginality: Urban Poverty and Politics in Rio de Janeiro.* Berkeley and Los Angeles: University of California Press.

Petersen, Karen. 1971. "Villagers in Cairo: Hypotheses versus Data." *American Journal of Sociology* 77 (November): 560–73.

Petran, Tabitha. 1987. *The Struggle over Lebanon.* New York: Monthly Review Press.

Phillips, Doris G. 1959. "Rural-to-Urban Migration in Iraq." *Economic Development and Cultural Change* 7 (July): 405–21.

Picard, Elisabeth. 1977. "Science politique, orientalisme, et sociologie au chevet du Liban." *Revue Francaise de science politique* 27 (August–October): 630–42.

———. 1988. *Liban, état de discorde: Des Fondations aux guerres fratricides.* Paris: Flammarion.

Pintak, Larry. 1988. *Beirut Outtakes: A T.V. Correspondent's Portrait of America's Encounter with Terror.* Lexington, Mass.: Lexington Books.

Pittaway, James. 1989. "Egypt: A Benign Brotherhood?" *The Atlantic Monthly,* January, 25–33.

Poggi, Gianfranco. 1978. *The Development of the Modern State: A Sociological Introduction.* Stanford, Calif.: Stanford University Press.

Polk, William R., and Richard L. Chambers, eds. 1968. *Beginnings of Modernization in the Middle East: The Nineteenth Century.* Chicago: University of Chicago Press.

Post, Erika. 1987. "Egypt's Elections." *Middle East Report* 17 (July–August): 17–22.

Purcell, Susan K. 1981. "Mexico: Clientelism, Corporatism, and Political Stability." In *Political Clientelism, Patronage, and Development.* See Eisenstadt and Lemarchand 1981.

Quataert, Donald. 1983. *Social Disintegration and Popular Resistance in the Ottoman Empire, 1881–1908: Reactions to European Economic Penetration.* New York: New York University Press.

Qubain, Fahim I. 1961. *Crisis in Lebanon.* Washington, D.C.: Middle East Institute.

Raad, Mansour (pseudonym). 1990. "Everyone Misunderstood the Depth of the Movement Identifying with Aoun" (interview). *Middle East Report* 20 (162): 11–14.

Rabinovitch, Itamar. 1988. "Arab Political Parties: Ideology and Ethnicity." In *Ethnicity, Pluralism, and the State in the Middle East,* edited by M. Esman and I. Rabinovitch, 155–72. Ithaca, N.Y.: Cornell University Press.

Rassam, Amal. 1977. "Al-Taba'iyya: Power, Patronage, and Marginal Groups in Northern Iraq." In *Patrons and Clients in Mediterranean Societies.* See Gellner and Waterbury 1977.

Raymond, André. 1968. "Quartiers et mouvements populaires au Caire au XVIIIème siècle." In *Political and Social Change in Modern Egypt.* See Holt 1968.

———. 1973–74. *Artisans et commercants au Caire au XVIIIème siècle.* 2 vols. Damascus: Institut Francais de Damas.

———. 1984. *The Great Arab Cities in the 16th–18th Centuries: An Introduction.* New York: New York University Press.

———. 1985. *Grandes villes Arabes à l'époque Ottomane.* Paris: Sindbad.

———. 1988. "Is There an Islamic City?" Unpublished paper, Princeton University.

Richard, Yann. 1985. "L'Organisation des Feda'iyan-e Islam, mouvement intégriste Musulman en Iran (1945–1956)." In *Radicalismes Islamiques* edited by Olivier Carré and Paul Dumont, 1:23–82. Paris: L'Harmattan.

———. 1987. "La Fonction parénétique du 'Alem: La prière du Vendredi en Iran depuis la révolution." Unpublished paper.

Richards, Alan, and John Waterbury. 1990. *A Political Economy of the Middle East: State, Class, and Economic Development.* Boulder, Colo.: Westview Press.

Rosen, Lawrence. 1984. *Bargaining for Reality: The Construction of Social Relations in a Muslim Community.* Chicago: University of Chicago Press.

Rotblat, Howard J. 1972. "Stability and Change in an Iranian Provincial Bazaar." Ph.D. diss. Department of Sociology, University of Chicago.

———. 1975. "Social Organization and Development in an Iranian Provincial Bazaar." *Economic Development and Cultural Change* 23 (January): 292–305.

Roussillon, Alain. 1987–88. "Islam, Islamisme, et démocratie: Recomposition du champ politique." *Peuples Méditerranéens* No. 41–42 (October–March): 303–39.

————. 1988. *Sociétés Islamiques de placements de fonds et 'ouverture economique.'* Cairo: C.E.D.E.J.

Rugh, Andrea B. 1978. "Religious Community and Social Control in a Low Income Area of Cairo." Ph.D. diss. American University, Washington D.C.

————. 1979. *Coping with Poverty in a Cairo Community.* Cairo Papers in Social Science, Monograph 1. Cairo: American University in Cairo Press.

————. 1984. *Family in Contemporary Egypt.* Syracuse, N.Y.: Syracuse University Press.

Sabari, Simha. 1981. *Mouvements populaires à Baghdad à l'Epoque 'Abbasside, IX–XI siècles.* Paris: Librairie d'Amérique et d'Orient, Jean Maisonneuve.

Sadowski, Yahya. 1987. "Egypt's Islamist Movement: A New Political and Economic Force." *Middle East Insight* (September): 37–45.

Salamé, Ghassan. 1986. *Lebanon's Injured Identities: Who Represents Whom during a Civil War.* Papers on Lebanon No. 2. Oxford: Center for Lebanese Studies.

————. 1988. "The City and the New Political Order: The Fertile Crescent." Unpublished paper.

Salehi, M. M. 1988. *Insurgency through Culture and Religion: The Islamic Revolution of Iran.* New York: Praeger.

Salem, Elie. 1973. *Modernization without Revolution: Lebanon's Experience.* Bloomington: Indiana University Press.

Salibi, Kamal S. 1965. *The Modern History of Lebanon.* London: Weidenfeld & Nicolson.

————. 1968. "The 1860 Upheaval in Damascus as Seen by al-Sayyid Muhammad Abu'l-Su'ud al-Hasibi, Notable and Later Naqib al-Ashraf of the City." In *Beginnings of Modernization in the Middle East.* See Polk and Chambers 1968.

————. 1976. *Crossroads to Civil War: Lebanon, 1958–1976.* Delmar: Caravan.

————. 1981. "The Lebanese Identity." In *Religion and Politics in the Middle East,* edited by Michael Curtis, 217–25. Boulder, Colo.: Westview Press.

————. 1988. *A House of Many Mansions: The History of Lebanon Reconsidered.* London: I. B. Tauris.

Saqqaf, Abdulaziz Y., ed. 1987. *The Middle East City: Ancient Traditions Confront a Modern World.* New York: Paragon House.

Schahgaldian, Nikola B. 1987. *The Iranian Military Under the Islamic Republic.* Santa Monica, Calif.: Rand Corporation.

———. 1989. *The Clerical Establishment in Iran.* Santa Monica, Calif.: Rand Corporation.

Schatkowski Schilcher, Linda. 1985. *Families in Politics: Damascene Factions and Estates of the 18th and 19th Centuries.* Stuttgart: Franz Steiner Verlag Wiesbaden GMBH.

Schmidt, Steffen, James C. Scott, Carl Landé, and Laura Guasti, eds. 1977. *Friends, Followers, and Factions: A Reader in Political Clientelism.* Berkeley and Los Angeles: University of California Press.

Scott, James C. 1972. "Patron-Client Politics and Political Change in Southeast Asia." *American Political Science Review* 66 (March): 91–113.

———. 1985. *Weapons of the Weak: Everyday Forms of Peasant Resistance.* New Haven: Yale University Press.

———. 1990. *Domination and the Arts of Resistance: Hidden Transcripts.* New Haven: Yale University Press.

Scoville, J. G. 1985. "The Labor Market in Prerevolutionary Iran." *World Development* 34 (October): 143–51.

Seddon, David. 1984. "Winter of Discontent: Economic Crisis in Tunisia and Morocco." *MERIP Reports* 14 (October): 7–16.

———. 1989. "Riots and Rebellion in North Africa: Political Responses to Economic Crisis in Tunisia, Morocco and Sudan. In *Power and Stability in the Middle East,* edited by Berch Berberoglu, 114–35. London: Zed Books.

Seurat, Michel. 1985. "Le Quartier de Bab Tebbane à Tripoli (Liban): Etude d'une 'Asabiyya urbaine." In *Mouvements communautaires et espaces urbains au Machreq,* edited by C.E.R.M.O.C. (Centre d'Etudes et de Recherches sur le Moyen-Orient Arabe Contemporain), 45–86. Beirut: CERMOC.

———. 1986. "La Ville Arabe Orientale." *Esprit* No. 111 (February): 9–14.

Sewell, Grandville H. 1964. "Squatter Settlements in Turkey: Analysis of a Social, Political, and Economic Problem." Ph.D. diss. MIT.

Shapira, Shimon. 1988. "The Origins of Hizballah." *Jerusalem Quarterly* No. 46 (Spring): 115–30.

Sheikholeslami, Ali Reza. 1986. "From Religious Accommodation to Religious Revolution: The Transformation of Shi'ism in Iran." In *The State, Religion, and Ethnic Politics: Afghanistan, Iran, and Pakistan*, edited by Ali Banuazizi and Myron Weiner, 227–55. Syracuse, N.Y.: Syracuse University Press.

Shils, Edward. 1966. "The Prospects for Lebanese Civility." In *Politics in Lebanon*. See Binder 1966b.

Shoshan, Boaz. 1980. "Grain Riots and the 'Moral Economy': Cairo, 1350–1517." *Journal of Interdisciplinary History* 10 (Winter): 459–78.

———. 1986. "The 'Politics of Notables' in Medieval Islam." *Asian and African Studies* 20:179–215.

Sick, Gary. 1986. *All Fall Down: America's Tragic Encounter with Iran*. New York: Penguin.

Singerman, Diane. 1993. *Family, Politics, and Networks in Urban Quarters of Cairo*. Princeton, N.J.: Princeton University Press.

Sivan, Emmanuel. 1985. Radical Islam: Medieval Theology and Modern Politics. New Haven: Yale University Press.

Smock, David, and Audrey Smock. 1975. *The Politics of Pluralism: A Comparative Study of Lebanon and Ghana*. New York: Elsevier.

Snider, Lewis. 1984. "The Lebanese Forces: Their Origins and Role in Lebanon's Politics." *Middle East Journal* 38 (Winter): 1–33.

Spooner, Brian. 1971. "Religion and Society Today: An Anthropological Perspective." In *Iran Faces the Seventies*, edited by E. Yarshater, 166–88. New York: Praeger.

Springborg, Robert. 1975. "Patterns of Association in the Egyptian Political Elite." In *Political Elites in the Middle East*, edited by George Lenczowski, 83–107. Washington, D.C.: American Institute for Public Policy Research.

———. 1982. *Family, Power, and Politics in Egypt: Sayyed Bey Marei—His Clan, Clients, and Cohorts*. Philadelphia: University of Pennsylvania Press.

———. 1989. *Mubarak's Egypt: Fragmentation of the Political Order*. Boulder, Colo.: Westview Press.

Staffa, Susan Jane. 1977. *Conquest and Fusion: The Social Evolution of Cairo, a.d. 642–1850.* Leiden: E. J. Brill.

Starr, Paul D. 1977. "Lebanon." In *Commoners, Climbers, and Notables,* edited by C. A. O. Van Nieuwenhuijze, 205–25. Leiden: E. J. Brill.

Stauffer, Thomas B. 1952. "Labor Unions in the Arab States." *Middle East Journal* 6 (1):83–88.

Stern, S. M. 1970. "The Constitution of the Islamic City." In *The Islamic City.* See Hourani and Stern 1970.

Stoakes, Frank. 1975. "The Supervigilantes: The Lebanese Kataeb Party as a Builder, Surrogate, and Defender of the State." *Middle Eastern Studies* 11 (October): 215–36.

Stork, Joe. 1989. "Notes from the Seventh Month." In *Intifada.* See Lockman and Beinin 1989.

Suleiman, Michael W. 1967. *Political Parties in Lebanon: The Challenge of a Fragmented Political Culture.* Ithaca, N.Y.: Cornell University Press.

———. 1972. "Crisis and Revolution in Lebanon." *Middle East Journal* 26 (Winter): 11–24.

Suzuki, Peter. 1966. "Peasants without Plows: Some Anatolians in Istanbul." *Rural Sociology* 31 (December): 428–38.

Tabari, Azar. 1983. "The Role of the Clergy in Modern Iranian Politics." In *Religion and Politics in Iran.* See Keddie 1983b.

Tabbarah, Riad. 1978. "Rural Development and Urbanization in Lebanon." *Population Bulletin of the United Nations Economic Commission for Western Asia* No. 14 (June): 3–25.

Tachau, Frank. 1984. "The Political Culture of Kemalist Turkey." In *Ataturk and the Modernization of Turkey,* edited by Jacob M. Landau, 57–76. Boulder, Colo.: Westview Press.

Taeschner, F. 1960. "'Ayyar." In *The Encyclopaedia of Islam, New Edition,* 1:794. Leiden: E. J. Brill.

———. 1965. "Futuwwa." In *The Encyclopaedia of Islam, New Edition,* 2:966–69. Leiden: E. J. Brill.

Taheri, Amir. 1978. "The Bazaar." *Kayhan International,* 2 October.

———. 1986. *The Spirit of Allah: Khomeini and the Iranian Revolution.* Bethesda: Adler & Adler.

———. 1987. *Holy Terror: The Inside Story of Islamic Terrorism.* London: Hutchinson.

———. 1988. *The Middle East behind the Headlines.* London: Hutchinson.

Tehranian, Majid. 1980. "Communication and Revolution in Iran: The Passing of a Paradigm." *Iranian Studies* 13 (1–4): 5–30.

Thaiss, Gustav. 1971. "Religion and Social Change in Iran: The Bazaar as a Case Study." In *Iran Faces the Seventies,* edited by E. Yarshater, 189–216. New York: Praeger.

———. 1972. "Religious Symbolism and Social Change: The Drama of Husain." In *Scholars, Saints, and Sufis.* See Keddie 1972d.

Tilly, Charles. 1970. "Race and Migration to the American City." In *The Metropolitan Enigma: Inquiries into the Nature and Dimensions of America's 'Urban Crisis,'* edited by James Q. Wilson, 144–69. New York: Anchor Books.

———. 1973. "The Chaos of the Living City." In *Ghetto Revolts: The Politics of Violence in American Cities,* edited by Joe R. Feagin and Harlan Hahn, 98–124. New York: Mcmillan.

———. 1975. "Revolutions and Collective Violence." In *Handbook of Political Science.* Vol. 3, *Macropolitical Theory,* edited by Fred I. Greenstein and Nelson W. Polsby, 483–555. Reading: Addison-Wesley.

———. 1978. *From Mobilization to Revolution.* Reading: Addison-Wesley.

Tilly, Charles, Louise Tilly, and Richard Tilly. 1975. *The Rebellious Century: 1830–1930.* Cambridge: Harvard University Press.

Tönnies, Ferdinand. 1940. *Fundamental Concepts of Sociology.* New York: American Book.

Vitullo, Anita. 1989. "Uprising in Gaza." In *Intifada.* See Lockman and Beinin 1989.

Walton, Thomas (pseudonym). 1980. "Economic Development and Revolutionary Upheavals in Iran." *Cambridge Journal of Economics* 4 (September): 275–92.

Waltz, Susan. 1986. "Islamist Appeal in Tunisia." *Middle East Journal* 40 (Autumn): 651–70.

Waterbury, John. 1972a. *North for the Trade: The Life and Times of a Berber Merchant.* Berkeley and Los Angeles: University of California Press.

———. 1972b. "Tribalism, Trade and Politics: the Transformation of the Swasa of Morocco." In *Arabs and Berbers: Ethnicity and Nation-Building in North Africa,* edited by Ernest Gellner and Charles Micaud, 231–57. Lexington: Lexington Books.

———. 1977. "An Attempt to Put Patrons and Clients in Their Place." In *Patrons and Clients in Mediterranean Societies.* See Gellner and Waterbury 1977.

———. 1978. *Egypt: Burdens of the Past, Options for the Future.* Bloomington: Indiana University Press.

———. 1979. "Clientelism Revisited." *Government and Opposition* 14 (Spring): 217–28.

———. 1983. *The Egypt of Nasser and Sadat: The Political Economy of Two Regimes.* Princeton, N.J.: Princeton University Press.

Weiner, Myron. 1987. "Political Change: Asia, Africa, and the Middle East." In *Understanding Political Development,* See Weiner and Huntington 1987.

Weiner , Myron, and Samuel P. Huntington, eds., 1987. *Understanding Political Development.* Boston: Little, Brown.

Weingrod, Alex. 1968. "Patrons, Patronage, and Political Parties." *Comparative Studies in Society and History* 10 (July): 377–400.

Weiss, Bernard G., and Arnold H. Green. 1982. *A Survey of Arab History.* Cairo: American University in Cairo.

Wirth, Eugen. 1982. "Villes Islamiques, villes Arabes, villes Orientales? Une problématique face au changement." In *La Ville Arabe dans L'Islam,* edited by A. Boudhiba and D. Chevallier, 193–201. Paris: C.E.R.E.S.–C.N.R.S.

Wirth, Louis. 1938. "Urbanism as a Way of Life." *American Journal of Sociology* 44 (July): 1–24.

World Bank. 1984. *World Development Report.* New York: Oxford University Press.

Wright, Robin. 1989. *In the Name of God: The Khomeini Decade.* New York: Simon & Schuster.

Yamak, Labib Z. 1966a. "Party Politics in the Lebanese Political System." In *Politics in Lebanon.* See Binder 1966b.

———. 1966b. *The Syrian Social Nationalist Party: An Ideological Analysis.* Cambridge: Harvard University Press.

Yavari d'Hellencourt, Nouchine. 1987. "Lutteurs devant l'éternel." In *Téhéran: Au Dessous Du Volcan* (special issue). *Autrement* No. 27: 207–12.

Yazdi, Majid. 1990. "Patterns of Clerical Behavior in Post-war Iran, 1941–53." *Middle Eastern Studies* 26 (July): 281–307.

Zabih, S. 1979. *Iran's Revolutionary Upheaval.* San Francisco: Alchemy Books.

Zamir, Meir. 1985. *The Formation of Modern Lebanon.* Ithaca, N.Y., and London: Cornell University Press.

Zartman, William I. 1988. "Introduction." In *The Durability of the Arab State.* See Dawisha and Zartman 1988.

Zonis, Marvin. 1971. *The Political Elite of Iran.* Princeton, N.J.: Princeton University Press.

———. 1983. "Iran: A Theory of Revolution from Accounts of the Revolution." *World Politics* 35 (July): 586–606.

———. 1991. *Majestic Failure: The Fall of the Shah.* Chicago: University of Chicago Press.

Zubaida, Sami. 1986. "The City in Islamic Ideas and Movements." In *Middle Eastern Cities in Comparative Perspective.* See Brown et al. 1986,

———. 1988a. *Islam, the People, and the State: Essays on Political Ideas and Movements in the Middle East.* New York: Routledge.

———. 1988b. "An Islamic State? The Case of Iran." *Middle East Report* 18 (July–August): 3–7.

Index